Religion and Royal Justice in Early Modern France

Habent sua fata libelli

Religion AND *Royal Justice*

IN EARLY MODERN FRANCE

The Paris Chambre de l'Edit, 1598–1665

Diane C. Margolf

Sixteenth Century Essays & Studies 67

Truman State University Press

Cover art: "Figvra Condemnationis Reorvm," from Jean Milles de Souvigny, *Praxis criminis persequendi* (Paris, 1541), courtesy of the Robbins Collection at the School of Law, University of California, Berkeley.
Cover designer: Teresa Wheeler
Type: Monotype Corp., Centaur
Printed by Thomson-Shore, Dexter, Michigan USA

Library of Congress Cataloging-in-Publication Data
Margolf, Diane Claire.
   Religion and royal justice in early modern France : the Paris Chambre de l'Edit, 1598–1665 / Diane C. Margolf.
      p.   cm. — (Sixteenth century essays & studies ; v. 67)
Includes bibliographical references and index.
   ISBN 1-931112-25-8 (Cloth, casebound : alk. paper) — ISBN 1-931112-26-6 (pbk. : alk. paper)
   1. Huguenots—Legal status, laws, etc.—France—History—17th century.
2. France. Chambre de l'Edit (Paris) I. Title. II. Series.
   KJV4207.H85 M37 2001
   342.44'0852—dc21

                                                        2003007961
                                                        Rev.

♾ The paper in this publication meets or exceeds the minimum requirements of the American National Standard for Information Sciences—Permanence of Paper for Printed Library Materials, ANSI Z39.48-1992.

Contents

Acknowledgments

This book began with an offhand reference to the special law courts mandated by the Edict of Nantes which I heard in a lecture during my first year in graduate school. In the intervening years, as it has developed from a seminar paper to a dissertation, through conference papers and essays to a monograph (with much revising in between), I have incurred many debts which it is now a pleasure to acknowledge. My research was funded by a Bourse Chateaubriand in 1987 through 1988, which enabled me to spend a second year reading seventeenth-century court documents in Paris, as well as later grants by the Department of History of the College of Charleston and the Professional Development Program at Colorado State University. A number of advisors, friends, and fellow scholars have sustained my work on the Chambre de l'Edit with their interest, comments, and suggestions: the late Harry Miskimin, Keith Luria, David Underdown, Lee Palmer Wandel, Amanda Eurich, Al Hamscher, Ron Love, Peter Sahlins, Maarten Ultee, Bertrand Van Ruymbeke, and Michael Wolfe. A special thanks to Ray Mentzer, who is in a sense the godfather of this project; had he not encouraged me to continue with it at a very early stage, it might never have reached the printed page. In Paris, Mme Marie-Noelle Baudouin-Matuszek provided invaluable assistance, friendship, and hospitality to a novice American graduate student, which have continued ever since our first meeting. The late M. Yves Metman offered some timely lessons in paleography, and Mme Marie-Aimée Belle (along with her daughter Nadège) taught me a great deal about the Parisians of today while I was studying those of the early modern era. I also acknowledge the staffs of the Archives Nationales (now the Centre d'Accueil et des Recherches des Archives Nationales), the Bibliothèque Nationale, the Bibliothèque de la Société de l'Histoire du Protestantisme Français, the Beinecke Rare Book and Manuscript Library, and Sterling Memorial Library at Yale University for their assistance.

Finally, I thank my parents for their love and support throughout my years of study, teaching, writing, and research. This book is dedicated to them.

Introduction

In February 1602, a Huguenot weaponry maker named Noel Billot stood before a panel of magistrates in a chamber of the Palais de Justice in Paris. A year earlier, the royal judge and prosecutor in Billot's native town of Mâcon had convicted him of "using at various times in public places seditious language and discourse tending to scandal, against the edicts and rules of pacification."[1] Billot had been ordered to leave Mâcon within three days or risk being expelled by the authorities, but he appealed to the Chambre de l'Edit, a special law court affiliated with the Paris parlement which heard lawsuits involving French Calvinists, or Huguenots. The Paris judges rejected the sentence of banishment and formally rebuked Billot for his disruptive behavior, then ordered him to return home to Mâcon, "to live there and comport himself modestly according to the king's edicts."[2]

The case of Noel Billot illustrates many of the issues explored in the pages that follow. This book is about litigants like Billot and the legal disputes they brought before the Paris Chambre de l'Edit in seventeenth-century France. The chamber's origins lay in the Wars of Religion of the later sixteenth century, when Huguenots feared the partisanship of the predominantly Catholic judiciary. In 1598, the Edict of Nantes declared an end to the warfare and provided a legal blueprint for future relations among Huguenots and Catholics in France. Its provisions reflected elements found in many previous edicts of pacification and offered an institutional guarantee of protection and privileges for the Huguenot minority: special law courts, composed of both Huguenot and Catholic magistrates, which would resolve disputes involving Huguenot litigants. Chambres mi-parties, so called because they included equal numbers of judges from both confessions, were

[1] Archives Nationales (hereafter A.N.) X2b 205, 5 February 1602: Noel Billot, fourbisseur...attainct et convaincu d'avoir usé divers fois en public de pluseurs langages et discours seditieux et tendant à scandalle contre les edicts et reglemens de pacification. (Punctuation and accents have been added for clarity in French quotations from these documents, but the original spelling has been preserved. All translations are my own unless otherwise noted.)

[2] A.N. X2b 205, 5 February 1602: [La cour] luy a permis et permet de se retirer en sa maison en ladite ville de Mascon pour y vivre et se comporter modestement suivant les edicts du Roy.

to be affiliated with the parlements of Grenoble, Bordeaux, Rouen, and Toulouse. A fourth court, christened the Chambre de l'Edit or "chamber of the edict," would be established for the Parlement of Paris. The Paris Chambre de l'Edit functioned under this mandate until formally dissolved by royal edict in 1669.

This book analyzes the Chambre de l'Edit's role in seventeenth-century France from several different perspectives. Because of its broad jurisdiction, the Chambre de l'Edit provides a unique avenue for examining the problems that Huguenots faced individually and collectively after 1598. The court's records allow us to study the issues of religious conflict, coexistence, and toleration long associated with the Edict of Nantes and its aftermath, using previously unexplored source materials. The chamber's work also reflects the monarchy's efforts to restore peace and enhance its authority in the French state and society, a development often referred to as "absolutism." Finally, the court's activities provide valuable insight into competing concepts of community and identity in seventeenth-century France. The effort to define, establish, and maintain order amid political, social, religious, and cultural change—a significant theme in early modern French history—clearly emerges in the Chambre de l'Edit's adjudication of legal disputes.

The chamber's written orders and decisions (*minutes d'arrêt*) for criminal cases during the period 1600–1665 form the principal documentary basis of this study. For the first decade (1600–1610), every criminal case for each year was examined; thereafter, samples were taken from the records at five-year intervals up to 1665. This produced a collection of approximately 3,600 *minutes d'arrêt*, spanning the period immediately following the Edict of Nantes through the early years of Louis XIV's personal reign. Though the Chambre de l'Edit judged civil as well as criminal matters, this study concentrates on the latter in order to focus on a central issue in the court's work: its enforcement of the Edict of Nantes. Criminal cases offer the most fruitful area for exploring the problems associated with the edict's mandate of peaceful coexistence among Huguenots and Catholics, for such cases usually involved behavior—verbal and physical violence, for example, or disputes about clandestine marriages and illegal burials—which directly challenged the law's requirements. Since most of the Chambre de l'Edit's cases were heard on appeal, one can also see how criminal offenses associated with the Edict of Nantes were dealt with by lesser courts, and how the chamber judges upheld, overturned, or modified the sentences and punishments decreed by local authorities.

The *minutes d'arrêt* present some frustrations for the historian eager to have a complete picture of the court's work. In some cases, the documents give the technical details about the proceedings in a given lawsuit but are silent regarding the substance of the dispute. A single lawsuit may spawn a bewildering array of countersuits and related accusations; other cases continue across several months or years in the records, only to disappear without a final decision. Some litigants are clearly identified as members of "the so-called reformed faith" [la religion préten-due réformée], but in other cases it is unclear which of the parties is Huguenot and which is Catholic. Huguenots might very well sue each other, and litigants' claims to the status and privileges of being Huguenot (and therefore entitled to judicial appeal before the Chambre de l'Edit) were sometimes challenged by their opponents. French royal judges exercised great latitude in deciding cases and spe-cific references to judicial precedents are rare, so one must infer the reasons for the judges' decisions from the available information. Moreover, the Paris Chambre de l'Edit's members included only one Huguenot. Analysis of confessional divisions among the court's judges is therefore more difficult than in the case of the provin-cial chambres mi-parties.[3]

Despite these problems, the Chambre de l'Edit's records reveal valuable infor-mation about the people who appealed to the court and the kinds of complaints they brought forth. Litigants are usually identified in the *minutes d'arrêt* by name, title or profession, family affiliation, and place of residence or origin. This pro-vides a view of the hundreds of men and women from all levels of French society (and sometimes from foreign countries) who appeared before the chamber magis-trates. The court heard accusations of blasphemy and insult, illicit marriages and contested inheritances, street fights, murders, thefts, and forgeries, proving that the Chambre de l'Edit in fact exercised the broad criminal jurisdiction which the Edict of Nantes had accorded it on paper. During the reign of Henry IV and for much of the seventeenth century, the Chambre de l'Edit was thus actively involved in the complex task of implementing the Edict of Nantes's provisions for religious coexistence and maintaining the peace among French subjects.

In interpreting the significance of the court's activities, this study attempts to present the Paris Chambre de l'Edit as a legal institution in cultural context. This means seeing the chamber not only as a special law court for Huguenots and a part of the royal judiciary, but also as a powerful symbol of the Huguenots' protected yet limited status in Catholic France. The meaning and importance of the court's work cannot be measured solely in terms of how many cases it heard or what kinds

---

[3]Such issues have been examined in recent studies of the chambre mi-partie for Languedoc. See Raymond A. Mentzer, "Bipartisan Justice and the Pacification of Late Sixteenth-Century Languedoc," in *Regnum, Religio et Ratio: Essays Presented to Robert M. Kingdon*, ed. Jerome Friedman (Kirks-ville, Mo.: Sixteenth Century Journal Publishers, 1987), 125–32; idem, "L'Edit de Nantes et la Chambre de Justice du Languedoc," in *Coexister dans l'intolérance: L'Edit de Nantes (1598)*, ed. Michel Grandjean and Bernard Roussel (Geneva: Labor et Fides, 1998), 321–38; and Stéphane Capot, *Jus-tice et religion en Languedoc au temps de l'Edit de Nantes: La Chambre de l'Edit de Castres, 1579–1679* (Paris: Ecole des Chartes, 1998).

of decisions it rendered, though that information is certainly essential to this study. As a symbol of the privileges guaranteed under the Edict of Nantes, the Chambre de l'Edit was vigorously defended by Huguenots from attacks by their Catholic opponents, with both sides appealing to the crown to protect or condemn the tribunal. What the court represented to Huguenots, Catholics, and the monarchy was perhaps as significant as its actual adjudication of legal disputes. The Chambre de l'Edit's symbolic value and everyday activities were both directly related to contemporary concerns about religious difference, law, and identity.[4]

For many people in seventeenth-century France, religious pluralism remained a serious threat to social and political order, which the Edict of Nantes did not resolve. Although peaceful coexistence was mandated by law and actually occurred in some localities, many Catholics abhorred the Huguenots' continued presence in France and looked to the Bourbon kings to combat the Calvinist heresy. At the same time, Huguenots tried to represent themselves to the monarchy as loyal, obedient subjects who did not disrupt society nearly as much as those Catholics who clamored for their destruction. Huguenots also relied upon a variety of institutions—consistories and synods, political assemblies, and deputies-general—to lead and preserve their communities. Yet they gradually lost their military garrisons, aristocratic leaders, legal privileges, and royal protection, a process that culminated in the revocation of the Edict of Nantes in 1685. The Huguenots' failures thus seemed to assure the success of both "royal religion" and the Catholic Reformation in France.[5]

The Paris Chambre de l'Edit sheds new light on the Huguenots' troubled history during this period. Litigants' disputes with family members, neighbors,

---

[4]The following works have been especially helpful in thinking about "cultural context": Lynn Hunt, ed., *The New Cultural History* (Berkeley: University of California Press, 1989); Roger Chartier, *Cultural History: Between Practices and Representations*, trans. Lydia Cochrane (Ithaca: Cornell University Press, 1985); William J. Bouwsma, *A Usable Past: Essays in European Cultural History* (Berkeley: University of California Press, 1990); Anne J. Cruz and Mary Elizabeth Perry, eds., *Culture and Control in Counter-Reformation Spain* (Minneapolis: University of Minnesota Press, 1992); Mack P. Holt, "Putting Religion Back into the Wars of Religion," *French Historical Studies* 18 (1993): 524–51; and Michael Wolfe, ed., *Changing Identities in Early Modern France* (Durham: Duke University Press, 1997).

[5] On the Huguenots' history during the seventeenth century, see Elisabeth Labrousse, *Une Foi, une loi, un roi? La révocation de l'Edit de Nantes* (Geneva: Labor et Fides, 1985); Janine Garrisson, *L'Edit de Nantes et sa révocation: Histoire d'une intolérance* (Paris: Seuil, 1985); Daniel Ligou, *Le Protestantisme en France de 1598 à 1715* (Paris: S.E.D.E.S., 1968). On the concept of "royal religion" in early modern France, see Dale Van Kley, *The Religious Origins of the French Revolution* (New Haven: Yale University Press, 1996); Jeffrey Merrick, *The Desacralization of the French Monarchy* (Baton Rouge: Louisiana State University Press, 1990); Michael Wolfe, *The Conversion of Henri IV* (Cambridge: Harvard University Press, 1993).

and local authorities were often at the heart of the cases that the chamber magistrates heard; the court's records thus offer a perspective on how royal judges sought to resolve such local and personal conflicts when they were appealed to a higher court. The Chambre de l'Edit's work also illustrates how religious identity was closely entwined with secular laws and privileges. In order to justify their appeals to the Chambre de l'Edit, many litigants framed their complaints as infractions of the Edict of Nantes or other laws concerning the Huguenots; other litigants claimed the status of Huguenots as the basis of their appeals, regardless of the crime at issue. Such efforts suggest that one's religious identity was not only a matter of belief and worship, but also was tied to the assertion of privileges that distinguished one confessional group from another. Most of all, the chamber's activities highlight the central paradox of the Huguenots' position in the French state. Appearing before the magistrates of the Paris Chambre de l'Edit, Huguenot litigants (and their opponents) could air grievances and protest mistreatment even as they submitted to the authority of royal justice. In short, they could simultaneously obey and challenge the law. Their disputes exemplified the Huguenots' energetic but ambivalent struggle with French authorities, especially the monarchy and the judiciary.

While the Chambre de l'Edit's work reflected the problems associated with religious pluralism in early modern France, it was also linked to issues concerning law and governance more generally during this period. In implementing the Edict of Nantes, the court carried out royal policies that were often prejudicial to the religious minority. This implies a linear, hierarchical connection between judges and litigants, king and subjects, Catholic majority and Huguenot minority: a straightforward relationship of domination by the rulers and submission (despite resistance) by the ruled.[6] Yet the chamber functioned within a complex of beliefs and practices about law and governance that were anything but straightforward. The court was not simply an instrument for protecting or persecuting Huguenots, but rather an arena where many issues about Huguenots were contested, and where the results of such contests were varied and uncertain. In the largest sense, the Paris Chambre de l'Edit was involved in the task of defining, establishing, and maintaining social and political order in seventeenth-century France.

Law itself was an essential element of order in society and the state, though like religion it was problematic. Even laws promoted by kings and enforced by judges could become double-edged swords, generating disorder and conflict rather

[6]See James Scott, *Domination and the Arts of Resistance: Hidden Transcripts* (New Haven: Yale University Press, 1990); June Starr and Jane F. Collier, eds., *History and Power in the Study of Law: New Directions in Legal Anthropology* (Ithaca: Cornell University Press, 1989).

than assuring peace and tranquility. A narrow judicial interpretation of the Edict of Nantes clearly helped to undermine the Huguenots' position in France as early as the reign of Henry IV. Louis XIV's formal revocation of that edict was preceded by a plethora of decrees that restricted the Huguenots' ability to hold public offices, join professions, worship publicly, assemble or present grievances, and educate their children. During the seventeenth century, it became increasingly difficult for Huguenots to invoke the law effectively to protect themselves or maintain their cohesiveness as a community. Yet the Huguenots were not alone: royal edicts aimed at regulating many other groups in French society, including clerics, artisans, professionals of all kinds, women, poor persons, and vagabonds. By implementing laws that defined and condemned certain groups or behaviors as criminal, the monarchy and the magistracy often collaborated to punish individual offenders, enhance each other's authority, and discipline society at large.

Such uses of the law, however, were not entirely one-sided, much less successful. Recent scholarship on law and crime in early modern Europe has tended to emphasize that law courts were not simply agents of centralizing states and their rulers. Rather, they were institutions used by all sorts of people to resolve disputes, regulate conduct, and advance or protect the interests of individuals, families, and communities. The records of both secular and ecclesiastical courts have revealed much about the contours of criminal behavior in early modern societies and about the distance that might exist between crimes defined in law and those that were actively prosecuted.[7] Numerous studies have focused on individuals whose trials for heresy, clandestine marriage, prophecy, and fraud illuminate social attitudes and behaviors, as well as the judgments of learned magistrates.[8] Crime and its prosecution represent a mirror image of the contemporary concern with law, discipline, and order, and both reflect that "struggle for stability" which characterized much of European culture generally in the seventeenth century.[9]

---

[7] John Bossy, ed., *Disputes and Settlements: Law and Human Relations in the West* (Cambridge: Cambridge University Press, 1982); André Abbiateci et al., *Crimes et criminalité en France sous l'ancien régime, XVIIe–XVIIIe siècles* (Paris: A. Colin, 1971); V.A.C. Gatrell et al., eds., *Crime and the Law: The Social History of Crime in Western Europe since 1500* (London: Europa Publications, 1980); Michael Weisser, *Crime and Punishment in Early Modern Europe* (New Jersey: Humanities Press, 1979).

[8] Examples include Natalie Zemon Davis, *The Return of Martin Guerre* (Cambridge: Harvard University Press, 1983); Carlo Ginzburg, *The Cheese and the Worms: The Cosmos of a Sixteenth-Century Miller*, trans. John and Anne Tedeschi (Baltimore: Johns Hopkins University Press, 1980); Gene A. Brucker, *Giovanni and Lusanna: Love and Marriage in Renaissance Florence* (Berkeley: University of California Press, 1986); and Richard L. Kagan, *Lucrecia's Dreams: Politics and Prophecy in Sixteenth-Century Spain* (Berkeley: University of California Press, 1990).

[9] Theodore K. Rabb, *The Struggle for Stability in Early Modern Europe* (New York: Oxford University Press, 1975).

The Paris Chambre de l'Edit's work illustrates this multifaceted role of law and legal institutions in the struggle for stability and order in France. The court's criminal lawsuits show that French men and women were not merely subject to the law, but also willing to invoke the law's protection when they believed themselves to be abused or wronged. Litigants appealed to courts, magistrates, and in theory to the king himself as the fount of justice in the realm, but they sometimes sought to delay, circumvent, or subvert royal justice. Small wonder that the legal system seemed to produce chaos and corruption instead of order and fairness, a perception which spurred criticisms ranging from literary lampoons to official attempts at legal reform, such as the Code Michaud of 1629 and the Ordonnance Criminelle of 1670. The Chambre de l'Edit was part of the larger problems associated with the administration of justice, but it also contributed to the role of law and legal institutions in helping to create a sense of national identity in early modern France.

The emergence of the nation-state has long been viewed as one of the most important features of early modern European history in general and of French history in particular. Historians have tended to emphasize the French monarchy's successful subordination or co-optation of political and social elites that resulted in absolutism.[10] The nature and meaning of French absolutism has generated a great deal of debate; for the purposes of this study, absolutism refers to the monarchy's efforts to regulate political, social, economic, religious, and artistic activities by French men and women, as well as to theories which justified such regulation. The violent political and religious upheavals of the later sixteenth century spurred both the expansion of the central government's power and the focusing of popular allegiance on the French crown. Far from disrupting the growth of royal authority, the Wars of Religion ultimately promoted reliance on the monarchy as the sole entity capable of unifying the disparate elements of the French state. In theory, the king possessed a combination of sacral and secular power which remained entwined well into the eighteenth century, and which no other French official or institution could claim. As defender of the Gallican church's "liberties" and the kingdom's fundamental laws (which included eliminating heresy), the king occupied a pivotal place in a complex web of political and religious beliefs and institutions. The early modern French state thus was built around the monarchy if not actually by the monarch. French kings and their representatives

---

[10]Richard Bonney, "Absolutism: What's in a Name?" *French History* I (1986): 93–117; David Parker, *The Making of French Absolutism* (London: Edward Arnold, 1983); Nannerl O. Keohane, *Philosophy and the State in France: The Renaissance to the Enlightenment* (Princeton: Princeton University Press, 1980); Keith Cameron, ed., *From Valois to Bourbon: Dynasty, State and Society in Early Modern France* (Exeter: University of Exeter Press, 1989).

sought to dominate almost every aspect of individual and corporate life: politics and lawmaking, work and trade, religious worship and education, the arts, literature, and language. The monarchy's success in this endeavor is debatable, but the effort alone left an indelible mark upon the history of early modern France.

Some scholars have questioned the value of concepts such as "absolutism" and "state building," especially as applied to France between the sixteenth and seventeenth centuries.[11] According to these arguments, France remained a hierarchical corporate society whose medieval heritage of decentralized authority did not give way easily or inevitably to royal power during the sixteenth and seventeenth centuries. Numerous groups and institutions—nobles, clerics, guilds, municipalities, and others—defended their traditional privileges and proved to be a real obstacle to the ambitions of Valois and Bourbon rulers. The revolts and rebellions that occurred throughout the period showed recurrent if not always successful challenges to royal authority at the local level. Contemporary political pamphlets indicated that theories about the king's absolute power did not entirely efface competing strands of political theory which emphasized the king's duties to those he governed, rather than their obligation to obey him.[12] French kings and royal officials sought to uphold and extend the crown's power, but they did not set out to construct the political abstraction known as the modern nation-state, of which they had no conception. Instead, royal authority increased due to a convergence of interests among governing elites, lay and clerical, aristocratic and bourgeois. Though not always harmonious, this alliance of interests tended to produce support for the French crown and its policies, producing that royal dominance of state and society which reached its height with the absolutism of Louis XIV.

Historians have also sought the origins of French nationalism amid such political developments. Without denying the formative influence of the French Revolution, some scholars have traced French national consciousness as far back as the medieval period, linking it to concepts of the French people, their monarchy, and their religious heritage in western Christianity as they emerged during

---

[11] For a brief summary of the debate, see James B. Collins, *The State in Early Modern France* (Cambridge: Cambridge University Press, 1995), 1–27.

[12] See William Beik, *Urban Protest in Seventeenth-Century France: The Culture of Retribution* (Cambridge: Cambridge University Press, 1997); A. Lloyd Moote, *The Revolt of the Judges: The Parlement of Paris and the Fronde, 1643–1652* (Princeton: Princeton University Press, 1971); Sharon Kettering, *Judicial Politics and Urban Revolt in Seventeenth-Century France: The Parlement of Aix, 1629–1659* (Princeton: Princeton University Press, 1978). On pamphlet literature, see Jeffrey Sawyer, *Printed Poison: Pamphlet Propaganda, Faction Politics, and the Public Sphere in Early Seventeeth-Century France* (Berkeley: University of California Press, 1990); Christian Jouhaud, *Mazarinades: La Fronde des mots* (Paris: Aubier, 1985); Joseph Klaits, *Printed Propaganda under Louis XIV* (Princeton: Princeton University Press, 1976).

that era.[13] Events such as the French victory in the Hundred Years' War expanded and refined this inchoate mixture of cohesion and chosenness, strengthening the symbolic ties between crown and people. In the sixteenth century, the Wars of Religion helped forge a new sense of loyalty to the monarch as the arbiter of confessional differences in the realm.[14] The revolution of 1789, which pitted those loyal to the new republic against both foreign armies and conspirators within France's borders, thus appears as simply one in a series of key events that shaped French national identity before the nineteenth century. Other studies have shown how this identity grew out of long-term interactions between center and periphery: between the inhabitants of the Cerdagne or Finistère, for example, and officials who tried to govern those distant provinces from Paris.[15] French laws of citizenship also helped to redefine national identity during the early modern period, while both religious missions and secular education revealed efforts to transform the French people into a unified citizenry through a common language.[16] French national identity was clearly a cultural construct, something which was created collectively over time rather than imposed by a single ruler or institution, and which derived from a combination of geography, history, politics, language, and religion.

Scholarship about the medieval and early modern roots of national identity and controversy about absolutism have thus encouraged historians to redefine the formation of the early modern French nation-state as a gradual but powerful process. This process emerged from the ordinary day-to-day business of governing locally and regionally as well as from politics and diplomacy at the royal court; it often reshaped traditional elements and institutions of governance without dramatically

[13]Joseph Strayer, "France: The Holy Land, the Chosen People and the Most Christian King," in *Action and Conviction in Early Modern Europe*, ed. Theodore K. Rabb and Jerrold E. Seigel (Princeton: Princeton University Press, 1969), 3–16; Colette Beaune, *The Birth of an Ideology: Myths and Symbols of Nation in Late Medieval France*, trans. Susan Huston (Berkeley: University of California Press, 1991).

[14]Christopher Allmand, *The Hundred Years' War: England and France at War, c. 1300–c. 1450* (Cambridge: Cambridge University Press, 1988), esp. 136–50; Myriam Yardeni, *La Conscience nationale en France pendant les guerres de religion, 1550–1590* (Louvain: Nauwelaerts, 1971).

[15]Peter Sahlins, *Boundaries: The Making of France and Spain in the Pyrenees* (Berkeley: University of California Press, 1989); Caroline Ford, *Creating the Nation in Provincial France: Religion and Identity in Brittany* (Princeton: Princeton University Press, 1993).

[16]Charlotte Wells, *Law and Citizenship in Early Modern France* (Baltimore: Johns Hopkins University Press, 1994); Peter Sahlins, "Fictions of a Catholic France: The Naturalization of Foreigners, 1685–1787," *Representations* 47 (1994): 85–110; David A. Bell, "Lingua Populi, Lingua Dei: Language, Religion and the Origins of French Revolutionary Nationalism," *American Historical Review* 100 (1995): 1403–37; Douglas Johnson, "The Making of the French Nation," in *The National Question in Europe in Historical Context*, ed. Roy Porter and Mikuláš Teich (Cambridge: Cambridge University Press, 1993), 35–62.

overturning or replacing them. This process also involved historical actors from the entire spectrum of French society who promoted, modified, or resisted absolutism according to their own lights. Far from being confined to the realm of political, legal, or institutional history, the cultural construction of national identity appears as yet another facet of that effort to establish (or restore) discipline and order in society noted above—an effort which both engaged and divided Catholics and Huguenots, laypersons and clerics, royal officials and ordinary folk.

The Paris Chambre de l'Edit stands at the intersection of these struggles concerning social order, royal authority, and religious difference, illustrating how a specific institution—in this case, a law court—could contribute to the cultural construction of national identity. By the seventeenth century, obedience to the monarchy and its laws was one of the key features of French national identity, and French kings sought to exact this obedience from Huguenots and Catholics alike. The Edict of Nantes did not make the two confessional groups equal to each other, but it did claim to make them equally subject to royal authority and justice. Mandated by law, religious pluralism helped generate lawsuits like those heard before the Chambre de l'Edit, which in turn heightened the debate about national identity and who possessed it. To Huguenots, their privileges as guaranteed by law and enforced by royal authority made them part of the nation. To many Catholics, those same privileges set the Huguenots apart and precluded their full participation in politics and society; only by conversion could Huguenots fully integrate themselves into the French body politic. Huguenots argued that neither their political loyalty nor their legitimate status in French society was compromised by religious difference. They professed their allegiance to the "imagined community" of the nation (led by the monarchy and dedicated to upholding Catholicism) while trying to maintain another "imagined community" of those who shared their religion.[17] They continued to believe that obedience to the law would sustain their place in society and legitimate their membership in the nation.

The criminal lawsuits adjudicated by the Paris Chambre de l'Edit thus reveal dilemmas of identity—national and otherwise—in early modern France. Identity has been described as "the understanding of what, culturally, one is."[18] It is directly related to the things one shares or does not share with others: physical environment and property, social and economic activities, beliefs and standards of behavior. Past experiences and future goals shape identity, situating groups and individuals in what they perceive as their history. Since it involves both self-definition and the

---

[17] Benedict Anderson, *Imagined Communities: Reflections on the Origin and Spread of Nationalism*, 2d ed. (London: Verso, 1991).

[18] Anthony Pagden and Nicolas Canny, "From Identity to Independence," in *Colonial Identity in the Atlantic World, 1500–1800*, ed. Anthony Pagden and Nicolas Canny (Princeton: Princeton University Press, 1987), 270.

acceptance of one's self-image by others, identity is rarely static or one-dimensional. A person's or group's identity may be imposed by others or asserted in resistance to such impositions, and collective identities can be challenged or fractured from within.[19] Identity thus helps to connect individual and collective experience, and it has become part of the cultural history of early modern Europe through studies of the self, the family, social groups, and colonial societies, as well as appearing implicitly or explicitly in discussions of French nationalism and citizenship.[20]

Identity also connects the issues of religious difference, law, governance, and social order that inform this study of the Paris Chambre de l'Edit. The Huguenots' identity—their self-definition and acceptance (or rejection) by others—provoked conflicts which laws concerning the Huguenots could neither prevent nor contain. Indeed, the laws themselves became important weapons in those conflicts. Appearing as plaintiffs and defendants before the court, Huguenots and Catholics often competed to present themselves as law-abiding French subjects, and to characterize each other as subversive or disobedient. The court's adjudication of criminal lawsuits shows how the actions of judges, lawyers, and litigants contributed to an emerging sense of French national identity. The court's work also reveals that the growing pretensions of royal authority developed in tandem with the demands of the king's subjects, individually and collectively, for royal protection, mercy, and justice. Both submission and resistance thus contributed to the monarchy's growing power and an emerging sense of national identity. The Huguenots' experience suggests that it became increasingly difficult to claim an identity or membership in a community that did not acknowledge the king's superior place in the polity, society, and culture—and that did not depend upon submission to the king's laws. In the end, being Huguenot became not only illegal, but also incompatible with being French.

---

[19]See Jon Butler, *The Huguenots in America: A Refugee People in New World Society* (Cambridge: Harvard University Press, 1983); Stephen J. Greenblatt, *Renaissance Self-Fashioning: From More to Shakespeare* (Chicago: University of Chicago Press, 1980); the essays in *Colonial Identity in the Atlantic World*, ed. Pagden and Canny, and in *Changing Identities in Early Modern France*, ed. Wolfe.

[20]See especially Natalie Zemon Davis, "Boundaries and the Sense of Self in Sixteenth-Century France," in *Reconstructing Individualism: Autonomy, Individuality and the Self in Western Thought*, ed. Thomas C. Heller et al. (Stanford: Stanford University Press, 1986), 53–63; Davis, "Ghosts, Kin and Progeny: Some Features of Family Life in Early Modern France," *Daedalus* 106, no. 2 (1977): 87–114; Jonathan Dewald, *Aristocratic Experience and the Origins of Modern Culture: France, 1570–1715* (Berkeley: University of California Press, 1980); Daniel Gordon, *Citizens without Sovereignty: Equality and Sociability in French Thought, 1670–1789* (Princeton: Princeton University Press, 1994). The "microhistories" listed in note 11 also concern issues of individual and collective identity to some degree; on nationalism and citizenship, see notes 16 through 19 above.

Understanding the Paris Chambre de l'Edit's work in relation to religious difference, governance, social order, and the cultural creation of national identity accounts for this book's purpose, structure, and conclusions. Chapter 1 considers the chamber's role in the troubled history of the Huguenots and the law in seventeenth-century France, describing the court's legal mandate as well as contemporary views of the court's purpose and significance. Chapter 2 analyzes the court's judges, litigants, and procedures. Chapters 3, 4, and 5 examine three categories of legal disputes brought before the court: lawsuits related to the Wars of Religion, in which the "memory" of the past was legally contested; cases related to the family and its key components (marriage, sexuality, and inheritance); and cases concerning local conflicts between Huguenots and Catholics over implementation of the Edict of Nantes's terms. Each of these categories represents an important source of disorder that the chamber judges tried to address.

The Paris Chambre de l'Edit thus offers new insights into the political, legal, and cultural history of early modern France. The court's *minutes d'arrêt* include heated debates about the difference between a war crime and a crime committed during wartime; families and communities divided or united by their legal disputes; and individuals who, in the face of misconduct by local officials, neighbors, relatives, or strangers, demanded that "force remain with the king and justice" (discussed in chap. 5). Legal procedure becomes a dynamic mode of interaction among the parties and the judges to whom they have appealed. The theme that permeates the court's business is the effort to restore peace and maintain order among all who petitioned for justice, as well as to address the complaints of one specific group in French society, the Huguenots. Royal authority—indeed, authority of all kinds—had been fragmented by the factional and religious conflicts of the later sixteenth century. The desire to renew popular allegiance to the crown, to restore the efficacy and integrity of law throughout the kingdom, to mend the social fabric, and to address the ongoing tensions surrounding religious difference all gave a larger purpose to the court's judgment of specific disputes. This study concludes that above all, the Paris Chambre de l'Edit dispensed royal justice to Huguenot and Catholic litigants. In doing so, the court insisted upon the petitioners' individual and collective acknowledgment of royal authority, thus strengthening the monarchy's claim to be an essential source of power and privilege, community and identity in early modern France.

"Le Port de Salut et repos de cet etat"

Huguenots & the Law in Seventeenth-Century France

IN APRIL 1598, HENRY IV DECLARED THAT BY THE GRACE OF GOD
the kingdom of France was finally at peace. His declaration encompassed not only
an end to the civil and religious warfare of the past thirty-six years, but also a
foundation for future unity and recovery. After considering the complaints and
demands of both Catholics and Huguenots, and having consulted his principal
councilors, the king was ready to provide his subjects with "a general law on all of
this, clear, precise, and absolute, by which they might be governed with regard to
all such differences as have hitherto sprung up, or may hereafter arise among
them, and by which both sides may be contented insofar as the spirit of the times
will permit."[1] The peace agreement known as the Edict of Nantes actually comprised several documents, including a set of secret articles and two *brevets* concerning royal subsidies and military protection for the Huguenots. A fourth
document—the general edict of pacification—outlined the terms under which
Huguenots would be permitted to live, work, and worship alongside French Catholics, and to litigate against them.[2]

---

[1]"The Edict of Nantes with Its Secret Articles and Brevets," trans. Jotham Parsons, in *The Edict
of Nantes: Five Essays and a New Translation*, ed. Richard L. Goodbar (Bloomington, Minn.: National
Huguenot Society, 1998), 42. Unless otherwise indicated, references are to articles in the general
edict. This translation is based on the French text of the Edict of Nantes reprinted in Roland Mousnier, *L'Assassinat d'Henri IV* (Paris: Gallimard, 1964), 294–334.

[2]For a summary of the Edict of Nantes's complex provisions, see Mack P. Holt, *The French Wars of
Religion, 1562–1629* (Cambridge: Cambridge University Press, 1995), 162–66. *Brevets* were executive

The Edict of Nantes has become the most famous of the many laws that defined the Huguenots' status and activities in early modern France. It made France's Calvinists a privileged though vulnerable minority, and it remained the touchstone of their claims to royal protection and fair treatment by other French men and women throughout the seventeenth century. The edict was intended to establish a regime of peaceful coexistence among Henry IV's subjects, though it was probably not meant to be a permanent solution to the problems of religious difference within the kingdom. Although it was amended and renewed by Henry's successors, the edict was often narrowly interpreted and applied by royal officials and judges (supported by members of the French Catholic clergy). Its formal revocation by Louis XIV in 1685 was merely the last in a long series of legal maneuvers against the Huguenots.[3]

Prior to the revocation, French men and women invoked and argued about the Edict of Nantes in pamphlets, treatises, letters, memoirs, and lawsuits. The fact that the edict could serve the interests of many different groups—Huguenots and Catholics, lawyers and polemicists, clerics, jurists, and monarchs—explains why it was such a powerful tool for both governance and resistance. Law in general, and this law in particular, greatly affected the Huguenots' status and helped to define their identity after the Wars of Religion, albeit in ambiguous ways. As one of the special law courts mandated by the edict and responsible for enforcing its provisions, the Paris Chambre de l'Edit played an important role in this process. The complex and troubled relationship between the Huguenots and the law during the seventeenth century is an essential context for understanding the court and its work.

orders issued on the king's authority alone, and unlike the general edict of pacification they were not registered by the parlements.

[3]Elisabeth Labrousse, "Calvinism in France, 1598–1685," in *International Calvinism, 1541–1715*, ed. Menna Prestwich (Oxford: Clarendon Press, 1985), 301; N. M. Sutherland, "The Huguenots and the Edict of Nantes," in *Huguenots in Britain and Their French Background, 1550–1800*, ed. Irene Scoloudi (London: Macmillan Press, 1987), 158–72; idem, "The Crown, the Huguenots and the Edict of Nantes," in *The Huguenot Connection: The Edict of Nantes, Its Revocation, and Early French Migration to South Carolina*, ed. Richard Golden (Dordrecht: Kluwer Academic Publishers, 1988), 28–48. On the Edict of Nantes's revocation, see Labrousse, *Une foi*; Garrisson, *L'Edit de Nantes et sa révocation*; Jean Quéniart, *La Révocation de l'Edit de Nantes: Protestants et catholiques en France de 1598 à 1685* (Paris: Desclée de Brouwer, 1985).

The Edict of Nantes formed a fragile bridge between the war-torn past of the later sixteenth century and the hope of a more peaceful future. Among other things, it was the last in a series of peace treaties negotiated among Huguenot and Catholic factions and the French crown during the Wars of Religion. The circumstances that produced this agreement were especially tense. Henry of Navarre became king of France upon the death of his cousin Henry III in 1589, but he was not universally recognized or welcomed by his subjects. After converting publicly to Catholicism in July 1593, he gradually won the support and submission of many Catholic nobles and urban elites. By 1595, however, his success had led to open war with Spain (which sought to rally opposition to the king among renegade leaders of the Catholic League), as well as increased fear and discontent among the Huguenots. Led by nobles such as the duc de Bouillon and the duc de La Trémoille, Huguenot political assemblies insisted upon substantial concessions from Henry IV as the price of their participation in the war against Spain.[4] As a peace treaty, the Edict of Nantes was shaped by the king's immediate struggles against rebellious subjects and foreign enemies; as a religious settlement, it was meant to placate both Huguenots and Catholics with a set of practical, temporary arrangements that would establish civil order until a more permanent solution to France's religious divisions could be achieved.

The Edict of Nantes comprised four documents that did not have equal legal or political standing. Indeed, Henry IV's most generous concessions to the Huguenots were also the most tenuous. In two *brevets* dated 3 and 30 April 1598, the king agreed to subsidize Huguenot pastors and *places de sûreté*—fortified towns that would be garrisoned either with royal troops or local militias for the Huguenots' protection. Yet the king could revoke the *brevets* at will; they would expire in eight years unless renewed and would become invalid at his death unless preserved by his successor. In the secret articles, Henry allowed for exceptions to the general edict's terms, notably concerning towns where Reformed worship was permitted or forbidden. Other clauses protected specific individuals like the king's supporter François de La Noue and his son Odet, who were exempted from legal proceedings brought against them during the 1580s.[5] Such arrangements mirrored Henry's efforts to appease Catholic nobles by granting them offices, lands, and pardons for their past actions, as well as his flexible policy toward municipal leaders in towns across France.[6] The secret articles and *brevets* thus illustrated the king's

---

[4] N. M. Sutherland, *The Huguenot Struggle for Recognition* (New Haven: Yale University Press, 1980); Wolfe, *The Conversion of Henri IV.*

[5] "Edict of Nantes," 62 (Secret Articles, art. 34), 65 (Secret Articles, art. 56).

[6] Annette Finley-Croswhite, *Henry IV and the Towns* (Cambridge: Cambridge University Press, 1999).

general policy of treating his Huguenot and Catholic subjects in an evenhanded manner in order to win their obedience and achieve peace.

This goal was also reflected in the general edict of 13 April 1598. It outlined a blueprint for peaceful coexistence between Huguenots and Catholics for the immediate future, in the form of a "perpetual and irrevocable" law backed by the authority of the Bourbon monarchy. According to the preamble, Henry intended to prevent religious differences from disrupting the peace which God had bestowed upon the kingdom and "to bring it about that he should be worshiped and adored by all our subjects; and if it has not yet pleased him to permit that this should be by one and the same form of religion, then it should at least be with the same intention, and under such a rule that there should arise no tumult and disturbance on account of it among them."[7] The king would impose peace among his subjects based upon their common adherence to the law, at least until such time as their religious differences could be reconciled or overcome.

Not surprisingly, both confessional groups viewed the edict with suspicion and dissatisfaction. For many Catholics, the settlement gave too much protection to heretics who still threatened the kingdom's moral and political well-being. The Assembly of the Clergy opposed the special law courts, church synods, and admission to French universities guaranteed by the edict for Huguenots. Royal magistrates in the predominantly Catholic parlements of Paris, Bordeaux, Toulouse, Aix-en-Provence, and Rennes resisted registering the edict; the parlement of Rouen would not do so until 1609.[8] On the other hand, Huguenots noted with alarm that the edict clearly endorsed Catholicism as the official religion of France. Catholic worship was to be restored in areas where it had been disrupted by the religious wars. Catholic clerics and religious communities could reclaim property and goods that had been confiscated by Huguenot authorities, and the purchasers of such property could apply for reimbursement from the crown for the losses they incurred. Huguenots were required to observe religious holidays according to the Catholic calendar, to acknowledge the authority of canon law in matters related to marriage, and to pay the Catholic Church's tithe.[9]

In keeping with its double goal of restoring Catholicism and protecting Calvinism, the edict weakened but did not destroy the Huguenots' ecclesiastical institutions. Inspired by the teaching of John Calvin and the influence of missionaries from Geneva, Huguenot communities had established a hierarchy of local

[7]"Edict of Nantes," 42. See also Mario Turchetti, "La Qualification de 'perpétuel et irrévocable' appliquée à l'Edit de Nantes (1598)," *Bulletin de la société de l'histoire du protestantisme français* [hereafter *B.S.H.P.F.*] 139 (1993): 41–78.

[8]Holt, *French Wars of Religion*, 167–69; Ligou, *Le Protestantisme en France*, 20–25.

[9]"Edict of Nantes," 42–43 (arts. 3, 4), 45–46 (arts. 20, 23, 25).

consistories, provincial synods and colloquys, and national synods during the 1550s. The Huguenot laity participated with ministers in these institutions by serving as elders (*anciens*) and deacons in the consistories, and as representatives to the colloquys and synods that met periodically during the later sixteenth century.[10] The Edict of Nantes upheld this ecclesiastical organization with two important modifications contained in the secret articles. First, Huguenot consistories, colloquies, and synods could only meet in places where "the public exercise of the said religion shall be undertaken…by permission of His Majesty"; such public worship was already restricted by the general edict's terms. In addition, national synods could only be convened with the king's permission.[11] Henry IV and his successors would allow Huguenot synods to meet periodically until 1659 but would insist that they consider only religious and doctrinal matters.

Other clauses in the Edict of Nantes permitted but also constrained Reformed religious practice. The articles concerning public and private worship (*liberté de culte*) reveal this pattern. Huguenot noblemen who possessed full legal jurisdiction over the people on their estates (*haute justice*) could hold religious services for a congregation of any size, as long as they themselves were present; lesser seigneurs could do so only for their families and groups of no more than thirty. Reformed worship could not take place at all within the jurisdiction of a Catholic seigneur without his permission. The death or conversion of an individual nobleman (or his descendants) could therefore jeopardize Reformed worship on his lands and among his dependents.[12] Outside the seigneury, Huguenots were guaranteed two places of public worship for each *bailliage* and *sénéchaussée*, but these were restricted to the outskirts of provincial towns. Existing places of worship were protected by the edict if they had held services since 1596 or if they had been authorized by the treaties of Nérac (1579) and Fleix (1580).[13] Many Huguenot communities, however, had found it difficult to support a minister financially or

---

[10]Holt, *French Wars of Religion*, 14–49; J.H.M. Salmon, *Society in Crisis: France in the Sixteenth Century* (New York: Methuen, 1975), 188–24; Mark Greengrass, *The French Reformation* (Oxford: Blackwell, 1987); Robert M. Kingdon, *Geneva and the Coming of the Wars of Religion in France* (Geneva: Droz, 1956); idem, *Geneva and the Consolidation of the French Protestant Movement* (Geneva: Droz, 1967). On lay participation in French Calvinist ecclesiastical institutions, see Samuel Mours, *Le Protestantisme en France au XVIe siècle* (Paris: Librairie Protestante, 1959), 114–18; Robert Mandrou et al., *Histoire des Protestants* (Toulouse: Privat, 1977), 72–85; Glenn S. Sunshine, "Geneva Meets Rome: The Development of the French Reformed Diaconate," *Sixteenth Century Journal* 26 (1995): 329–46; Labrousse, "Calvinism in France," 285–93.

[11]"Edict of Nantes," 62 (Secret Articles, art. 34); Ligou, *Le Protestantisme en France*, 16.

[12]"Edict of Nantes," 43–44, (arts. 7, 8).

[13]"Edict of Nantes," 44 (arts. 9–11).

to maintain their congregations during the later sixteenth century. It has been esti-
mated that the number of Reformed churches in France had fallen by about 30
percent during the period of 1570 through 1598, a circumstance which mitigated
the edict's protection.[14] Moreover, Reformed worship was explicitly banned at the
French royal court, in Paris, and within a five-league radius of that city. Even
books concerning "the so-called reformed religion" [la religion prétendue
réformée] could only be printed and sold in towns where Reformed worship was
legally permitted.[15] As a result, the edict's many specific conditions simultaneously protected and restricted the Huguenots' public worship.

In contrast to the limited protection given to the French Reformed churches
and public worship, the Edict of Nantes sought to dismantle the Huguenots'
political organization. During the first half of the sixteenth century, Calvinism
had spread rapidly among the French nobility, urban elites, and various occupa-
tional groups, as well as in some areas of the countryside. The Saint Bartholomew's Day massacre of August 1572 sparked a series of assemblies among the
Huguenots of southern and western France to organize political and military
resistance to their Catholic enemies and the monarchy that had apparently
betrayed them. By 1573, the Huguenots of the Midi had launched a kind of fed-
eral republic that later included Reformed communities throughout France. In
this "Protestant state," Huguenot provincial governors administered regional
affairs in concert with councils and assemblies composed of nobles, ministers,
lawyers, and notaries. Another council conducted financial, diplomatic, and political affairs at the national level, aided by an annual assembly of deputies from the
provinces. Henri de Bourbon, prince de Condé, Henri de Montmorency-Damville, and finally Henry of Navarre himself served in turn as protector of the
Huguenot churches and communities—the individual designated to lead military
actions and defense.[16] The uneven geography of Huguenot strength, along with
internal conflicts among the Huguenot leaders, councils, and assemblies, prevented this political regime from being completely united or effective during the
Wars of Religion. Yet it represented as great a threat to Henry IV's goals of restoring peace and obedience to the French crown as its counterpart, the Catholic
League.

---

[14]Mandrou et al., *Histoire des Protestants*, 67–69. Using figures first provided by Samuel Mours,
Janine Garrisson estimates that the number of Reformed churches in northern France dropped from
514 in 1570 to 346 in 1598; the Midi churches' number fell from 729 to 501 in the same time
period.

[15]"Edict of Nantes," 44–45 (arts. 13–15, 21).

[16]Holt, *French Wars of Religion*, 98–120; Janine Garrisson, *Les Protestants du Midi, 1559–1598* (Toulouse: Privat, 1980).

The Edict of Nantes thus dissolved all Huguenot provincial assemblies and councils, along with other leagues and associations. In the general edict, the king particularly forbade his subjects to raise money or troops, to construct fortifications, or conduct diplomatic negotiations without royal permission. Article 77 absolved Huguenots of responsibility for the activities that their political assemblies and councils had conducted during wartime, including tax and toll collections, military garrisons, and diplomacy with foreign powers—in short, "of all which has been done, deliberated, written, and ordered by the said assemblies and councils." Neither the men who had commanded and carried out such actions nor their widows and heirs could be prosecuted at law.[17] The edict abolished the past deeds of the Huguenot and Catholic political regimes, as well as outlawing such organizations for the future.

In place of their own "state within a state," the Huguenots would have to depend upon the king and his officials to uphold the edict's terms, and this was perhaps the greatest limitation imposed upon the Calvinist minority. In addition to the bipartisan law courts affiliated with the parlements (described in detail below), the king would appoint special commissioners to assure that the edict was implemented properly in the provinces. *Baillis*, *sénéchaux*, and *procureurs généraux* throughout France were commanded to enforce its tenets rigorously.[18] For the Huguenots, the price of this protection was loyalty to the king and their own obedience to the law. Article 6 of the general edict implied such a quid pro quo:

> And to leave no occasion for troubles and differences among our subjects, we have permitted and do permit those of the so-called Reformed religion to live and dwell in all cities and places of this our kingdom and the lands of our obedience, without being questioned, vexed, or molested, nor constrained to do anything with regard to religion contrary to their conscience, nor on account of it to be searched out in their houses and the places where they wish to dwell, bearing themselves otherwise according to what is in our present edict.[19]

For Henry IV, the Edict of Nantes was intended to achieve a measure of peace and order among Huguenots and Catholics that would help restore France's glory, unity, and power. He promised to make sure that the edict was "strictly observed

---

[17]"Edict of Nantes," 54 (art. 76), 56–57 (art. 82), 55 (art. 77), the source of the quoted statement.

[18]On the royal commissioners, see François Garrisson, *Essai sur les commissions d'application de l'Edit de Nantes, règne Henri IV* (Montpellier: Déhan, 1950); Elisabeth Rabut, *Le Roi, l'église et le temple: L'execution de l'Edit de Nantes en Dauphiné* (Grenoble: Editions La Pensée Sauvage, 1987).

[19]"Edict of Nantes," 43 (art. 6).

without allowing it to be infringed any way," but he also prayed that God would make his subjects realize "that in the observance of this ordinance consists (next to their duty towards God and towards all) the principal foundation of their union, concord, tranquility and repose, and of the reestablishment of this whole state in its first splendor, opulence, and strength."[20]

Henry's double goal of rebuilding France and preserving its Calvinist minority no doubt derived from his close ties to both the Huguenot cause and the French crown. The son of Antoine de Bourbon and Jeanne d'Albret, queen of Navarre and a formidable Huguenot leader in her own right, Henry was raised and educated at the royal courts of Navarre and France. He became the titular chief of the French Calvinists in 1569 at the age of fifteen and managed to retain the loyalty of most Huguenots despite his conversion to Catholicism in 1572, at the time of his marriage to Marguerite de Valois. Henry had apparently reflected upon his potential destiny as ruler of France even before June 1584, when the death of King Henry III's younger brother François, duc d'Anjou, made him heir to the throne. In a letter written to Henri de Montmorency-Damville in 1576, he declared, "I realize that not only is my private interest joined with the public, but that, after my lord the king and his brother, I have a greater interest in the conservation and reestablishment of this kingdom than anyone in the world."[21] Henry of Navarre's claim to have a personal stake in France's future foreshadowed the purpose he expressed years later in issuing the Edict of Nantes. Being well acquainted with the Huguenots' capacity for organization and resistance, he was determined to prevent them from challenging the monarchy's power or the kingdom's return to peace and stability. He would restore France to greatness by insisting upon his subjects' submission to royal authority despite religious difference.

The Edict of Nantes therefore was not a declaration of religious toleration or freedom of conscience, but rather a law intended to regulate religious divisions in the interests of peace. The edict protected Calvinism and restored Catholicism as France's official religion, but it did so within the tradition of Gallicanism—the monarchy's special power to defend the Christian faith within France's borders. Since the late medieval period, French kings and jurists had invoked Gallicanism to extend royal control over clerical appointments, church taxes, and religious policy, usually at the expense of papal authority. As the Wars of Religion drew to a close, Gallicanism helped to bolster Henry IV's demand for French Catholics'

---

[20]"Edict of Nantes," 42.

[21]Quoted in Jean-Pierre Babelon, *Henri IV* (Paris: Fayard, 1981), 226: Je reconnais que non seulement mon intérêt particulier est conjoint avec le public, mais que, après la personne de mon roi, mon seigneur, et de Monsieur son frère, j'ai plus grand intérêt à la conservation et rétablissement de ce royaume que personne de ce monde.

loyalty and submission, especially after his own public conversion to that faith. It also reinforced his claim to the Huguenots' allegiance, since they were French subjects and fellow Christians. Most of all, the Gallican tradition supported Henry's likely goal of eventually reconciling his subjects in a common allegiance to Catholicism and the crown, embodied in the formula, "une foi, une loi, un roi."[22] According to the edict's terms, the king became the arbiter of confessional differences via the law, something that fit well into Gallican conceptions of royal authority in religious matters.

The edict also endowed the Huguenots with a set of specific privileges that both protected and constrained their activities. In general, privileges entitled persons and groups to do things that others could not, such as wear certain kinds of clothing. Privileges also exempted some people from obligations that others had to fulfill, such as paying taxes or accepting a certain court's jurisdiction. Privilege thus served as an important matrix of corporate identity and interaction in early modern French society, establishing distinctions between clergy and laity, nobles and wealthy commoners, and the members of various professions and trades. Towns jealously guarded the "liberties" contained in their charters, and peasants—the least privileged group in French society—might protest their overlords' or the crown's infringement of customary practices regarding common lands and forest use as violating a kind of privilege. Privilege often depended for its effectiveness on the acknowledgment of those who lived within the system, yet privileges could also be expressed in the form of laws, as the example of sumptuary legislation shows. Such laws might not prevent persons from exercising privileges to which they were not entitled, but privileges expressed in the form of law could be enforced by means other than social recognition.[23]

[22]Holt, *French Wars of Religion*, 14–49; on Gallicanism in a broader seventeenth-century context, see William J. Bouwsma, "Gallicanism and the Nature of Christendom," in Bouwsma, *A Usable Past*, 308–24; George Rothrock, "The Gallican Resurgence after the Death of Henry IV," *The Historian* 24 (1961): 1–25.

[23]On sumptuary laws, see Diane Owen Hughes, "Sumptuary Law and Social Relations in Renaissance Italy," in *Disputes and Settlements: Law and Human Relations in the West*, ed. John Bossy (Cambridge: Cambridge University Press, 1982), 69–99; Catherine Kovesi Killerby, "Practical Problems in the Enforcement of Italian Sumptuary Law, 1200–1500," in *Crime, Society and the Law in Renaissance Italy*, ed. Trevor Dean and Kate Lowe (Cambridge: Cambridge University Press, 1994), 99–120. For France, much of the research on problems of privilege has focused on the nobility: see especially George Huppert, *Les Bourgeois Gentilhommes: An Essay on the Definition of Elites in Renaissance France* (Chicago: University of Chicago Press, 1977); Jonathan Dewald, *Formation of a Provincial Nobility: The Magistrates of the Parlement of Rouen, 1499–1610* (Princeton: Princeton University Press, 1980); Ellery Schalk, *From Valor to Pedigree: Ideas of Nobility in France in the Sixteenth and Seventeenth Centuries* (Princeton: Princeton University Press, 1986). More generally, see Roland Mousnier, *The Institutions of France under the Absolute Monarchy, 1598–1789*, trans. Brian Pearce (Chicago: University of Chicago Press, 1979), 113–68;

In granting the Huguenots privileges regarding worship, education, employment, and justice, the Edict of Nantes left them with an ambiguous legacy while strengthening the power of the French crown and its officials to control this particular corporate group. Like Catholics, Huguenots were required to honor the law, keep the peace, and obey the king, but their privileges effectively set them apart within French society. Their separate places of worship, cemeteries, and law courts gave them a kind of public recognition, but separation also reinforced the view that they remained a threat to the French state—a view still held by many Catholics.[24] The Huguenots would have to depend upon the monarchy to defend their protected but limited position in Catholic France. When they believed the Edict of Nantes had been violated, they often appealed to the king or his magistrates in the Paris Chambre de l'Edit for justice.

Like other elements of the Edict of Nantes, its provisions for bipartisan law courts can be traced back to earlier peace treaties issued during the Wars of Religion, when the Huguenots battled for protection from their Catholic opponents in the royal judiciary. The Edict of Saint Germain (1570) nullified all judgments and legal proceedings against Huguenots since 1567 and allowed Huguenot litigants to demand that a specific number of parlement magistrates abstain from judging their appeals.[25] Over the next six years, such requests evolved from recusing judges to separate law courts. Huguenot political assemblies proposed the establishment of Protestant parlements or special tribunals composed of judges from the Grand Conseil, a sovereign court of law within the king's council.[26] The Edict of Beaulieu (also known as the Peace of Monsieur) of May 1576 ordered the creation of chambres mi-parties in all eight parlements. These chambers would possess equal numbers of Huguenot and Catholic judges and would judge any criminal or civil dispute involving a Huguenot litigant. The courts' Huguenot magistrates were assured the same privileges, status, and honors as their Catholic counterparts.[27]

William Beik, *Absolutism and Society in Seventeenth-Century France* (Cambridge: Cambridge University Press, 1985), 3–33; David Parker, "The Social Foundations of French Absolutism, 1610–1630," *Past and Present* 53 (1971): 67–89.

[24]Janine Garrisson, *Henri IV* (Paris: Seuil, 1984), 276–81; Bernard Dompnier, *Le Venin de l'hérésie: L'image du protestantisme et combat catholique pendant le XVIIe siècle* (Paris: Le Centurion, 1985); Grandjean and Roussel, eds., *Coexister dans l'intolérance.*

[25]The text of the edict of Saint Germain is published in Eugène Haag and Émil Haag, *La France protestante*, vol. 1, *Pièces justificatives* (Paris: J. Cherbuliez, 1846–59), 96–97.

[26]Léonce Anquez, *Histoire des assemblées politiques des réformés en France, 1573–1622* (Paris: A. Durand, 1859), 120–21.

[27]For the text of the Edict of Beaulieu, see Haag and Haag, *Pièces justificatives*, 127–41.

In 1577, however, the Edict of Poitiers and secret articles negotiated by King Henry III with Henry of Navarre and the prince de Condé significantly altered these arrangements. The special chambers attached to the parlements would include Catholic and Huguenot judges but not necessarily in equal numbers, and they would be selected by the king on Navarre's recommendation.[28] The Edict of Poitiers was implemented with greater success than the Edict of Beaulieu; chambres exceptionnelles (law courts with various combinations of Huguenot and Catholic magistrates) were established at Paris, Grenoble, and Bordeaux. The chamber that opened at Lisle-en-Albigeois in June 1579 to serve the province of Languedoc was evenly divided between Huguenot and Catholic judges and thus a true chambre mi-partie.[29]

The bipartisan chambers' history during the decades that followed was one of constant suspicion and turmoil. In attempting to enforce the Edict of Poitiers, the French crown negotiated two additional agreements that supported the 1577 edict's terms. The treaty of Nérac (1579) forbade other sovereign courts from adjudicating cases involving Huguenots while the special chambers were being founded. While conducting inquiries into criminal cases, judges of each religion were required to work with an assistant (adjoint) of the other faith. The treaty of Fleix, issued in November 1580, condemned the intervention of other law courts in Huguenot litigation and enjoined royal officials to obey the special chambers' decisions and decrees.[30] The chief problem with all of these agreements was the French crown's inability to enforce their provisions among local judicial officials or the Catholic populace. Deputies at the Huguenot political assemblies held between 1581 and 1584 complained about the parlements' hostility to the special

---

[28]François-André Isambert et al., *Recueil général des anciennes lois françaises* (Paris: Belin-Leprieur, 1833), 14:300–41, contains the text of the Edict of Poitiers and the secret articles.

[29]Anquez, *Histoire des assemblées politiques*, 125–26; M. Sacaze, "Les Chambres mi-parties des anciens parlements: La Chambre de l'Edit du Languedoc, 1576–1679," *B.S.H.P.F.* 3 (1855): 362–77; Raymond A. Mentzer, "The Formation of the Chambre de l'Edit of Languedoc," *Proceedings of the Annual Meeting of the Western Society for French History* 8 (1980): 47–56; Capot, *Justice et religion en Languedoc*. The terminology used to describe these courts is a bit confusing. "Chambre de l'Edit" originally dates from the Edict of Beaulieu though it is used in the seventeenth century to describe the courts mandated by the Edict of Nantes. "Chambre de l'Edit" is sometimes used interchangeably with "chambre mi-partie" although not all of the special courts had equal numbers of Huguenot and Catholic judges, as was the case in Languedoc. "Chambres triparties" referred to courts with two presidents (one of each faith) and a group of judges unevenly divided between Huguenots and Catholics.

[30]The texts of these treaties appear in Haag and Haag, *Pièces justificatives*, 159–67 (treaty of Nérac) and 171–78 (treaty of Fleix); see also Anquez, *Histoire des assemblées politiques*, 126–29. For a comparative summary of each treaty, along with the other edicts and declarations issued during the Wars of Religion, see Sutherland, *Huguenot Struggle for Recognition*, 334–72.

chambers, especially in the southern provinces, as well as the crown's delays in appointing Huguenot candidates to judicial offices. The treaty of Nemours (1585) surely confirmed the Huguenots' worst fears about securing protection through the royal judiciary: it revoked the Huguenots' eligibility for offices, military strongholds, and public worship, as well as abolishing the bipartisan law courts. The Edict of Union issued in 1588 further cemented the alliance between Henry III and the Catholic League at the Huguenots' expense.[31]

Henry of Navarre's troubled accession to the throne as Henry IV the following year brought new conflicts concerning the chambres exceptionnelles. In November 1590 Henry revoked all such law courts, yet the Edict of Mantes (1591) appeared to reverse that decision: it annulled the decrees of 1585 and 1588 and restored previous edicts that had upheld the special chambers. At Huguenot political assemblies that met during the period of 1594 through 1598, deputies demanded chambres mi-parties for all of France's parlements and threatened to ignore royal tribunals entirely if the king did not accede to their wishes. Henry responded by confirming only the chambers already founded at Paris and Languedoc, though he offered to create a temporary bipartisan court at Tours and to permit recusation of suspect judges. Despite the Huguenots' insistence on privileged access to the royal judiciary as both magistrates and litigants, the king apparently regarded the special law courts as unjust and symbolic of divisions that eventually would have to be abolished among his subjects.[32] Nevertheless, provisions for bipartisan law courts and the administration of justice generally comprised roughly one-third of the Edict of Nantes's articles in the general edict; five other clauses pertaining to the courts appeared among the secret articles. The edict's terms reflected both the Huguenots' long-standing concerns about their position as litigants, magistrates, and seekers of judicial office, and Henry IV's desire to limit the "separateness" of the special chambers.

The edict restricted the number of chambres mi-parties to three, maintaining the chamber in Languedoc (which now met in the town of Castres) and mandating two other such courts for the parlements of Grenoble and Bordeaux. This entailed creating new judicial offices for Huguenots in both parlements (seven at Bordeaux and four at Grenoble), and the king himself would choose the Catholic magistrates to serve in these chambres mi-parties. No bipartisan chambers would be affiliated with the parlements of Aix or Dijon: Provence was included in the

[31] Anquez, *Histoire des assemblées politiques*, 129–33. The texts of the treaty of Nemours and the Edict of Union appear in Haag and Haag, *Pièces justificatives*, 184–87 and 201–3, respectively.

[32] Sutherland, *Huguenot Struggle for Recognition*, 293–99, 311–23; Anquez, *Histoire des assemblées politiques*, 131–33. Anquez quotes Henry as describing the chambres mi-parties in 1596 as "une alteration de la justice et une marque insigne de la division qu'il serait bien nécessaire d'ôter" (186).

Grenoble court's jurisdiction, and Huguenots in Burgundy could appeal their cases to the chambers at Grenoble or Paris.[33] The edict also mitigated the chambres mi-parties' distinctive identity and independence in relation to their respective parlements. Article 35 declared the Grenoble chamber "united and incorporated with the body of the said parlement." Its Huguenot magistrates were made full members of the parlement and therefore, the article continued, "the presidents and councilors of the so-called Reformed religion...shall at first be distributed among the other chambers and then extracted and taken out of them, to be employed and to serve in the one which we newly order."[34] Article 36 promised that the Languedoc and Bordeaux chambers would be likewise incorporated into their respective parlements "when...the causes which moved us to establish them shall cease and no longer take place among our subjects."[35] Such clauses reflected Henry IV's view of the courts as a temporary measure, as well as his efforts to emphasize the chambers' ties to, rather than their independence from, the parlements.

The Chambre de l'Edit ordained for the Parlement of Paris illustrated these aspects of royal policy even more clearly. It would consist of a president and sixteen councilors but would receive only one of the four Huguenot magistrates who were to serve in the parlement as a whole. The Paris chamber's geographical jurisdiction matched that of the parlement, covering the provinces of Picardy, Champagne, Touraine, Poitou, Anjou, and Saintonge, as well as Ile-de-France and the areas surrounding the city. It also included Normandy and Brittany, at least until similar chambers could be founded for the parlements of Rouen and Rennes. Finally, the Paris Chambre de l'Edit was supposed to resolve lawsuits for which the provincial chambres mi-parties had rendered split decisions.[36] Thus, the chamber that exercised the broadest legal and geographical competence was also fully integrated into its affiliated parlement and involved the least participation of Huguenot judges.

Along with embedding the bipartisan law courts within their respective parlements, the edict emphasized the chambers' specific jurisdiction over the Huguenots and recalled earlier efforts to give the religious minority legal protection. As sovereign courts of appeal, the special chambers could adjudicate virtually any civil or criminal case in which at least one of the parties was Huguenot. Such cases could include infractions of the edict itself and therefore covered a wide range of matters related to the public exercise of Reformed religion. The chambers were

[33]"Edict of Nantes," 47 (arts. 31–33).
[34]"Edict of Nantes," 48 (art. 35).
[35]"Edict of Nantes," 48 (art. 36).
[36]"Edict of Nantes," 46–47 (art. 30), 49 (art. 47).

authorized to probate wills involving Huguenots, and the secret articles of May 1598 gave them cognizance of disputes about the validity of Huguenot marriages.[37] These provisions recalled the chambers' main purpose, at least from the Huguenots' perspective: to provide equity and protection for Huguenot litigants who found themselves facing hostility and prejudice from their Catholic opponents and judges. The edict also attempted to regulate legal proceedings involving Huguenots that were conducted by lesser local judicial officials. Those who conducted inquiries into civil matters were required to work with *adjoints* of the other religion, and a similar system was mandated for criminal investigations and trials before the *prévôts des maréchaux* or their lieutenants. Huguenots and Catholics could also impugn suspect judges who served in the local law courts.[38] Like so many other clauses in the edict, these arrangements echoed those of earlier peace treaties and demonstrated the belief—apparently shared by Huguenots, Catholics, and monarch alike—that reforming the administration of justice in the aftermath of civil and religious conflict meant regulating every level of the judiciary.

The Edict of Nantes thus represented a watershed in the Huguenots' battle for privileged access to royal justice. During the Wars of Religion, Huguenots had demanded special law courts in order to assure themselves a secure place in society and a share of the power and status available through judicial office, but the arrangements mandated by various peace treaties proved impossible to enforce. After 1598, the Edict of Nantes became the basis of what N. M. Sutherland has called "the Huguenot struggle for recognition," and many Huguenots regarded the edict as a permanent set of privileges which the king had pledged to uphold. Henry IV clearly held a different view of the edict and its guarantees of judicial protection for the Huguenot minority. He had given the bipartisan law courts a fresh mandate "so that justice [might] be given and administered to our subjects without any suspicion, hatred, or favor, as being one of the principal means of maintaining them in peace and concord."[39] Yet he also saw the courts, and indeed the edict's provisions as a whole, as a response to immediate circumstances of political and religious conflict. From his perspective, the chambers' true purpose was to alleviate such conflict and pave the way for a time when such tribunals would be unnecessary. This paradox reinforced the entire edict's primary aim: to promote the return of peace and order under royal authority in France, until Huguenots and Catholics were fully reconciled and unified.

---

[37]"Edict of Nantes," 47–48 (art. 34), 50 (art. 51), 52 (art. 62), 63 (Secret Articles, art. 41).
[38]"Edict of Nantes," 52 (arts. 61, 65) and 53 (arts. 66–67).
[39]"Edict of Nantes," 46 (art. 30).

Henry IV's support for bipartisan law courts, even as a temporary measure, also reflected a policy that had been pursued by his predecessors: to strengthen the monarchy's place and power amid the chaos of France's judicial institutions. In theory, all justice flowed from the king; in fact, justice was administered by a variety of persons and corporate bodies whose authority and jurisdictions frequently overlapped or conflicted. Seigneurs and municipal officers such as *consuls, maires,* and *échevins* often possessed some power to administer justice on their estates and in towns, respectively. The courts of the *baillis* and *sénéchaux* dealt with legal disputes in the provinces, aided by their subordinates and the *lieutenants de roi* created to assist them in 1523 and 1554. The parlements topped the royal judicial hierarchy, with the Paris court claiming superiority among the sovereign courts. The parlements were second only to the Grand Conseil and the king himself in their authority to decide judicial appeals, along with some cases heard in the first instance. A host of other royal tribunals stood outside this hierarchy, such as the courts of the admiralty, royal waters and forests, and constableship known collectively as the *Table de Marbre.*[40]

This sketch of the French judiciary suggests a patchwork of institutions rather than an organized system for implementing laws and settling disputes. During the early sixteenth century, however, several factors favored the slow ascendancy of royal law courts and the monarchy's judicial authority. Studies of Roman law produced by Renaissance French and Italian jurists enhanced the image of the king as lawgiver, though providing justice had long been considered an important attribute of kingship and royal glory. Representing the king as the guardian of public peace allowed jurists to enlarge the *cas royaux*—the category of civil and criminal matters that involved royal interests—and thus extend the jurisdiction of royal law courts. French kings attempted to reform the judicial machinery: Charles VII launched an effort to codify French customary laws with the ordinance of Montil-les-Tours (1454), while the ordinance of Villers-Cotterêts (1539) issued by Francis I aimed at making French courts operate more efficiently and fairly. Such reforms emphasized the use of written proceedings and the need for trained, professional magistrates and lawyers to exercise the judicial authority delegated by the king.[41]

---

[40]For details on these institutions see Salmon, *Society in Crisis,* 60–78; Roger Doucet, *Les Institutions de France au XVIe siècle,* 2 vols. (Paris: Picard, 1948); Bernard Barbiche, *Les Institutions de la monarchie française à l'époque moderne* (Paris: Presses Universitaires de France, 1999); R.J. Knecht, *French Renaissance Monarchy: Francis I and Henry II* (London: Longman, 1984), 14–19.

[41]On these developments, see William F. Church, *Constitutional Thought in Sixteenth-Century France* (Cambridge: Harvard University Press, 1941); Donald R. Kelley, *The Foundations of Modern Historical Scholarship: Language, Law and History in the French Renaissance* (New York: Columbia University Press, 1970);

Other changes in the legal system stemmed from the crown's pressing need to finance foreign wars and an increasing royal debt in the sixteenth century. French kings increased the sales of judicial offices and created new offices to sell in order to raise funds for the monarchy. Francis I added three chambers to the Parlement of Paris, thereby increasing the number of judges and lesser legal officials who served in the court, while Henry II established another set of law courts, the *presidiaux*, both to raise money and to deal with the problem of unlimited simultaneous judicial appeals. Lawsuits involving small sums or minor matters were supposed to be adjudicated by the *presidiaux* instead of the overburdened parlements. The parlements opposed the new courts, however, and the *presidiaux* never succeeded in fulfilling their task. Royal manipulation of the judiciary had other consequences: the expansion of venal judicial offices brought new opportunities for Frenchmen who sought social and political advancement for themselves and their families. It also exacerbated tensions between the monarchy and magistrates who were anxious to preserve their corporate privileges, independence, and identity.[42]

The advent of the Protestant Reformation and later the Wars of Religion further complicated the administration of justice in the realm. Catholic and Huguenot aristocratic factions struggled for influence over the Valois monarchs who succeeded Henry II, while towns, villages, and even families found themselves split between adherents to Catholicism and converts to the Reformed faith. Divisions within community, church, and polity produced heated debates about the nature of legitimate governance, the relationship between rulers and their subjects, and the authority of "magistrates"—governing elites other than the king, including judicial officials. In the Midi, the *gens de robe* as a group proved receptive to the new religion: Janine Garrisson has shown the preponderance of Huguenot judges in provincial and presidial courts, as well as their participation in the Reformed ministry and political assemblies.[43] France's parlements, including the Parlement

---

Julian H. Franklin, *Jean Bodin and the Sixteenth Century Revolution in the Methodology of Law and History* (New York: Columbia University Press, 1963); Frédéric Cheyette, "La Justice et le pouvoir à la fin du moyen âge français," *Revue historique de droit français et étranger*, 4th series 40, no. 3 (1963): 373–94.

[42]René David, *French Law: Its Structures, Sources and Methodology*, trans. Michael Kindred (Baton Rouge: Louisiana State University Press, 1972), 1–10; François Olivier-Martin, *Histoire du droit français des origines à la Révolution* (Paris: Domat Montchrestien, 1951), 301–12; Adhémar Esmein, *Cours élémentaire d'histoire du droit français* (Paris, 1921), 332–421; J.H. Shennan, "The Parlement and the Law," in *The Parlement of Paris* (Ithaca: Cornell University Press, 1968), chap. 2.

[43]Janine Garrisson, "Vers une autre religion et une autre Eglise, 1538-1598?" in Mandrou, *Histoire des Protestants*, 60–76 On the debate about legitimate governance in contemporary political theory, see Julian H. Franklin, ed., *Constitutionalism and Resistance in Sixteenth-Century France* (New York: Pegasus, 1969).

of Toulouse, remained predominantly Catholic, yet the magistrates were divided by the events of the 1580s and 1590s—the rise of the Catholic League, the rebellion against Henry III, and the turmoil surrounding Henry IV's succession to the throne. Healing those divisions and restoring order in the royal judiciary thus became an important part of the Bourbon king's peacemaking efforts.[44]

In light of the fragmentation of judicial authority that occurred in the later sixteenth century and Henry IV's policy of restoring both peace to his kingdom and power to the French crown, the Edict of Nantes's articles concerning bipartisan law courts take on new meaning. The edict reflected long-standing Huguenot demands for legal recognition and privileged access to royal justice, but it also exemplified the efforts of French kings to achieve greater power over the judiciary. Since dispensing justice was a fundamental attribute of French kingship, the problem of defining the Huguenots' legal status in the Edict of Nantes offered Henry IV a chance to reassert the monarchy's pivotal role in judicial matters. Royal magistrates and local judicial officials throughout France had shown divided loyalties during the Wars of Religion. It was especially important to cement their allegiance and insist upon their obedience to the crown, because they would be responsible for maintaining peace under the law.

The Huguenots' history after 1598 was marked by two major themes: the variable but generally repressive policies of the French crown, and the Reformed community's own internal divisions and weaknesses. The Huguenots' strength and cohesion were threatened by demographic decline as well as the ambiguous protection of the Edict of Nantes. Conversions to Catholicism made inroads among the Huguenot nobility, while the ambitions and discontents of some Huguenot nobles produced open rebellion in the 1620s. Catholic clerics and members of the new religious orders preached the need to eliminate heresy from France, though research on local communities and families has shown that Huguenots and Catholics crossed confessional boundaries to do business, pursue education, and marry. "Even while ongoing social and commercial interactions may have knitted members of the two faiths more tightly together," notes Philip Benedict, "a powerful cultural dynamic thus worked to heighten awareness of confessional difference."[45]

---

[44]Nancy L. Roelker, *One King, One Faith: The Parlement of Paris and the Religious Reformations of the Sixteenth Century* (Berkeley: University of California Press, 1996); Linda Taber, "Religious Dissent within the Parlement of Paris in the Mid-Sixteenth Century: A Reassessment," *French Historical Studies* 16 (1990): 684–99; and Michel de Waele, *Les Relations entre le parlement de Paris et Henri IV* (Paris: Publisud, 2000).

[45]Philip Benedict, "Un roi, une loi, deux fois: Parameters for the History of Catholic-Reformed Co-existence in France, 1555–1685," in *Tolerance and Intolerance in the European Reformation*, ed. Ole Peter Grell and Bob Scribner (Cambridge: Cambridge University Press, 1996), 65–93.

The French crown and the bipartisan law courts struggled to navigate the crosscurrents of cohesion and separation between Huguenots and Catholics.

As the monarch who revoked the Edict of Nantes in 1685, Louis XIV has borne much of the blame (and received much of the attention) for the crown's repression of France's Protestant minority. Yet Henry IV fought the Huguenots' efforts to expand the edict's provisions in their favor. He was unable to avoid authorizing political assemblies in 1601 (Sainte-Foy), 1605 (Châtellerault), and 1608 (Jargeau), but he attempted to regulate their size, membership, and competence. For their part, the assemblies drew up cahiers of grievances concerning violations of the edict that the king was expected to address. Henry did agree to establish the *députation générale*, which allowed Huguenots to have one or two individuals represent their interests at the royal court, and he permitted Reformed church synods to meet in 1601, 1603, 1607, and 1609. He also retained Huguenot nobles in his household and council, notably Maximilien de Béthune, duc de Sully. But other leaders questioned the king's true intentions toward the Huguenots and his ability to protect them.[46]

Henry IV's assassination in May 1610 plunged France into a period of turmoil and increased the Huguenots' concerns about their position. They distrusted the pro-Catholic and pro-Spanish foreign policy promoted by the queen mother and regent, Marie de Médicis and her favorite, Carlo Concini, despite the crown's renewal of the Edict of Nantes. Both the regent and Louis XIII himself viewed the Huguenots as potentially rebellious subjects, and such fears proved justified on several occasions. The annexation of Béarn, a Bourbon principality where Jeanne d'Albret had imposed Calvinism in the sixteenth century, stirred Huguenot discontent: integrating Béarn fully into the French state meant restoring Catholicism and enforcing the Edict of Nantes's restrictions on the Reformed church and communities.[47] The annexation provoked a rebellion led by Henri, duc de Rohan, and his younger brother Benjamin, seigneur de Soubise, as well as a split in the Huguenot party between the militant minority who joined the revolt and those who refused to support it. Foreign policy issues became a factor as Huguenot rebels sought aid

[46]Sutherland, "The Huguenots and the Edict," 162–63; Anquez, *Histoire des assemblées politiques*, 183–86, 208–10. See also James S. Valone, *Huguenot Politics, 1601–1622* (Lewiston, N.Y.: E. Mellen Press, 1994); Arthur L. Herman, "Protestant Churches in a Catholic Kingdom: Political Assemblies in the Thought of Philippe Duplessis-Mornay," *Sixteenth Century Journal* 21 (1990): 543–57. On the Protestant *députation générale*, which lasted until 1685, see Solange Deyon, *Du Loyalisme au refus: Les protestants français et leur député général entre la Fronde et la Révocation* (Lille: Université de Lille III, 1976).

[47]Holt, *French Wars of Religion*, 173–76; Ligou, *Le Protestantisme en France*, 54–71; Christian Desplat, "Louis XIII and the Union of Béarn to France," in *Conquest and Coalescence: The Shaping of the State in Early Modern Europe*, ed. Mark Greengrass (London: Edward Arnold, 1991), 68–83.

from England, the United Provinces of the Netherlands, and Spain. The siege of La Rochelle (1628–1629) represented the apogee of Huguenot resistance to the crown. Led by the king and his chief minister, Cardinal Richelieu, royal forces subdued the city and later crushed the remnants of Rohan's support in Languedoc.[48] The revolt was formally settled by the Peace of Alès (1629), which upheld the religious and judicial protection set forth in the Edict of Nantes but eliminated the Huguenots' military garrisons and political assemblies. It also left the Huguenots entirely dependent upon the king's goodwill for its support, since no *brevets* granting financial subsidies accompanied this treaty. Rohan's defeat marked a shift in the Huguenots' leadership from the nobility to the churches, opening what Elisabeth Labrousse has called "a 'clerical' phase" in the Huguenots' history.[49]

On the other side of the confessional divide, many among the French Catholic clergy and laity rejected the central government's apparent leniency toward those of the Reformed faith. The Assemblies of the Clergy persistently complained about the Huguenots' protection under the Edict of Nantes; in their view, the Huguenots' legal privileges were an affront to both church and state.[50] As it took shape in seventeenth-century France, the Catholic Reformation emphasized strengthening piety and discipline within the church, especially among the clergy and congregations of rural parishes. Such efforts involved the participation of lay men and women as well as members of the newer religious orders, including the Jesuits, and involved vigorous programs of catechism, preaching, and prayer.[51] Catholic reformers also sought to persuade French Protestants to return to the fold: conversions to Catholicism, especially among Huguenot nobles, were widely publicized as victories in the cause of true religion and rewarded by the crown. Of

[48]Holt, *French Wars of Religion*, 172–89; David Parker, *La Rochelle and the French Monarchy: Conflict and Order in Seventeenth-Century France* (London: Royal Historical Society, 1980).

[49]Holt, *French Wars of Religion*, 183–84; Labrousse, "Calvinism in France," 302.

[50]On the Assemblies of the Clergy, see Pierre Blet, *Le Clergé de France et la monarchie: Étude sur les assemblées générales du clergé, de 1615 à 1666*, 2 vols. (Rome: Librairie éditrice de l'Université grégorienne, 1959).

[51]Philip Hoffman, *Church and Community in the Diocese of Lyon, 1500–1789* (New Haven: Yale University Press, 1984); Denis Richet, "La Contre-Réforme catholique en France dans la première moitié du XVIIe siècle," in *De la Réforme à la révolution: Études sur la France moderne* (Paris: Aubier, 1991), 83–95; Andrew Barnes, "The Social Transformation of the French Parish Clergy, 1500–1800," in *Culture and Identity in Early Modern Europe: Essays in Honor of Natalie Zemon Davis*, ed. Barbara Diefendorf and Carla Hesse (Ann Arbor: University of Michigan Press, 1993), 139–57; J. Michael Hayden and Malcolm R. Greenshields, "The Clergy of Seventeenth-Century France: Self-Perception and Society's Perception," *French Historical Studies* 18, no. 1 (1993): 145–72. For a broader view, see Ruth Kleinman, "The Unquiet Truce: An Exploration of Catholic Feeling against the Huguenots in France, 1646–1664," *French Historical Studies* 4 (1965): 170–88.

course, efforts to encourage public conversions could polarize local communities by insisting upon boundaries that separated Huguenots from Catholics, and the pressures and incentives for conversion were not always successful: highlighting the Huguenots' isolation within Catholic France sometimes heightened their sense of election even if it gradually weakened their numbers.[52] Most of all, the Catholic reformers' activities challenged the legitimacy of confessional coexistence, whether as royal policy, legal privilege, or social practice.

As a result of these and other pressures, the Huguenot population declined during the seventeenth century. According to the most recent estimates, France's Calvinists numbered approximately 900,000 in 1610 and would drop to 730,000 by 1681. This was a far cry from the mid-sixteenth century, when the Reformed church could claim approximately 1.8 million members or 10 percent of France's total population.[53] The seventeenth-century Huguenot population also remained unevenly distributed and divided along both social and regional lines. French Calvinists retained a strong presence throughout the Midi and western France, encompassing both urban and rural areas, whereas north of the Loire they were found mainly among merchants, artisans, and craftsmen in towns such as Rouen and Caen. Such divisions had consequences beyond the mere number of Huguenot inhabitants in a given area: Elisabeth Labrousse has argued that while the scattered Reformed communities in the north tended to favor assiduous obedience to royal authority, many of their counterparts in the south and southwest adopted a more combative attitude toward the French crown and its officials, as illustrated in their support for the rebellion led by Rohan and Soubise.[54]

Under the circumstances, maintaining their cohesion and collective identity proved extremely difficult for the Huguenots, and they looked to their pastors, academies, synods, and consistories to provide the education and social discipline necessary for that purpose. All of these institutions, however, faced serious obstacles. The leading Reformed academies at Saumur, Sedan, Montauban, and Die instructed the sons of elite Huguenot families, but they struggled with controversies surrounding the theology of grace, which complicated the task of training a

---

[52]Keith P. Luria, "Rituals of Conversion: Catholics and Protestants in Seventeenth-Century Poitou," in *Culture and Identity in Early Modern Europe*, 65–82; Susan Rosa, "'Il était possible aussi que cette conversion fût sincere': Turenne's Conversion in Context," *French Historical Studies* 18, no. 3 (1994): 632–66; Dompnier, *Le Venin de l'hérésie*, 139–221.

[53]Philip Benedict, *The Huguenot Population of France, 1600–1685: The Demographic Fate and Customs of a Religious Minority*. Transactions of the American Philosophical Society, 2d series, 81, no. 5 (Philadelphia: American Philosophical Society, 1991), 7–9, 75–77. Benedict's estimates revise the figures compiled by Samuel Mours, *Essai sommaire de géographie du protestantisme français au XVIIe siècle* (Paris: Librairie Protestante, 1966). On the sixteenth century, see Greengrass, *The French Reformation*, 43.

[54]Labrousse, *Une foi*, 59; Prestwich, *International Calvinism*, 178–85.

new generation of pastors. The academies also suffered from chronic financial problems, understaffing, and increasingly hostile competition from their Jesuit counterparts.[55] The Reformed churches' synods were supposed to assure unity in matters of doctrine and discipline among the Huguenot congregations across France. Yet national synods could convene only with the king's permission and, after 1623, with a royal commissioner in attendance to observe the proceedings. The synods' difficulties in dealing with financial problems and doctrinal disputes increased in tandem with the crown's insistence that the deputies avoid any discussion of Huguenot complaints about royal policies.[56] Consistories played an important role in sustaining Reformed communities at the local level by supervising moral conduct, education, and poor relief; but pastors and elders sometimes tempered their punishment of misconduct among the faithful, recognizing that too much severity might provoke individuals to leave the community rather than seek reintegration into it.[57] In elite circles, individual Huguenots found themselves welcomed and patronized as financiers, artists, intellectuals, and literary figures. The Reformed church at Charenton outside Paris comprised a prestigious congregation, and its pastors could claim a certain preeminence among the French clergy. The individual and collective fortunes of most Huguenots, however, were much more precarious.

What role did the bipartisan law courts play in the Huguenots' travails during this period? In contrast to the fortified towns, political assemblies, and church synods, the chambres mi-parties and Chambres de l'Édit survived well into the personal reign of Louis XIV: the courts for Paris and Rouen were abolished by royal decree in 1669, and the chamber at Castres was eliminated a decade later. The chambers' status as courts of appeal and their broad legal jurisdiction gave them wide influence, in contrast to the more limited scope of local institutions such as the consistory. Yet the chambers also embodied that ambiguous combination of protection and limitation that defined the Huguenots' status in the seventeenth century. As a result, Huguenot leaders frequently appealed to the French

[55]Ligou, *Le Protestantisme en France*, 141–69; Prestwich, *International Calvinism*, 185–88; Elizabeth K. Hudson, "The Protestant Struggle for Survival in Early Bourbon France: The Case of the Huguenot Schools," *Archiv für Reformationsgeschichte* 76 (1985): 271–95.

[56]Prestwich, *International Calvinism*, 188–91; Labrousse, "Calvinism in France," 288–89; Ligou, *Le Protestantisme en France*, 126–40. National synods met infrequently after 1626 and were suppressed after 1659.

[57]Labrousse, "Calvinism in France," 291; Raymond A. Mentzer, "Ecclesiastical Discipline and Communal Reorganization among the Protestants of Southern France," *European History Quarterly* 21 (1991): 163–83; Solange Bertheau, "Le Consistoire dans les églises réformées du Moyen Poitou au XVIIe siècle," *B.S.H.P.F.* 116 (1970): 332–59, 513–49; Alfred Soman and Elisabeth Labrousse, "Le Registre consistorial de Coutras, 1582–1584," *B.S.H.P.F.* 126 (1980): 195–228.

crown to preserve the bipartisan law courts from attack, even though they were not entirely satisfied with the courts' ability to defend the religious minority.

Such appeals often appeared in the cahiers of grievances periodically presented by the French Reformed community's representatives to the monarchy. For example, a cahier for August 1602 requested that the king avoid transferring lawsuits from the special chambers to the Grand Conseil, arguing that the Huguenots' general privileges in the Edict of Nantes (art. 47) outweighed the legal privileges of individuals who might qualify for such a change of jurisdiction.[58] In another cahier presented four years later, the king was asked to maintain the chambers' jurisdiction over all lawsuits involving Huguenot individuals or communities, denying such jurisdiction to the parlements in accordance with article 34 in the Edict of Nantes. The same complaint resurfaced in the cahiers of April 1609 and April 1612.[59] In each case, the king agreed to the request, though in 1606 Henry IV stipulated that the parlements neither could nor should deny justice to Huguenots who chose to appeal to them rather than use the bipartisan chambers.[60] As late as 1625, Louis XIII was asked to uphold the chambers' jurisdiction as defined in the Edict of Nantes and conducted "prior to recent events"—perhaps an effort to avoid having the courts penalized for Soubise's seizure of Ile de Ré and Oléron earlier that year.[61]

Huguenots requested that the king protect not only the bipartisan chambers, but also the litigants who sought to use them. The cahier of August 1606 demanded that Henry IV order judicial officers to accept documents that identified litigants as Calvinists as if they had been obtained from judges or notaries.

[58]*Decisions royales sur les principales difficultez de l'Edict de Nantes. Par Responses et Expressions faites et ordonées au Conseil d'Estat, sur les Cayers des plaints et remonstrances qu'en ont esté presentées au Roy* (Paris, 1643), 44–45 (August 1602 cahier, art. 37): "il a esté octroyé des evocations des Chambres de l'Edit au Grand Conseil, sous pretexte des privileges accordez par sa Majesté...attendu que le privilege general accordé ausdits supplians est de plus grande consideration, Supplient vostre Majesté qu'il luy plaise declarer qu tous lesdits privileges ne pourront d'oresnavant nuire ny prejudicier ausdits supplians et de ne plus accorder de telles evocations pour les privileges particuliers."

[59]*Decisions royales,* 74–75 (August 1606 cahier, arts. 36, 40), 79 (April 1609 cahier, art. 26), 112–13 (April 1612 cahier, art. 7).

[60]*Decisions royales,* 74 (August 1606 cahier, art. 36): "Les Parlemens ne peuvent ny ne doivent denier la Justice à ceux de ladite Religion qui voudront y proceder; Ne pourrons toutesfois les Arrests qui y sont intervenus, estre executez que contre ceux qui y auront procedé volontairement."

[61]*Decisions royales,* 165 (July 1625 cahier, art. 12): "que lesdites Chambres cognoissoit de toutes matières qui leur sont attribuées par le 34 article dudict Edit, ainsi qu'il se pratiquoit avant les derniers mouvemens, et particulièrement des Elections Consulaires des villes et lieux de la Religion, Reglemens de Justice, affaires de Communauté, Colleges et Hospitaux." The king affirmed the request, citing both the edict and unspecified *arrêts du conseil.* On Soubise's actions, see Holt, *French Wars of Religion,* 182–85; Sutherland, "The Crown, the Huguenots and the Edict of Nantes," 45–48.

Such documents included baptismal and marriage registers kept by Reformed churches, or certificates issued by Calvinist pastors or elders.[62] This implied that when it came to the legal validity of such records, Reformed religious officials were on a par with notaries and judges, as well as Catholic clerics (who also maintained records of baptisms and marriages in their parishes). On this and later occasions, the crown insisted that magistrates, notaries, and other officials should treat Huguenot and Catholic litigants equally. In response to a similar complaint made in September 1610, the king (or rather his regents) enjoined judicial officers "to have the same care for those of the said religion as for Catholics, as much for the conservation of innocence as for the investigation and punishment of crimes."[63] The cahier for the following year reflected the crown's insistence not only that Huguenots be accepted as royal notaries, but also that Catholic notaries register Huguenot contracts, wills, and other acts on pain of deprivation of their offices.[64]

The Huguenots also complained about problems they encountered in proving their religious affiliation when they began legal proceedings. Huguenots objected to having to call themselves members of "the so-called reformed religion" [la religion prétendue réformée]. In addition, judicial officials often demanded *attestations*—written affirmations of an individual's membership in a specific Reformed church, issued by the pastor—as proof of a Huguenot's confessional and legal identity. In a cahier from 1612, the Huguenots petitioned the crown to prevent royal notaries and other legal officers from insisting that they use the phrase "religion prétendue réformée" to identify themselves in their judicial acts. The king and his regents responded that according to the edicts, this was the required legal designation for French Calvinists. Yet in order to avoid conflicts about the *attestations'* language,

> His Majesty agrees that the said attestations may be done in the form prescribed below: "I, so and so, minister of the church established in

[62]*Decisions royales,* 70 (August 1606 cahier, art. 21): "Que les extraicts des registres tenus pour les Baptesmes et Mariages, ensemble les certificates qu'on requiert de ceux de ladite Religion, pour introduire leurs causes dans les Chambres, seront autant valuables, estans expediez sous le seing des Ministres et Anciens, que s'ils avoient este faits par leur rapport devant le Magistrat ou Notaires, afin d'eviter frais aux parties, et grande distraction ausdits Ministres et Anciens."

[63]*Decisions royales,* 85 (September 1610 cahier): d'avoir le mesme soin de ceux de ladite Religion que des Catholiques, tant pour la conservation de l'innocence, que recherche et punition des crimes....

[64]*Decisions royales,* 105 (July 1611 cahier). In maintaining that Huguenots could become royal notaries, however, the crown avoided endorsing the demand that two new offices be created for Huguenot notaries.

such and such place according to the Edict, certify that so and so is a member of the said church." After which notaries will write, "Before us, Notaries, there has appeared the minister named above, dwelling in…and who acknowledges having written and signed the above, as true. Done, etc." His Majesty also agrees that the barristers and attorneys who plead will use these words: Of the status of the Edict.[65]

Despite the king's orders, the problems that Huguenots encountered in proving their status to the judicial authorities' satisfaction apparently continued. According to a cahier presented in May 1620, judges were demanding written proof of a Huguenot litigant's religious affiliation if witnesses' testimony was offered, or proof by witnesses if documentation had been obtained—"a diversity which indicates a clear injustice" [diversité qui marque une injustice manifeste]. The Huguenots requested that such proofs be handled "according to the common law, that is, by writing or by witnesses, at the plaintiffs' choice." This time Louis XIII referred the matter to the bipartisan chambers to be settled according to the relevant edicts and ordinances.[66]

The Huguenots' complaints and the crown's responses illustrate a concern about abuses of the religious minority's privileged access to royal justice that was shared by the French Reformed churches. Meeting in 1601, the synod of Gergeau [Jargeau] ordered Huguenots to obtain *attestations* from their own churches and forbade "the Pastors of Churches in which the Courts of the Edict be established" to vouch for anyone outside their own congregations unless the individual was known to them personally. The reason for such a command: "divers Abuses…committed in giving Attestations for the removing of Law-Suits from Inferiour Courts, to the Courts of the Edict."[67] The Code Michaud, a royal ordinance issued in 1629 to reorganize and reform French laws and legal procedures, shows that such problems persisted in the reign of Louis XIII. In the code's article 105, Huguenots were accused of intervening in lawsuits simply to divert the proceedings to their special

---

[65]*Decisions royales*, 129–30 (April 1612 cahier, art. 6): Sa Majesté trouve bon que lesdites attestations soient faites en la forme cy-dessous prescrite. 'Je tel Ministre de l'Eglise establie en tel lieu suivant l'Edict, certifie que tel est un des membres de ladite Eglise.' En suite de quoy les Notaires souscriront, "Pardevant nous Notaires, etc., est comparu un tel Ministre cy-dessus denommé, demeurant à, etc., lequel a recognu avoit ecrit et signé ce que dessus, et contenir veritté. Fait, etc.' Comme aussi Sa Majesté [est] agreable que les Advocats et Procureurs parlant ou plaidant, useront de ces mots: De la qualité de l'Edict.

[66]*Decisions royales*, 147–48 (May 1620 cahier, art. 11): suivant le droict commun, c'est à sçavoir, par ecrit, ou par temoins, au choix des demandeurs.

[67]John Quick, *Synodican in Gallia Reformata: Or, the Acts, Decisions, Decrees and Canons of those Famous National Councils of the Reformed Churches in France* (London: Parkhurst and Robinson, 1692), 1:217.

chambers and away from the appropriate tribunals, a practice that caused "great disorder in justice" [un grand desordre en la justice]. It was also noted that Catholics sometimes pretended to be adherents of "the so-called reformed religion" for the same purpose; to prevent this, the Code Michaud ordered all judges to obtain *attestations* from Huguenot litigants and notarized statements from Catholics who claimed to have adopted the Reformed faith.[68] Thus throughout the early seventeenth century, the Huguenots petitioned the French crown to protect them from the ploys used by judicial officials to delay their proceedings, while the French Reformed churches fulminated against those who used *attestations* as a clever maneuver in litigation. Small wonder that by 1629, the Code Michaud and other royal decrees depicted the Huguenots, their law courts, and their legal privileges as subversive of true order and justice.

Other tensions among the Huguenots, the French Reformed churches, and the crown focused specifically on the bipartisan chambers. In a cahier of grievances presented in July 1611, Huguenots complained that split decisions and recusations of judges were causing delays in litigation before the chambers, and further delays occurred when such matters were referred to the king's council. The crown responded by noting that in case of a split decision, a lawsuit could be remanded to another bipartisan court, but denied a proposal that the litigants themselves should choose where the appeal would be heard: "It is for the King in his Council to assign Judges."[69] Similar complaints about the special chambers and the king's council appeared in the cahier for May 1620; Louis XIII ordered both bipartisan courts and the parlements to observe the Edict of Nantes' requirements for prompt justice.[70] On other occasions, the Huguenots protested efforts by other judicial officials to hinder the bipartisan chambers' work. Such interference took many forms: refusals by local court clerks to forward documents concerning Huguenots' lawsuits to the chambers; decrees by the parlements of Aix, Dijon, and Rennes against sergeants who carried out orders issued by the special chambers of Paris and Grenoble in the parlements' jurisdictions; and refusals by Catholic judges to use Protestant *adjoints* when investigating criminal cases involving Huguenots.[71] These complaints suggest that local officials and royal magistrates found ways to

---

[68] The text of the Code Michaud is reprinted in Isambert, *Recueil général*, 16:257–58 (art. 105), 258–59 (arts. 106, 108).

[69] *Decisions royales*, 105–6 (July 1611 cahier, art. 29): C'est au Roy en son Conseil de donner les Juges.

[70] *Decisions royales*, 148–49 (May 1620 cahier), which specifically cites the Edict of Nantes articles *particuliers* 1 and 6.

[71] *Decisions royales*, 76 (August 1606 cahier, art. 42), 104–5 (July 1611 cahier, art. 26), 141–42 (August 1617 cahier, art. 37).

undermine the bipartisan courts' work despite the crown's insistence on obedience to the law and justice for the king's Protestant subjects.

In keeping with their other demands about the bipartisan courts, Huguenots insisted that the chamber magistrates be accepted as full-fledged members of the royal judiciary, and they looked to the king to enforce that acceptance in the face of opposition from the parlements. The cahier for August 1602 requested that Huguenot judges in the parlements of Paris, Grenoble, and Rouen have "a deliberative voice in all of their chambers' business...and generally will be employed in all of the commissions and other functions related to the office of councilor in the said courts as the Catholics, without distinction of matter or person."[72] Four years later, the Huguenots' cahier pointed out the special vulnerability of the Paris Chambre de l'Edit. The court still had only one Huguenot councilor in its ranks, and he was often absent from the court due to illness or recusation—he who, "because of his faith, was more narrowly obliged than the Catholics [serving in the court] to safeguard the suppliants' interests." This was of great concern "since the goods, lives, and honor of so many persons of the said religion have been committed to the said chamber's jurisdiction."[73] To resolve this problem (and to strengthen the Huguenots' presence on the court), the king was asked to have all six Huguenot magistrates in the Paris parlement serve in the Chambre de l'Edit, or at least to appoint three of them to the chamber. Henry IV refused, but he did agree that when the lone Huguenot magistrate was absent from the Chambre de l'Edit, the most senior of the other five Protestant judges could replace him temporarily.[74] Such complaints continued in the reign of Louis XIII, for in 1620 and 1625 Huguenots again requested the king's support in maintaining the "honors, privileges, and authorities" of Protestant magistrates in the bipartisan law courts.[75]

The grievance expressed in 1606, however, highlights the double nature of the special chambers as both royal tribunals and Huguenot institutions—law courts that, from the Protestants' point of view, were obligated to protect and

[72]*Decisions royales*, 40–41 (August 1602 cahier, art. 26): "que lesdits Presidens et Conseillers auront séance et voix deliberative en toutes les affaires de leurs Chambres...et generalement seront employez en toutes les commissions et autres fonctions dependans de la charge de Conseiller esdites Cours comme les Catholiques, sans distinction de cause ou de personne."

[73]*Decisions royales*, 72–73 (August 1606 cahier): par la conformité de sa créance [il] soit obligé plus étroitement que les Catholicques à prendre garde à l'intérêt des supplians...puis que les biens, vies et honneurs de tant de personnes de ladite Religion sont commis à la Jurisdiction de ladite Chambre.

[74]*Decisions royales*, 73 (August 1606 cahier).

[75]*Decisions royales*, 146 (May 1620 cahier, art. 6), 165 (July 1625, art. 12): "que les Officiers des Chambres My-Parties qui sont de la Religion, soient maintenus en tous les honneurs, privilegez et authoritez qui leur sont attribuez par l'article 35 de l'Edict de Nantes, et 48 des particuliers."

advance their individual and collective interests. The French Reformed church clearly expected the Huguenot magistrates who served in the bipartisan chambers to represent the religious community to which they belonged. The synod held at Saint Maixent in 1609 directed the deputies of provinces in which special chambers had been established "to wait upon the Lords presidents, and councilors of those Mixed Courts professing the Reformed Religion, and to exhort them to persevere in their zeal and good affection to the general welfare of the Churches, and of their poor oppressed Members, who have recourse to them for justice against their oppressors." The same message was to be conveyed to the judges in writing.[76] The synod of Alès (1620) forbade Huguenot lawyers "to plead in such Causes as tend to the suppression of the word of God being preached, nor to the setting up of Mass, nor in any wise shall they be suffered to give Counsel or Assistance unto the Romish Church-men in those Causes which have a tendency directly or indirectly to the oppression of the [Reformed] Church."[77] Three years later, the synod of Charenton acknowledged "that Advocates are intrusted with many Secrets, and [are] obliged by the Duties of their Office and Calling to conceal Matters confided to them by their Clients." In response to a query from the deputies of Dauphiné, therefore, the synod declared that consistories could not use their powers of censure to compel a lawyer to reveal such confidential information unless it concerned high treason.[78] Reformed church leaders clearly expected Huguenot lawyers and judges, especially those who served in the bipartisan chambers, to defend the privileges and interests of their confessional community. Yet they also recognized that Huguenot members of the legal profession faced potential conflicts in fulfilling the demands of the law, their profession, and the religious minority they were supposed to represent.

For the synods, however, such conflicts were most evident in relation to the consistory, whose members included lay elders and deacons. In 1563, the synod of Lyon decreed that a magistrate might serve in the consistory, "provided it do not hinder him in the exercise of his publick Office, nor be prejudicial to the Church."[79] When asked what to do if consistory members knew of "a most heinous crime," deputies at the synod of Vitré (1583) stated that the offender "ought not to be impeached, unless before a Magistrate of our Religion, and it shall be done by way of Intelligence, and not by that of Delator or Accuser."[80] Conversely, the synod of Vitré that met in 1617 emphasized that Huguenot magistrates should

---

[76]Quick, *Synodicon in Gallia Reformata*, 1:326.

[77]Quick, *Synodicon in Gallia Reformata*, 2:9.

[78]Quick, *Synodicon in Gallia Reformata*, 2:98.

[79]Quick, *Synodicon in Gallia Reformata*, 1:32.

[80]Quick, *Synodicon in Gallia Reformata*, 1:145.

not abuse their knowledge of consistory affairs when acting in their capacity as secular judges. The deputies insisted that "all Magistrates professing the Reformed Religion shall be intreated not to require any such confessions [concerning misconduct] from our Pastors or Elders; and in case they should persist in those demands, they also shall be sharply censured by the Consistories."[81] Concerns about the overlapping and potentially conflicting duties of consistory members who were also judges lasted well into the seventeenth century. Echoing the principle announced in 1563, the synod of Charenton (1644) decreed that magistrates could serve as elders "provided that the exercise of the one of the charges, hinder not the other, and that it be not prejudiciall to the Church."[82]

Even when judges were not consistory members, the questions of whether, when, and how consistories should report their knowledge of crimes to the civil authorities were complicated. The synod of Lyon left such decisions to "the conscience of the Minister, who must prudently consider all circumstances," but in 1579 the synod of Figeac decreed that "Consistories shall not give in Evidence against any Person, by Act, or any other way unto the Magistrate; And the Members of those Consistories shall not reveal to any Person the Confessions of Penitents." Two years later, Huguenot deputies meeting at La Rochelle amended this article, allowing the consistory itself to permit individual members of the congregation to reveal such information.[83] During the reign of Henry IV, the synod of Gap (1603) forbade ministers who received information about crimes to reveal their knowledge to civil authorities unless the offense was high treason, and the synod of Tonneins elaborated upon this principle in 1614:

> [T]he Canon of our Discipline forbidding the discovery unto a Civil Judicature of matters transacted in the Consistory ought not to be restrained to the sole confessions of Crimes, but is to be understood in the most comprehensive sence [sic] of all things whatsoever, excepting only such riots and outrages, whose fact being notorious, it may be lawful to inform the Magistrate....[84]

Pastors and elders were thus responsible for keeping confidential their knowledge of minor quarrels and misdeeds within their congregations, and for distinguishing

---

[81]Quick, *Synodican in Gallia Reformata,* 1:480.

[82]"The Generall and Particular Acts and Articles of the Late National Synod of the Reformed Churches of France, Assembled by the Permission of the King at Charenton near Paris, beginning the 26th of December, 1644" (London, 1645), 40 (chap. 4, art. 6).

[83]Quick, *Synodican in Gallia Reformata,* 1:38 (Lyon), 130 (Figeac), 137 (La Rochelle).

[84]Quick, *Synodican in Gallia Reformata,* 1:229 (Gap), 409 (Tonneins).

between crimes that threatened the state and those that merited only the consistory's sanction.[85]

In a larger sense, the French Reformed synods were struggling to define a boundary between consistories and secular law courts, including the bipartisan chambers. This struggle involved concerns not only about shared personnel (Huguenot judges who served as elders), but also about overlapping jurisdictions. The consistory has been described as "a religious court responsible for watching over the behavior of the faithful," and consistories attempted to suppress or punish many offenses that could be prosecuted as crimes before secular law courts.[86] A spiritual duty to uphold godly discipline justified the consistory's surveillance of public and private conduct, producing an intimate knowledge of a Reformed community's affairs that was not supposed to be shared too freely (if at all) with civil magistrates. Although its sanctions were limited to noncorporal penalties (fines, public apologies, and excommunication), the consistory did possess a certain authority to settle disputes and punish offenders—an authority that had to be carefully differentiated from that of the king's law courts. A pronouncement by the synod of Lyon (1563) implied that the consistory's jurisdiction ended when it came to property disputes: "Although the Body of the Consistory may advise, and admonish disagreeing Persons to terminate their Controversies and Suits at Law," the deputies argued, "yet that very Consistory shall never consent to be the Judge or Arbitrator of those Controversies betwixt Persons at Variance about Worldly Goods and Estates."[87]

---

[85]In addition to works cited above (n. 58) on Calvinist consistories, see Raymond A. Mentzer, ed., *Sin and the Calvinists: Morals Control and the Consistory in the Reformed Tradition* (Kirksville, Mo.: Sixteenth Century Journal Publishers, 1994); idem, "'Disciplina Nervus Ecclesiae': The Calvinist Reform of Morals at Nîmes," *Sixteenth Century Journal* 18 (1987): 89–115; Janine Estèbe and Bernard Vogler, "La Genèse d'une société protestante: Étude comparée de quelques registres consistoriaux languedociens et palatins vers 1600," *Annales: Economies, Sociétés, Civilisations* 31 (1976): 362–88; Katharine Jackson Lualdi and Anne T. Thayer, eds., *Penitence in the Age of Reformations* (Aldershot: Ashgate, 2000). When it reissued the Reformed churches' discipline in 1644, the synod of Charenton upheld this principle by forbidding consistory members individually or collectively to testify before civil magistrates regarding offenses recounted to them in confidence by members of their congregations. The synod also advised consistories to consider the gravity and frequency of an offender's action before reporting him or her to civil authorities: "As for scandalous vices, and dammageable to the Common-wealth, the faithfull ought to further and assist the magistrate against them which are impenitent and persevere in their evill; But in the behalfe of them which shall have fayled for once and prosecute not their failings, one Ecclesiasticall censure shall suffice." "The Generall and Particular Acts," 52–53 (chap. 4, arts. 28–30).

[86]Quoted in Labrousse, "Calvinism in France," 290.

[87]Quick, *Synodican in Gallia Reformata*, 1:32.

The synod's suggestion that consistories should persuade Huguenot litigants to avoid "Controversies and Suits at Law" altogether, however, suggests a certain ambivalence about the role of secular justice in the Reformed churches and communities. Litigation could disrupt the concord, unity, and discipline within a Reformed community that the consistory was supposed to preserve. Indeed, recourse to secular justice could imply that the consistory had failed in its duty to prevent such ruptures by counseling the parties to resolve their differences amicably. Even after 1598, when the Huguenots' collective existence was tied to royal law and its enforcement by the king and his courts, Reformed church leaders wanted the contentious practices of litigation kept separate from the conduct of church affairs. Meeting in 1607, the synod of La Rochelle clearly expressed this view:

> To prevent for the future that evil custom crept into the Churches...by reading and examining an infinite number of Acts passed before secular Judges which may finally bring in upon us that base Chicanery, so much practiced by crafty Lawyers, and utterly unworthy of the Gravity of these Assemblies...all such manner of proceedings are most expressly forbidden, and all persons are commanded to keep themselves to a native plainness and simplicity, as best suiting with Church affairs....[88]

The relationship between Reformed consistories and law courts remained troubled, especially when Huguenots used one institution to challenge the other. At the synod of Alès in 1620, deputies from Saintonge asked "what course we might take with them, who take out from the courts of Parliament Prohibitions against the Orders and Censures of the Church as if they were intolerable abuses." They were told to regard such persons "as Rebels against the Discipline of our Church, and to inflict upon them the last and heaviest censure of Excommunication, provided that they have first endeavoured by the ways of Love and Kindness, and Grave Religious Counsels to reduce such Persons unto their Duty." More problems arose when civil magistrates' demands conflicted with the Reformed churches' requirements. In 1631, the synod at Charenton noted that "thro' a deplorable Infirmity," some Reformed communities had bowed to court decrees to decorate their houses and light candles for the festival of the Holy Sacrament. The synod ordered consistories to rebuke those who had complied with the judges' decrees and to relieve from their offices any pastors or elders who had obeyed.[89] Meeting again at Charenton in 1644, the synod castigated churches that

---

[88]Quick, *Synodican in Gallia Reformata*, 1:270–71.
[89]Quick, *Synodican in Gallia Reformata*, 2:37, 295.

had refused to support their pastors and elders when they were "Sued at Law, and Imprisoned for following the Duties of their Places and Callings." The deputies urged Huguenots who were suing each other to avoid law courts and consistories alike:

> They of the Religion, which have processes and differences as well civill as criminall, shall be seriously exhorted by the Pastours to indeavour an accord between themselves by the arbitrement of them which are of the Religion without going to law.... A certaine complaint being made, that the Consistories too much trench upon the Magistrate, taking Cognisance of Processes, to determine them.[90]

Consistories were not the only Reformed ecclesiastical institutions suspected of "trench[ing] upon the Magistrate." Long before 1644, the French crown took a lively interest in the synods' own quasi-judicial functions. When permitted to meet, the national synods provided a forum where consistory decisions could be reviewed in relation to the ecclesiastical discipline that governed all Reformed communities in France; they also supervised the Huguenot academies and the conduct of Reformed pastors.[91] Bourbon monarchs repeatedly sought to confine the synods' deliberations to purely doctrinal matters, though not always with success. The synod of La Rochelle (1607), for example, noted with displeasure that

> divers persons, to trouble and vex their adverse Parties, do plunge them in infinite Charges and Expences, drawing their Processes both Civil and Criminal before other Courts than the Chambers of the Edict; Our Deputies are charged to make report of it unto his Majesty, and in this particular to be favourable not only to the Bodies of the Churches, but even unto particular Persons.[92]

As the century wore on, royal commissioners who attended and addressed the synods warned the deputies against making such complaints to the crown. In 1637, the synod of Alençon's members were told that although "some things may be enacted by the Government and Civil Magistrate, which for want of knowledg [sic] of their true Springs and Motives, may seem prejudicial to the Liberty of your Consciences...his Majesty doth expressly forbid all and every one of you, to tax or condemn his Government for any evil Designs against your Religion."[93] Seven years

---

[90]"The Generall and Particular Acts," 42 (chap. 4, art. 14).
[91]Labrousse, "Calvinism in France," 287–88, 291. See also Labrousse, *Une foi*, 45–60.
[92]Quick, *Synodican in Gallia Reformata*, 1:305.
[93]Quick, *Synodican in Gallia Reformata*, 1:326.

later, the sieur de Cumont outlined the proper course of redress for Huguenot grievances. "You have Chembre [sic] mi-parties...and other Courts of Justice, established by Edicts to doe you Justice, and to repaire the Contraventions unto the Edicts if any shall happen," he stated, "for the which you may procure Remedy, before the counsell of the King, and there present your requests, according to the accustomed manner, your Synod having no power to judge in such matters."[94] The Huguenots were thus reminded that their ecclesiastical institutions were not to be confused with royal law courts, and that if they wanted redress for the injustices they claimed to have suffered, they would have to appeal to the king and his council—and to the bipartisan chambers established by the Edict of Nantes.

In the preamble to the Edict of Nantes, Henry IV gave thanks that the disorder and confusion that had plagued France at his accession had been overcome at last: "we...have now reached a harbor of safety and repose for this state," he declared.[95] But neither the edict nor the regime of religious pluralism it mandated truly fulfilled this vision of peace and order. Instead, the law itself became a fertile source of further conflict among Huguenots, Catholics, and the French crown. As outlined in the edict, the Huguenots' privileges made them a protected but vulnerable minority in Catholic France; they became a rather suspect corporate body that could not expand and that was dependent upon the crown and the magistracy for its survival. Over time, the Huguenots would face increasing pressures to convert to Catholicism as the only way to be truly reconciled and reunited with the rest of France, and to be truly obedient subjects of the king. But in 1598, a program of legally mandated religious coexistence (however temporary) seemed the best way to restore peace and order to the kingdom.

The relationship between the Huguenots and the law after 1598, however, was fraught with paradoxes. The most obvious of these is well known: despite its guarantees of protection, the Edict of Nantes imposed real limitations on the Huguenots' activities and collective existence. A narrow interpretation of the edict eventually enabled the French monarchy and magistracy to transform the Huguenots' legal protection into persecution. Even during the reign of Henry IV, however, the French crown clearly insisted upon a strict reading of the edict's terms. Moreover, the privileges that the edict accorded to the Huguenots represented a double-edged sword: in defining the religious minority as a protected corporate

---

[94]"The Generall and Particular Acts," 6.
[95]"Edict of Nantes," 41.

group, they also emphasized the Huguenots' continued separation from the rest of Catholic France.

The bipartisan law courts established by the edict embodied these paradoxes. The Paris Chambre de l'Edit, along with the chambres mi-parties in the provincial parlements, offered the Huguenots a guarantee of privileged access to royal justice as both litigants and magistrates. The very existence of such tribunals implied that the Huguenots' lives, property, and security would receive special protection by "their" law courts and "their" judges. Yet the chambers were closely tied to their affiliated parlements, making it difficult for them to function as separate "Huguenot" institutions. This was especially true of the Paris chamber, which included only one Protestant judge despite its extensive geographical and legal jurisdiction. In their cahiers of grievances, Huguenot leaders argued that the courts' work was hindered by interference from local judicial officials as well as the parlements, and they deplored the apparent harassment of Huguenot litigants through the use and abuse of *attestations*. The Reformed churches' synods likewise worried about Huguenot judges and lawyers who faced competing demands from the confessional community they were supposed to represent and the professional corps to which they belonged. Nevertheless, Henry IV and Louis XIII were constantly entreated to protect the bipartisan chambers and maintain their jurisdiction.

The Huguenots' privileged access to royal justice raised other problems as well, notably concerning the relationship between secular law courts and consistories. Meeting in national synods during the sixteenth and seventeenth centuries, Reformed church leaders noted the potential conflicts of interest that could arise when judges and lawyers served as consistory members, along with the dangers of consistories' sharing information with civil magistrates about congregants' misdeeds. Synod deputies thus struggled to define a boundary between Reformed consistory and secular tribunal, and the relative authority of each institution over the faithful. The task was complicated not only by shared personnel, but also by interests that both conflicted and overlapped. Consistories were responsible for maintaining faith, concord, and social discipline within Reformed communities, and they might punish certain sins that were also crimes in secular law; small wonder that they were accused of "trench[ing] upon the Magistrate."[96] Royal magistrates were responsible for maintaining social order, but unlike consistories their authority extended to Huguenots and Catholics alike. Moreover, such judges required obedience to laws and royal edicts that were not always favorable to the religious minority and that might conflict with synodal or consistorial decrees.

---

[96]"The Generall and Particular Acts," 42 (chap. 4, art. 14).

The world of secular justice was associated with delays, corruption, and "base Chicanery,"[97] and consistories were supposed to advise their congregants to settle their disputes informally and amicably. When it came to defending the bipartisan chambers, however, the Huguenots insisted upon the legal privileges that distinguished them—and theoretically protected them—from their Catholic opponents.

Throughout much of the seventeenth century, the Huguenots were in effect subject to two legal systems. One was expressed in the French Reformed church's ecclesiastical discipline as implemented by synods and consistories. The other was embodied in the Edict of Nantes (along with subsequent royal edicts that regulated the Huguenots' status) and was enforced by secular law courts, notably the bipartisan chambers. For the French crown, the distinction between the two systems was clear: Reformed consistories and synods were not to be confused with law courts, and their jurisdiction was confined to religious matters. The bipartisan chambers, however, were mandated by royal edict and embedded within the royal judiciary. The crown could expect to exercise considerable control over them, which was consistent with its policy of extending the reach of royal justice and limiting the judicial powers of other corporate bodies within the realm. The bipartisan chambers therefore represented a legitimate avenue for judicial redress. If Huguenots were encouraged by their pastors, elders, and deacons to avoid "going to law" against each other, they were enjoined by their kings to seek royal justice when they believed they had been wronged or that their privileges had been violated. In appealing to the bipartisan chambers, Huguenots could simultaneously obey the law, exercise a privilege, and air their grievances. We turn now to one of the courts that heard such appeals: the Paris Chambre de l'Edit.

[97]"The Generall and Particular Acts," 42 (chap. 4, art. 14).

"Our processes are judged by the ticket on the bagges"

Magistrates, Litigants, & the Paris Chambre de l'Edit

IN 1628, AN ANONYMOUS PAMPHLET ADDRESSED BY THE FRENCH Reformed churches to the English Parliament included the following complaint about the Huguenots' experiences in the French judicial system:

> As for the regard of the offices and dignities whereunto we ought to be indifferently admitted with our other Country men and fellow Citizens, it is this which our Enemies have impugned and prevented with all sorts of passion and violence.... Our processes are judged by the ticket on the bagges, so that those of a contrary religion boldly sue all manner of actions against us how unjust so ever, being confident that the contrary Judge of our Religion will make them gaine their Causes....[1]

The pamphlet reflected the Huguenots' grievances as both officeholders and litigants in the French judiciary. The Edict of Nantes had promised Huguenots access to government posts, schools, and professions of all kinds, yet Catholics opposed the Huguenots' full acceptance into the "offices and dignities" that they managed to obtain, including those in the royal law courts. Despite the edict's emphasis on fair treatment for Huguenot plaintiffs and defendants, the law courts apparently had made the situation worse: Catholics relied on magistrates of their

[1] "The Apologie of the Reformed Churches of France, Wherein are expressed the Reasons, why they have joined their armies to those of the King of Great Brittaine. Translated according to the French coppie" (London, 1628), 23–25.

religion to deliver partisan judgments against Huguenot litigants. Most of all, Catholics had acted with "passion and violence" to undermine the "good peace and lasting repose" between the two confessions that was the whole purpose of the edict's specific clauses.[2] These inequities surely justified the Huguenots' rebellion against the French crown, which had failed to enforce the law or provide true justice to the Huguenot minority.

Though not mentioned specifically in the pamphlet, the Paris Chambre de l'Edit was implicated in these complaints. Throughout the Wars of Religion, Huguenots had demanded that the crown protect them from the prejudice of the royal law courts, especially the parlements. The bipartisan chambers mandated by the Edict of Nantes were supposed to accomplish this by allowing Huguenot litigants to appeal to courts that included Huguenot magistrates. Establishing the chambers would also provide a limited number of judicial offices for Huguenots in the legal profession. Among the bipartisan courts, the Paris Chambre de l'Edit was something of an anomaly. The Paris court exercised a broad geographical jurisdiction and could hear all kinds of legal disputes on appeal. Yet it offered the least opportunity for Huguenot office seekers, since its ranks included only one Protestant judge; for the same reason, it also offered perhaps the least judicial protection for Huguenot plaintiffs and defendants. In spite of these limitations, Huguenots from across the spectrum of French society appealed to the Chambre de l'Edit. Their willingness to invoke the court's authority gave real substance to the chamber's jurisdiction as outlined in the Edict of Nantes. The Chambre de l'Edit was also embedded within one of the most powerful and complex institutions in early modern France: the Parlement of Paris. The chamber's close but troubled affiliation with the parlement helped to define its relationship to the Huguenot minority. This chapter thus explores the history and composition of the Chambre de l'Edit's magistracy, as well as providing an overview of the litigants who petitioned the chamber for justice and the procedures they used to do so.

As mandated by the Edict of Nantes, the Chambre de l'Edit was situated within the Parlement of Paris, arguably the most powerful law court in the French royal judiciary. The Parlement of Paris had evolved from the royal council into a separate judicial institution during the thirteenth and fourteenth centuries. It claimed

---

[2] "Edict of Nantes," 41 (preamble to the general edict). Arts. 22 (p. 45) and 27 (p. 46) guarantee the Huguenots' access to schools and offices; arts. 30–67 (pp. 46–53) include the arrangements for special law courts, rules for judicial proceedings involving Huguenots, and other related matters.

preeminence among France's other provincial parlements, as well as a special responsibility to safeguard the kingdom's fundamental laws and the Gallican liberties of the Catholic Church in France. By the early seventeenth century, the Parlement of Paris had further subdivided into various chambers that dealt with different areas of the court's business. The most important of these was the Grand Chambre. Its members included both lay and clerical judges (though the former outnumbered the latter), princes and peers of the realm, and honorary councilors known as *maîtres des requêtes*. Judges known as *présidents à mortier* (so named because of the black velvet cap or *mortier* which signified their office) formed the core of the Grand Chambre's magistracy. As the most experienced and responsible of the parlement's judges, they corrected and delivered the chamber's decisions, assured that court orders were carried out, and supervised the chamber councilors' conduct. By virtue of his seniority among the *présidents à mortier*, the parlement's First President (*prémier président*) usually led the Grand Chambre's plenary sessions, as well as presiding over its review of royal ordinances and receptions of new members.[3]

The Parlement of Paris also included five Chambres des Enquêtes, which handled lawsuits involving written evidence and depositions rather than oral pleadings, and two Chambres des Requêtes, which reviewed petitions from persons claiming the privilege of direct appeal to the parlement for justice (known as *committimus*) and disputes about letters of grace, pardon, and remission issued by the royal chancery. Another chamber known as the Tournelle dealt with criminal lawsuits. Established in 1454 and modified by Francis I during the sixteenth century, the Tournelle was staffed by *présidents à mortier* and lay councilors from the Grand Chambre and Chambres des Enquêtes who served in rotation, a system that lasted into the eighteenth century. Finally, the Chambre des Vacations handled the parlement's litigation during the court's summer recess. It could deliver definitive verdicts in criminal cases, but its decisions in civil matters often required further approval.[4]

[3]Barbiche, *Les Institutions de la monarchie française*, 89–114, 335–58; Shennan, *The Parlement of Paris*, 32–36; François Aubert, *Le Parlement de Paris de l'origine à François Ier, 1250–1515* (Paris, 1894), I:11–18, 139–40. For information about the parlement's history, personnel and procedures in relation to its archives, see Monique Langlois, "Serie X: Parlement de Paris," in *Guide des recherches dans les fonds judiciaires de l'Ancien Régime*, ed. Michel Antoine (Paris: Archives Nationales, 1958), 65–151.

[4]Shennan, *Parlement of Paris*, 37–42; Aubert, *Le Parlement de Paris*, I:18–43; and Barbiche, *Les Institutions*, 342–43. The Tournelle shared its jurisdiction with the Grand Chambre, which could hear cases involving the most serious crimes, and the Chambres des Enquêtes, which could hear criminal cases involving petty offenses on appeal. Aubert attributes the name "Tournelle" to the tower (*tour*) in the Palais de Justice where the court usually met; other historians associate it with the rotation of its members, who served in turn (*en tour*).

When it officially opened in February 1599, the Chambre de l'Edit took its place within this constellation of law courts that comprised the Parlement of Paris. Like the Tournelle, it was staffed by magistrates drawn from the ranks of the *présidents à mortier* and lay councilors who served in rotation. The Chambre de l'Edit judges sometimes joined those of the Grand Chambre and Tournelle to deliberate important cases heard by the court, such as the trial of Henry IV's assassin, François Ravaillac.[5] In general the Chambre de l'Edit followed the same routines as the parlement's other chambers. Its sessions officially opened after the feast of St. Martin in November and the *séance de rentrée*, a two-day ceremony during which the magistrates and other judicial officers attended high mass in the chapel of the Palais de Justice and renewed the oaths of their profession. The judges then began their weekly round of deliberations: the Grand Chambre met every morning and several afternoons a week, while other chambers met two or three times a week. The parlement followed this calendar (with breaks for holidays such as Christmas and Easter, as well as important ceremonial occasions) from November until the following September.[6]

Three other men affiliated with the Parlement of Paris played an important role in the Chambre de l'Edit's work: the royal prosecutor [procureur général du roi] and the royal advocates (*avocats du roi* or *avocats généraux*). Collectively, these men were known as "the king's men" [gens du roi] or *parquet*, a reference to the area of the courtroom where they worked. From the fourteenth century on, the royal prosecutor's main duty was to represent and safeguard the king's interests in any lawsuit before the court; his recommendations about a case were often part of the proceedings and the judges' deliberations. The royal prosecutor could join with private individuals as a plaintiff in their litigation or initiate a judicial investigation by a royal magistrate, and with an *appel à minima*, he could appeal verdicts that seemed too lenient. Finally, he was responsible for making sure that royal edicts and ordinances were publicized throughout the kingdom by his counterparts at the local level, the *substituts du procureur du roi*. The royal advocates pleaded before the court on the king's behalf and communicated the royal prosecutor's opinions.[7]

---

[5] Edouard Maugis, *Histoire du parlement de Paris de l'avènement des rois Valois à la mort d'Henri IV*, 3 vols. (Paris, 1914–16; repr. New York, 1967), 2:209–12. The parlement's records indicate when the Chambre de l'Edit assembled with other chambers, as in the case of Ravaillac: A.N. X2b 254, 27 May 1610.

[6] Shennan, *Parlement of Paris*, 29–31; Maugis, *Histoire du parlement de Paris*, 1:272–82, 340–67; Aubert, *Le Parlement de Paris*, 1:176–204.

[7] Shennan, *Parlement of Paris*, 67–71 (*procureur général*), 44–45 (*avocats du roi*); Aubert, *Le Parlement de Paris*, 1:141–75; Barbiche, *Les Institutions*, 337–38.

A horde of lesser judicial officials also participated in the daily work of the Parlement of Paris. The Palais de Justice teemed with notaries (*notaires*), court clerks (*greffiers*), and their assistants, as well as the sergeants (*sergents*), bailiffs (*baillis*) and ushers (*huissiers*) who were mainly responsible for carrying out the court's orders. Lawyers who pleaded before the court (*avocats*) and those who represented their clients' interests in other ways (*procureurs*) formed a higher echelon of legal professionals affiliated with the parlement. Such lawyers in turn employed clerks who were known collectively as the *Basoche* (Basilica), their own nickname for the Palais de Justice itself. By the sixteenth century, the Basochiens were famous for their disruptive behavior and their comic theatrical productions.[8] Although most of these men left little personal imprint on the Chambre de l'Edit's records, they played an essential role in the court's ordinary round of legal business.

The Chambre de l'Edit's distinctive place within the Parlement of Paris was due primarily to two factors: its composition and jurisdiction. A number of factors, however, tended to undermine the court's distinctiveness, strengthening instead its ties to the parlement as a whole. The Huguenot magistrates helped give the chamber its unique place in the parlement, but they faced serious problems in exercising and retaining their judicial offices. On the other hand, Catholic judges who served in the court rotated frequently; they, too, had little chance (and perhaps little desire) to make the Chambre de l'Edit an important part of their professional service and advancement. Moreover, their marriage alliances, social contacts, and participation in other areas of the parlement's work reinforced their ties to the royal magistracy and all that it represented.

The Parlement of Paris's judges were an elite group defined by the shared responsibilities, values, and privileges of the legal profession, as well as education and occupation. Lawyers and magistrates were a vital element of Renaissance society and culture. As both agents of change and proponents of order, they helped expand the concept of political sovereignty and enhance the "myth of recovered culture" throughout Western Europe.[9] France was no exception to this pattern:

---

[8]Shennan, *Parlement of Paris*, 45–49; Aubert, *Le Parlement de Paris*, 1:205–60. According to Shennan, the distinction between *avocats* and *procureurs* was roughly the same as that between English barristers and solicitors. See also Charles Bataillard, *Moeurs judiciaires de la France du XVIe siècle au XIXe siècle* (Paris, 1878); André Damien, *Les Avocats du temps passé: Essai sur la vie quotidienne des avocats au cours des âges* (Versailles: H. Lefebvre, 1973); Roland Delachenal, *Histoire des avocats au parlement de Paris, 1300–1600* (Paris, 1885); Marcel Rousselet, *Histoire de la magistrature*, 2 vols. (Paris, 1956); André Dupin, ed., *Profession d'avocat: Recueil des pièces concernant l'exercice de cette profession* (Paris, 1832); David A. Bell, *Lawyers and Citizens: The Making of a Political Elite in Old Regime France* (New York: Oxford University Press, 1994).

[9]William J. Bouwsma, "Lawyers and Early Modern Culture," *American Historical Review* 78, no. 2 (1978): 303–27, reprinted in Bouwsma, *A Usable Past*, 129–53. See also Lauro Martines, *Lawyers and Statecraft in Renaissance Florence* (Princeton: Princeton University Press, 1968).

men trained in the law contributed to an emerging notion of French "nation" during the fourteenth and fifteenth centuries, when jurisprudence in royal law courts was part of France's battle to expel the English during the Hundred Years' War. French lawyers also drew upon Roman law precepts to bolster the Valois rulers' claims to judicial authority at the expense of other groups and institutions. Critical approaches to the study of Roman law developed by French and Italian jurists encouraged new perspectives on politics and history, linking lawyers, humanist scholars, and princes in the intellectual and cultural activity of the Renaissance.[10]

During the sixteenth century, French royal magistrates also developed a sense of collective identity and purpose which was directly linked to contemporary debates about the nature of nobility, and which revolved around the ideal of the "perfect magistrate." French judges perceived themselves as learned, virtuous, and compassionate—qualities that were both necessary and desirable in men who had considerable judicial and political power. At the highest levels of the judiciary, magistrates could exercise a moral influence that extended from their own corps to the legal profession more generally, and ultimately to society as a whole. Punishing criminals and enforcing specific laws required a larger effort to administer justice and impose order on a disorderly and often violent society. This effort reinforced the magistrates' connection to the French monarchy, the ultimate earthly source of all justice. In theory, royal judges like those in the parlements exercised a judicial authority delegated by the king; in the courtroom they represented the crown, the ultimate source of judgment and mercy.[11]

Changes in the legal procedures used to prosecute and punish criminals also enhanced the magistrate's role in the administration of royal justice. During the late medieval period, accusatorial procedure gradually gave way to inquisitorial procedure in most of France's law courts. As the name suggests, accusatorial procedure emphasized the role of the accuser; it depended upon oral testimony and direct confrontations by the parties to settle a dispute. The judge was mainly responsible for assuring that the parties followed the customary rules, rituals, and

[10] André Bossuat, "The Maxim, 'The King Is Emperor in His Kingdom': Its Use in the Fifteenth Century before the Parlement of Paris," in *The Recovery of France in the Fifteenth Century*, ed. P. S. Lewis, trans. G. Martin (London, 1971), 185–95; Kelley, *The Foundations of Modern Historical Scholarship*; George Huppert, *The Idea of Perfect History* (Urbana: University of Illinois Press, 1970).

[11] Raymond A. Mentzer, "The Self-Image of the Magistrate in Sixteenth-Century France," *Criminal Justice History* 5 (1984): 23–43; Colin Kaiser, "Les Cours souveraines au XVIe siècle: Morale et Contre-Réforme," *Annales: Economies, Sociétés, Civilisations* 37 (1982): 15–31; Arlette Lebigre, *La Justice du roi: La vie judiciaire dans l'ancienne France* (Paris: Albin Michel, 1988); Barbiche, *Les Institutions*, 47–51.

formulas, including trial by battle or ordeal.[12] By contrast, inquisitorial procedure relied upon written depositions and gave judges a more active role in initiating and investigating the prosecution of criminal acts.[13] The ordinance of Blois (1498) issued by Louis XII and the ordinance of Villers-Cotterêts (1539) issued by Francis I confirmed this transition. Judges and prosecutors were responsible for investigating reported misdeeds, questioning witnesses, deciding on the use of judicial torture, and communicating their findings to the parties. In deciding criminal cases, magistrates would determine guilt or innocence based on evidence, testimony, and a body of written law. Francis I ordered royal judicial officials to carry out their duties "in order to accomplish the good of our justice, the shortening of legal proceedings, and the succor of our subjects."[14]

By the early sixteenth century, prosecuting criminals in France's royal law courts thus involved an elaborate series of initiatives and responses in which royal magistrates exercised considerable power. Prompted by the complaint of an ordinary individual, a royal prosecutor, or the common report of a criminal act, a magistrate interrogated witnesses and collected their written depositions in a dossier (the *information*). The accused person would also be questioned, and the royal prosecutor or his representative would comment on the case. Depending on the gravity of the crime, the judge would proceed by *procès ordinaire*, which involved only financial penalties, or *procès extraordinaire*, which could include capital or corporal punishments. *Procès extraordinaire* entailed reexamining witnesses and allowing the accused to confront them (*récolement et confrontation*); the accused could also present evidence against the witnesses' credibility (*faits des reproches*). The royal prosecutor would offer recommendations about the case, and then the judge who had been designated as *rapporteur* for the lawsuit would prepare a summary of the charges, evidence, and

---

[12]On the history of French criminal procedure, see Albéric Allard, *Histoire de la justice criminelle au XVIe siècle* (Paris, 1868); Adhémar Esmein, *Histoire de la procédure criminelle en France* (Paris, 1882); idem, *Cours élémentaire* (Paris, 1921); Aubert, *Le Parlement de Paris*; John Langbein, *Prosecuting Crime in the Renaissance* (Cambridge: Harvard University Press, 1974); David, *French Law*; Arlette Lebigre, *Les Institutions de l'Ancien Régime* (Paris: Les Cours de Droit, 1976); Jean Imbert, "Principes généraux de la procédure pénale, XVIIe–XVIIIe siècles," in Jean Imbert, *Quelques procès criminels des XVIIe et XVIIIe siècles* (Paris: Presses Universitaires de France, 1964), 1–12.

[13]Lebigre, *Les Institutions* 162–75; Esmein, *Cours élémentaire*, 343–88; Allard, *Histoire de la justice criminelle*, 149–52. See also John P. Dawson, *A History of Lay Judges* (Cambridge: Harvard University Press, 1960); Edward Peters, *Inquisition* (New York: Free Press, 1988).

[14]The text of the ordinance of Blois appears in Isambert et al., *Recueil général*, 11:323–79; arts. 127–96 specifically cover legal procedure. The text of the ordinance of Villers-Cotterêts appears in the same work (13:600–40); arts. 144–67 cover legal procedure. The quotation is from the edict's preamble: pour aucunement pourvoir au bien de notre justice, abbreviation des procès, et soulagement de nos sujets (p. 600).

proceedings. At this point, the court could consider ordering judicial torture to obtain the accused person's confession. The judges would then consider the *rapporteur's* summary and pronounce their verdict and punishment.[15] Although they were expected to follow specific laws and jurisprudence, the magistrates had considerable latitude in rendering their decisions.

Whether the rest of French society accepted the magistrates' perception of their own wisdom and virtue, of course, is open to question. The early modern concept of the magistrate as an exemplary figure may have developed in part as a response to contemporary criticisms of corruption and incompetence within judicial ranks. Complaints about the payment of fees or gifts (*épices*) to judges and other legal officials, as well as excessive delays and complications in litigation, appear frequently in pamphlets, memoirs, and official documents from the sixteenth and seventeenth centuries—including those written by lawyers and magistrates who advocated legal reform.[16] These specific grievances, however, were part of a larger and more complex feature of the early modern French judiciary: the confusion of public responsibility and private interest. As Robert Harding has noted, it was difficult to establish boundaries between corrupt and ethical conduct by public officials when nepotism, patronage, and favoritism were acceptable grounds for making such appointments. The notion of "public service" competed against other individual and corporate loyalties, privileges, and ambitions, and the problem could become especially acute when such officials represented royal authority at the same time as they pursued personal or familial advancement.[17]

For magistrates in the Parlement of Paris, the volatile combination of royal judicial authority, elite social and professional status, and suspected corruption crystallized around venality of office. Government positions of all sorts could be bought, sold, and often inherited in early modern France, but judicial offices were

---

[15]Esmein, *Histoire,* 140–52; Aubert, *Le Parlement de Paris,* 2:209–20. See also Doucet, *Les Institutions de France,* 2:534–41. On judicial torture, see John Langbein, *Torture and the Law of Proof* (Chicago: Chicago University Press, 1976); Alfred Soman, "La Justice criminelle aux XVIe–XVIIe siècles: Le parlement de Paris et les sièges subalternes," in *La Faute, la répression et le pardon. Actes du 107e Congrès National des Sociétés Savantes* (Brest: Comité des travaux historiques et scientifiques, 1982), 1:15–52.

[16]Kaiser, "Les Cours," 16–17. See also Jeffrey Sawyer, "Judicial Corruption and Legal Reform in Early Seventeenth-Century France," *Law and History Review* 6, no. 1 (1988): 95–118; Robert Carey, *Judicial Reform before the Revolution of 1789* (Cambridge: Harvard University Press, 1981). On sources of parlement judges' income in the seventeenth century, see Albert N. Hamscher, *The Parlement of Paris after the Fronde, 1653–1673* (Pittsburgh: University of Pittsburgh Press, 1976), 63–68.

[17]Robert Harding, "Corruption and the Moral Boundaries of Patronage in the Renaissance," in *Patronage in the Renaissance,* ed. Guy Fitch Lytle and Stephen Orgel (Princeton: Princeton University Press, 1981), 41–64. See also Sharon Kettering, *Patrons, Brokers and Clients in Seventeenth-Century France* (New York: Oxford University Press, 1986).

among the most desirable. The French crown's practice of selling judicial posts (and creating new ones for that purpose) increased during the sixteenth and seventeenth centuries, a situation that was both defended and deplored by its beneficiaries. On the one hand, many judicial offices conferred noble status on the purchaser and, if retained within his family for several generations, upon his descendants. Venality of office thus functioned as a means of social mobility, offering wealthy but nonnoble Frenchmen entry into the aristocracy's ranks. It also strengthened the magistrates' sense of cohesion and corporate identity: they saw themselves as a "nobility of the robe" [noblesse de robe], deriving their privileges and status from their role in administering royal justice and defending France's legal heritage. The robe nobility gradually consolidated its ranks through marriage and practices that enabled its members to inherit offices from each other. *Survivance* allowed magistrates to vacate their positions in favor of a designated successor (usually a son, son-in-law, or brother) who "inherited" the office upon his predecessor's death, advancement, or transfer to another post. Established in 1604, the *droit annuel* (also known as the *paulette*) allowed officeholders to retain their posts in return for a yearly payment. It was popular with the monarchy and officeholders alike, for it provided a steady source of revenue for the crown while bringing a certain amount of stability to a system that had been characterized by confusion throughout much of the sixteenth century. The monarchy's continuing sale and manipulation of judicial offices, however, fostered concerns among robe nobles about the dilution of their status.[18]

The Parlement of Paris, and royal magistrates generally, claimed an essential place in French government that combined both submission to and independence from the crown. Scholars have argued about whether judges in provincial royal courts saw themselves primarily as representatives of the crown in their localities or as a local elite responsible for communicating local concerns to the central government; the role of such royal officials in promoting or restraining the monarchy's growing power has also been debated.[19] Magistrates in the Paris parlement,

---

[18] The classic study of venality of judicial offices for this period is Roland Mousnier, *La Vénalité des offices sous Henri IV et Louis XIII*, 2d ed. (Paris: Presses Universitaires de France, 1971). See also William Doyle, *Venality: The Sale of Offices in Eighteenth-Century France* (New York: Oxford University Press, 1996); chap. 1 provides a good summary of venality's origins and development in the sixteenth and seventeenth centuries. On change, continuity, and definition in the French nobility, see J.H.M. Salmon, "Storm over the Noblesse," *Journal of Modern History* 53 (1981): 252–57; Schalk, *From Valor to Pedigree*; Arlette Jouanna, *Le Devoir de revolte: La noblesse française et la gestation de l'état moderne, 1559–1661* (Paris: Fayard, 1989).

[19] Jonathan Dewald, "The 'Perfect Magistrate': Parlementaires and Crime in Sixteenth-Century Rouen," *Archiv für Reformationsgeschichte* 67 (1976): 284–99; Jonathan K. Powis, "Order, Religion and the Magistrates of a Provincial Parlement in Sixteenth-Century France," *Archiv für Reformationsgeschichte*

however, were especially conscious of their role as the guardians of France's fundamental laws and political integrity in relation to the French crown and the French people. They could and did resist registering royal edicts and decrees that seemed to challenge France's legal traditions or the power of the parlement itself. In general, the parlementaires were also defenders of Gallicanism: they saw themselves as responsible for helping to protect the Catholic Church in France from papal or other foreign domination, a task that became complicated during the religious and political turmoil of the later sixteenth century.[20] Tensions surrounding the parlement's role in governance in relation to the crown surfaced in the rituals that accompanied important acts of state: royal funerals, coronations, official entries into major cities, and *lits de justice*. In these ceremonial enactments of political power, the magistrates represented royal justice—an aspect of the king's authority that made them essential participants in governance. Scholars have argued, however, that the crown increasingly dominated such events during the seventeenth century, challenging the magistrates' pretensions to even a symbolic share in the monarchy's power.[21]

Controversies surrounding religious reform posed serious challenges to the already complex relationship between the crown and its law courts. The Parlement of Paris played a key role in the religious, political, and legal conflicts that beset the French crown and the city of Paris during the sixteenth century. The magistrates were not exempt from the appeal of the Protestant reformers' message, though relatively few of them became Protestants themselves. Their determination to defend Gallican traditions and to preserve the French constitution's delicate balance among crown, church, justice, and people made most of the parlementaires equally suspicious of Protestant heresy and ultramontane claims.[22] Since it was impossible for them to separate religious issues from their political, legal, and

---

71 (1980): 180–97; Ralph E. Giesey, "State-Building in Early Modern France: The Role of Royal Officialdom," *Journal of Modern History* 55 (1983): 191–207.

[20]Roelker, *One King, One Faith*; de Waele, *Les Relations*. On Gallicanism generally, see Victor Martin, *Les Origines du gallicanisme*, 2 vols. (Paris: Blond & Gay, 1939); Church, *Constitutional Thought*; William J. Bouwsma, "Gallicanism and the Nature of Christendom," in Bouwsma, *A Usable Past*, 308–24.

[21]Ralph E. Giesey, *The Royal Funeral Ceremony in Renaissance France* (Geneva: Droz, 1960); Giesey, "The King Imagined," in *The Political Culture of the Old Regime*, ed. Keith M. Baker (New York: Oxford University Press, 1988), 41–59; Lawrence M. Bryant, *The King and the City in the Parisian Royal Entry Ceremony* (Geneva: Droz, 1986); Sarah Hanley, *The Lit de Justice of the Kings of France* (Princeton: Princeton University Press, 1983).

[22]In addition to the studies by Roelker and de Waele, see Taber, "Religious Dissent within the Parlement of Paris," 684–99; Barbara B. Diefendorf, *Beneath the Cross: Catholics and Huguenots in Sixteenth-Century Paris* (New York: Oxford University Press, 1991).

social implications, the magistrates were also sensitive to the problem of prosecuting heretics. They protested Henry II's attempt to establish an inquisition for France, and many showed a marked lack of enthusiasm for the "burning chamber" [chambre ardente], a special panel of judges drawn from the Paris parlement's ranks to prosecute heretics during the period of 1548 through 1550. Though royal magistrates often took the lead in attempting to eliminate the Protestant heresy from France during the 1560s, their efforts proved ineffective. The Huguenot minority survived and fought back, the crown experimented with religious toleration, and the kingdom descended into the chaos of civil war.[23]

The legal recognition accorded to the Huguenots periodically during the Wars of Religion helped feed the discontent of many Catholics with the crown's policies and the apparent leniency of royal magistrates toward heretics. Such discontents spurred the formation of the Catholic League, whose members looked to the duc de Guise rather than King Henry III for leadership in the war on heresy. Paris proved to be an important source of support for Catholic political and religious opposition: following the Day of Barricades (12 May 1588), the king was forced to flee the city, and Guise formed an uneasy alliance with a faction of the Parisian Catholic League known as the Sixteen. Composed of clerics, merchants, minor government officials, and lawyers, the Sixteen played an important role in the kingdom's and the city's politics until Paris surrendered to Henry IV in 1594.[24]

The relationship between the Sixteen and the Parlement of Paris was one of mutual distrust that deteriorated into outright hostility. The Sixteen and their supporters viewed the magistrates as the embodiment of official corruption and moral laxity that helped account for the French people's misery.[25] After the Day

[23]E. William Monter, *Judging the French Reformation: Heresy Trials by Sixteenth-Century Parlements* (Cambridge: Harvard University Press, 1999); N.M. Sutherland, "Was There an Inquisition in Reformation France?" in *Princes, Politics and Religion, 1547–1589* (London: Hambledon, 1984), 13–29; Raymond A. Mentzer, *Heresy Proceedings in Languedoc, 1500–1560.* Transactions of the American Philosophical Society, 2d series 74:5 (Philadelphia: American Philosophical Society, 1984). On the "burning chamber," see Noel Weiss, *La Chambre ardente: Etude sur la liberté de conscience en France sous François Ier et Henri II* (Paris, 1889); Roelker, *One King, One Faith,* 219–22.

[24]Denis Richet, "Sociocultural Aspects of Religious Conflicts in Paris during the Second Half of the Sixteenth Century," in *Ritual, Religion and the Sacred: Selections from the Annales,* ed. Robert Forster and Orest Ranum (Baltimore: Johns Hopkins University Press, 1982), 182–212; Elie Barnavi, *Le Parti de dieu* (Louvain: Nauwelaerts, 1980); Arlette Lebigre, *La Révolution des curés: Paris, 1588–1594* (Paris: Albin Michel, 1980); J.H.M. Salmon, "The Paris Sixteen, 1584–1594: The Social Analysis of a Revolutionary Movement," reprinted in Salmon, *Renaissance and Revolt* (Cambridge: Cambridge University Press, 1987), 235–66. For an excellent overview of the Catholic League's role in the Wars of Religion, see Holt, *The French Wars of Religion,* 121–52.

[25]Elie Barnavi and Robert Descimon, *La Sainte Ligue, le juge et la potence* (Paris: Hachette, 1985).

of Barricades, First President Achille de Harlay refused Guise's request to convene the court, observing that "when the prince's majesty has been violated, the magistrate no longer has any authority."[26] When Guise and his brother, the cardinal of Lorraine, were assassinated on Henry III's orders in December 1588, the Sixteen purged the parlement's ranks by imprisoning twenty-two magistrates in the Bastille and replacing Harlay as First President. In March 1589 the king ordered those magistrates loyal to the crown to join a royalist parlement in exile established at Tours; magistrates would leave Paris for Tours over the next five years.[27]

Divided loyalties and internal dissent plagued both law courts. In Paris, the Catholic League's close association with the papacy and Spain encouraged those powers to intervene more openly and frequently in French affairs, a situation which conflicted with the parlementaires' traditional defense of France's political and religious integrity. Many Paris judges resisted the Sixteen's attempt to nominate magistrates to the court, nor would they summarily punish royalist sympathizers and suspected heretics. Their insistence on proper legal procedures for criminal prosecutions was a careful but powerful way of resisting the Sixteen's policies. On the other hand, Parisians who were more and more discontented with food shortages and heavy taxes levied to support the civil war blamed the magistrates, whom they still regarded as implicated in the city's governance.[28] Meanwhile, the parlement meeting at Tours bitterly debated whether to accept into its ranks magistrates who had delayed answering Henry III's summons and struggled to assert its own legitimacy as a royal tribunal.[29] Similar royal law courts loyal to the king were mandated for Châlons-sur-Marne, Carcassonne, Caen, Pertuis, and Flavigny, in opposition to the League-dominated tribunals at Troyes, Toulouse, Rouen, Aix, and Dijon, respectively.[30] The power struggle between the king and the Catholic League thus fractured the royal judiciary through much of the kingdom, as well as in Paris itself.

[26] Quoted in Lebigre, *La Révolution des curés*, 141–42: Quand la majesté du prince est violée, le magistrat n'a plus d'autorité.

[27] Maugis, *Histoire du parlement de Paris*, 2:54–99. Michel de Waele emphasizes that leaving Paris for Tours had social as well as political implications for the magistrates, whose corporate and individual identity was closely bound to the city; de Waele, *Les Relations*, 139–67.

[28] Salmon, *Renaissance and Revolt*, 250–52; Roelker, *One King, One Faith*, 356–85; de Waele, *Les Relations*, 309–33. On the League's relations with Spain, see DeLamar Jensen, *Diplomacy and Dogmatism: Bernardino de Mendoza and the French Catholic League* (Cambridge: Harvard University Press, 1964).

[29] Maugis, *Histoire du parlement de Paris*, 2:61–99, 136–62; Roelker, *One King, One Faith*, 356–437; de Waele, *Les Relations*, 213–40.

[30] Maugis, *Histoire du parlement de Paris*, 2:179–83. On the court at Châlons-sur-Marne, see Mark Konnert, "Urban Values versus Religious Passion: Châlons-sur-Marne during the Wars of Religion," *Sixteenth Century Journal* 20 (1989): 387–406.

The assassination of Henry III in July 1589 and the accession of Henry of Navarre—now Henry IV—to the French throne brought the tensions among the Catholic League, the Sixteen, and the Parlement of Paris to a climax. While the new king fought to wrest control of his capital and his kingdom from the Catholic League's armies and their Spanish allies, the Sixteen tried to tighten their domination of the city through purges, arrests, and executions. The parlement's lack of cooperation only confirmed the Sixteen's view of the court as their principal enemy; they responded by summarily executing First President Barnabé Brisson and two other judges in November 1591. Within a week, however, Mayenne entered the city and ordered the radical leaders who had attempted a "coup against the parlement" hanged or expelled. The magistrates themselves refused to convene the court for two weeks and later pursued the Sixteen's accomplices.[31]

By 1591, the Sixteen, the Catholic League, and the Paris parlement's magistrates were facing a serious constitutional crisis. At issue was the question of Henry IV's legitimacy as king of France and the relationship among religion, politics, and law in determining the succession to the throne. The roots of the crisis lay in a dilemma which all French Catholics had confronted even before Henry's accession: could a heretic be a legitimate king of France?[32] In the 1580s, the Catholic League had designated the elderly but pious Charles, cardinal de Bourbon, as a viable rival to Navarre, arguing that religious orthodoxy superseded Salic Law in determining the succession. The League recognized Bourbon as "King Charles X" after Henry III's death in 1589, but the cardinal's death in May 1590 left the League without an alternative "king" to support. The League urgently needed such a leader: although Gregory XIV issued a papal bull in 1591 denying Henry IV's legitimacy as king and excommunicating his followers, Henry's armies had already inflicted serious defeats on League forces at Arques (1589), Ivry (1590), and Chartres (1591).

In January 1593 Mayenne convened an Estates-General in Paris to resolve the succession question, presumably by electing a suitable Catholic. Led by the Sixteen, a pro-Spanish faction advocated marrying the chosen candidate to the Infanta Isabella, whose grandparents were the French monarchs Henry II and Catherine de Médicis. When the Estates-General held its final debates in June 1593, the parlement met in a plenary session. The deputies and the magistrates

---

[31]Salmon, *Renaissance and Revolt*, 252–59; Barnavi and Descimon, *La Sainte Ligue*, 152–75. For a comparison of the events in Paris with the League's activities in other French cities, see Holt, *French Wars of Religion*, 135–48.

[32]On the Catholics' dilemmas throughout this period, see Mack Holt, *The Duke of Anjou and the Politique Struggle during the Wars of Religion* (Cambridge: Cambridge University Press, 1986); Wolfe, *The Conversion of Henri IV.*

resolved to uphold the kingdom's fundamental laws and to oppose the accession of any foreign prince to the French throne. Henry IV's formal conversion to Catholicism a month later further weakened the League's resistance: in an elaborate public ceremony at St. Denis, the former Huguenot chieftain renounced Calvinism and effectively eliminated the final obstacle to Catholic acceptance of his rule.[33] Despite their internal divisions and conflicts, the parlement magistrates played a key role in both the constitutional crisis and its resolution, reasserting their traditional position as the defenders of France's laws, traditions, and rulers.[34]

The task of reuniting the kingdom, however, was far from over. Henry's bloodless entry into Paris in March 1594 allowed him to reclaim the capital from Spanish troops and the radical Leaguers who had dominated its political leadership. Most of the remaining members of the Paris Sixteen and their followers were exiled rather than executed. This was in keeping with Henry's general policy of amnesty toward his former enemies: by offering (or promising) gifts of money, honors, and offices, Henry persuaded many municipal governors, militia leaders, clerics, nobles, and other officials to return to royal service. Despite some lingering hostility and suspicion, judges from the law courts established at Tours and Châlons-sur-Marne were gradually reintegrated into the parlement at Paris, most of whose members also managed to keep their offices.[35] Eventually, Catholic magistrates from this reconstituted parlement would fill the ranks of the Paris Chambre de l'Edit.

During the period of 1594 through 1598, the parlement magistrates struggled to establish good relations with the king and to fully regain what they regarded as their rightful place in French governance. The tensions surrounding this effort culminated in another moment of crisis: the ratification of the Edict of Nantes. The Huguenots had been pressuring the king for a legal guarantee of their privileges since his accession. Although he had revoked the punitive laws issued by Henry III in 1585 and 1588 with the Edict of Mantes (1591), its terms did not satisfy all of the Huguenots' concerns. As Henry consolidated his power as king, the Huguenots renewed their demands for a comprehensive royal edict that would protect them. The Paris parlement's magistrates had generally supported the Edict of Mantes but had expressed serious reservations about the clause that allowed

---

[33]Holt, *French Wars of Religion*, 120–49; David Buisseret, *Henry IV* (London: George Unwin and Allen, 1984), 41-43.

[34]Roelker, *One King, One Faith*, 441–72; de Waele, *Les Relations*, 333–55; Shennan, *Parlement of Paris*, 227–32; Maugis, *Histoire du parlement de Paris*, 2:93–135.

[35]Buisseret, *Henry IV*, 46–54 ; Barnavi, *Le Parti de Dieu*, 239–55; Lebigre, *La Révolution des curés*, 225–54; Roelker, *One King, One Faith*, 434–39; de Waele, *Les Relations*, 240–48. On Henry's policy of amnesty toward French towns in particular, see Finley-Croswhite, *Henry IV and the Towns*.

Huguenots to hold offices. Responding to such complaints in August 1592, one of Henry's most trusted advisors, Philippe Duplessis Mornay, noted that this attitude contradicted the king's will, the law's intentions, and public justice.[36] A second interim royal declaration issued in November 1594 and ratified by the parlement in January 1595 provoked similar discontents among the magistrates, who remained largely opposed to admitting Huguenots to offices in the sovereign courts and elsewhere. Allowing such men to enter the judiciary could only cause conflict within the court and undermine justice itself: as parlementaire Guillaume Deslandes put it, "one heretic judge could do more harm than an entire army of soldiers."[37]

These debates were apparently a kind of dress rehearsal for the later confrontation between king and magistrates following Henry IV's decree of the Edict of Nantes in April 1598.[38] When the edict was presented to the court for approval in January 1599, the magistrates balked at the clauses concerning the chambres mi-parties and Huguenot officeholding. Even after Henry summoned a delegation of judges to the Louvre to insist on their obedience, the parlementaires continued to debate its terms. The Paris parlement finally registered the edict in late February, but Huguenot officeholding in the court would prove to be a sensitive issue once the Paris Chambre de l'Edit began to function.

The sixteenth century's legacy to the Paris parlement and the Chambre de l'Edit was thus a mixture of conflict and reconciliation. Royal magistrates had played an important part in the constitutional crisis of the 1580s and 1590s. Indeed, that crisis highlighted the multiple roles of the "perfect magistrate" in early modern France: member of a judicial and civic elite, guardian of France's legal heritage, and participant in royal governance. The parlementaires' experiences during the turmoil of the later sixteenth century showed the ties among religious, political, and legal matters—ties that could not be untangled for most of the magistrates. Though many of them questioned the wisdom—and indeed the justice—of establishing special law courts and judicial offices for Huguenots, in the end they

[36] Quoted in de Waele, *Les Relations*, 360: "c'est contre le volonté du roi, l'intention des edits, et la justice de la société publique." Duplessis Mornay's remarks were addressed to Louis Servin, who would serve as royal advocate in the Paris parlement and frequently appear before the Chambre de l'Edit.

[37] De Waele, *Les Relations*, 362–67. The quotation appears on p. 365: un juge hérétique pouvait faire plus de mal qu'une armée entière de gendarmes.

[38] De Waele, *Les Relations*, 371–82; Roelker, *One King, One Faith*, 444–50. Both authors use the earlier debates about Huguenot officeholding as a guide to the magistrates' likely opinions about the Edict of Nantes, since detailed records of the parlement's final discussions of that edict (between late January and 25 February, when it was finally approved) have not survived. The parlement had also objected strenuously to earlier (and unsuccessful) efforts to establish bipartisan law courts: see de Waele, *Les Relations*, 366–74; Roelker, *One King, One Faith*, 118, 324.

approved these and other provisions in the Edict of Nantes as a necessary step in restoring order to the realm. When the Paris Chambre de l'Edit began to judge criminal lawsuits, its judges worked within the context of a renewed monarchy, a period of relative peace, and a regime of religious coexistence mandated by law.

During the period of 1600 through 1610, a total of sixty-two magistrates from the Parlement of Paris served in the Chambre de l'Edit. This number includes the court's five presidents, as well as the four Huguenot councilors whose presence helped define the chamber's place in the parlement and the royal judiciary generally. Since only one Huguenot judge served in the Paris Chambre de l'Edit at any time, the court's purpose of providing fair justice for Huguenot litigants depended a great deal upon the corps of Catholic magistrates. The court's records, along with other sources, allow us to identify most of these judges.[39]

Such an analysis reveals several important features of the Chambre de l'Edit's composition. The chamber's judges changed frequently during this period, with some councilors leaving and others entering the court's ranks every year. Excluding the chamber's presidents, there were fifty-seven councilors for the period in question; of these, forty served for three years or less. Only four judges—Pierre Catinat, Cyprien Perot, Nicolas Violé, and Nicolas Le Camus—remained in the Chambre de l'Edit for seven years or more. The terms served by the chamber's presidents reflect a similar pattern. Jacques-Auguste de Thou presided over the court for four years, while Jean Forget, Antoine Séguier, Edouard Molé, and Antoine Le Camus did so for two years or less. In addition, the total number of judges who comprised the Chambre de l'Edit fluctuated slightly over time, dropping to fourteen in 1605 and 1607 and rising to nineteen in 1609. Usually the court included the sixteen members required according to the Edict of Nantes.[40]

---

[39] In addition to Roelker, de Waele, and Maugis, see François La Chesnaye-Desbois, *Dictionnaire de la noblesse*, 19 vols., 3d ed. (Paris, 1863–1877); Henri de Carsalade du Pont, *La Municipalité Parisienne à l'époque d'Henri IV* (Paris: Éditions Cujas, 1971); Barbara B. Diefendorf, *The Paris City Councillors in the Sixteenth Century: The Politics of Patrimony* (Princeton: Princeton University Press, 1983); Haag and Haag, *La France protestante*; Anquez, *Histoire des assemblées politiques*; Pierre de l'Estoile, *Mémoires-Journaux*, ed. G. Brunet et al., 12 vols. (Paris, 1875–1896). Two of the judges produced memoirs of their own: Nicolas-Edouard Olier, *Journal de Nicolas-Edouard Olier, conseiller au Parlement, 1593–1602*, ed. L. Sandret (Paris, 1876); Jacques-Auguste de Thou, *Mémoires*, in *Nouvelle collection des mémoires pour servir à l'histoire de France*, ed. Joseph François Michaud and Jean-Joseph-François Poujoulat, 1st series, vol. 11 (Paris, 1838). For further details on the Chambre de l'Edit's composition, see Catherine Dubief, "La Chambre de l'Edit du Parlement de Paris" (unpublished Mémoire pour le diplôme d'études supérieures d'histoire du droit et des faits sociaux, Université de Paris II, 1972), Bibliothèque de la Société de l'Histoire du Protestantisme Français MSS 2857; Diane C. Margolf, "The Paris Chambre de l'Edit: Protestant, Catholic and Royal Justice in Early Modern France" (Ph.D. diss., Yale University, 1990), chap. 2.

[40] "Edict of Nantes," 46–47 (art. 30).

A variety of factors could account for these variations in the chamber's membership: absences due to illness or incapacity, delays in the official reception of new judges, or complications in the transfer of judicial posts from one officeholder to another. Above all, changes in the court's composition suggest that no individual judge or group of judges could influence the Chambre de l'Edit's adjudication of lawsuits for very long.

The chamber's Catholic presidents and councilors were diverse in background and experience. While some of them had entered the Parlement of Paris twenty or thirty years earlier, twenty-two of them (just over one-third) attained their offices under Henry IV (that is, between 1594 and 1610). The senior Catholic magistrates who served in the Chambre de l'Edit included men who had joined the royalist "parlements" established at Tours and Châlons-sur-Marne, abandoning Paris under the leadership of the Catholic League and the Sixteen. There were others, however, whose past actions might have given Huguenot judges and litigants pause. When Henry III issued letters patent in May 1589 designating as rebels forty-four officials who had refused to join the law court at Tours, the list included three future members of the Chambre de l'Edit: Jean Midorge, Jean Courtin, and Edouard Molé.[41] Molé served as the Paris parlement's *procureur général* during the Catholic League's regime but remained a *conseiller* after the city surrendered to Henry IV; he became a *president à mortier* in 1602 and presided over the Chambre de l'Edit itself in 1605 and 1610.[42] Midorge, a member of the Chambre de l'Edit in 1606, served in both the League parlement and as an officer in the municipal militia. His loyalty to the Sixteen apparently waned as their aims became more extreme and their methods more violent: in May 1590, he himself was attacked by a mob and nearly drowned in the Seine.[43] Jean Courtin, along with Etienne Tournebus and François Gaudart, also served in the League parlement, though the details of their activities remain obscure. All three would later join the Chambre de l'Edit's ranks—Courtin for two years, Tournebus and Gaudart for six years. Despite the Catholic League's avowed aim of eliminating heresy, membership in the League parlement did not preclude magistrates from service in the Chambre de l'Edit.

Along with judges who had participated in the recent political turmoil, the court's ranks included some of the most famous French jurists of their day. Jacques-Auguste de Thou presided over the court from 1601 to 1603 and again in 1608. During the Wars of Religion, de Thou served both Henry III and Henry

[41] Maugis, *Histoire du parlement de Paris*, 2:137.

[42] Maugis, *Histoire du parlement de Paris*, 3:278, 299. See also Barnavi, *Le Parti de dieu*, 205, on Molé's conduct in the League parlement.

[43] Barnavi, *Le Parti de dieu*, 183; Salmon, "Paris Sixteen," 251.

IV as an ambassador and political advisor; he participated in the negotiations that produced the Edict of Nantes and also achieved fame as a historian.[44] Royal advocates Louis Servin and Cardin Le Bret, who appeared frequently before the Chambre de l'Edit, were also experienced jurists who contributed to the legal and political debates of their day. Servin published a collection of his arguments in court cases, as well as a Latin polemic about Venice's dispute with the papacy.[45] Le Bret, who entered the Parlement of Paris in December 1604, wrote a treatise entitled *De la Souveraineté du Roy* [On the King's Sovereignty], which placed the crime of treason *(lèse-majesté)* within the context of French constitutional law, recent political events and Le Bret's own experiences as a royal judicial official.[46]

Even the Chambre de l'Edit's less prominent magistrates were fully integrated into the social and political elite that the parlement's magistracy represented. Venality of office partly accounted for this: as noted above, the *droit annuel* enabled officeholders to retain judicial posts in their families, while *survivance* allowed officeholders to transfer their posts to designated successors, usually within their families. Philbert Turin (or Thurin) resigned his office of *conseiller* in the parlement to his son François in February 1608, having served in the parlement since 1566. The elder Turin apparently received a special dispensation that delayed the transfer until the end of the court's session, which allowed him to finish out his term in the Chambre de l'Edit.[47]

Marriage was another key mechanism by which parlementaires consolidated their wealth and status or advanced their family fortunes. The Chambre de l'Edit judges were no exception: by marrying their colleagues' daughters and sisters, they reinforced professional relationships with kinship ties. Nicolas Le Camus spent

---

[44]Roelker, *One King, One Faith*, 356–439 passim; de Waele, *Les Relations*, 309–73 passim; Anquez, *Histoire des assemblées politiques*, 68–79; Diefendorf, *Paris City Councillors*, 130–34; Buisseret, *Henry IV*, 96. On de Thou's scholarly career, see Henry Harisse, *Le Président de Thou et ses descendants* (Paris, 1905); Christophe Dupuy, *Jacques-Auguste de Thou and the Index: Letters from Christophe Dupuy, 1603–1607*, ed. Alfred Soman (Geneva: Droz, 1972). When de Thou met with deputies from the Huguenot political assembly of Châtellerault in 1597, he might have encountered his future Huguenot colleague in the Chambre de l'Edit, Jean Rochelle du Coudray.

[45]L'Estoile, *Mémoires-Journaux*, 8:118, 258, 261; Maugis, *Histoire du parlement de Paris*, 3:338–39, Michel Popoff, ed., *Prosopographie des gens du parlement de Paris, 1266–1753* (Saint-Nazaire-le-Désert: Références, 1996), 970. See also William J. Bouwsma, "The Venetian Interdict and the Problem of Order," in Bouwsma, *A Usable Past*, 97–111.

[46]Maugis, *Histoire du parlement de Paris*, 3:334. See also La Chesnay-Desbois, *Dictionnaire*, vol. 4, s.v. "Bret, Le"; Popoff, *Prosopographie*, 960. On Le Bret's theory of sovereignty, see Ralph E. Giesey, Lanny Haldy, and James Millhorn, "Cardin Le Bret and Lese Majesty," *Law and History Review* 4 (1986): 23–54.

[47]Maugis, *Histoire du parlement de Paris*, 3:232, 303.

three of his nine years as a Chambre de l'Edit councilor working with his uncle, Jacques II Sanguin, who in turn was related to the de Thou family by marriage.[48] Guillaume Bénard, a member of the court's ranks for six years, married the sister of Jean Forget, chamber president. Bénard's daughter Marie in turn married Cyprien Perrot, a chamber judge for seven years; according to the court's records, the two men served there together in 1603 and 1606.[49] Family ties such as these not only connected the magistrates to each other, but also embedded them firmly within the larger social and professional world of the Paris parlement.

What of the Chambre de l'Edit's Huguenot members? Four such judges rotated through the court during the first decade of the seventeenth century: Jean Garrault, Pierre Berger, Jacques Chalmont du Breuil, and Jean Rochelle du Coudray. How they entered the parlement's ranks, and their experiences prior to serving in the chamber, contrast with those of the Catholic judges. Their offices were recent creations, not inherited positions: according to the Edict of Nantes's terms, Henry IV agreed to establish four offices in the Paris parlement specifically for Huguenots, and to appoint Huguenot candidates to two other offices when they fell vacant.[50] In December 1599, the Huguenot political assembly at Saumur recommended that the king appoint Garrault, Berger, and du Breuil to three of those offices. Garrault, a former judge in the parlement of Rennes, had been a member of the royal household of Navarre; Berger and du Breuil were lawyers who had been active in the Huguenot political assemblies of the 1580s and 1590s as deputies from the town of La Rochelle.[51] The assembly submitted these nominations to the king through its representative at the royal court, Jean Rochelle du Coudray. The three candidates proved acceptable, but when problems arose over a fourth nominee the following January, the assembly nominated du Coudray himself. Eventually, all four were received as parlement judges, Garrault and Berger in 1600 and du Breuil and du Coudray a year later.[52] In contrast to their Catholic

---

[48]Maugis, *Histoire du parlement de Paris*, 3:261–62 (Jacques II Sanguin), 314 (Nicolas Le Camus). See also La Chesnaye-Desbois, *Dictionnaire*, vol. 4, s.v. "Camus." Sanguin's father, also named Jacques, had married Barbe de Thou, Jacques-Auguste de Thou's aunt; see Carsalade du Pont, *La Municipalité Parisienne*, 58–60; Dupuy, *Jacques-Auguste de Thou and the Index*, 16.

[49]Maugis, *Histoire du parlement de Paris*, 3:240 (Guillaume Bénard), 292 (Cyprien Perrot).

[50]"Edict of Nantes," 46–47 (art. 30).

[51]Haag and Haag, *La France protestante*, 3:315–16 (Chalmont du Breuil), 8:457–58 (Rochelle du Coudray). The latter's role in the political assembly at Loudun is noted in Anquez, *Histoire des assemblées politiques*, 68–79.

[52]Maugis, *Histoire du parlement de Paris*, 3:316–17. See also Anquez, *Histoire des assemblées politiques*, 202. Pierre de l'Estoile recorded Garrault's and Berger's entry into the parlement's ranks; see l'Estoile *Mémoires-Journaux*, 7:236.

counterparts, these judges were linked to the Huguenot political assemblies and the faction that had once been led by Henry of Navarre, now King Henry IV. Like the Catholics, however, they were evidently able judges. In May 1601, Pierre l'Estoile recorded that du Coudray "was examined in the court of parlement and inducted into it, among the councilors, after having greatly satisfied his judges and given by his answers singular proof of his competence."[53] According to l'Estoile, Jean Garrault also was "a respectable man, worthy of his office," while Pierre Berger was described as having "the reputation of a respectable man, a good judge, and uncorrupted."[54]

Religious conversion, however, began to complicate the distribution of Huguenot and Catholic judges (and their offices) in the Chambre de l'Edit. In 1608 Pierre Berger resigned his office to his son, who was also a promising lawyer. But when Pierre II Berger abjured the Reformed faith in 1613, Huguenot leaders argued that since a "Protestant" judicial office was now held by a Catholic, a new office and officeholder were needed to maintain the Edict of Nantes's provision for six Protestants in the parlement.[55] On the other hand, two Catholic judges named François Le Coq and Jean de Villemereau adopted the Reformed faith in 1615 and 1616, respectively. This seemed to increase the number of Protestants in the parlement to seven, likewise violating the edict's terms.[56] Both sides appealed to the crown: the parlement protested the Huguenots' apparent manipulation of judicial offices, while Huguenot leaders demanded that the king force the court to accept Le Coq and Villemereau. In 1619 François de Bonne, duc de Lesdiguières, appealed to Louis XIII to support the beleaguered Huguenot judges, "for the said Parlement's refusal implies that your subjects are unworthy of offices, contrary to

[53] L'Estoile, *Mémoires-Journaux*, 7:292–93: un nommé Ducoudray fût examiné en la Cour de Parlement et reçu en icelle, au nombre des Conseillers, après avoir fort contenté ses juges et donné par ses réponses, un singulier témoignange de sa suffisance. L'Estoile apparently became further acquainted with Rochelle du Coudray and his family; among his journal entries for 1608 he recorded the deaths of "two young women of my acquaintance, both of whom will be missed because of their judgment and virtue, the one from the suburb of Saint-Germain, named Mademoiselle du Coudray, wife of the court councilor du Coudray, of the [Reformed] religion." [deux jeunes femmes de ma connoissance, toutes deux regrettables pour leur probité et vertu, l'une au fauxbourg Saint-Germain, nommée Mademoiselle du Coldray, femme du Conseiller en la Cour, du Couldray, de la Religion.] (9:173).

[54] L'Estoile, *Mémoires-Journaux*, 9:137: un homme de bien et digne de sa charge; 9:282: réputation d'homme de bien, bon juge, et non corrompu.

[55] Maugis, *Histoire du parlement de Paris*, 3:316 (Pierre Berger), 324 (Pierre II Berger); Mousnier, *Vénalité*, 598–600; Jacques Pannier, *L'Eglise réformée de Paris sous Louis XIII, 1610–1621* (Paris, 1922), 183–85. Pannier states that it was the elder Berger who converted, but comments by Mousnier and l'Estoile (cited above) support the view that it was the younger Berger.

[56] Mousnier, *Vénalité*, 598–601; Pannier, *L'Eglise réformée sous Louis XIII, 1610–1621*, 183–93.

the disposition of your edicts which expressly admit them [to offices] as natural Frenchmen and not foreigners."[57] The dispute continued until August 1620, when the court was forced to accept the two judges by royal command.[58]

In the Chambre de l'Edit's early years, the court's judges were divided by their history and experience, as well as by religion. The chamber combined Catholic judges who had shown divided loyalties during the period of the Catholic League's and the Sixteen's domination of Paris—as well as a few who had been affiliated with the Huguenots' political assemblies during the same period. Some of the court's Catholic members possessed years of judicial experience, while others had only recently joined the parlement's ranks. Most of them were united by family ties and by their common membership in the parlement itself. Recent studies of the parlement during the later sixteenth century have emphasized both conflict and continuity in the magistrates' mentality—their personal and professional understanding of their role in the French state, especially in relation to Catholicism and the crown.[59] The Catholic magistrates' full integration in the parlement, rather than their temporary service in the Chambre de l'Edit, represented the most important element of their corporate identity.

The Protestant magistrates' position was more problematic. Throughout the Wars of Religion, the Huguenots had complained of prejudicial treatment by the parlements' Catholic judges and demanded protection in the form of special law courts or guaranteed judicial offices (or both). Huguenot political assemblies of the 1590s—many of whose deputies were lawyers—petitioned Henry IV repeatedly for guaranteed access to judicial office; such demands no doubt reflected the deputies' social and professional ambitions as well as their concerns about fairness before the courts.[60] Berger, Garrault, du Breuil, and du Coudray thus did not

---

[57]François de Bonne, duc de Lesdiguières, *Lettre et Advis envoyé au Roy, par Monsieur le Mareschal de Lesdiguières* (Tours, 1610): Car le refus dudit Parlement fait presuppose vosdits subjects indignes des charges, contre la disposition de vos Edicts, qui les y admettre expressement comme naturels François et non estrangers. The letter was written and published prior to the Huguenot political assembly at Loudun, which also demanded the judges' acceptance in office: see Pannier, *L'Eglise réformée sous Louis XIII, 1610–1621*, 187–88. Lesdiguières himself converted to Catholicism in 1621.

[58]Mousnier, *Vénalité*, 598–601; Pannier, *L'Eglise réformée sous Louis XIII, 1610–1621*, 183–88. The text of the parlement's *arrêt* on the acceptance of the two judges is reprinted in Pannier, 656: it states that the two judges' successors must be Catholic, and that the court will not accept more than six Protestant magistrates as specified in the Edict of Nantes. Elsewhere Pannier identifies François Le Coq as a parlement judge during the period from 1621 to 1629 but notes that he did not serve in the Chambre de l'Edit: see Pannier, *L'Eglise réformée de Paris sous Louis XIII, 1621–1629*, 2 vols. (Paris: H. Champion, 1931), 1:332–33.

[59]Roelker, *One King, One Faith*, 441–72; de Waele, *Les Relations*, 409–16.

[60]Joseph Airo-Farulla, "Les Protestants et l'acquisition des offices à la fin du XVIe siècle," *Bulletin de la Société de l'Histoire du Protestantisme Français* 116 (1970): 509–12.

achieve their offices in the traditional way, through the familial and professional networks of the Parisian magistracy. Instead, they owed their positions directly to the Edict of Nantes's requirements, which many parlementaires had opposed and which would continue to be disputed in the seventeenth century. Although the four Protestant judges were apparently accepted into the parlement's ranks as men of the law, the question of whether Protestants could or should hold judicial office remained unsettled; indeed, the debate quickly revived in the wake of several officeholders' conversions. The one thing that should have united the court's Huguenot and Catholic members—their mutual commitment to the fair administration of royal justice—was compromised by the presence of religious difference in their ranks, and by the continuing perception of religious difference as a threat to political, religious, and social order.[61]

The main features outlined above for the Chambre de l'Edit's Catholic magistrates continued throughout the court's history in the seventeenth century.[62] The court's Catholic members rotated frequently into and out of the chamber, as revealed by a sample of *arrêts* taken for the period 1615–1665.[63] Both the individual magistrates and the number of judges serving at any given time appear to have fluctuated throughout the period in question. The judges themselves, however, were still drawn from the leading families of the robe nobility, and their names are readily familiar to students of the Paris parlement during the seventeenth and eighteenth centuries: Longueil, Molé, Méliand, Petau, Bailleul, Le Coigneux, Pithou, Bullion, Sevin, and de Creil. The parlement's royal advocates who appeared in the chamber's records displayed a similar kind of professional continuity, for Jérôme II Bignon and Denis Talon both replaced relatives in those offices.[64] The Chambre de l'Edit's Catholic members thus remained tied to the

[61] Dompnier, *Le Venin de l'hérésie*, 75–82.

[62] The following section relies greatly on Moote, *Revolt of the Judges;* Hamscher, *Parlement of Paris after the Fronde.*

[63] Concurrent service in the parlement by members of the same family makes it difficult to identify individual judges with certainty, but the evidence suggests frequent changes in the Chambre de l'Edit's composition. Of the nineteen names that appear in the court's records for 1615, only four reappear in the records for 1620. In 1625 the court included three out of ten judges who had served in it before; of the nine names which appear in 1630, only one resurfaces five years later. Eleven of the thirteen councilors in the court's records for 1640 were new, and two of the twelve names that appear in records from 1645 are also among the thirteen listed for 1660, as is one from the panel for 1655.

[64] Moote, *Revolt of the Judges,* 287; Hamscher, *Parlement of Paris after the Fronde,* 127–29. Hamscher has illustrated the family ties among the parlementaires especially for the 1650s, showing how younger members were invariably related to their elders and to each other; see 28–30. See also Popoff, *Prosopographie,* 959 (Bignon), 970 (Talon).

social, political, and professional world of the parlement magistracy, just as the court's earliest members had been.

What of the chamber's Protestant judges? The court resisted accepting Protestant converts François Le Coq and Jean de Villemereau into its ranks until forced to do so by royal *lettres de jussion*. The parlement judges reacted similarly after Jean Rochelle du Coudray's death: they sought to have his office suppressed and managed to deny admission to another Protestant office seeker, Abimélec de Cumont, sieur de Boisgrolier, for more than two years.[65] Records of the elders for Paris's Reformed church at Charenton, when read in conjunction with the Chambre de l'Edit's records, suggest some connections between the two groups: family names which appear in both sources include De Murat, Mandat, and Chandieu.[66] Identifying individuals with certainty remains difficult, the more so because Protestants and Catholics might be connected through marriage and godparentage. Even during the sixteenth century, there were family ties between Catholic magistrates and Reformed families, and recent studies of early modern French elites have shown the existence of confessional divisions within families as well as their persistence across generations.[67]

Perhaps more importantly, the Paris parlement found ways to capitalize on the Huguenot judges' vulnerable position within the court. The parlement's Catholic magistrates continued to view their Protestant counterparts as outsiders. As such, they could not really enjoy the same privileges and status as other judges, and every effort would be made to emphasize the limitations they faced. In a letter to Philippe Duplessis Mornay dated December 1618, François Le Coq explained the

[65]Pannier, *L'Eglise réformée sous Louis XIII, 1610–1621*, 186–91. According to another work by Pannier, Le Coq was succeeded by both his son and grandson in office. Although the parlement's *arrêt* of August 1620 specified that Le Coq's successor must be Catholic, his descendants apparently remained Protestant. He identifies both de Cumont and Isaac II du Candal as Protestant judges in the Paris parlement but not necessarily as members of the Chambre de l'Edit; see Pannier, *L'Eglise réformée sous Louis XIII, 1621–1629*, 1:332–33.

[66]Pannier, *L'Eglise réformée sous Louis XIII, 1621–1629*, 2:74–79.

[67]Jacques Pannier, *L'Eglise réformée sous Henri IV* (Paris, 1911), 183; Dubief, "La Chambre de l'Edit," 1–28 and appendix. See also Barbara B. Diefendorf, "Houses Divided: Religious Schism in Sixteenth-Century Parisian Families," in *Urban Life in the Renaissance*, ed. Susan Zimmerman and Robert Weissman (Newark: University of Delaware Press, 1989), 80–99; Diefendorf, "Give Us Back Our Children: Patriarchal Authority and Parental Consent to Religious Vocations in Early Counter-Reformation France," *Journal of Modern History* 68 (1996): 265–82; J.H.M. Salmon, "Protestant Jurists and Theologians in Early Modern France: The Family of Cappel," in Salmon, *Renaissance and Revolt* (Cambridge: Cambridge University Press, 1987), 54–72; Raymond A. Mentzer, *Blood and Belief: Family Survival and Confessional Identity among the Provincial Huguenot Nobility* (West Lafayette: Purdue University Press, 1994).

difficulties of his position as both judicial officeholder and convert to the Reformed faith:

> First, I am beyond hope of being able to resign my place to my son when I wish, as the others can do whether of one or the other faith, which is more unacceptable to me than any other thing they can do to me, for they hold it as a maxim that my office, having come from a Catholic, must necessarily belong to a Catholic, which is against our edicts, but they say that they are the interpreters [of the edicts], that is to say judges in their own cause....[68]

Le Coq also complained that he was being excluded from serving in the Chambre de l'Edit "because I am not one of the six created by the Edict of Nantes to serve in it...I have an office and yet I do not, since I cannot freely dispose of it and do not enjoy the privileges that the others do." Le Coq predicted that his office would certainly be eliminated after his death.[69] Le Coq's comments suggest that Protestant judges could be in the Paris parlement but not of the court, and that the Chambre de l'Edit was fully subordinate to the larger parlement. The fact that they were few in number (as defined by the Edict of Nantes) made it all the more difficult for them to assert any real influence in the parlement or the chamber.

Ironically, this situation may account for the fact that contemporary complaints about the bipartisan chambers and their judges rarely mentioned the Paris court. For the French crown at least, the Paris chamber's relative weakness within its affiliated parlement was a model for the other bipartisan law courts, as indicated in the Code Michaud (1629). Issued by Louis XIII in an effort to reform abuses within the royal judiciary, the code contained several articles specifically aimed at the chambres mi-parties. The king ordered the bipartisan chambers

[68]Bibliothèque de la Société de l'Histoire du Protestantisme Français MS Papiers Duplessis Mornay No. 753.10, fol. 101. Lettre de M. Le Coq à M. Mornay (Paris, 8 December 1618): premierement je suis hors d'esperance de pouvoir resigner ma place à mon fils quand bon me semblera ainsi que peuvent faire les autres tant d'une que d'autre religion, ce qui m'est plus insupportable q[ue] toutte autre chose qu'ils puissant faire contre moy car ils tiennent pour maxime que mon office estant venue d'un catholiq[ue] il est necessairement affecté à un catholiq[ue], ce qui est contre nos edits, mais ils disent qu'ils en sont les interpretes c'est à dire juges en leur propre cause.

[69]Lettre de M. Le Coq à M. Mornay (Paris, 8 December 1618): je suis exclus de la chambre de l'edict car estant ceste annee en mon rang pour y entrer on ne m'y a pas voulu mettre par ce que je ne suis pas l'un des six crées par l'edict de nantes pour y servir.... J'ay un office et je n'en ay point puis que je n'en puis librem[ent] disposer et ne jouis point des privileges qu font les autres. Elsewhere in the letter Le Coq states that "quand je viendrois à deceder il est tres certain q[ue] mon office seroit suprimé."

meeting at Beziers and Agen to be reunited *(reunis)* with their respective parlements at Toulouse and Bordeaux, which would fully incorporate the chambers as the Paris parlement did ("en la manière qui se pratique en notre parlement de Paris"). This would halt the constant wrangling between the chambers and the parlements, as well as ending the oppression of the king's subjects that had resulted from the courts' quarrels.[70] It would also honor the Edict of Nantes's terms: after all, Henry IV had indicated that the chambers would be incorporated into the provincial parlements "when the causes which moved us to establish them shall cease and no longer take place among our subjects."[71]

The Code Michaud reflected another problem related to the bipartisan chambers: the judges' religious prejudices. Huguenots and Catholics alike claimed that judges of both confessions allowed favoritism toward members of their faith (and prejudice against those of the other confession) to taint their treatment of lawsuits and litigants. Again, such complaints invariably focused on the chambres mi-parties: since they possessed equal numbers of Protestant and Catholic magistrates, religious partisanship would literally split the courts' verdicts and prolong their proceedings. The Code Michaud specifically claimed that in such cases, Protestants were given the lightest criminal penalties or escaped punishment altogether. In order to prevent the Protestant judges' favoritism from producing such injustices, the code mandated that split decisions should be appealed according to the Edict of Nantes's terms.[72]

Similar complaints of Protestant judicial prejudice continued to surface in the seventeenth century, appearing outside official documents like the Code Michaud. For example, a *mémoire* addressed to Louis XIV claimed that Protestant magistrates offered favorable treatment not only to other Protestants, but also to Catholics who were willing to convert. "From this," the author wrote, "a great number of perversions occur every day, such that we have the shame and displeasure of seeing the loss of souls and the destruction of justice."[73] In 1680 royal advocate Denis Talon argued that Protestants were "incapable of judicature," even in seigneurial courts. The legal profession itself insisted that its members be Catholic, a requirement that superseded the Edict of Nantes's guarantees of Protestant

---

[70]The text of the Code Michaud appears in Isambert et al., *Recueil général*, 16:223–344. Art. 102 (pp. 255–56) contains the order regarding the Beziers and Agen chambers' incorporation.

[71]"Edict of Nantes," 48 (art. 36).

[72]Isambert et al., *Recueil général*, 16:257–58. (Code Michaud, art. 104).

[73]A.N. TT430, dossier 31, no. 97, "Mémoire du Duc d'Elzès," fol. 2: il arrive tous les jours grand nombre de perversions, en sorte que nous avons la honte et le deplaisir de voir la perte des ames et l'aneantissement de la justice. Though undated, the memoir was written in response to controversy over an *arrêt* issued by the Parlement of Toulouse in February 1665.

access to offices and dignities. Moreover, judges who were not Catholic lacked the moral capacity to serve in the judiciary. "One cannot be surprised if an infinity of scandalous actions and profanations of the most august mysteries of religion have not been repressed with severity," Talon stated, "when Judges guilty of a false doctrine secretly approve actions of impiety and libertinism."[74] Protestant judges thus threatened to subvert the administration of royal justice from within the judiciary itself. Religious difference and judicial office were fundamentally incompatible.

Talon's comments echoed fears and criticisms that had long been expressed about the inability of Protestant judges to be "perfect magistrates" who exemplified moral virtue and legal wisdom, suppressed disorder, and enforced laws in the king's name. Though Huguenots complained about the prejudice of Catholic judges, the magistracy and the monarchy tended to focus on the other side of the problem: the Code Michaud, for example, condemns the leniency and favoritism of Protestant judges in the chambres mi-parties but makes no mention of similar conduct by Catholic magistrates. Throughout much of the seventeenth century, the Huguenots' special law courts and judicial offices were seen as a source of disorder and injustice.

The Paris Chambre de l'Edit existed within this context of religious divisions, conflicting interests, and suspicion of prejudice. If the court was rarely singled out for criticism on the grounds of religious partisanship, this was no doubt due to the fact that from its inception, the chamber was largely embedded in and subordinate to the Paris parlement. Protestant magistrates might have been allowed within its ranks according to the Edict of Nantes's terms, but they could be isolated in other ways from full participation in the court's activities and privileges. The difficulties experienced by Huguenot councilors in the world of the Parisian royal magistracy stemmed not only from religious difference, but also from its social, political and moral implications. In short, Protestant judges might be tolerated but they could never truly belong.[75] The Chambre de l'Edit, however, derived its identity as a "Protestant" law court as much from its petitioners as from its panel of magistrates.

[74]"Arrest du Parlement, Qui ordonne la Destitution des Officiers des Justices subalterns faisans profession de la R.P.R., 23 August 1680," in *Recueil des édits, declarations, et arrêts du conseil, rendus au sujet de la religion prétendue réformée depuis 1679 jusqu'à present* (Paris, 1701): l'on ne doit pa[s] s'etonner si une infinité d'actions scandaleuses et de profanations des mystères les plus augustes de la Religion, n'ont pas été reprimez avec severité, lorsque les Juges prevenus d'une fausse doctrine approvent en secret les actions d'impieté et de libertinage....

[75]On the equivocal meanings of "tolerance" in the sixteenth and seventeenth centuries, see Mario Turchetti, "'Concorde ou tolérance' de 1562 à 1598," *Revue historique* 556 (1985): 341–55; Nicolas Piqué and Ghislain Waterlot, eds., *Tolérance et réforme: Éléments pour une généalogie du concept de tolérance* (Paris and Montréal: L'Harmattan, 1999).

Despite all complaints and suspicions of prejudice or ineffectiveness, many litigants appealed to the court for justice. The French men and women who appeared before the Chambre de l'Edit were perhaps the ultimate source of the court's work, for they invoked or accepted the court's authority to settle their disputes. As revealed by the chamber's records, these litigants constituted a much larger and more diverse group than the judges, for individuals from across the spectrum of French society appealed to the Chambre de l'Edit.

A sample of one thousand cases heard by the court from 1600 to 1610 shows the geographical distribution of judicial appeals to the chamber during that period. The *arrêts* for 697 of those cases indicate the law court (and the place) where the case was first heard. Sentences were appealed to the Paris Chambre de l'Edit from a variety of royal tribunals and judicial officers: the *sénéchal* of Poitou or his *lieutenant criminel* at Poitiers, the *bailli* of Touraine or his lieutenant at Chinon, the governor of La Rochelle or the parlement of Brittany at Rennes. Appeals from municipal and many seigneurial jurisdictions can also be grouped together roughly according to the administrative regions of seventeenth-century France. Table 2.1, column 2, reflects the results of this analysis.

These figures show several important features of judicial appeals to the Chambre de l'Edit. First, the breadth of the chamber's judicial competence clearly matched that of the Paris parlement itself, which covered much of northern, northwestern, and central France. Few of the appeals came from the provincial bipartisan chambers: three from the court at Castres, two from the court at Nérac, one from the court at Rouen, and none at all from the one at Grenoble. Paris and its environs were the most fertile source of business for the Paris chamber, followed by Brittany, Anjou, and Touraine.

How does this pattern in judicial appeals compare to the distribution of the Reformed population in seventeenth-century France? According to the research of Samuel Mours, the western provinces of Poitou and Saintonge-Aunis had the largest numbers of Huguenots, followed by Normandy and Paris (which Mours grouped with Champagne, Chartres, and Picardy).[76] In contrast, Brittany possessed a relatively small Reformed population, though it appears prominently among the areas supplying judicial appeals to the Chambre de l'Edit. Its most active congregations, however, were found at Rennes and Nantes—two cities whose law courts' decisions were frequently appealed to the chamber.[77] More recently, Philip Benedict's analysis of parish and census records shows a pattern of irregular demographic decline among the Huguenots, with their numbers dropping significantly

---

[76]Samuel Mours, *Les Eglises réformées en France* (Paris: Librairie Protestante, 1958), 163–68; idem, *Essai sommaire.*

[77]Mours, *Les Eglises réformées,* 161–62.

TABLE 2.1: GEOGRAPHICAL DISTRIBUTION OF JUDICIAL APPEALS
TO THE PARIS CHAMBRE DE L'EDIT

AREA (BY 1610 DISTRIBUTION)	CASES (NO.)	
	1600–1610	1615–1665
Poitou	167	52
Paris (including Champagne, Picardy, Boulonnais, Beauvais, and Ile-de-France)	160	–
Paris	–	88
Brittany	55	22
Maine	47	5
Anjou	45	5
Touraine	43	8
Angoumois	28	7
Orléanais	27	11
Berry	23	8
Normandy	11	7
La Marche	11	5
Bourgogne	10	4
Lyonnais	10	–
Lyonnais / Maconnais	–	6
Dauphiné	–	5
Languedoc	6	7
Auvergne	4	–
Guyenne	3	10
Limousin	–	3
Provence	1	1
Other (one appeal per jurisdiction)	46	77
Total	697	331

during the first half of the seventeenth century. Though urban Reformed communities were especially marked by this pattern, regional variations also occurred. The northern congregations dwindled rapidly during the years leading up to 1685, whereas congregations in the Midi remained relatively numerous and strong.[78]

[78]Benedict, *Huguenot Population of France*, 77. The comparison with Mours is somewhat approximate because his figures are organized according to the Reformed churches' provincial colloquies, whose boundaries may not correspond exactly with the regions and jurisdictions indicated above. In

Despite the Huguenots' apparently waning strength and numbers in northern France, Paris and its environs, along with Poitou and Brittany, were the source of many judicial appeals to the Chambre de l'Edit even after 1610. An analysis of cases from the later decades of the seventeenth century shows substantial continuity with the situation described above. Table 2.1, column 3, is based on a sample of 331 arrêts for the period 1615 to 1665. Although based on a smaller sample of cases spread out over a broader chronological period, the overall pattern of judicial appeals remained much the same as in the first decade of the seventeenth century. Most of the court's business still originated in the northern and western provinces rather than those of the south and east, where the Huguenots' demographic strength was greatest and where regional bipartisan chambers could handle their legal disputes.

The Chambre de l'Edit's records also reveal important information about the litigants themselves: names, places of residence, occupations, gender, and family affiliation. Though litigation was a time-consuming and costly enterprise, it was by no means confined to the wealthy and leisured classes. Families, guilds, groups of creditors and debtors, inhabitants of towns and villages, and individuals from every stratum of French society had an interest in using the legal system to regulate behavior, enforce contracts, and punish offenders. Even relatively poor people could pursue lawsuits on appeal if a royal prosecutor was willing to join their case as a *partie civile*. If law courts had not yet become the "tribunals of the nation" of the eighteenth century, they did provide a forum for airing and resolving disputes. They also served to disseminate knowledge of the law even to those outside the legal profession and the judiciary itself.[79]

The Chambre de l'Edit reflected this widespread use of royal justice, receiving appeals from aristocrats and artisans, clerics and laypersons, men and women. Litigants before the court included some of France's most illustrious nobles. Damoiselle Henriette de Rohan, dame de La Garnache and Beauvau sur Mer, appealed to the court in 1615 concerning a dispute with a messenger.[80] Charlotte de Nassau, duchesse de la Trémoille, was involved in several disputes over the administration of seigneurial lands which the court adjudicated.[81] Armand Nompar de Caumont, duc de La Force, brought suit before the court in August 1660 against

---

addition, some of his figures are taken from late seventeenth-century sources.

[79] Sarah Maza, "Le Tribunal de la nation: Les mémoires judiciaires et l'opinion publique à la fin de l'Ancien Régime," *Annales: Economies, Sociétés, Civilisations* 42 (1987): 73–90.

[80] A.N. X2b 286, 9 February 1615. Her opposing party was Jacques Richer, "messager de Nantes et Angers, facteur de Mace Rabut, messager d'Angers et Paris."

[81] A.N. X2b 286, 3 February 1615; X2b 319, 19 June 1620.

a councilor in the king's household, while François de Villedon, sieur de Chavreliere appealed his conviction for illegal hunting on François de Roye de La Rochefoucauld's lands in 1665.[82] The court's records abound with plaintiffs and defendants who belonged to the lesser ranks of the nobility—ecuyers, sieurs, and seigneurs—along with their wives, widows, sisters, and daughters.

Not all of the chamber's litigants came from the aristocracy. In 1620, master clockmaker Abraham Cuzin appealed to the Chambre de l'Edit in his dispute with Edmé Nicot, a judicial official in Nivernais.[83] Louis Le Scellier, a Huguenot laborer from a village near Beauvais, petitioned the court, as did Jean Simon, a haberdasher (*mercier*).[84] The court also dealt with appeals from tanners and candlemakers, tailors and jewelers, soldiers and printers. Workers in the textile industry—identified as *tixier, maître tisserand, peigneur de laine,* and *sayettier*—also sued before the court. A merchant from Sedan named Jacques Doree appealed his case against the master cloth dyers and weavers of Amiens; two merchants from Lyon filed an accusation of forgery against Helie Bouchereau, a merchant from La Rochelle and their opponent in a lawsuit.[85] A Parisian *maître brodeur* named Jehan Talon, along with his wife and servant, petitioned the court regarding their dispute with *maître brodeur* Daniel Peschel and his wife.[86] Doctors, surgeons, notaries, and lawyers also appeared in the Chambre de l'Edit's records as petitioners for the court's judgment of their disputes. In 1615 Antoine and Isaac Arnauld sued a Huguenot lawyer named Cezard Dupleix (also spelled de Plais), accusing him of writing and distributing defamatory literature about them, while surgeon Nicolas Remy brought his case before the court in 1620.[87]

The Paris Chambre de l'Edit's business also included a sprinkling of lawsuits involving foreigners, mainly from Protestant countries: England, Scotland, Flanders, and the Netherlands. Epipheman Eveschan and Sarra Ramizet (no doubt a phonetic spelling of "Sarah Ramsay"), who were English and Scots, respectively, sued before the court in 1605.[88] Three years later the court heard a forgery case which pitted Valentin Conoques and his wife against Thomas Cotteils, a London

---

[82] A.N. X2b 483, 12 January 1645 (Caumont); X2b 697, 11 May 1665 (Villedon).

[83] A.N. X2b 319, 22 and 27 June 1620.

[84] A.N.X2b 623, 14 January 1660 (Le Scellier); X2b 697, 7 May 1665 (Simon).

[85] A.N. X2b 210, 18 December 1602 (Doree); X2b 241, 28 April 1608 (Bouchereau).

[86] A.N. X2b 236, 15 June 1607.

[87] A.N. X2b 286, 22 and 29 January, 17 February 1615 (Arnauld); X2b 316, 15 January 1620 (Remy). The Arnaulds were members of a distinguished Parisian judicial family; in the *arrêt*, Antoine Arnauld is identified as "avocat en la cour" while Isaac is listed as "conseiller d'état et intendant général des finances." See also Michel de Waele, "Les opinions politiques d'un avocat parisien sous Henri IV: Antoine Arnauld," *Renaissance and Reform / Renaissance et Réforme* 17 (1993): 51–60.

[88] A.N. X2b 225, 27 May 1605.

merchant; another lawsuit involving two English merchants and Jacques Guiton, a municipal official from La Rochelle, was brought before the chamber magistrates later that year.[89] Not all such cases stemmed from disputes between French and foreign merchants. When Daniel Naboresquin, a Polish nobleman visiting Paris, appeared before the court in January 1604, he claimed that a servant had robbed him of gold worth 300 *écus* a year earlier. He also accused judicial officials of mishandling the case; arguing that the thief had escaped through their negligence, he demanded that they reimburse him for his losses. The provost of Paris had rejected his case, and the Chambre de l'Edit likewise sent him away empty-handed.[90] In some instances, the foreign nationals' religion clearly accounted for the substance of their litigation before the chamber magistrates. For example, in 1602 two Englishmen and two Flemings appealed a fine imposed by judicial officials in St. Mâlo, where one of the Flemings lived. The court ordered the recipient of the fine—the bishop of St. Mâlo—to refund the money, with the following admonition:

> The court enjoins the inhabitants of Saint Malo and all of the king's subjects to live in good amity together, so that those of the so-called reformed religion, whether the king's subjects or foreigners [estrangers], may not be investigated, vexed or molested for their religion, nor because of their religion sought in the houses or places where they wish to live, conducting themselves peaceably and without scandal, according to the edicts.[91]

In addition to nobles, artisans, and foreigners, clerics of both religious confessions appeared before the Chambre de l'Edit. The Edict of Nantes stipulated that the chamber would deal with criminal lawsuits involving Catholic clerics as plaintiffs against Protestants; when such clerics were defendants, the case belonged to the sovereign courts.[92] Thus Charles de Ruelle, sieur des Presles, appealed to the court in 1607 regarding his dispute with Mathias Lachou, a priest

---

[89] A.N. X2b 240, 6 February 1608 (Cotteils); X2b 208, 19 July 1602 (Guiton).

[90] A.N. X2b 217, 16 January 1604. In commenting on the case, the royal advocate emphasized that the thief might not have possessed any of the stolen gold at the time of his capture, as Naboresquin claimed; perhaps he suspected Naboresquin of acting in complicity with his servant to double the value of his money with an accusation of judicial misconduct! The chamber's verdict appears in a later *arrêt*: X2b 217, 20 February 1604.

[91] A.N. X2b 211, 19 February 1603. See also X2b 214, 19 July and 1 August 1603.

[92] "Edict of Nantes," 47–48 (art. 34). Maintaining the distinction between plaintiffs and defendants, however, was difficult: litigants often multiplied their legal actions against each other, blurring the original distinction between *demandeur* and *défendeur*. The article further specifies that the bipartisan chambers could not adjudicate cases involving the Catholic Church's funds or property; these, too, are to be remanded to the sovereign courts.

and canon from St. Mâlo.[93] Priest François Rose, along with several members of his parish, sued David Brisbarre and five others, while the clergy of the diocese of Châlons brought suit against Jacques Liberon, a *manouvrier* from the village of Saint Germain La Ville.[94] Reformed ministers also appeared before the Chambre de l'Edit as litigants. Jacques Mestayer, a pastor from Lusignan, protested an order for his arrest that had been issued at the request of the Franciscans of Lusignan; since the chamber judges had already agreed to hear his case, they forbade Mestayer's arrest.[95] In 1645, another pastor named Louis de Faucanbourg joined the Protestant inhabitants of Senlis in suing Henry d'Orleans, duc de Longueville, and Marie de Bourbon, princesse de Cavignan.[96]

Ecclesiastical leaders of both confessions criticized the Chambre de l'Edit and other bipartisan law courts, though for different reasons. As we have seen, the French Reformed churches' synods often gave consistories and congregants a mixed message regarding recourse to royal justice: it was important to maintain the Huguenots' legal privileges and essential to obey the king's laws, but Huguenots should avoid suing each other. The French Catholic clergy, on the other hand, consistently railed against the protection and privileges enjoyed by members of the "so-called reformed religion," including the bipartisan courts' claim to any jurisdiction over Catholic clerics. According to Pierre Blet, this eventually led the clergy and the royal judiciary to make common cause against the Huguenot minority, despite the fact that the church and the royal law courts had their own jurisdictional disputes. In addition, many Catholic clerics continued to view the Huguenots as fundamentally mired in heresy; whatever the law might say, they deserved to be treated as a subversive element within society and the state.[97]

Huguenot litigants who appealed to the Paris Chambre de l'Edit thus asserted a legal privilege that highlighted their status as a corporate group within Catholic France. That status, of course, was often contested and even rejected by those around them as part of the ongoing struggle over the political and religious settlement embodied in the Edict of Nantes. Like the Huguenot magistrates who served on the court and in the Parlement of Paris, however, Huguenot litigants were also accused specifically of fostering disorder in the administration of royal justice. In their capacity as judges, Huguenots were charged with favoritism toward their coreligionists; as litigants, they were criticized for abusing their privilege of judicial appeal with fraudulent claims.

[93] A.N. X2b 238, 29 August 1607.
[94] A.N. X2b 389, 19 June 1630 (Rose); X2b 697, 13 May 1665 (Châlons).
[95] A.N. X2b 286, 5 January 1615.
[96] A.N. X2b 483, 11 January 1645.
[97] Blet, *Le Clergé de France;* see especially 1:9–111, 2:386–88. See also Dompnier, *Le Venin de l'hérésie.*

The Chambre de l'Edit's records provide examples of litigants whose legal status (*qualité*) as Protestants was challenged. Written evidence of such status was often required: thus Charles de La Ruelle brought a certificate from a Reformed minister and elders to prove his religious affiliation.[98] In 1620 a plaintiff before the court produced a certificate indicating that he had adopted the Reformed faith three years earlier, but his opponents countered with a written affirmation from a priest certifying that the man was in fact Catholic.[99] Such challenges might come from the *gens du roi*: in 1615, royal advocate Cardin Le Bret questioned the claims of Vincent Polle, Jean Marchant, and Guillaume Pointel to be Protestant and therefore entitled to appeal their cases to the Chambre de l'Edit.[100] When nobleman Arthur de Cahiduc appealed a lawsuit to the chamber in 1629, he cited not only a certificate but also his other cases pending before the court as evidence of his religious affiliation and legal privileges. His opponent's lawyer, however, argued that Cahiduc was in fact Catholic. Royal advocate Jérôme Bignon noted that several witnesses supported this, claiming that Cahiduc had received the sacraments at Easter in his local parish church. Caught between the possibility that Cahiduc was deceiving the court or the victim of slander, Bignon recommended further investigation of Cahiduc's religious status, even though this meant delaying the proceedings.[101]

The French crown also took heed of accusations that the Huguenots were abusing their legal privileges, as evidenced by several articles in the Code Michaud. Article 105 acknowledged that flaws in the judicial system allowed litigants to divert their disputes away from the appropriate judges, but Protestants in particular "often lent their names" [pretent souvent leur nom] to cases in which they had no direct interest, thus producing "a great disorder in justice" [un grand désordre en la justice]. Moreover, other persons falsely claimed to be Protestant in order to withdraw their cases from the courts and jurisdictions where they belonged! To curb these abuses, the code ordered that Protestants who wanted their cases heard by the bipartisan chambers would have to follow the appropriate procedures within certain time limits. Those who "feigned" being Protestant would be punished, and royal judges were admonished to assure that all *attestations* of Protestant status were legally valid.[102]

[98] A.N. X2b 238, 29 August 1607.
[99] A.N. X2b 316, 29 January 1620. The court ultimately rejected the case.
[100] A.N. X2b 286, 7 January 1615. Both documents bear this date.
[101] A.N. X2a 237, 23 January 1630: "qu'il fault d'un coste qu'il y ayt Illusion à Justice et de l'aultre Calomnye et quand telles occations se presentent on ne considere poinct ce que peult accelerer ou retarder les affaires des parties." The court agreed to postpone the proceedings while the issue was investigated.
[102] Isambert et al., *Recueil général*, 16:257–58 (art. 105), 258 (art. 106), 258–59 (art. 108).

On the other hand, Huguenot litigants might be denied the use of some procedures available to Catholics. For example, secular magistrates could enlist the aid of Catholic clerics in collecting evidence about a crime by issuing a *monitoire*. The *monitoire* was a court order requiring local priests to publicize criminal charges, though without naming the parties in the case. Persons with knowledge of the crime were supposed to report to the priest on pain of excommunication; the cleric would then forward their names to the court clerk for further proceedings.[103] When Protestant Antoinette de La Motte demanded a *monitoire* in her case against Jean Le Machon and his nephew, their lawyer protested that "the said La Motte is not receivable [in her request] given the repugnant status that she claims and that, being of the so-called reformed religion, she cannot take advantage of any ecclesiastical censures, which belong only to Catholics."[104] Nicole Goujat petitioned the Chambre de l'Edit to enforce a *monitoire* that had already been issued to obtain information about her husband's murder. Specifically, she wanted the court to confiscate the temporal goods of clerics who had delayed in reporting their findings to the court clerk.[105] By 1660 a solution had apparently been found for this problem. Acknowledging that he could not obtain a *monitoire* under his own name, Protestant Gabriel de Briqueville requested the chamber's permission to have the royal prosecutor do so. The court had already granted a similar petition from Briqueville's opponent—his wife, Philippes de Liscous.[106]

Like the criticisms of Protestant magistrates, accusations that Protestant litigants abused their legal privileges highlighted the troubled connection between religious difference and the administration of royal justice in seventeenth-century France. Such accusations, however, were also related to the changes in judicial procedure outlined above. These changes were less directly related to religion as such, or even to the problems of religious coexistence between Catholics and Huguenots, than to the expanding power of the monarchy and the royal judiciary.

The French king's duty to provide justice for his subjects was a powerful means of enhancing royal authority in the French state. The creation and sale of judicial offices, the proliferation of royal law courts, and the extension of such courts' jurisdiction all seem to suggest that the monarchy was effectively using the royal judiciary to increase and centralize its power at the expense of other legal

[103]Allard, *Histoire de la justice criminelle*, 186–88. See also Charles-Joseph Ferrière, *Dictionnaire de droit et de pratique* (Paris, 1762), 2:222–24.

[104]A.N. X2b 193, 5 February 1600: ladite de La Motte estre non Recepvable actendu mesme sa qualité repugnante à ce qu'elle pretend et qu'elle estant de la religion pretendue reformee n'a le pourvoir de s'aider d'aucunes sensures eclesiastique[s] ce qui apprtient seullement aux Catholiques.

[105]A.N. X2b 251, 19 November 1609.

[106]A.N. X2b 631, 18 August 1660 (Briqueville); X2b 630, 30 July 1660 (Liscous).

institutions. The intricacies and inconsistencies of judicial procedure, however, assured that this far-reaching royal judicial authority in fact remained fragmented. Paradoxically, the very complexity of the legal system gave it flexibility, or at least left it open to manipulation. If French monarchs and magistrates sometimes tried to use the mythic unity and power of royal justice to the crown's advantage, resourceful litigants and their lawyers often used judicial procedure to prolong lawsuits, outwit opposing parties, and circumvent courts, judges and punishments.

Judicial procedure—the series of formal actions used by litigants to pursue a legal action and by judges to decide a given case—thus formed an essential part of the justice rendered by France's royal law courts, including the Paris Chambre de l'Edit. As we have seen, the magistrate played a central role in the inquisitorial procedures used in the royal judiciary. Decisions of guilt or innocence could depend on whether the parties had assiduously followed the proper steps in their proceedings, as well as the judge's opinion of the case's merits. Procedure could even become a weapon in a lawsuit: by multiplying the legal actions concerning different aspects of a case, by impugning judges and using appeals to transfer the case from one court to another, litigants could try to overwhelm their adversaries with legal costs and the hardships of imprisonment. Outright illegalities, such as suborning witnesses or falsifying documents, could also prolong or divert a lawsuit's course.

There were in fact many opportunities to delay or derail the procedures mandated by royal edicts and judicial practice, and most of them surfaced in the Chambre de l'Edit's records. For example, an accused person might contest or fail to answer a court's summons to appear. Magistrates often punished such negligence, but they might also grant a postponement and continue with proceedings concerning the substance of the legal dispute.[107] Witnesses and litigants alike often requested postponements from the Chambre de l'Edit, citing ill health, family responsibilities, old age, bad weather, and distance to justify their claims.[108] Litigants who persisted in their refusal to appear could be condemned *par contumace* or at least be denied their judicial appeal, though such verdicts could also be challenged. Those who traveled to Paris to pursue their cases often complained of being unjustly detained by excessive delays or imprisonment. In May 1602, Antoinette de La Motte claimed that the Chambre de l'Edit had granted seven months' worth of delays to Jean Le Machon and his nephew, thus preventing a fair resolution of her

---

[107] Allard, *Histoire de la justice criminelle*, 189–99; Doucet, *Les Institutions de France*, 2:540–41; Aubert, *Le Parlement de Paris*, 2:26–35.

[108] For example, Nicolas Girardeau requested a postponement of six months due to "his old age and his being responsible for a large household" [attendu son viel aage et qu'il est chargé d'un grand ménage]; the court granted him only six weeks. A.N. X2b 241, 29 March 1608.

case against them. The two men countered by arguing that La Motte's legal maneuvers had kept them prisoners in the Conciergerie for three years.[109] In his petition to the court, Jacques de Bray, sieur de Saint Michel claimed that his opponents had deliberately prolonged their litigation "to ruin the said suppliant with a long detention and great costs...and by this means prevent him from proving his innocence."[110] Finally, a host of problems surrounded the collection and presentation of written evidence. Delays in transporting such documents to Paris would prompt complaints from plaintiffs and defendants whose cases languished until the records arrived. Litigants might also claim that their adversaries had falsified documents, such as contracts, wills, or bills of sale, that were at the heart of their legal dispute. Seen in this context, accusations that Protestants intervened in cases to divert them to the bipartisan chambers—or that Catholics feigned being Protestant for the same purpose—are yet another example of widespread judicial abuses by litigants.

Among the many elements of criminal procedure, judicial appeal itself is perhaps the most important for understanding the Paris Chambre de l'Edit: after all, the chamber was essentially a court of appeal for Huguenots and their adversaries. Yet it was also part of the general development of appellate jurisdiction for royal law courts, notably the Parlement of Paris. Judicial appeals to royal law courts offered litigants the chance to challenge the decisions of local courts, and royal tribunals could likewise use judicial appeal to draw legal disputes into their jurisdictions. As Alfred Soman has argued, the theory and practice of judicial appeal from lesser courts to the Paris parlement was already gaining force by the end of the sixteenth century, well before it was officially mandated by the Ordonnance criminelle of 1670.[111]

The royal judiciary also claimed cognizance of criminal cases through the concept of *cas royaux*. The notion of *cas royaux* (royal cases)—or offenses against the king and his interests—dated from the thirteenth century, but the category was never fully defined. According to royal ordinances, *custumals*, and legal treatises it usually included treason, violations of royal safeguards, forgery of coin or royal seals, violence against royal officials, illicit assemblies and the bearing of arms, and crimes committed in the king's forests or on major roads and waterways. Such lists generally concluded with the phrase "and other cases touching the royal prerogative" [et autres cas touchant au droit royal], implying that additional serious but

---

[109] A.N. X2b 207, 14 May 1602; X2b 209, 6 September 1602.

[110] A.N. X2b 286, 9 January 1615: de ruyner ledit suppliant par une longue detention et grands frais...et l'empescher par ce moyen de justifier son Inocence. He also complained about the diseases *(maladies)* that had affected his health while in prison.

[111] Alfred Soman, "Aux Origines de l'appel de droit dans l'Ordonnance Criminelle de 1670," *XVIIe siècle* 32 (1980): 21–35; Soman, "La Justice criminelle aux XVIe–XVIIe siècles."

unspecified crimes might also fall within the jurisdiction of the king's courts.[112] The vagueness of *cas royaux* made it useful for extending the legal interpretation of the kings' "interests," and for enlarging the royal law courts' jurisdiction.

Finally, the initiatives of both the French crown and ordinary litigants helped to extend and strengthen the royal judiciary's authority. In the thirteenth and fourteenth centuries, criminal cases could be appealed from lesser royal law courts, such as those of the provincial *bailli* or *sénéchal*, to the Parlement of Paris and finally to the king himself. Over time this helped to undermine the power and independence of seigneurial courts.[113] As the ultimate source of all justice in the realm, the king also retained the power to review or intervene directly in any judicial proceeding. Through *évocation*, the king and his council thus could transfer a lawsuit from one court to another.[114] The king's subjects could also request such transfers, just as they could petition for letters of pardon. Litigants could challenge a court's jurisdiction or verdict for a variety of other reasons: errors of fact or law (*proposition d'erreur*); family ties between the judges and parties in the lawsuit (*parentelle*); or conflict of jurisdiction (*règlement de juges*). The royal chancery could also provide *lettres de relief d'appel*, allowing the petitioner to pursue an appeal despite an impediment to such proceedings.[115] By the early seventeenth century, jurisprudence had established that criminal cases involving certain crimes that carried corporal or capital punishments, such as witchcraft, should be automatically appealed to the Parlement of Paris.[116]

Judicial appeal was thus a dynamic mechanism that tended to subordinate local law courts to the highest echelons of royal justice. It also connected ordinary persons to the king's justice. Like the adoption of inquisitorial procedure for judging criminal cases, the development of judicial appeal and its underlying legal principles helped French kings and royal magistrates expand their power by drawing more and more lawsuits within their reach, and by encouraging the king's subjects to seek redress from his law courts. This development also helps to explain the

---

[112]Allard, *Histoire de la justice criminelle*, 50–56; Esmein, *Cours élémentaire*, 410–12; Jean Brissaud, *A History of French Private Law*, translated by J. Garner, Continental Legal History, vol. 9 (New York: Rothman, 1969), 225–26; Doucet, *Les Institutions de France*, 2:523–26.

[113]Esmein, *Cours élémentaire*, 415–19. See also Esmein, *Histoire*, 24–31.

[114]On the significance of this for the seventeenth century, see David Parker, "Sovereignty, Absolutism and the Function of the Law in Seventeenth-Century France," *Past and Present*, 122 (1989): 36–74; Albert N. Hamscher, *The Conseil Privé and the Parlements in the Age of Louis XIV: A Study in French Absolutism*. Transactions of the American Philosophical Society 77, no. 2 (Philadelphia: American Philosophical Society, 1987).

[115]Esmein, *Cours élémentaire*, 415–18, 422–24; Brissaud, *History of French Private Law*, 430–32; Aubert, *Le Parlement de Paris*, 2:21–25.

[116]Allard, *Histoire de la justice criminelle*, 59; Soman, "Aux Origines de l'appel de droit."

complaints about delays, excessive complexity, and corruption that were often voiced about the legal system in the sixteenth and seventeenth centuries.

Yet judicial appeal held advantages for litigants as well as the crown and the royal judiciary. Although simultaneous appeals in different jurisdictions were prohibited, they certainly occurred; in fact, the number of times a person could undertake such legal actions was apparently limited only by his or her persistence, wealth, and ingenuity.[117] The same appellate procedures that seemed to contribute to the crown's and the royal law courts' growing power were also open to manipulation by litigants and their lawyers, offering ways for the resourceful (or the unscrupulous) to turn the system of royal justice to their own advantage. Until it was abolished in 1669, the Paris Chambre de l'Edit was part of this complex network of procedures, institutions, and jurisdictions, attempting in its own way to administer royal justice.

As a court of appeal for France's Protestant minority, the Paris Chambre de l'Edit adjudicated criminal lawsuits in the seventeenth century despite the fact that many Catholics opposed its existence. The court not only heard legal disputes involving Huguenots, but also represented the Huguenots' legal privileges as outlined in the Edict of Nantes in the most concrete way. Unlike the chambres mi-parties in the provinces, the Paris chamber only possessed one Protestant judge; it was fully embedded within the Parlement of Paris from its inception, making it less able to assert much independence from the parlement. Like the chambres mi-parties, however, it gave Huguenots access to royal justice as both officeholders and litigants.

Huguenots soon found, however, that their legal privileges were truly a double-edged sword. As the anonymous pamphleteer of 1628 complained, many Catholics opposed the idea that Protestants "ought to be indifferently admitted" to offices. The Huguenot magistrates who served in the Chambre de l'Edit were viewed and treated as outsiders within the royal judiciary for decades before the edicts, decrees, and *arrêts* that formally excluded them from office were issued.[118] Demands and debates about Protestant officeholding began in the sixteenth century, when venality of office and changes in judicial procedure were also reshaping

---

[117]Esmein, *Cours élémentaire*, 418–19; Doucet, *Les Institutions de France*, 2:532–34.

[118]Both before and after the Edict of Fontainebleau, which revoked the Edict of Nantes, royal decrees were issued that imposed restrictions on Huguenot lawyers and judges; even Catholic magistrates with Protestant wives were forbidden to judge cases involving Catholic clerics, Reformed ministers, or individuals of either confession. These culminated in an *arrêt du conseil* of 23 November 1685

the royal judiciary. If the constitutional crisis of the 1580s and 1590s ultimately led Parisian magistrates to uphold France's fundamental laws in favor of Henry IV, the judges were far less enthusiastic about the king's edict mandating religious coexistence. In particular, they opposed the Edict of Nantes's provisions for bipartisan law courts and judicial offices essentially reserved for Protestants. They did so not only because they sought to maintain the Parisian magistracy's social and corporate identity, but because for them that identity was inextricably tied to the kingdom's (and the king's) religion, Catholicism. Not surprisingly, the notion that religious difference made Protestants incapable of being royal magistrates became a theme expressed throughout the seventeenth century, though perhaps with intermittent intensity. By 1680, the bipartisan law courts had been abolished and royal advocate Talon could declare that Protestants were "incapable of judicature."

Huguenots faced similar challenges when they exercised their judicial privileges as plaintiffs or defendants. The 1628 pamphleteer denounced the prejudice of Catholic judges against Protestant litigants, claiming that "our processes are judged by the ticket on the bagges." Yet Catholic polemicists leveled similar accusations of favoritism against Protestant magistrates. Such arguments were apparently more convincing to the French crown than those of the Huguenots: the Code Michaud condemned Protestant magistrates in the chambres mi-parties for excessive leniency toward their coreligionists but made no mention of Catholic magistrates' engaging in similar misconduct. The Code Michaud also condemned litigants who abused the privilege of judicial appeal based on religious status, whether they were Huguenots who pretended to have an interest in a given dispute or Catholics who pretended to be Protestant. In the end, the Huguenot litigants' judicial privileges were seen as not only unnecessary, but also as a perversion of royal justice.

The Huguenots' efforts to assert their judicial privileges also reinforced their continuing dependence on the monarchy and royal magistracy for protection. The fact that the Huguenots' corporate status was defined by royal edict made them vulnerable: they opened themselves to attack when they asserted their collective privileges, whether as judicial officeholders or as litigants. Although privileges were an integral part of the legal system and indeed of early modern French society, those associated with religious difference were viewed as unjust, illegitimate, and destructive. Instead of restoring order, they seemed to threaten the "good peace and lasting repose" that the Edict of Nantes had promised. When it came to royal

---

which ordered all Protestant councilors in the parlement of Paris to resign their offices immediately. See *Recueil des édits, declarations et arrêts*, 202–5 (20 January 1685), 243–44 (10 July 1685), 294–95 (5 November 1685), 299–300 (17 November 1695), 302–3 (23 November 1695).

justice, Huguenots' and Catholics' perceptions were in fact the mirror image of each other: each group saw itself as threatened by the other's judicial privileges.

The chief beneficiary of this situation was the French crown. The fact that each group appealed to the king to support its position contributed to the extension of the king's justice, just as appellate procedure helped to expand the sovereign courts' authority. The willingness of many French men and women to appeal their cases to the Paris Chambre de l'Edit, however, gave legitimacy to the court's function and competence as outlined in the Edict of Nantes. The chapters that follow will explore the nature of some of those disputes.

CHAPTER 3

"Le remède de la sage oubliance"

Memory, Litigation, & the Paris Chambre de l'Edit

ON 4 JANUARY 1600, YSAAC MARIETTE, SIEUR DE LA TOUSCHE, AND five confederates appealed to the Paris Chambre de l'Edit for justice and protection from their past. The *bailli* and *lieutenant criminel* of Orléans had ordered all six men seized and their goods confiscated at the request of damoiselle Nicole de Bourbel and Bonny Le Page, two widows who apparently held the men responsible for their husbands' deaths. The chamber magistrates suspended execution of the local judges' order and decided that the Paris court would hear the parties' arguments, which were presented two months later.[1]

In his summation of the case, the royal prosecutor described the substance of the dispute. He recounted how in 1590, Mariette and his followers were told that supporters of the Catholic League were hiding in Bourbel's house; encountering resistance when they attempted to investigate, Mariette and the other men ended by burning the place. The prosecutor, however, emphasized that the men had acted out of zealous service to the king and not because of any private quarrel with Bourbel or her family. He added that one of Bourbel's sons had also served the king in wartime—a testament to her own loyalty to the French crown. "All the same," he concluded, "the deed having thus occurred and [given] the edicts for the forgetting of similar deeds, it cannot be that there is any reason to investigate further." The chamber magistrates accepted this evaluation and dismissed the case, declaring the parties *hors de cour et de procès*.[2]

[1] A.N. X2b 193, 4 January 1600.
[2] A.N. X2b 194, 15 March 1600: Touttefois le faict estant ainsy passé et les edicts pour l'oubliance de faicts semblables, il n'estant pas qu'il y ayt lieu d'en faire nulle recherche.

This lawsuit exemplifies a small but significant category of the Chambre de l'Edit's business in the early seventeenth century: legal disputes concerning the Wars of Religion. Such cases often involved the widows, children, or relatives of men killed during the decades of civil conflict, and litigants usually sought restitution for the loss of lives or property resulting from wartime events. Regardless of their specific grievances, the parties in these disputes all participated in a larger ongoing dispute about how the Wars of Religion should be remembered or forgotten, given that a new regime of peaceful coexistence between Huguenots and Catholics had been decreed. A close analysis of this criminal litigation reveals the efforts of plaintiffs, defendants, and lawyers to describe past experiences in accordance with legal requirements, especially those contained in the Edict of Nantes. In adjudicating lawsuits about memory and *oubliance*, the chamber judges had to decide among competing versions of recent history, weighing appeals for justice that recalled the past against the edict's declaration that the Wars of Religion were to be officially forgotten. This litigation illustrates the Chambre de l'Edit's role in implementing a policy of *oubliance*, as well as the court's efforts to promote a common obedience to the law that would overcome the divisive effects of past conflict and continuing religious difference.

The twin themes of memory and forgetting appear in the Edict of Nantes's opening article, in which Henry IV declared that "the memory of everything which has occurred on one side and the other since the beginning of the month of March 1585 up to our accession to the crown, and during the other preceding troubles and on account of them, shall remain extinct and dormant as though they had never happened."[3] The edict's second article expanded upon this sweeping statement by prohibiting specific behaviors related to the remembrance of the Huguenots' and Catholics' wartime past that could disrupt public order in the present:

> We forbid all our subjects...[to renew] the memory of those things, attacking, resenting, injuring, or provoking one another by reproaches for what has occurred, for whatever cause and pretext there may be; [to dispute] these things, contesting, quarreling, or outraging or offending by word or deed; but they shall restrain themselves and live peaceably together like brothers, friends, and common citizens, under

---

[3]"Edict of Nantes," 42 (art. I).

the penalty of being punished as infractors of the peace and disturbers of the public repose.[4]

Other articles in the edict further supported these declarations about forgetting the past. Like previous peace treaties issued during the sixteenth century, the Edict of Nantes granted amnesty to many of those whose conduct during the Wars of Religion might have led to legal prosecution. Huguenot leaders, their families, followers, and communities were specifically protected from the consequences of having levied troops, minted coin, constructed fortifications, destroyed towns, homes, and churches, established law courts, and negotiated with foreign powers. A similar provision halted any legal proceedings against those responsible for captures (*prises*) on land or sea. Persons imprisoned because of "the troubles" or their religious affiliation were to be released, and no one was to be sued for taxes or financial subsidies levied prior to Henry IV's accession to the throne.[5] In general, these and other clauses attest to the widespread fragmentation of authority during the Wars of Religion, when the Huguenot "state within a state" and the Catholic Leagues had competed with the French crown for governance of the realm. By 1598, Henry IV had already won many former Catholic opponents to his side without bloodshed, and he was trying to placate Huguenot leaders who had become fearful and rebellious since the king's conversion in 1593. The Edict of Nantes's amnesty thus announced the restoration of royal authority by annulling previous challenges to that authority, and by calling upon Huguenots and Catholics alike to act as obedient subjects and fellow citizens despite their troubled history.[6]

The edict, however, also contained clauses that would allow a renewal of past conflicts, undermining the policy of *oubliance*. Destructive acts that had been committed against the orders of those in command could still be prosecuted, yet such lawsuits could lead to a reopening of hostilities if such accusations were not limited somehow. Therefore, the edict restricted the category of prosecutable offenses to execrable cases (*cas execrables*): rape, violations of passports and safeguards, and unbounded killing or pillage. The *cas execrables* also included rape, arson, murder,

---

[4]"Edict of Nantes," 42 (art. 2).

[5]"Edict of Nantes," 54–57 (arts. 73, 75, 76, 83).

[6]On the Edict of Nantes's amnesty and its broader context, see Michael Wolfe, "Amnesty and Oubliance at the End of the French Wars of Religion," *Cahiers d'histoire* 16 (1996): 45–68; Diane C. Margolf, "The Edict of Nantes' Amnesty: Appeals to the Chambre de l'Edit, 1600–1610," *Proceedings of the Annual Conference of the Western Society for French History* 16 (1988): 49–55; Sutherland, *Huguenot Struggle for Recognition*; Kathleen A. Parrow, *From Defense to Resistance: Justification of Violence during the French Wars of Religion*, Transactions of the American Philosophical Society 83:6 (Philadelphia: American Philosophical Society, 1993).

and theft done "by betrayal and lying in wait, outside the regular course of hostilities, and for the exercise of vengeance, against the duties of war."[7] Crimes that had occurred among persons fighting on the same side or without a military commander's order were likewise subject to prosecution and punishment. The Edict of Nantes's amnesty clauses thus distinguished between actions that had been carried out "according to the necessity, law, and order of war" and crimes committed during the Wars of Religion but not because of the conflict.[8] Events of the first sort were supposed to be excused and forgotten, but the latter could and did become the subject of legal dispute.

A second factor that complicated the edict's stated policy of putting the past to rest concerned previous judicial proceedings against Huguenots. Most lawsuits, verdicts, and confiscations that had been rendered against French Protestants during the wars were annulled. Such cases reverted to the stage in the proceedings prior to whatever judicial decision had been reached "during the troubles," even if a final sentence had already been carried out. The written records and material evidence of such actions were to be destroyed:

> We order that [the previous judgments and decrees against Huguenots] shall be struck out and excluded from the registers of the courts, both sovereign and inferior. We likewise wish that all marks, vestiges and monuments of the said executions, books and defamatory acts against their persons, memory and posterity, shall be destroyed and effaced....[9]

The only exceptions were judgments rendered by inferior law courts in towns that had been under Huguenot control, a qualification that strongly implies that this provision was addressed to Huguenots who felt that they had suffered unfair condemnation at the hands of a prejudiced judiciary during the civil conflict. The effort to obliterate such legal proceedings against Huguenots extended to those who had died or fled France during the Wars of Religion, as well as those who had participated in the fighting and survived. Finally, the edict imposed perpetual silence *(silence perpetuel)* on royal prosecutors concerning everything ordered or done by the Huguenot political assemblies and councils, regardless of any judicial decisions or proceedings to the contrary.[10]

---

[7]"Edict of Nantes," 57 (arts. 85–86).

[8]"Edict of Nantes," 57 (art. 87).

[9]"Edict of Nantes," 51 (art. 58). The article refers earlier to "all sentences, court decrees, procedures, seizures, sales, and decrees made and given against persons of the so-called Reformed religion, living or dead."

[10]"Edict of Nantes," 51 (art. 58), 55 (art. 77).

The Edict of Nantes's statements about memory and *oubliance* thus represented a legal bridge spanning past, present, and future. Its specific clauses belonged to a tradition of amnesty aimed at reconciling former enemies and restoring public order. These goals were especially important because the edict also sanctioned the religious differences that had been at the heart of France's civil wars for almost forty years, giving legal protection and privileges to Huguenots while restoring Catholicism as the official religion of the French state. The law's apparently simple command to forget the past was actually a complex policy involving selective remembrance rather than complete amnesia. While the edict forbade some legal prosecutions of past actions, it invited others. Indeed, the Edict of Nantes essentially created a category of potential litigation by overturning legal decisions and actions taken during the wartime period, reopening such cases for anyone willing to pursue such matters in the hope of achieving a different verdict. The policy of *oubliance* thus encouraged Huguenots and Catholics to revive parts of their troubled history by appealing to royal justice for redress of their wartime grievances. Past wrongs could be corrected through formal legal proceedings and by royal judges, rather than the quarrels, provocations, and violence which the edict forbade. Memory and *oubliance* thus became the subject of legal dispute before the Paris Chambre de l'Edit.

Lawsuits concerning incidents that had happened during the Wars of Religion form a small but clearly identifiable category among the criminal cases heard by the Chambre de l'Edit, comprising a total of fifty-seven lawsuits for the decade 1600–1610. Such cases never dominated the Chambre de l'Edit's business, even in the war's immediate aftermath: out of 114 cases presented to the court in 1600 alone, only fourteen dealt with matters directly related to the Wars of Religion. The number of such lawsuits also dropped during the course of the decade, from eleven in 1602 to three in 1609; there were none at all in 1610. Documents for this type of legal dispute always refer to "things which occurred during the troubles" [choses advenues pendant les troubles] or "deeds declared covered by the king's edicts" [faicts déclarés couverts par les edicts du roy]. The specific deeds at issue included destruction or thefts of property, ransoms, and deaths that had occurred during military attacks. Some litigants appealed to the court to reverse judicial decisions of the past, claiming that the convicted person had been a victim of partisan judgment or private vengeance. Other people petitioned to have the chamber magistrates quash accusations of their own misconduct, arguing that their actions were excused by the circumstances of war and the royal edicts that forbade further investigation of such matters.

In adjudicating these disputes, the court tended to dismiss the litigants' complaints more often than it issued condemnations or acquittals. Sixteen out of the fifty-seven cases ended in one of the parties' being convicted or acquitted; another sixteen cases remained inconclusive or were remanded to another law court for resolution or further investigation of the charges. The Chambre de l'Edit dismissed twenty-five lawsuits, declaring the parties *hors de cour et de procès* or the incident in question "abolished," "extinguished," or "covered" *(aboli, éteint, couvert)* by royal edicts of pacification. Those who were condemned for their wartime misconduct were usually sentenced to financial penalties, such as fines, monetary reparations, charitable donations, or the return of stolen or confiscated property.

The real significance of war-related lawsuits, however, lies in what they reveal about the policy of *oubliance* as implemented by the Chambre de l'Edit. Magistrates, lawyers, prosecutors, and litigants all participated in the process of interpreting the Edict of Nantes's provisions about remembering and forgetting the Wars of Religion. Lawyers for plaintiffs and defendants alike tried to describe past events in ways that would fit the law's requirements in order to win a favorable decision from the court. The Chambre de l'Edit thus offered litigants a judicial forum for their complaints, an audience for their tales of past wrongs, and an opportunity to have their version of events vindicated by legal judgment.

In these cases, the disputants often invoked the past in a double sense: first, by describing the wartime event that formed the core of their grievance, and second, by connecting that event to an even more remote past so as to remove it from the context of the religious wars themselves. Damoiselle Claude de Sainte Melaine's four-year lawsuit against Pierre Le Cornu, sieur Duplessis de Cosme, exemplifies this double use of the past. Sainte Melaine sued Le Cornu for murdering her husband, Jehan Le Michel, sieur de Cricquebeuf, and submitted a written plea explaining her case to the Chambre de l'Edit in January 1600. She admitted that her husband had died defending Château Montjean, a stronghold in Anjou which he had held for Henry IV and which Le Cornu had captured for the Catholic League in October 1591. But through her lawyer, Sainte Melaine claimed that Le Cornu's conduct had surpassed the ordinary violence of war, and that her husband's death was a prosecutable crime rather than simply the result of pitched battle between opposing military forces.

Sainte Melaine and her lawyer Galland presented three arguments against Le Cornu, all of which revolved around the Edict of Nantes's distinction between acts of war and "execrable cases." First, she noted that Le Cornu had given her husband a letter of safeguard in September 1591, promising him the League's and Le Cornu's personal protection. She also presented two other letters from Le Cornu that had offered further assurances of his favor; one of these preceded Le Cornu's attack on Montjean by only one or two days. According to Sainte Melaine, Le Cornu's actions represented "broken good faith" [la foy rompue] and a clear violation of safeguard.[11] Sainte Melaine also associated her opponent's behavior during the assault with the kind of violence condemned in the Edict of Nantes. While promising her husband protection, Le Cornu had allegedly suborned two of Cricquebeuf's servants to breach the château's defenses. He then attacked at midnight, scaling the walls with ladders and killing everyone in his path. Sainte Melaine herself had been driven from Montjean and her dying husband's side at two o'clock in the morning; she was forced to seek refuge at a nearby farm "naked beneath her chemise without any comfort" [nue en chemise sans aucune commodité]. Other women who remained behind had been raped in Le Cornu's presence before he withdrew the next day to Craon with his spoils. Emphasizing Le Cornu's excessive brutality as a military commander, Sainte Melaine turned the Edict of Nantes's admonition to forget past conflicts on its head:

> It is not necessary to represent the life and actions [of Le Cornu] during his stay in the said castle...it is not necessary to revive the actions extinguished and buried by the edict's general *oubliance.* The destruction of eighty castles and gentlemen's homes and the ruin of all the surrounding countryside are testimony to his cruelty.[12]

Sainte Melaine's final argument against Le Cornu centered on what she perceived as the true reason for her husband's death at Le Cornu's hands. During their youth before the wars, she asserted, the two men had fought openly, and "deadly enmity" [inimitiés capitalles] had long existed between their families. Religious and military conflict in the region had merely provided Le Cornu with "the means to enrich himself, increase and augment his fortune, and moreover to revenge his private hatred" of Cricquebeuf.[13] Sainte Melaine claimed that having been captured by some of Le Cornu's soldiers, her husband had negotiated a ransom of eight thousand *écus.* Instead of honoring this arrangement, Le Cornu himself had ordered Cricquebeuf's execution, telling him that "he had waited twenty years for this outcome."[14] The widow and her lawyer thus concluded that

[11]A.N. X2b 193, 7 January 1600, Galland pour dame Claude de Sainte Melaine. The plea reproduces the text of the letter in question, which was dated 13 September 1591.

[12]A.N. X2b 193, 7 January 1600, Galland pour dame Claude de Saincte Melaine: Il n'est besoing de representer quelle a esté la vie et les actions [of Le Cornu] pendant son sejour audict chasteau...il ne faut point faire revivre les actions estaintes et ensevelies par l'oubliance generalle des edicts. Le rasement de quatre vingts chasteaux et maisons de gentilhommes et la ruyne de tout le plat pays sont tesmoignanges de sa cruaulté.

[13]A.N. X2b 193, 7 January 1600, Galland pour dame Claude de Sainte Melaine: un moyen pour s'enrichir, acroistre et augmenter sa fortune et davantage pour venger ses inimitions particulières.

[14]A.N. X2b 193, 7 January 1600, Galland pour dame Claude de Sainte Melaine: il y avoit vingt ans qu'il luy garder ceste issu.

her husband's death was an act of revenge that originated in Le Cornu's personal hatred of Cricquebeuf—a hatred that predated the military conflict in which her husband had lost his life, and that could not be hidden or excused by the circumstances of war.

In trying to refute Sainte Melaine's accusations, Le Cornu and his lawyer Constant placed these events in the context of a very different past and depicted Sainte Melaine herself as the true criminal. Le Cornu claimed that the letters of safeguard and friendship that Sainte Melaine had presented to the court were forgeries that had been done at her behest.[15] Even if the letters had been genuine, they could not have forestalled a surprise attack on Montjean, since such tactics were legitimate in wartime. Le Cornu also denied her charges of excessive violence, arguing that only three or four men had perished on each side. The pillage that accompanied the assault, he argued, had been in keeping with "such encounters full of furor and blood" [telles rencontres plegnes de fureur et de sang]. Most of all, Le Cornu depicted Cricquebeuf as a courageous soldier rather than the victim of personal vengeance:

> Seeing himself surprised at night and yet wanting to show in this last act of his life that a man of his profession should never die except with his weapons in hand, he seized a halberd to defend himself...[he] was wounded by a sword blow and died of this wound two days later.[16]

Le Cornu thus presented himself and his opponent as two soldiers who had acted within the context of the military conflict between Henry IV and the Catholic League, and the laws of war more generally. Le Cornu had also paid a price for fighting on the losing side: ill and impoverished, he was now the grateful recipient of both divine and royal pardon. Sainte Melaine, on the other hand, had resorted to illegal means to seek vengeance against him, violating the king's edicts with her lawsuit about a past that was supposed to be forgotten. Le Cornu's defense ultimately depended upon the double argument that his actions were acceptable amid open warfare and that hers were disloyal in peacetime.

The legal disputes between Claude de Sainte Melaine and Pierre Le Cornu had begun in November 1591 and would not be settled until September 1602,

---

[15]Le Cornu had already begun a lawsuit against Sainte Melaine on charges of forgery in 1599; this case continued in tandem with her suit against him until the court rendered verdicts in both cases; A.N. X2b 209, 7 September 1602.

[16]A.N. X2b 193, 7 January 1600, Constant pour Pierre Le Cornu: se voyant surpris de nuict et voulant neantmoings encorres tesmoigner en ce dernier acte de sa vye qu'un homme de sa profession ne doibt jamais mourir que les Armes en la main, Il prinse un hallebarde pour se defender...[il] fut blecé d'un coup d'espee dont il mourut deux jours après.

when the Chambre de l'Edit delivered a verdict largely in Sainte Melaine's favor. Le Cornu was sentenced to pay three thousand *écus* in reparations, five hundred *écus* in donations to various municipal charities in Paris, and the costs of all proceedings. The magistrates dismissed Le Cornu's suit against Sainte Melaine for forgery, though they commanded officials in Anjou and Maine to apprehend the accused forger and bring him to Paris for questioning. The court made one concession to Le Cornu by ordering that in the future, he could not be prosecuted for his wartime activities or as a result of his litigation against Sainte Melaine.[17] As it happened, he was already facing such charges: Samuel, Louis, and Jeanne Lefebvre had accused him of murdering their father Ciprien in 1578 and had brought their complaint before the Chambre de l'Edit in February 1600. Just ten days after Le Cornu lost his dispute with Sainte Melaine, the chamber magistrates rejected the Lefebvre children's case.[18] The court thus supported Claude de Sainte Melaine's claim to have suffered a grievance even as it required *oubliance* for any other crimes Pierre Le Cornu might have committed during the Wars of Religion.

A lawsuit brought by the children of Pierre Denyau, sieur de La Seicherie, against the monastic community of Saint François d'Ollonne in Poitou provides another example of how litigants contested the policy of forgetting the wartime past. Jean, Marie, Mathieu, and Suzanne Denyau appeared before the Chambre de l'Edit in February 1602 to protest their late father's condemnation by the *lieutenant criminel* of Angers two years earlier. Convicted of having burned and sacked the monastery in April 1568, Pierre Denyau had been condemned to have his right hand cut off before being hanged and to pay twelve thousand *livres* in reparations. The Denyau children objected to this sentence on the grounds that the monks of Saint François d'Ollonne had first sued their father for his actions in 1585, some seventeen years after the monastery's destruction. Pierre Denyau's own judicial appeals had been ignored or blocked by his opponents. Most of all, the incident had occurred while the Catholics of Poitou were openly at war with the Huguenots of the region, including Denyau. Although Condé's army at Chartres had received word of a peace declaration in late March 1568 that might have allayed hostilities, the news of it had traveled slowly, reaching Orléans on 3 April, Nantes on 11 April, Poitiers on 13 April, and La Rochelle on 21 April. Like Pierre Le Cornu, the Denyau children argued that the entire matter belonged to a war-scarred era that now lay beyond the law's reach. "The research of all things past

---

[17]A.N. X2b 209, 7 September 1602. Sainte Melaine had great difficulty in collecting her reparations from Le Cornu, and documents concerning this suit continue to surface among the court's records until 1604.

[18]A.N. X2b 209, 17 September 1602.

has been prohibited," their pleading stated, "especially burned churches."[19] Accordingly, the Denyaus requested that the Chambre de l'Edit annul the earlier proceedings against their father, declare the incident closed, and obtain costs and reparations from their opponents.

The monks of Saint François d'Ollonne and their lawyer, however, claimed that Pierre Denyau's actions had been anything but an act of war. They argued that in 1566, Denyau had lost a legal dispute with the monastery over gifts and legacies made by his uncle and had harbored a grudge against the religious community for the next two years. Though the region was at peace in 1568, Denyau had conspired with a group of friends and relatives to attack the monastery, destroying it completely in a violent two-day rampage. Personal vengeance, rather than religious fervor or wartime conflict, explained both the motive and the brutality of the assault:

> The arson, thefts, and sacrileges were committed by the said Seiche-rie, driven by private hatred and revenge because of the said proceed-ings [of 1566] and not because of contrary religion...given that at the time of the said arson, there was no longer any trouble and that peace had been made and the hostilities extinguished.[20]

The monks' account dissociated Denyau's actions from the contexts of both war-fare and religious difference, emphasizing instead that this was an extraordinary act of individual revenge that deserved to be remembered, prosecuted, and pun-ished. Denyau had already been convicted of his crimes by a judge in Angers in May 1599, though the sentence had been delivered *par contumace* (meaning that Denyau himself had not appeared to answer the charges or suffer the penalties). The monks now demanded that the Chambre de l'Edit uphold the local magis-trate's sentence, including the costs and reparations owed by Denyau's heirs.

These competing versions of Pierre Denyau's actions and the monastery's destruction received a final gloss from *avocat du roi* Louis Servin, one of the king's legal representatives in the Parlement of Paris. Servin opened his summation of the case with an eloquent description of Piety lamenting wartime sacrileges and Peace holding a burning torch to destroy the instruments of war, while Justice attempted to reconcile their competing claims for her support. He went on to

---

[19]A.N. X2b 205, 13 February 1602: La recherche de toutes choses passees a esté defendues, particulièrement des eglises bruslees.

[20]A.N. X2b 205, 13 February 1602: L'incendie, volleries et sacrileges avait esté faictes par ledict Seicherie, poussé d'une haine et vengeance particullière à l'occasion desdicts procès [of 1566] et non pour le faict de Relligion contraire...attendu que lors de ladicte incendie il n'y avoit plus aucun trouble et que le paix estoit faict et les voyes d'hostilité esteintes.

note that the king's edicts had pardoned more recent incidents of arson and mayhem committed by members of the Catholic League. Lawsuits like this one would only provoke further religious and political conflict, which was contrary to the goal of restoring peace. "The Church, like the state," he argued, "cannot maintain itself in the peace which is suitable to them both if an opening is made for accusations about such deeds; it is expedient to pursue what the times require."[21] Servin then recommended that the court apply "the remedy of wise forgetfulness" [le remède de la sage oubliance] to this dispute by quashing the proceedings and declaring the entire matter closed.

The Chambre de l'Edit accepted Servin's recommendation and dismissed the case in February 1602, though a second petition from the Denyau children offers an interesting epilogue to their legal dispute. According to this document, a gibbet and effigy of Pierre Denyau had been erected publicly in front of the monastery after his conviction *par contumace* in 1599. (The petition states that the effigy was punished in place of Denyau himself, though whether this was because he had already died or had simply managed to avoid arrest at the time is unclear.) In light of the Chambre de l'Edit's verdict, the Denyau children demanded that the gibbet be dismantled with equal publicity—on market day and in the presence of municipal officials—and that all insults to their father's memory be punishable by a fine of five hundred *écus*. The chamber magistrates responded by ordering that the gibbet and effigy be removed "without noise or scandal" [sans bruit et scandal], and the dispute then disappears from the court's records.[22] Once again, the Chambre de l'Edit adjudicated the competing claims of remembrance and *oubliance*, attempting to strike a balance between those claims in the interest of maintaining a fragile peace.

Along with arguments about past events and their connection to warfare, religious difference, and personal revenge, many war-related cases included disputes about the distinction between soldiers and civilians. In September 1600, for example, François Delahaye and Gilles Chaudet appealed to the Chambre de l'Edit for return of the ransom and goods that Jacques de La Ferrière had extorted from them in 1591. La Ferrière had been commander of the garrison of Vezins in Anjou for Henry IV; in responding to the charges, he stated that he had done "what was permitted by the usage and ordinary practice of military discipline...against those who made war against him."[23] Delahaye and Chaudet countered by claiming that

[21]A.N. X2b 205, 13 February 1602: L'eglise comme l'estat ne se pouvant maintenir au Repos qu leur est convenable si l'ouverture est faicte aux accusations de tells faits; il est expedient de suivre ce que requiert le temps.

[22]A.N. X2b 206, 19 March 1602.

[23]A.N. X2b 197, 6 September 1600: il n'aye faict que ce que luy a esté permis par l'usage et

they "had not been at war against the king in any fashion" [n'ont faict la guerre contre le Roy en façon quelconque] and that attacks against civilians were not excused by the king's edicts. Since La Ferrière also presented letters patent issued to him personally in 1599 exempting him from punishment, the court dismissed the charges against him. Less than a year later, however, La Ferrière himself petitioned the Chambre de l'Edit because of another dispute about his wartime conduct. Hillaire Ogeron, Jacques Demazières, and Renée Letheulle, widow of Claude Ogeron, had accused him of having attacked them one night in 1594, pillaging their homes and then holding them for ransom at Vezins. They emphasized the injustice of this, given that they "were not making war and [were] paying the king's taxes, and all the same were constrained to pay ransom by force and violence used against their persons."[24] In August 1599, the seneschal of Anjou had convicted La Ferrière for these actions; in appealing the sentence to the Chambre de l'Edit two years later, La Ferrière repeated his earlier arguments about protection from prosecution for wartime deeds. He also noted that one of his accusers had had two sons in the service of a local League seigneur, suggesting that his opponents had been involved in the religious and civil conflict despite their claims to have been only peaceful taxpayers. The chamber judges again rejected the whole dispute, sending the parties away without penalty on either side.

The court dealt with a complaint from a group of Catholics from Chevannes, near Auxerre, in similar fashion. The plaintiffs were suing the soldiers who had seized and sold their livestock in December 1592, despite the fact that they had not been actively fighting against the king. Like Claude de Sainte Melaine, the plaintiffs argued that the soldiers' actions—which included "sacrileges, burnings, murders, pillaging" [sacrileges, bruslemens, meutres, pilleries]—exceeded the bounds of wartime violence and could not be covered by the edicts.[25] The accused men described their past deeds as part of the conduct of war, depicting the incident as a pitched battle rather than a theft. Engaged for the king against the Catholic League at Auxerre and hearing that League troops were in Chevannes selling livestock that had been taken from royal forces, they had successfully attacked the place, "which did not happen without great conflict, burned houses, and persons killed, and all this occurred by way of hostility."[26] The Chambre de l'Edit followed

---

pratique ordinaire en discipline militaire...contre tous ceux qui luy faisoient la guerre.

[24] A.N. X2b 201, 20 June 1601: ne faisans la guerre et paiant les tailles au Roy et touttefois par force et viollances exercées sur leurs personnes auroient esté contraincts à paier Rançon.

[25] A.N. X2b 200, 4 April 1601. In fact, these are some of the deeds specifically defined as *cas execrables* in the Edict of Nantes (art. 86).

[26] A.N. X2b 200, 4 April 1601: ce que n'estoit advenu sans grand conflict, maisons bruslés et personnes tués, et tout cela exploicté par voyes d'hostillité.

royal advocate Louis Servin's recommendation to drop the matter, once again subordinating the parties' conflicting remembrance of past events to the aims of peace and *oubliance*.

In one instance, the chamber magistrates reversed their own decision concerning a case of theft in wartime. Claude d'Orgemont, sieur de Mery, appealed to the Chambre de l'Edit in December 1600, demanding the return of stolen jewelry, furnishings, silver, horses, and livestock or compensation for their value up to eight thousand *écus*. Jacob de Bourdon, sieur de la Couldraye claimed that he had seized the goods while capturing château Mery, a League stronghold, for Henry III in 1589. D'Orgemont denied this, arguing that both he and Bourdon had been in the king's service at the time; Bourdon had acted "under the veil of hospitality" [soubs le voile d'hospitallité] rather than according to the laws of war.[27] Acknowledging the letters patent that Bourdon had obtained from the royal chancery declaring the incident at Mery a military act, the chamber magistrates dismissed the suit in July 1602, but d'Orgemont managed to revive the case and won a favorable judgment two years later. The Chambre de l'Edit sentenced Bourdon's widow and brother to pay him twenty thousand *livres tournois* in reparations. In addition to d'Orgemont's keen legal maneuvers, the court may have been influenced by his apparent rise in status from "chevallier Sieur de Mery" (as he styled himself in 1602) to "chevallier de l'ordre du Roy [et] gentilhomme de sa chambre," his title in 1604.[28]

D'Orgemont's case also highlights another factor in many legal disputes stemming from the Wars of Religion: royal pardons issued by the chancery, known as *lettres de rémission* and *abolition*. Such documents allowed the king to pardon individuals for their crimes or to remit the penalties imposed for their offenses.[29] When the letters dealt with wartime incidents, they generally proclaimed the military nature of the person's conduct and often contained the king's avowal that the individual had acted in his service or at his command. Litigants sometimes presented letters

[27] A.N. X2b 198, 13 December 1600.

[28] A.N. X2b 208, 30 July 1602; X2b 221, 7 September 1604.

[29] *Lettres d'abolition* provided complete amnesty for an offense, while *lettres de rémission* concerned capital crimes committed involuntarily or in self-defense, acknowledging the intention of the act. The king could also issue letters of pardon for lesser crimes: Esmein, *Cours élémentaire*, 425–27; Antoine Furetière, *Dictionnaire universel* (La Haye and Rotterdam, 1690; repr. Geneva: Slatkine, 1970), s.v. "Abolition" and "Remission." For the use and significance of such letters, see Wolfe, "Amnesty and Oubliance"; Claude Gauvard, "L'Image du roi justicier en France à la fin du Moyen Age, d'après les lettres de rémission," in *La Faute, la répression et le pardon: Actes du 107e Congrès National des Sociétés Savantes* (Brest, 1982), I:165–92; Claude Gauvard, *"De Grace Especial": Crime, état et société en France à la fin du Moyen Age* (Paris: Publications de la Sorbonne, 1991); Natalie Zemon Davis, *Fiction in the Archives: Pardon Tales and Their Tellers in Sixteenth Century France* (Stanford: Stanford University Press, 1987).

of remission and abolition to the Chambre de l'Edit to justify or strengthen their claims to be exempt from prosecution. Isaac Journee, sieur de La Ronce, appealed to the court in March 1603 to protest the lawsuit that Jehan Liennart, Gilles Mocquet, and their wives had brought against him at Rennes. At issue was the death of François Chanterel, a relative of Liennart's and Mocquet's by marriage who had died while serving as a soldier under Journee's command at the garrison of Bordaige. Journee did not deny killing Chanterel, but a letter of remission issued by Henry IV in May 1598 emphasized Journee's long and faithful service to the king in Brittany, as well as the special circumstances that explained his actions. Suspecting Chanterel of treason, Journee had addressed him with "soft words and gracious remonstrances" [parolles douces et gratieuses remonstrances], but Chanterel had responded with insults and drew his sword. Journee had acted to defend both his honor and the garrison under his command. The Chambre de l'Edit officially registered Journee's letter of remission and ordered his release from prison, declaring Chanterel's death "covered and abolished by the edicts of pacification."[30]

A letter of abolition from Henry IV in July 1601 also helped expedite the appeal of Benjamin and Anne Girault, siblings who petitioned the court in December of that year. The letter stated that despite an agreement between the late king (Henry III) and Henry of Navarre that protected the honor, property, and reputation of those who had died in Navarre's service during the period of 1585 through 1589, the property of Thomas Girault, sieur de La Mothe Charente, had been confiscated and later acquired by clerics belonging to the chapter of Saint André d'Angoulême. The chapter refused to recognize the Girault children's status as legitimate heirs, resulting in fruitless litigation in Paris and Angoumois. In restoring the Giraults' inheritance and ordering the Parlement of Paris to enforce their claims, Henry IV noted that the Edict of Nantes had explicitly overturned judicial sentences against Huguenots like Thomas Girault. Moreover, the king himself possessed superior knowledge of this particular case, "inasmuch as there is no one who knows better than we what command we gave to the late sieur de La Mothe Charente, as a result of which he was condemned and executed and his goods confiscated."[31] The chamber magistrates decreed that

---

[30]A.N. X2b 213, 6 May 1603. The text of the king's letter appears in the *arrêt* containing the court's verdict. For documents related to Journee's case, see X2b 212, 5 March, 12 March, and 18 March 1603; the proceedings against him at Rennes had begun in April 1599.

[31]A.N. X2b 204, 3 December 1601. The text of the king's letter accompanies this *arrêt* as a separate document dated 11 July 1601: d'aultant qu'il n'y a personne qui sache mieulx que nous quelle estoit le commandement que nous avions donné audict feu Sieur de La Mothe Charente, à cause duquel il a esté condamné et executé à mort et ses biens confisqués.

Thomas Girault's sentence should be erased from local court records, paving the way for his son and daughter to regain their inheritance.[32]

As the cases of Jacob de Bourdon and Pierre Le Cornu show, however, the court did not always allow royal pardons to protect individuals completely from prosecution for wartime misconduct. This was true in the case of François Jehan Charles de Pardheillan, sieur de Panias (or Panjas) and royal governor of Auzan in Armagnac. Pardheillan and three associates were accused of murdering Jehan and Arnauld La Fontan and François d'Ambes in 1592. The four men were being prosecuted before the chambres mi-parties at Castres and Nérac, as well as royal authorities at Armagnac, when their case was transferred to the Paris Chambre de l'Edit by order of the king and his council.[33] The king's letter of abolition on behalf of Pardheillan and his accomplices was addressed specifically to the chamber judges and ruthlessly ordered an end to the proceedings:

> We know...why and how the death of the said de La Fontans and d'Ambes occurred, which for several great and important reasons which move us we will not permit to be mentioned here...we impose perpetual silence on this matter, both now and for the future; we set aside by these words signed by our hand all the proceedings, judgments and orders which may have intervened because of this deed.[34]

The Chambre de l'Edit formally accepted this letter and by implication the king's command to halt the trial, but the judges stipulated that the letter applied only to Pardheillan himself and one of his accomplices, Michel du Pré. Another of Pardheillan's men named Jacques Besquet, who had already been sentenced to the galleys for life by the Castres court, received no such protection. In a case like this one, the king himself might intervene to limit the prosecution of wartime misconduct, but the Chambre de l'Edit judges tried to have the last word in matters of legal *oubliance*.

---

[32]A.N. X2b 209, 30 August 1602.

[33]A.N. X2b 220, 2 July and 17 August 1604; the latter document contains the court's verdict, and the *lettre d'abolition* (dated 29 August 1603) accompanies the same *arrêt*.

[34]A.N. X2b 220, 17 August 1604 (text of the letter of abolition, 29 August 1603): Nous scavons...pourquoy et comment le deceds desdicts de La Fontan et d'Ambes est advenu dont pour plusieurs grands et importantes considerations à ce nous mouvans ne voullans ester icy faict aulcune mention...[nous] sur ce impose et imposons scillence perpetual tant pour le present que pour l'advenir, mis et mettons au neant par ces dictes presantes signees de notre main touttes les procedures, jugemens et arrests qui pour Raison dudict faict peuvent estre Intervenus. The letter states elsewhere that d'Ambes and the La Fontans had been plotting to capture the town of Eauze and possibly attack the king himself ("surprendre n[ot]re ville d'Eauze et d'attempter mesmes à n[ot]re personne") when Henry ordered Pardheillan to have the men seized.

Although some litigants produced royal letters of pardon to explain or excuse their actions during the Wars of Religion, most simply invoked the edicts of pacification that applied to all French subjects, and the chamber magistrates usually did the same in delivering their verdicts. When Isaac Robin sought redress for thefts and crimes stemming from the capture of Château d'Angle in Poitou in 1588, the court declared that the matter was abolished by the edicts of pacification.[35] Ester Rolland requested that the Chambre de l'Edit overturn a judgment that had labeled the seizure of some goods belonging to her late mother as a legitimate military capture *(bonne prise)* in 1589. The court denied her petition, and Rolland failed to obtain damages for her losses.[36] In other cases, however, restitution of money or property was part of the court's effort to redress past wrongs. The chamber magistrates nullified Mathurin Gouyn's ransom obligation to Claude Ollivier, sieur de La Grelerie, which dated from 1586, but the judges also ordered Gouyn to refund the money that Ollivier had already repaid him because of an earlier judicial sentence in Gouyn's favor.[37] Similarly, the court ordered Pierre Le Cornu (in yet another lawsuit) to repay the sum of 1250 *écus* he had extorted from Jean de Lannay, sieur de La Mothelais, in 1595, despite a truce that had been declared by Henry IV and the duc de Mercoeur.[38]

References to the king's edicts or the circumstances of war did not always persuade the Chambre de l'Edit to "forget" past misdeeds. In June 1602, an apothecary named Jacques Chevreuil accused André Bonnyeau, a royal sergeant from Poitou, of assaulting and robbing him after dragging him about the woods from one place to another in July 1598. Bonnyeau was convicted by the seneschal of Poitou for this offense, but in appealing his case to the Chambre de l'Edit, his lawyer argued that "because of the edicts [Chevreuil] should be declared ineligible [in his appeal]... and the deed in question declared extinguished and abolished."[39] The royal advocate opposed this attempt to associate Bonnyeau's action with the edict's amnesty, noting that July 1598 was not "the height of the war" [le fort de la guerre]. The court agreed and ordered the original sentence against Bonnyeau to be carried out. If the chamber judges were reluctant to permit too much remembrance of past conflicts, they were equally unwilling to extend the protection of *oubliance* too far into the present.

[35] A.N. X2b 241, 6 March 1608.
[36] A.N. X2b 222, 11 December 1604. In an *arrêt* dated 2 December 1604, the property is described as "a certain quantity of wine and provisions" [une certaine quantité de vin et hardes].
[37] A.N. X2b 235, 17 March 1607.
[38] A.N. X2b 194, 16 March 1600.
[39] A.N. X2b 207, 12 June 1602: en consequence des edicts... [Chevreuil] soit declare non recevable... et le faict dont est question declaré extaint et aboly.

Judicial appeals for redress of past injustices thus revolved around several important factors: the nature of the deed (act of war or personal vengeance, legitimate property loss or theft); timing (when the disputed event occurred, what else was going on at the time or in the area); and the parties' status (soldiers on opposing sides, disinterested civilians). Such issues became even more complicated when they involved the relatives, heirs, and descendants of those whose conduct was in question. Widows like Claude de Sainte Melaine appeared frequently before the Chambre de l'Edit to demand prosecution of their husbands' killers, often acting on behalf of their children. Jeanne Louet accused David de Remberge, sieur de Retail, and Magdelon Marin, sieur de Laulnay, of having murdered her husband in 1598. Documents from her case, which spanned four years, refer to her not only as a widowed mother, but also as legal guardian (*tutrice et curatrice*) of her minor children.[40] Jehanne Dechart had prosecuted her husband's murderer in her double capacity as widow and guardian of an unborn child. When the accused man appealed his case to the Chambre de l'Edit, the court reduced his death sentence to perpetual banishment but upheld Dechart's claim to six hundred *écus* from his confiscated property.[41] Ysabeau de Gaubert, widow of Michel d'Argnoust, sieur de Berville, sued the men she held responsible for her husband's death in 1579. Damoiselle Gratienne d'Argnoust, Michel's only daughter and heir, joined Gaubert in this lawsuit, though the Chambre de l'Edit ultimately dismissed their case.[42] On the other hand, widow Margueritte Poussard, dame du Breuil Goullard, and her son successfully appealed a sentence delivered against her husband by a royal judge at Montmorillon in December 1584, which included seizure of their goods. The chamber judges nullified the judgment and ordered Poussard's opponents—the children and heirs of François de La Tousche, sieur de Montagues—to repay any monies that they or their father had received as a result of the earlier verdict, along with costs and damages.[43]

Petitions for royal justice to redress past wrongs sometimes spanned generations and reached decades backward in time. The most intriguing case of this kind involved six men from three different families. Henri Cavelier, Clement Lefebvre,

[40]A.N. X2b 206–9, April–September 1602; X2b 224–226, April–August 1605. *Tutelle* referred to legal responsibility for the person of a minor child, while *curatelle* denoted care of the minor's property and legal interests; see Furetière, *Dictionnaire universel*, s.v. "Curatelle," "Curateur," "Tutelle," and "Tuteur."

[41]A.N. X2b 200, 17 March 1601. Dechart is described as suing "tant en son nom que comme tutrice du posthume dont elle estoit enceinte." Her opponent is identified as Jehan de Caireforcq, former schoolteacher and later soldier from Béarn.

[42]A.N. X2b 209, 4 September 1602.

[43]A.N. X2b 231, 5 May 1606.

and Pierre de Couldraye were three merchants from Rouen who had been robbed and murdered in 1576. Twenty-six years later, their sons and heirs sued René Hervé, sieur de Ruffé, and several accomplices for the deed. The merchants' sons claimed that it had been impossible for them to pursue the matter at the time because "they were still minors and young, destitute of means and under the authority of guardians who neglected them."[44] Moreover, a previous lawsuit against Ruffé and his associates had been bungled by the person representing the merchants' families, perhaps because of collusion with the accused. Now that they had reached adulthood, the merchants' sons were ready to summon the murderers to justice, along with their widows and heirs. Indeed, the embattled Ruffé was eventually joined by Cecille de Monceau, widow of one of his alleged accomplices.[45] Disputed accounts of the robbery/murder went on for two years; the royal advocate described the case as unique ("speciale en soy mesme") and advised the court to allow the appellants to seek restitution of their fathers' stolen money, if not reparations for the three murders. In the end, the Chambre de l'Edit rejected the lawsuit and declared the matter legally closed (préscripte), but the case itself illustrates the strength of remembrance and resistance to the policy of oubliance.[46]

Lawsuits concerning wartime events and past injustices also dealt with memory as reputation—the worth, honor, and renown of an individual and family. The Chambre de l'Edit often supported petitions that aimed at restoring a person's good reputaton from damage suffered during the Wars of Religion. As discussed above, Pierre Denyau's children expressed this concern when they asked to have a concrete public reminder of their father's condemnation—a gibbet and effigy—ceremoniously removed; the court granted the request but ordered that it be done without fanfare. Lawsuits brought by family members often linked considerations of material goods with those of reputation. When Thomas Girault's children demanded that their father's conviction be obliterated from local court records, they sought not only the return of his property, but also restoration of his good name as stipulated in Henry IV's letter of remission: "[we] restore and reestablish his memory as worthy of honor."[47] In a similar case presented in April 1602, the

---

[44]A.N. X2b 210, 7 December 1602: ils ont tousjours esté mineurs et en bas aage, desimé de moyens et soubs la puissance de tuteurs qui les ont Negligés.

[45]A.N. X2b 213, 16 June 1603. Monceau is described as a *dame d'honneur* of Catherine de Bourbon, Henry IV's sister and a staunch Calvinist. The Chambre de l'Edit initially refused to hear the case brought by the merchants' sons; only after Ruffé and Monceau appealed to the court was the suit accepted and judged.

[46]A.N. X2b 217, 11 February 1604.

[47]A.N. X2b 204, 3 December 1601: [nous] Remectons et Restablissons sa memoire comme digne d'honneur.

court authorized Pierre de Bremeur to erase the stain of a death sentence issued against his father *par contumace* in November 1591. Bremeur claimed that his father had died without ever knowing of his conviction; seven years later, the elder Bremeur's property had been unjustly seized by Jacques Le Lieur, sieur de Ruanville, thus depriving Pierre of his inheritance. When the chamber judges permitted Pierre de Bremeur to "clear the memory" [purger la mémoire] of his father, they also authorized him to seek the return of the confiscated property.[48] Six years later, the court allowed Jonas de Bessé, royal governor of Talmont, to vindicate his father, who had been convicted *par contumace* for murder in September 1576.[49]

The Chambre de l'Edit's efforts to balance the demands for restoration of property and honor against the claims of *oubliance* are best illustrated by the court's response to an appeal from the widow and children of a man named Jullart. The petitioners argued that Jullart had been unjustly seized as a prisoner of war, abused, and summarily executed in 1592. The defendants' lawyers, however, countered by citing "the edicts of pacification of the troubles which covered, extinguished and abolished all that happened during the said troubles and forbidden the investigation of such things."[50] The chamber magistrates declared the matter closed, a decision that effectively upheld Jullart's execution. Yet in delivering this verdict, the court also severely restricted the impact this would have on Jullart's family and reputation:

> Nothing may be imputed to the memory of the late Jullart and his family; [the court] forbids all persons to reproach the appellants and their posterity and orders that the said sentence will be struck from the registers at Rochefort and the fines adjudged by that court, if any have been paid, will be given to the appellants.[51]

Once again, we see the double legacy of *oubliance* as enforced by the Paris Chambre de l'Edit: the same edicts that precluded further investigation of Jullart's death also justified the court's protection of his memory and posterity, even to the point of ordering financial reimbursement to his family and destruction of the record of

---

[48]A.N. X2b 206, 19 April 1602.

[49]A.N. X2b 242, 5 May 1608.

[50]A.N. 2b 199, 31 January 1601: les edicts de pacification des troubles qui ont couvert exteinct et aboly tout ce qui s'est passé Durant desdicts troubles et deffendu la recherche des choses semblables.

[51]A.N. X2b 199, 31 January 1601: il en puisse estre aucune chose impute à la mémoire dudict deffunt Jullart et de ses siens; faictes deffences à toutes personnes d'en rien improperer aux appellans et à leur posterité, ordonne que ladite sentence sera rayée des registres de Rochefort et les amendes adjugés par icelle si aucunes ont été payées seront rendues aux appellans.

his condemnation. Like the other lawsuits analyzed above, this case clearly shows the court's efforts to settle current disputes about a conflicted past in the interest of maintaining peace and public order for the future.

In adjudicating lawsuits that stemmed from the Wars of Religion, the Chambre de l'Edit became an arena for battles about remembering and forgetting history and identity in seventeenth-century France. "In a single society (and within a single individual," according to Nathan Wachtel, "several memories coexist and even oppose each other, memories that are the object of struggles, strategies and power relations: sometimes official, dominant memories upheld by institutions; sometimes latent, secret recollections, those of the dominated groups, for instance. The task of the historian now consists of analyzing the forms, mechanisms and function of these recollections in the lives of social groups, as well as their interactions and conflicts."[52] Lawsuits concerning *oubliance* exemplify such "struggles, strategies and power relations," as litigants contested each other's accounts and interpretations of past events and royal magistrates tried to adjudicate memory. It is not surprising that memory should have played an important role in laws and legal disputes during this period. In the famous case of Martin Guerre's return to the village of Artigat, Arnaud du Tilh's remembrance of persons, places, and experiences from Martin's past represented some of the strongest evidence supporting his claim to be Martin Guerre, while other people's memories formed a corollary body of proof that both confirmed and refuted his claim. The magistrates of the Parlement of Toulouse weighed the conflicting evidence of memory in judging a dispute over an individual's identity.[53] But in the lawsuits before the Paris Chambre de l'Edit, memory was the very substance of dispute, not just part of the evidence, and both memory and *oubliance* were tied to larger issues of history and identity.

Historian John Gillis has described both memory and identity as "representations or constructions of reality, subjective rather than objective phenomena." Writing in the early twentieth century, sociologist Maurice Halbwachs laid the foundation for this view with his work on the "social frameworks of memory." Halbwachs argued that groups, such as family, social class, and religious confession, always shape the memories of their individual members. Storytelling, holidays, and

[52]Nathan Wachtel, "Memory and History: An Introduction," *History and Anthropology* 2 (1986): 218.

[53]Davis, *The Return of Martin Guerre.*

other commemorative events, rituals, and material archives all help to preserve a group's history, and all reflect the group's perception of what is worth remembering. Through such artifacts and events, individuals can identify with and even "remember" a past they themselves never experienced. Yet memory, as Wachtel pointed out, can be the product of conflict rather than consensus. Forgetting, on the other hand, may foster cohesion where remembrance only encourages further division and strife. Like these modern scholars, the judges, lawyers, and litigants of early modern France recognized the power of memory to connect individuals to the rest of society, to relate and explain past and present, and to create or suppress collective perceptions of the past.[54]

Lawsuits heard by the Paris Chambre de l'Edit illuminate this subjective, creative interaction of remembrance and forgetting. Along with memoirs, published histories, commemorative events, and monuments, this litigation constituted a *lieu de mémoire*—the concrete trace of a past that had itself disappeared.[55] The tensions surrounding *oubliance* in general were embedded in the law: the Edict of Nantes proclaimed that much of the wartime past was to be regarded as "something that had never happened." Yet the edict also allowed certain incidents to be remembered and revived as judicial grievances. The Chambre de l'Edit's handling of such disputes shows how events from the Wars of Religion were often contested before

---

[54]John R. Gillis, "Memory and Identity: The History of a Relationship," in *Commemorations: The Politics of National Identity*, ed. John R. Gillis (Princeton: Princeton University Press, 1994), 3. Maurice Halbwachs, *On Collective Memory*, ed. and trans. Lewis A. Coser (Chicago: University of Chicago Press, 1992), 21–26, 92–93; Halbwachs, *The Collective Memory*, trans. Francis Ditter and Vida Ditter (New York: Columbia University Press, 1980). Peter Burke, "History as Social Memory," in *Memory: History, Culture and the Mind*, ed. Thomas Butler (Oxford: Blackwell, 1989), 108. In addition to the works cited above on memory and history, see Jacques Le Goff, *History and Memory*, trans. Steven Rendall and Elizabeth Claman (New York: Columbia University Press, 1992); Pierre Nora, ed., *Les Lieux de mémoire*, 3 vols. (Paris: Gallimard, 1984); Paul Connerton, *How Societies Remember* (Cambridge: Cambridge University Press, 1985); David Lowenthal, *The Past Is a Foreign Country* (Cambridge: Cambridge University Press, 1985); Eric J. Hobsbawm and Terence O. Ranger, eds., *The Invention of Tradition* (Cambridge: Cambridge University Press, 1983); Keith M. Baker, "Memory and Practice: Politics and the Representation of the Past in Eighteenth-Century France," *Representations* 11 (1985): 134–64; Patrick H. Hutton, *History as an Art of Memory* (Hanover, N.H.: University Presses of New England, 1993); Sahlins, *Boundaries*; David Cressy, *Bonfires and Bells: National Memory and the Protestant Calendar in Elizabethan and Stuart England* (Berkeley: University of California Press, 1990); J.G.A. Pocock, *The Ancient Constitution and the Feudal Law*, 2d ed. (Cambridge: Cambridge University Press, 1987), esp. chap. 1.

[55]See Pierre Nora, "Between Memory and History: Les Lieux de Mémoire," *Representations* 26 (1989): 7–25; Natalie Zemon Davis and Randolph Starn, "Introduction to Special Issue on Memory and Counter-Memory," *Representations* 26 (1989): 1–6.

being relegated to a past that had been declared closed, abolished, and "forgotten." Moreover, the court's enforcement of *oubliance* was not just about hearing arguments and issuing orders, for it depended upon the litigants' active participation. Drawing upon legal definitions of what could and could not be remembered, French men and women presented their recollections of wartime events to the court, implicitly acknowledging the magistrates' authority to judge the past. The court's verdict might indicate official acceptance of claims that a given event was a crime (worthy of remembrance and punishment), or it might define the incident as part of "the recent troubles" that had to be forgotten. Whether those who lost their appeals actually accepted such decisions and substituted the official version of what had happened for their own interpretations of disputed events is something that the court records cannot reveal. But in Wachtel's terms, the Chambre de l'Edit (the official institution) and Huguenot litigants (the dominated group) together produced a "memory" and history of the Wars of Religion through the process of criminal litigation.

The court's work also reflects a complex relationship between memory and history that had been developing since the Renaissance, especially in the world of law and politics.[56] The Chambre de l'Edit's judgment of past events was influenced by present political aims. When the court adjudicated cases about *oubliance*, it did so with an eye to restoring the social order and political obedience that peacetime and the king's edicts required. The sixteenth-century past could be revived in the seventeenth-century courtroom, but claims of past injustices often had to give way before the chamber magistrates' principal goal of maintaining peace and order in the present. By the same token, history (or at least the judicial record of it) could be revised through criminal lawsuits and judicial verdicts. As we have seen, the Chambre de l'Edit responded to some appeals by reversing judgments, removing effigies, and restoring property and honor. Even when the court refused such requests, its decisions left traces in the historical record. Contrary to the Edict of Nantes's emphasis on forgetting, the wartime past was being contested and sometimes changed, rather than obliterated.

Legal disputes about the Wars of Religion were also helping to forge a sense of French national identity among the participants. Some of the key features of this identity were already in place by the early seventeenth century. The monarchy had become an important symbol of a realm that retained strong regional divisions and differences. French kings were gradually expanding their power relative

[56]Kelley, *Foundations of Modern Historical Scholarship*; Huppert, *Idea of Perfect History*; Orest Ranum, *Artisans of Glory: Writers and Historical Thought in Seventeenth-Century France* (Chapel Hill: University of North Carolina Press, 1980).

96 ❧ RELIGION AND ROYAL JUSTICE IN EARLY MODERN FRANCE

to other groups that participated in governance (nobility, clergy, guilds, town councils), though not without encountering resistance. Kings and magistrates alike claimed to defend the "Gallican liberties" of the Catholic Church in France, which further entwined religious and political allegiance.[57] An emerging notion of Frenchness, which revolved around adherence to both the monarchy and Catholicism, was seriously challenged during the French Reformation and Wars of Religion. The central government failed to halt the spread of heresy in the early sixteenth century, and conflicts among Huguenots, Catholics, and the crown dominated France's internal and international politics during the later 1500s. These conflicts were all the more divisive because they occurred on multiple levels: loyalties to family, municipality, seigneur, and king were often reinforced or ruptured because of religious difference.

The turbulent events of the sixteenth century, however, ultimately strengthened rather than weakened the sense of national consciousness that had been slowly taking shape since the medieval period, especially insofar as it centered on the monarchy. By 1598, Henry IV had defeated his opponents (both foreign and domestic) through a combination of military victories, financial and political incentives, and religious conversion, all of which helped to consolidate his legitimacy as king of France and to justify his demand for loyalty from his Catholic and Huguenot subjects. Religious and civil warfare gave way to a royal edict that promised an end to the violence and disorder that had resulted from confessional divisions and political rivalries, in return for unified obedience to one king and his law. The same edict assured Huguenots a protected, if limited, place in an officially Catholic kingdom, transforming them—at least in law—from dangerous heretics into a privileged religious minority. And the royal judiciary, which had suffered its own internal divisions during the religious wars, was now called upon to play a major role in implementing the peaceful coexistence mandated by the Edict of Nantes.[58]

Yet the peace decreed by the king could not be accomplished by royal or judicial fiat. Despite a consensus about the need for peace and order, disputes about

[57]William F. Church, "France," in *National Consciousness, History and Political Culture in Early Modern Europe*, ed. Orest Ranum (Baltimore: Johns Hopkins University Press, 1975), 43–66; Beaune, *Birth of an Ideology*; Strayer, "France," 3–16.

[58]Yardeni, *La Conscience nationale*; Denis Crouzet, *Les Guerriers de dieu: La Violence au temps des troubles de religion*, 2 vols. (Paris: Seyssel, 1990); Diefendorf, *Beneath the Cross*; Roelker, *One King, One Faith*; Wolfe, *Conversion of Henri IV*; Mack P. Holt, "Burgundians into Frenchmen: Catholic Identity in Sixteenth Century Burgundy," in *Changing Identities in Early Modern France*, ed. Michael Wolfe (Durham: Duke University Press, 1997), 345–70; Sutherland, *The Huguenot Struggle for Recognition*. For a longterm view of the development of "royal religion," see Van Kley, *Religious Origins*.

the Huguenots' status would continue. Moreover, Huguenots' and Catholics' perceptions of themselves and of each other remained linked to remembrance of their recent history, just as the Edict of Nantes itself spurred litigation about the Wars of Religion despite its emphasis on forgetting past conflicts. Faced with such disputes, the Paris Chambre de l'Edit tried to use "the remedy of wise forgetfulness" [le remède de la sage oubliance] to reinforce those elements of the law that insisted that former enemies become "brothers, friends and fellow citizens"—or at least that they behave as such.[59] Through their decisions, the chamber magistrates presented obedience to the king, the court, and the law itself as the keystone of a collective political identity that encompassed Huguenots and Catholics alike, superseding both past and present religious differences.

Ironically, the Huguenots' existence as a protected but still suspect religious minority thus helped to advance an emerging definition of national identity that would ultimately exclude them. Catholics who had rebelled against the monarchy during the Wars of Religion could be reintegrated into French society and state in ways that their Calvinist counterparts could not. The Huguenots' allegiance to their faith, their churches, and their communities would become increasingly incompatible with the officially sanctioned place of Catholicism in seventeenth-century politics, society, and culture, despite their frequent protestations of loyalty to the crown.[60] With the historian's gift of hindsight, we know that obedience to the Bourbon kings and royal law would not be enough to prevent a Huguenot rebellion against Louis XIII or to forestall Louis XIV's revocation of the Edict of Nantes in 1685. But in the first decade of the seventeenth century, lawsuits about *oubliance* showed that a conception of the loyal, law-abiding French subject— whether Huguenot or Catholic—who had overcome the memory of past conflict was being actively promoted in the Paris Chambre de l'Edit.

[59]A.N. X2b 205, 13 February 1602.
[60]David Parker, "The Huguenots in Seventeenth-Century France," in *Minorities in History*, ed A.C. Hepburn (New York: St. Martin's Press, 1979), 11–30; Elisabeth Labrousse, "The Wars of Religion in Seventeenth-Century Huguenot Thought," in *The Massacre of Saint Bartholomew: Reappraisals and Documents*, ed. Alfred Soman (The Hague: M. Nijhoff, 1974), 243–51.

"Comme père commun de tous nos sujets"

The Family, the Law, & the Paris Chambre de l'Edit

IN JANUARY 1599, HENRY IV SUMMONED A GROUP OF MAGISTRATES
from the Parlement of Paris to the Louvre to demand that the court ratify the
Edict of Nantes. At first, he addressed the delegation with these words:

> You see me in my private quarters, where I come to speak to you, not
> in royal attire, like my predecessors, nor with sword and cape, nor as a
> prince who comes to address foreign ambassadors, but dressed in a
> doublet, like a father, to speak frankly to his children.[1]

The soothing quality of the king's opening remarks quickly disappeared in the
harangue that followed. He berated the royal judges for their ingratitude and seditious intrigues; he threatened those who continued to incite opposition to the
edict and his policies. "Only do what I command," he concluded, "or rather what
I request. You will act not only for me, but also for yourselves and for the good of
peace."[2]

---

[1] L'Estoile, *Memoires-Journaux*, 7:164, quoted in Mousnier, *L'Assassinat d'Henri IV*, 335: Vous me
voiez en mon cabinet, où je viens parler à vous, non point en habit roial, comme mes prédécesseurs,
ni avec l'espee et la cappe, ni comme un prince qui vient parler aux ambassadeurs estrangers, mais
vestu comme un père de famille, en pourpoint, pour parler franchement à ses enfants. The king's
statement echoes views about the relationship between sovereign and paternal power expressed earlier
in the sixteenth century by Jean Bodin in his *Six Books of the Republic*, trans. M.J. Tooley (New York:
Barnes & Noble, 1967), bk. I, chap. 2.

[2] L'Estoile, *Memoires-Journaux*, quoted in Mousnier, *L'Assassinat d'Henri IV*, 337: Faites seulement

The double rhetoric of this speech is both eloquent and instructive. In presenting himself as a father rather than a king appearing in state, Henry IV emphasized the paternal quality of his royal power. At the same time he implicitly reduced the parlement magistrates to the subordinate status of both subjects and children. Abandoning the persona of the solicitous parent, he adopted that of an irate sovereign; he demanded the judges' obedience, even as he argued that they would be acting for the common good and their own self-interest. Far from being contradictory, these two personae reinforced each other and gave the king's command/request additional force. Like a father seeking to maintain order within his household, Henry was trying to restore peace and order among his divided subjects. The Edict of Nantes was essential for his purpose, and he successfully insisted that the Paris magistrates approve the law without further delay.

Henry's deliberate identification of royal with paternal authority invoked the family as a powerful metaphor for the state. Yet in France as elsewhere in early modern Europe, family relationships were more than just analogies for political ties of authority and obedience. Secular and religious leaders agreed that the family was the foundation of an orderly state, a godly community (whether Catholic or Protestant), and a productive society. Sources ranging from royal and ecclesiastical decrees to pamphlets, sermons, treatises, wills, and contracts show how contemporaries tried to shape family relationships through a combination of legal requirements and exemplary models. Lay and clerical authors offered advice about how men and women should behave in their familial roles as dutiful sons and daughters, virtuous husbands and wives, model parents, and responsible household managers. On the other hand, laws concerning marriage, inheritance, and guardianship sought to regulate family formation and property transmission across generations. Lawsuits about such matters could be brought before both secular and church courts, where judges acted to settle disputes, punish offenders, and further interpret the relevant laws.[3]

---

ce que je vous commande, ou plus tost dont je vous prie. Vous ne ferez pas seulement pour moi, mais aussi pour vous et pour le bien de la paix.

[3]Amid the enormous literature on these developments, the following works have proven especially helpful: Beatrice Gottlieb, *The Family in the Western World from the Black Death to the Industrial Age* (New York: Oxford University Press, 1993); James A. Brundage, *Law, Sex and Christian Society in Medieval Europe* (Chicago: University of Chicago Press, 1987); Jack Goody et al., *Family and Inheritance: Rural Society in Western Europe, 1200–1800* (Cambridge: Cambridge University Press, 1976); Philippe Ariès, ed., *A History of Private Life*, vol. 3, *Passions of the Renaissance*, ed. Roger Chartier, trans. Arthur Goldhammer (Cambridge: Harvard University Press, 1989); Hans Medick and David Sabean, eds., *Interest and Emotion: Essays on the Study of Family and Kinship* (Cambridge: Cambridge University Press, 1984); Lyndal Roper, *The Holy Household: Women and Morals in Reformation Augsburg* (New York: Oxford University Press,

Early modern France is an especially fertile field for studying the struggle for control and influence over families. Rules of inheritance, patterns of family and household organization, and marriage rituals differed from region to region, reflecting the variable influences of Roman law, local custom, and social class and occupation. On the other hand, royal edicts concerning marriage, inheritance, and parental authority over children applied to all French subjects, regardless of regional custom or social class. Such laws were issued throughout the sixteenth and seventeenth centuries.[4] The Catholic Church also exercised considerable authority in determining the validity of marriage and parentage, though this was sometimes tempered by the "Gallican liberties" of the French church and the monarchy. For example, the Council of Trent's decrees on marriage were not fully adopted in France, though many of the Tridentine requirements were incorporated into a royal edict issued in 1579.[5] During the sixteenth century, Huguenots developed their own rules about marriage and baptism based on the teachings of John Calvin and the disciplines established by the French Reformed churches. After the Wars of Religion, however, the Edict of Nantes emphasized that disputes among Huguenots about marriage and inheritance would be settled by royal magistrates, rather than by Reformed consistories or synods.[6] Like their Catholic

---

1989); Jean-Louis Flandrin, *Families in Former Times,* translated by Richard Southern (Cambridge: Cambridge University Press, 1979), originally published as *Familles: Parenté, maison, sexualité dans l'ancienne société* (Paris: Hachette, 1976). On lawsuits and family in early modern France, see Sarah Hanley, "Engendering the State: Family Formation and State Building in Early Modern France," *French Historical Studies* 16 (1989): 4–27; James Farr, *Authority and Sexuality in Early Modern Burgundy, 1550–1730* (New York: Oxford University Press, 1995); James F. Traer, *Marriage and the Family in Eighteenth-Century France* (Ithaca: Cornell University Press, 1980). The role of the Calvinist consistory in France is discussed below.

[4]Emmanuel Le Roy Ladurie, "A System of Customary Law: Family Structures and Inheritance Customs in Sixteenth-Century France," in *Family and Society: Selections from the Annales: Economies, Sociétés, Civilisations,* ed. Robert Forster and Orest Ranum, trans. Patricia Ranum and Elborg Forster (Baltimore: Johns Hopkins University Press, 1976), 75–103; Olivier-Martin, *Histoire de droit français;* Brissaud, *History of French Private Law.*

[5]Adhémar Esmein, *Le Mariage en droit canonique,* 2 vols. (Paris: Recueil Sirey, 1935); Jean Gaudemet, *Le Mariage en occident: Les moeurs et le droit* (Paris: Cerf, 1987); *Canons and Decrees of the Council of Trent,* trans. Henry Joseph Schroeder (St. Louis: B. Herder, 1941), 180–90; Traer, *Marriage and the Family,* 22–47. On regional variations in French marriage practices, see Jean-Baptiste Molin and Protais Mutembe, *Le Rituel du mariage en France du XIIe au XVIe siècle* (Paris: Beauchesne, 1976).

[6]Pierre Bels, *Le Mariage des protestants français jusqu'en 1685* (Paris: Librairie général de droit et de jurisprudence, 1968); J.-C. Groshens, *Les Institutions et le régime juridique des cultes protestants* (Paris: Librairie génerale de droit et de jurisprudence, 1957); Pierre Taillandier, *Le Mariage des protestants français sous*

counterparts, French Calvinists found themselves subject to overlapping and sometimes conflicting rules about family matters, and litigation about marriage, inheritance, and guardianship formed a constant feature of the Paris Chambre de l'Edit's work in the seventeenth century.

This chapter examines family-related lawsuits heard by the Chambre de l'Edit from several perspectives. Cases concerning the validity of marriages, guardianship, and contested inheritances reveal the court's effort to enforce royal laws and restore order within families. In addition, legal disputes could unite as well as divide family members: the court's records reveal much about the interests, loyalties, and obligations that fostered cooperation among relatives who were involved in litigation, as well as provoking conflicts among them. Finally, the family was an important battleground in the war for confessional allegiance in seventeenth-century France, though religious difference played an ambiguous role in these disputes. In general, the Chambre de l'Edit's work reflects a common goal of Huguenot, Catholic, and royal policy: to promote order and obedience within the family as the foundation of a peaceful, orderly state.

"Family" was a multivalent concept to people in early modern France. It referred not only to persons living in a common household *(ménage)*, but also to lineage *(lignage)*, a line of descent linking individuals to their ancestors, their immediate relatives, and a more distant posterity. For aristocrats and members of the middling classes, lineage connected family members to their collective past and guided their plans for the future—what Natalie Zemon Davis has called "the arrow of family fortunes in historical time."[7] On the other hand, the *ménage* existed in the present, immediate moments of a family's history. A married couple and their children usually stood at the core of the *ménage*, but households could include collateral relatives (aunts, uncles, cousins, grandparents), as well as servants or apprentices. In practice, household and lineage were clearly linked: the goods and property that a family acquired, managed, or sold to preserve the lineage also sustained the household, and families pursued strategies that aimed at maintaining or

---

l'ancien régime (Clermont-Ferrand, 1919); Ernest-Charles-François Bonifas, *Le Mariage des protestants depuis la Réforme jusqu'à 1789* (Paris: L. Boyer, 1901); René Voeltzel, "Le Droit matrimonial dans les anciennes églises réformées de France, 1559–1660," *Revue de droit canonique* 29 (1977): 154–77. On the Edict of Nantes's provisions, see below.

[7]Davis, "Ghosts, Kin and Progeny," in *Daedalus* 106:2 (1977): 87–114.

enhancing lineage through the advantageous marriages and productive careers of individual family members.[8]

The sixteenth and seventeenth centuries brought important developments in family structure and the nature of family ties. According to some historians, a focus on the nuclear family replaced a more extended notion of kinship that had prevailed during the medieval period. While families were still viewed as significant units of economic production, education, and political or social alliance, moralists promoted new ideals of behavior and sentiment that emphasized the family as an important center of emotional and moral support. Demographic factors, however, could weaken rather than strengthen the nuclear family's structure and affective ties. The death of one spouse often meant rapid remarriage for the survivor, which in turn could complicate inheritances, dowries, and guardianships for children from the first union.[9] The Chambre de l'Edit's records provide ample evidence of family ties as well as family friction, helping to illuminate the interests that bound relatives together or caused them to sue each other.

The early modern family is also associated with patriarchy. Drawing upon Christian scripture, classical philosophy, and Roman law, many legists and moralists argued that predominant authority in the family rightfully belonged to the male head of the household. Protestant reformers supported such views by praising family life over celibacy and emphasizing paternal responsibility for both the material and spiritual welfare of wives, children, and other household members. Amid the many upheavals of the sixteenth and seventeenth centuries, this emphasis on the husband/father/master's authority may have reflected a yearning for order that made obedience within one's family a value of paramount importance.[10] In addition, women were often perceived as naturally prone to weakness, irrationality, and sexual disorder. The need to curb women's propensity for sexual

---

[8]Davis, "Ghosts, Kin and Progeny"; Robert Wheaton, "Affinity and Descent in Seventeenth-Century Bordeaux," in *Family and Sexuality in French History*, ed. Robert Wheaton and Tamara Hareven (Philadelphia: University of Pennsylvania Press, 1980), 111–34; Roland Mousnier, *La Famille, l'enfant et l'éducation en France et Grande Bretagne, XVIe au XVIIIe siècles* (Paris: Centre de documentation Universitaire, 1975). On property, see Goody et al., *Family and Inheritance*; Ralph Giesey, "Rules of Inheritance and Strategies of Mobility in Pre-Revolutionary France," *American Historical Review* 82:2 (1977): 271–89.

[9]David Hunt, *Parents and Children in History: The Psychology of Family Life in Early Modern France* (New York: Basic Books, 1970); Philippe Ariès, *Centuries of Childhood: A Social History of Family Life*, trans. Robert Baldick (New York: Knopf, 1962); Micheline Baulant, "The Scattered Family: Another Aspect of Seventeenth-Century Demography," in *Family and Society*, 104–16. For another perspective on these issues, see Christiane Klapisch-Zuber, "La 'Mère cruelle': Maternité, veuvage et dot dans la Florence des XIV–XVe siècles," *Annales: Economies, Sociétés, Civilisations* 38 (1983): 1097–109.

[10]Susan D. Amussen, *An Ordered Society: Gender and Class in Early Modern England* (Oxford: Blackwell, 1988).

misconduct reinforced the insistence on male control that appears in laws, sermons, treatises, and other sources from this era. Sarah Hanley has argued that in early modern France, kings, judges, and lawyers created a "family-state compact" that put marriage, inheritance, and reproduction under secular rather than ecclesiastical authority. Acting as both heads of households and state officials, members of the French judiciary and royal bureaucracy enforced patriarchy largely at women's expense throughout the sixteenth and seventeenth centuries.[11]

Patriarchy, however, was not the only model of family authority available in early modern France, nor was it uncontested. French Protestant leaders meeting at the national synod of Verteuil in 1567 admonished parents not to force their children into marriage, even as they called for children who married without their parents' or guardians' consent to be punished.[12] François de Sales described marriage as "the nursery of Christianity" and exhorted husbands and wives to mutual fidelity, affection, and compassion, though his views were not widely shared by other Catholic reformers.[13] Recent scholarship has shown that women sometimes found ways to exercise initiative and agency despite the subordination that patriarchy required, invoking laws, contemporary mores, and public opinion successfully in their own defense.[14] As we shall see, women acting in their roles as wives, mothers, widows, and guardians often petitioned the Chambre de l'Edit on behalf of themselves or other family members, while some appeared as independent litigants before the court.

[11]Hanley, "Engendering the State"; Hanley, "Family and State in Early Modern France: The Marriage Pact," in *Connecting Spheres: Women in the Western World from 1550 to the Present*, ed. Marilyn Boxer and Jean Quataert (New York: Oxford University Press, 1987); idem., "Social Sites of Political Practice in France: Lawsuits, Civil Rights and the Separation of Powers in Domestic and State Government, 1500–1800," *American Historical Review* 102 (1997): 27–52. For another perspective, see Julie Hardwick, *The Practice of Patriarchy: Gender and Household Authority in Early Modern France* (University Park: Pennsylvania State University Press, 1998).

[12]Quick, *Synodican in Gallia Reformata*, 1:80–81 (decree 1, arts. 3, 7).

[13]François de Sales, *Introduction to the Devout Life*, trans. John K. Ryan (London: Longmans, Green, 1953), 236–41. See also Robin Briggs, "The Church and the Family in Seventeenth-Century France," in *Communities of Belief: Cultural and Social Tension in Early Modern France* (Oxford: Clarendon Press, 1989), 235–76.

[14]Hanley, "Engendering the State," 16–21; Harry A. Miskimin, "Widows Not So Merry: Women and the Courts in Late Medieval France," in *Upon My Husband's Death: Widows in the Literature and Histories of Medieval Europe*, ed. Louise Mirrer (Ann Arbor: University of Michigan Press, 1992), 207–19; Natalie Zemon Davis, "Women on Top," in *Society and Culture in Early Modern France* (Stanford: Stanford University Press, 1975); Gayle K. Brunelle, "Dangerous Liaisons: Mésalliance and Early Modern French Noblewomen," *French Historical Studies* 19 (1995): 75–103; Farr, *Authority and Sexuality*; Hardwick, *Practice of Patriarchy*.

The family was also a prime example of the uneasy division between public and private life that existed in early modern European societies. According to Philippe Ariès, it was during this period that the family "separated itself more sharply from the public realm. It extended its influence at the expense of the anonymous sociability of street and square." Ariès and others have acknowledged, however, that such changes were part of a complex, gradual redefining of the boundaries between public and private roles and activities.[15] In fact, the "public" and "private" elements remained closely linked. The artisan household (in which labor was divided among husbands, wives, children, servants, and apprentices) was still an important element of economic production, while among the middling and upper classes, family ties were essential in acquiring wealth, status, and political advancement.[16] The family was also perceived as the building block of an orderly society; the personal conduct of individual family members represented a microcosm of polity and society. When Louis XIII condemned clandestine marriages (that is, marriages contracted without parental consent) in a royal decree of 1639, he declared that "the natural reverence of children toward their parents is the link to the subjects' legitimate obedience toward their sovereign," while marriage itself was "the seminary of states" [le seminaire des états].[17]

Like other law courts that dealt with family disputes, the Chambre de l'Edit provides a valuable vantage point for observing the interplay between the public and private elements of family relationships. When appealing to the court, family members presented their disputes in a public arena composed of judges, lawyers, clerks, witnesses, and other observers; they also invoked or accepted the public authority of the judiciary and the crown to settle their conflicts. On the other hand, the magistrates who judged such cases were not simply addressing the complaints of private individuals about marriages, inheritances, and guardianship. They were also regulating activities that were seen to have important consequences for families and society in general. Adjudicating lawsuits about such matters thus helped to reinforce the family as both a public and private institution.

Despite a common interest in sustaining orderly families, secular and religious authorities often competed for influence and jurisdiction in family matters,

[15]Philippe Ariès, "Introduction," in *A History of Private Life*, vol. 3, *Passions of the Renaissance*, 8. See also Nicole Castan, "The Public and the Private," in the same collection, 403–46.

[16]For one example, see Joseph Bergin, *The Rise of Richelieu* (New Haven: Yale University Press, 1991); Bergin, *Cardinal Richelieu: Power and the Pursuit of Wealth* (New Haven: Yale University Press, 1985).

[17]"Declaration sur les formalités du mariage," in Isambert et al., *Recueil général*, 16:520: dans lesquelles [familles] la naturelle reverence des enfans envers leurs parens, est le lien de la legitime obeissance des sujets envers leur souverain. The declaration was issued in November 1639 and registered by the Parlement of Paris later that same year.

especially concerning the validity of marriage. Marriage represented both a spiritual union and a contractual arrangement; it also stood at the nexus of other family relationships. An illegal or invalid marriage could adversely affect the status of children and heirs, as well as determine or influence how property was divided and inherited among family members. Royal ordinances, canon law, and regulations issued by the French Reformed churches thus converged upon the problem of defining a valid marriage. These overlapping and sometimes conflicting rules about marriage, however, proved to be a source of legal disputes that ultimately tended to reinforce the royal judiciary's authority over Huguenots and Catholics alike.

In medieval canon law, marriage involved notions of both sacrament and contract—the germ of a distinction between the religious and social aspects of marriage that French jurists would later exploit. According to twelfth-century canonists, a valid marriage depended upon the spouses' own consent, yet the western Christian church prescribed no specific form of celebrating such unions. The legal distinction between an immediate exchange of vows ("sponsalia per verba de praesenti") and a promise to wed in the future or upon fulfillment of some condition ("sponsalia per verba de futuro") was not always clear, and confusion about such promises sometimes led to litigation before church courts. Canon law also recognized impediments to marriage, some of which could provide grounds for annulment. These included family ties within prohibited limits (making the spouses too closely related to each other to be legally wed), solemn vows to enter religious orders (taken prior to the marriage), bigamy, impotence, and circumstances that impeded the parties' free consent to marry, such as forcible abduction, mistaken identity, or fraud. Since the Church regarded valid marriages as sacraments that formed a permanent spiritual bond between the spouses, canon law required substantial proofs before dissolving such unions.[18]

The Catholic Church's doctrines on marriage were reviewed and clarified at the final sessions of the Council of Trent, which met intermittently from 1545 to 1563. The council declared that marriage remained a sacrament and that valid marriages were officially indissoluble even in the face of adultery, heresy, or desertion. Moreover, the spouses' mutual consent remained the essential basis of a legal union: those who married without their parents' or relatives' permission could be punished, but their marriages remained valid. In the decree Tametsi, however, the council specified how marriages were to be contracted and celebrated more precisely than ever before. Couples were ordered to exchange their vows in the presence of several witnesses and the local priest, who would record the marriage in

---

[18]Esmein, *Le Mariage*, 1:99–150, 228–448; Brissaud, *History of French Private Law*, 101–5, 112–29; Gaudemet, *Le Mariage en occident*, 175–93.

the parish register. The emphasis on publicity was partly intended to address the problem of clandestine marriages, which often resulted in lawsuits before church courts because their secrecy made them difficult to prove.[19] The Tridentine decrees on marriage thus aimed at clarifying the Catholic Church's doctrine for the faithful, as well as responding to Protestant reformers' criticisms.

The reformers' own interpretations of marriage remained rooted in the canon law tradition but differed from the Tridentine decrees in several respects. Martin Luther, John Calvin, Huldrych Zwingli, and others rejected marriage as a sacrament, finding no scriptural basis for such a claim. Yet they praised and promoted the value of marriage as a spiritual and social institution. Marriage provided a licit outlet for human sexuality (aimed at procreation, rather than pleasure); it was a worthy vocation for the majority of people who were incapable of celibacy, and whose weakness led to abuses and sin. Led by a godly husband and wife, the household could become a locus of spiritual instruction and wholesome religious practice, in contrast to the corrupt and unproductive communities of nuns and monks that the reformers vilified. While retaining some of canon law's requirements regarding marriage, Protestant reformers proposed a simpler set of prohibited degrees of kinship. Most of all, the Protestant concept of marriage included the possibility of divorce. Adultery, desertion, and impotence were possible grounds for dissolving a union and allowing the parties to remarry.[20]

In France, Protestant regulations concerning marriage were inspired by the teachings of John Calvin and Genevan example. Such regulations appeared in the ecclesiastical disciplines formulated and promoted by the French Reformed churches' national synods, notably those of Verteuil (1567), La Rochelle (1571), and Nîmes (1572). According to these rules, betrothals had to be announced to the local consistory and publicized for several weeks before the wedding ceremony itself, when a Reformed minister officially married the couple in the presence of

[19]Esmein, Le Mariage, 2:156–252, 330–45; Gaudemet, Le Mariage en occident, 286–95. On the problem of clandestine marriage and the litigation it provoked, see especially Beatrice Gottlieb, "The Problem of Clandestine Marriage," in Family and Sexuality in French History, 49–83.

[20]Esmein, Le Mariage, 2:141–56; Gaudemet, Le Mariage en occident, 278–85; Thomas Max Safley, Let No Man Put Asunder: The Control of Marriage in the German Southwest, A Comparative Study, 1550–1600, Sixteenth Century Essays & Studies, vol. 2 (Kirksville, Mo.: Sixteenth Century Journal Publishers, 1984), 28–38. See also Raymond A. Mentzer, "The Reformed Churches of France and Medieval Canon Law," in Canon Law in Protestant Lands, ed. Richard Helmholz (Berlin: Duncker & Humblot, 1992); E. William Monter, "The Consistory of Geneva, 1559–1569," in Renaissance, Reformation and Resurgence: Colloquium on Calvin and Calvin Studies, ed. P. DeKlerk (Grand Rapids, Mich: Calvin Theological Seminary, 1976), 63–84; Robert M. Kingdon, "The Control of Morals by the Earliest Calvinists," in Renaissance, Reformation and Resurgence, 95–106, along with the comments by Robert D. Linder and W. Fred Graham on these essays, respectively.

witnesses and relatives. The consistory was responsible for verifying that both spouses professed the reformed faith and that no impediments existed to the match.[21] The Reformed churches emphasized the importance of parental consent: minors ("les jeunes gens qui son[t] en bas aage," as stated in the discipline of 1571–72) needed their parents' permission to contract a marriage, and even individuals who were of age "nevertheless will do their fathers and mothers the honor of not contracting a marriage without first informing them of it."[22] Transgressors risked censure by the consistory, which could also intervene in cases where parents unreasonably opposed their children's marriages. The French Reformed churches' emphasis on parental consent, public celebration, and pastoral blessing clearly reflected the Protestants' view of marriage as an essential foundation for godly families and communities.

Despite their emphasis on the consistory's role in supervising the conduct of betrothal and marriage, the French Reformed churches also acknowledged the power of secular judges to determine a marriage's legality. The synod of Verteuil ordered that betrothed couples who disobeyed the consistory's advice and tried to separate should be sent to "the Civil Magistrate, who may, if he please, compel them to celebrate [the marriage]."[23] The advent of the religious wars further opened the way for "the civil magistrate" to intervene in such matters. The Edict of Beaulieu (1576) specifically gave royal magistrates jurisdiction over marriage disputes if the defendant (or both parties) were Calvinist. Disputes involving Catholic defendants would be settled by a Catholic ecclesiastical court (*officialité*).[24] Synodal decrees also urged the faithful to comply with royal edicts concerning marriage that, like the Reformed churches' disciplines, required parental consent and public ceremonies as conditions of a valid union.

The French Reformed churches' disciplines also addressed the problem of dissolving marriages among the faithful, and national synods pronounced upon such matters in the sixteenth and seventeenth centuries.[25] Consistories were supposed to

---

[21]For the synod of Verteuil, see Quick, *Synodican in Gallia Reformata*, 1:80–82; Voeltzel, "Le Droit matrimonial," 156–58. The text of the La Rochelle/Nîmes discipline appears in Glenn S. Sunshine, "French Protestantism on the Eve of St. Bartholomew: The Ecclesiastical Discipline of the French Reformed Churches, 1571–1572," *French History* 4:3 (1990): 340–77, esp. 371–73.

[22]Sunshine, "French Protestantism," 372 (art. 14), 371 (art. 1): [ceux qui sont en aage] feront neantmoins cest honneur a leurs peres et meres de ne contracter marriage sans leurs en communiquer premierement, et a faute de ce seront censurez au Concistoire.

[23]Quick, *Synodican in Gallia Reformata*, 1:82 (decree 4, art. 1).

[24]The text of the Edict of Beaulieu appears in Isambert et al., *Recueil général*, 14:283–84 (art. 10).

[25]Mentzer, "Reformed Churches of France," 179–81; Voeltzel, "Le Droit matrimonial," 171–77. See also Roderick Phillips, *Putting Asunder: A History of Divorce in Western Society* (Cambridge: Cambridge University Press, 1988).

implement the disciplines' articles on marriage and to mediate marital conflicts at the local level. As in the case of marriage formation, however, the Reformed churches acknowledged the authority of secular justice in disputes about such matters. Marriages could be dissolved on the grounds of adultery or abandonment, but a consistory could not grant the betrayed spouse permission to remarry until the grounds had been proven before a secular judge. As early as 1559, the Paris national synod declared that in cases where a Calvinist spouse had been convicted of adultery, "none of the Churches shall dissolve the marriage, lest they should intrench upon the Authority of the Civil Magistrate."[26] In 1565 another national synod warned consistories not to "intermeddle with the Execution of [a] Divorce and Dissolution of the Marriage...because it of right belongs unto the Civil Magistrate."[27] In 1637, a royal commissioner reiterated this principle when he reminded deputies at the synod of Alençon of the secular court's jurisidiction: "your Churches shall acquiesce in, and conform unto all Orders of the Civil Magistrate in this Particular, about the disannulling of marriages, and to take an especial care for the future, that this Default be repaired."[28]

Along with the Catholic and Reformed churches' rules, royal edicts decreed by the French crown during the sixteenth century constituted a third set of laws concerning marriage. The Edict of Blois, issued by Henry III in 1579, echoed some of the Council of Trent's provisions: couples were required to marry publicly, after the proclamation of banns and in the presence of four witnesses. According to the edict, however, the officiating priest was responsible for assuring that the spouses had obtained their parents' or guardians' consent—something that was not required in canon law. The edict also forbade notaries to authorize any exchange of vows that took place without public ceremony or parental consent, on pain of bodily punishment. Royal clerks were ordered to collect the parish records of marriages, births, and deaths annually, to swear to the truth of their contents, and to provide information from those records on request.[29]

Other royal decrees dealt with the problems of secret unions and second marriages. According to an edict issued in 1556, minor children—that is, women under the age of twenty-five and men under the age of thirty—who married without their parents' or guardians' consent were to be disinherited. Those who had advised or aided such clandestine marriages also risked punishment by royal

---

[26]Quick, *Synodican in Gallia Reformata*, 1:6 (art. 37).

[27]Quick, *Synodican in Gallia Reformata*, 1:65 (synod of Paris, art. 22).

[28]Quick, *Synodican in Gallia Reformata*, 2:326 (synod of Alençon, art. 7).

[29]The text of the Edict of Blois appears in Isambert et al., *Recueil général*, 14:380–463; esp. arts. 40, 44, 181. The ordinance of Villers Cotterêts (1536) required parish priests to keep records of births and deaths; see ibid., 13:610–11, arts. 50–56.

magistrates.[30] Clandestine pregnancies were similarly condemned: another ordinance from 1556 required pregnant women to have witnesses present at their deliveries, and a woman who concealed her pregnancy and gave birth in secret to a child who subsequently died was deemed guilty of infanticide.[31] The French crown also attempted to regulate second marriages in order to protect children and heirs whose inheritances were threatened or dissipated due to a parent's remarriage. Widows were forbidden to give goods acquired from their first husbands to their second husbands, and they could make only limited legacies to a second husband's family.[32] The Edict of Blois contained a similar provision aimed specifically at widows who married their servants: such women could neither sell nor donate their property, and any gifts, contracts, or sales that derived from their second marriages were declared null.[33]

The efforts of secular and religious authorities to regulate marriage resulted in rules and jurisdictions that often overlapped and sometimes conflicted. Royal edicts did not cover the sacramental or spiritual aspect of marriage, but royal judges could uphold or revoke a marriage's civil effects. Such judges could also impose penalties that were not available to episcopal courts or consistories, including disinheritance.[34] The French Reformed churches tried to regulate betrothal and marriage through their consistories, yet they acknowledged the authority of royal tribunals in such matters. On the other hand, the Catholic clergy protested the secular judiciary's intrusion into its jurisdiction. Responding to complaints by French clerics, Henry III issued an edict in 1580 that forbade royal judges to take over cases of disputed marriages pending before ecclesiastical courts. Yet the same edict ordered Catholic clerics to enforce the Edict of Blois's provisions against marriages made without parental consent, which were not invalid in canon law.[35] Henry IV would also forbid royal judges to interfere in ecclesiastical courts' proceedings unless the litigants themselves had filed an *appel comme d'abus* claiming that the church court had exceeded its jurisdiction.[36]

---

[30]Isambert et al., *Recueil général*, 14:469–71.

[31]Isambert et al., *Recueil général*, 14:471–73.

[32]Isambert et al., *Recueil général*, 14:36–37. Judgments by the Parlement of Paris show that these rules were enforced against widowers who remarried as well.

[33]Isambert et al., *Recueil général*, 14:423–24.

[34]Esmein, *Le Mariage*, 1:36–48; Pierre-Clément Timbal, "L'Esprit du droit privé au XVIIe siècle," *XVIIe siècle*, 58–59 (1963): 30–39.

[35]Isambert et al., *Recueil général*, 14:465–77 (edict of 1580).

[36]Isambert et al., *Recueil général*, 15:303–13 (edict of 1606). The *appel comme d'abus* originated in the fourteenth and fifteenth centuries but became fully established in French legal procedure during this period; see Albéric Allard, *Histoire de la justice criminelle*, 135–38; Doucet, *Les Institutions de la France*, 2:786, 789.

Situated within this profusion of laws, jurisdictions, and tribunals, the Paris Chambre de l'Edit derived its mandate to judge disputed marriages from the Edict of Nantes. Article 23 of the general edict required Huguenots to observe "the laws of the Catholic, Apostolic and Roman Church received in this our kingdom [les loix de l'Eglise catholique, apostolique et romaine, reçues en cettuy nôtre royaume]" regarding marriage and prohibited degrees of kinship. The phrasing was significant: it meant that Huguenots, like French Catholics, had to comply with those elements of canon law that had been endorsed by royal edicts, rather than with the Catholic Church's doctrines as such.[37] The secret articles signed at Nantes in May 1598 echoed the provisions of the Edict of Beaulieu thirty years earlier on the validity of marriages. Royal judges would hear cases involving Huguenot defendants or if both parties were Huguenots; only if the defendant were Catholic would the case be judged in a Catholic ecclesiastical court. Moreover, such cases could be appealed to the bipartisan chambers.[38] Huguenots who had married within prohibited degrees of kinship were not to be harassed, disinherited, or have their marriages annulled. Instead, they were ordered to present their cases to the king for resolution. Marriages involving priests and other religious were protected, although the spouses and their children could enjoy only limited rights of inheritance from their families.[39]

The Edict of Nantes also contained provisions regarding inheritance and disposition of property. Article 18 of the general edict, for example, forbade Huguenots and Catholics to force or induce the baptism, confirmation, or conversion of each other's children against their parents' will. Disinheriting one's relatives "solely out of hatred or concern for religion" was forbidden, and the edict outlawed all such disinheritances for the past and future. Finally, the secret articles upheld the validity of charitable gifts and legacies to Reformed ministers, students, or paupers despite any judicial decisions to the contrary.[40]

The Edict of Nantes's clauses, along with the laws and regulations issued by the monarchy earlier in the sixteenth century, thus formed the basis of many lawsuits brought before the Paris Chambre de l'Edit in the seventeenth century. Royal edicts overlapped and sometimes conflicted with the Catholic Church's and the French Reformed churches' decrees concerning marriage, especially on the question of parental consent as a condition of valid marriage. Although the chamber magistrates were no doubt aware of the religious authorities' rules, they were

[37]"Edict of Nantes," 45 (art. 23).

[38]"Edict of Nantes," 63 (Secret Articles, art. 41).

[39]"Edict of Nantes," 62–63 (Secret Articles, arts. 39, 40, 42).

[40]"Edict of Nantes," 45 (art. 18), 46 (art. 26), 52 (art. 62), 62–63 (Secret Articles, arts. 39, 40, 42).

required to enforce royal laws that regulated marriage and inheritance, upheld parental authority, and protected the interests of minor children—laws that applied to all French men and women.

Clandestine marriage and *rapt* were two crimes related to marriage formation that appeared regularly in the Chambre de l'Edit's records. According to royal decrees, clandestine marriages were those contracted secretly by minors without their family's approval; such unions were condemned repeatedly by the French crown and by royal magistrates during the sixteenth and seventeenth centuries. The French Reformed church likewise emphasized parental permission and public celebration as important elements of valid marriages among Protestants. Since the Council of Trent had upheld the spouses' consent as the foundation of a licit union, however, a clandestine marriage might be valid (though not desirable) in the eyes of Catholic authorities.

The crime of *rapt* was often related to the problem of clandestine marriage, and its changing definition illustrates how royal law courts gradually extended their jurisdiction into the area of marriage. *Rapt* originally referred to the forcible abduction of a woman to compel her to marry her captor. In some cases, the "abduction" could unite the woman willingly with her captor, allowing her to marry against her family's wishes. Despite this possible ambiguity, *rapt* was usually characterized by the use of force and the victim's displacement from her residence. According to the Council of Trent, *rapt* did not invalidate a marriage as long as the woman consented freely to the union after being released from her abductor's control.[41] During the sixteenth century, however, the French crown redefined this crime. The Edict of Blois (1579) condemned to death "those who were found to have suborned a minor son or a daughter...under pretext of marriage or other disguise, against the desire, knowledge, will, or express consent of [the son's or daughter's] fathers, mothers, and tutors." Anyone who counseled or abetted such marriages was to be punished, including priests who conducted the wedding ceremony, and the spouses' own consent or collusion was immaterial.[42] Thus from *rapt* by abduction sprang *rapt* by seduction—executed by enticement or persuasion rather than main force.

Though distinguishable in law, *rapt* and clandestine marriage were often linked in lawsuits about illicit marriages. *Rapt* involved the very methods (persuasion or

[41]Esmein, *Le Mariage*, 1:435–37, 2:279–86. See also Kathryn Gravdal, *Ravishing Maidens: Writing Rape in Medieval French Literature and Law* (Philadelphia: University of Pennsylvania Press, 1991), esp. 1–11; Mark Cummings, "Elopement, Family and the Courts: The Crime of *Rapt* in Early Modern France," *Proceedings of the Annual Meeting of the Western Society for French History* 4 (1976): 118–25; Hanley, "Engendering the State."

[42]Isambert et al., *Recueil général*, 14:391–92 (arts. 40, 42).

force) that might be used to contract a marriage secretly and without family approval. Parents and guardians used charges of *rapt* and clandestine marriage to thwart unions that they opposed, and royal magistrates often supported their efforts. According to one analysis of *rapt* cases heard by the parlements of Paris and Rouen in the seventeenth and eighteenth centuries, royal judges initially condemned marriages that resulted from *rapt de séduction* only when there were other circumstances that clearly invalidated the union. By the eighteenth century, however, *rapt* itself was sufficient cause for such decisions: it was presumed that the lack of parental consent caused the subornation.[43]

The tendency to connect and even conflate *rapt* with clandestine marriage (and to condemn both crimes) appears in cases heard before the Paris Chambre de l'Edit throughout the seventeenth century. In August 1602, for example, the court reviewed an appeal by royal councilor Antoine de La Planche concerning the clandestine marriage of his son Jerôme and Berthelemye Flé. The chamber magistrates nullified the couple's union and banished Flé from Paris for nine years, declaring her guilty of "having induced the said Jerôme [de La Planche] to pursue the said marriage by deceiving and without the consent of his father and for having abused the church's sacrament."[44] The court also meted out stiff punishments to those who had abetted the crime. Nicolas Garet, the notary who had supplied the marriage contract, was suspended from office for three months. Nicolas Fatin, the priest who had performed the wedding ceremony, was remanded to an ecclesiastical judge for further proceedings under the watchful eye of royal officials. Even Claude Gagnieres, a witness at the wedding, was fined fifty *écus* and banished for five years. As for Jerôme de La Planche, he was neither a coplaintiff with his father nor a codefendant with his wife. But he was sentenced to appear in court bareheaded and kneeling before his father to beg forgiveness for his defiance of parental authority.[45]

Parents who contested the legality of their children's marriages did not always receive favorable judgments from the Chambre de l'Edit. In June 1600, the court heard the appeal of Jehanne de La Palve, a widow who opposed her daughter Marie's marriage to René de Seillons. Having accused Seillons of *rapt*, La Palve found herself litigating against not only her daughter and son-in-law, but also

---

[43]Georges Pacilly, "Contribution à l'histoire de la théorie du rapt de séduction: Etude de jurisprudence," *Tijdschrift voor Rechtsgeschiedenis* 13 (1934): 306–18. See also Léon Duguit, "Etude historique sur le rapt de séduction," *Nouvelle revue historique du droit français et étranger* 10 (1886): 586–685.

[44]A.N. X2b 209, 31 August 1602: pour avoir induct ledict Hierosme a passe[r] oultre audict marriage au desceu et sans le consentement de son pere et avoir abuse du sacrament de l'eglise.

[45]A.N. X2b 206, 19 April 1602; X2b 209, 31 August 1602; the latter document contains the court's verdict.

Seillons's half-sister and her husband, the governor of Brest. Two of the chamber magistrates questioned Marie, perhaps to determine if she had willingly married a man her mother so adamantly rejected. But two months later, the court upheld the marriage by dismissing the case without costs.[46] François Arnaudeau, sieur de la Moriniere, and his wife accused Jean Favereau of *rapt*, but the presidial court at Poitiers rejected their claim; when they appealed to the Chambre de l'Edit, they lost their case again but escaped paying the costs of their appeal.[47] And after declaring Jeanne Azemart's marriage to Pierre Fizes invalid, the chamber magistrates commanded Azemart's parents, two brothers, a priest, and a notary to appear before the local magistrate at Montpellier for further questioning about how the marriage had been contracted.[48]

In some cases, the Chambre de l'Edit's decisions dealt with disputes about a marriage's legality by forcing the matter back upon the spouses and their families. For example, widow Jeanne Houssaye petitioned the court in 1660 to abolish the clandestine marriage that had united her daughter Marie Huberson (also a widow) with Jacques Veron, *portmanteau du Roy*. The judges agreed that the union was "invalidly contracted and celebrated" [non vallablement contracté et celle-bré]—and then ordered a new, legal celebration of the wedding after the spouses and their families had come to terms.[49] When widow Jeanne Savary accused Michel Le Gal, sieur de La Porte, of *rapt* against her daughter Jeanne Le Texier, the court ordered him to pay Le Texier ten thousand *livres* to help her marry, unless he wished to marry her himself. Le Gal could thus acknowledge his union with Le Texier by marrying her legally, or his financial penalty would make it possible for her to marry someone else. Either way, it seems the court was intent on providing Jeanne Le Texier with a legal, valid marriage.[50] The chamber magistrates handled the dispute between Jean Pierre, sieur de la Rochberanger, and damoiselle Marie Carré in a similar fashion. The daughter of a Reformed minister, Carré had accused Pierre of *rapt*. After being found guilty by the royal judge at Chatellerault, Pierre appealed to the Chambre de l'Edit. The Paris court sentenced Pierre to pay Carré four thousand *livres tournois* in damages unless he preferred to marry her

---

[46]A.N. X2b 195, 16 June 1600. See also X2b 195, 22 June 1600; X2b 196, 2 August 1600, contains the court's verdict.

[47]A.N. X2b 630, 31 July 1660.

[48]A.N. X1b 4397, 8 August 1654.

[49]A.N. X2b 626, 21 April 1660: "[La cour] declare le marriage dont est question non valablement contracte et cellebre et en consequence ordonne qu'il sera procedde a nouvelle celebration dudit marriage et les conventions prealablement reglees entre les parties et leurs parans."

[50]A.N. X2b 316, 29 January 1620. Six months later, Savary again appealed to the court; she charged Le Gal with violent conduct toward her daughter, who had in fact married someone else: X2b 319, 26 June 1620.

himself.[51] In each case, the court's ruling allowed for the accusation of *rapt* to result in a valid marriage, provided that the spouses and their families made the appropriate arrangements.

Accusations of *rapt* and clandestine marriage might also allow families to litigate about other matters, such as inheritance. When Jean Palisson, sieur de La Vau, and his wife Renée Donault brought their dispute with Renée's father before the Chambre de l'Edit in 1600, Renée's age at the time of her marriage seemed to be the key issue. François de Donault, sieur de La Tour de Rancay, accused Palisson of *rapt*, claiming that his daughter had been only twenty years old when she married and therefore a minor who needed his permission to marry legally. Renée and her husband insisted that she was twenty-five at the time (the legal age of majority) and could marry as she wished. Moreover, their union had been anything but secret: it was properly publicized and approved by other relatives. Since Donault had not accused Palisson of *rapt* until a year after the couple's wedding (and following the birth of their first child), their lawyer offered a different motive for the charges. He suggested that Donault's second wife had provoked the lawsuit to get Renée disinherited, which was the required penalty for minor children who married without their family's consent. Noting that the question of Renée's age and status as a minor could be settled by referring to her baptism record, her parents' marriage contract, and the testimony of other living relatives, the Chambre de l'Edit remanded the case to local judges for a final decision.[52]

The chamber's verdicts in cases of *rapt* and clandestine marriage were not just about enforcing royal decrees. This litigation also reveals the concerns about the social and moral consequences of illicit unions. Such concerns formed the context of the laws themselves and were shared by families and royal officials, especially when the situation involved an illustrious individual. After learning of Gaspard de Coligny's secret agreement to marry Henriette Mortier, Coligny's mother Marguerite Dailly and other relatives sued Mortier, her parents, and Coligny himself in 1615. Coligny is described as being about thirty years old and thus legally of

[51]A.N. XIb 4397, 11 August 1651. Interpreting the spouses' intentions in this case is especially complicated. Since Pierre appealed his case to the Chambre de l'Edit, it seems that he wished to avoid being (or becoming) Carré's husband. Yet Carré had made the initial complaint of *rapt;* she may have wanted to force him to marry her, or she may have wanted their union dissolved. Pierre's appeal to the Paris court was a financial mistake: the Chatellerault judge had only sentenced him to marry Carré and pay the costs of the proceedings, but the Chambre de l'Edit imposed a payment of two hundred *livres tournois* in alms as well as the four thousand *livres* for Carré and costs. The *arrêt* does not record whether he married Carré or paid the penalties that the court required.

[52]A.N. X2b 194, 17 March 1600. The chamber judges remanded the case to the *bailli* of Berry or his lieutenant at Bourges. It had been appealed from a judge at Issoudun, who Palisson's lawyer claimed was in league with Donault and his second wife.

age to wed without parental consent. But in assessing the case, royal advocate Louis Servin emphasized "the inequality between the said Henriette Mortier and the person and quality of the said Coligny [l'inégalité de ladite Henriette Mortier à la personne et qualité dud(it) de Coligny]." "The state and the public have an interest," he declared, in protecting Coligny from the "blandishments, attachments, and distraction" which Henriette Mortier apparently represented, and which threatened to make Coligny "distance himself from the counsel of his mother and relatives...to enter into any unequal marriage against their will."[53] The chamber judges agreed: they declared the union invalid, ordered the marriage contract delivered to Dailly, and forbade the couple to see each other in future.

A case from 1605 involving reciprocal charges of *rapt* further illustrates the court's tendency to condemn marriages that were socially unsuitable as well as illegal. Gabriel Durant, a *procureur* in the Parlement of Paris, accused Henri Bullion of finagling his daughter Marguerite into a secret wedding.[54] Bullion's mother, Charlotte Lamoignon, responded by bringing a countersuit naming Marguerite and her parents as the guilty parties. Arguing before the chamber magistrates, Louis Servin outlined the reasons for abolishing the marriage. Both Henri and Marguerite were minors who could not marry without their families' consent, despite their written vows of betrothal. The wedding ceremony had been conducted by a priest who had already run afoul of the authorities for his involvement in clandestine marriages. It had also taken place in a parish where neither the spouses nor their families resided, and with none of the public solemnities that the Tridentine and royal decrees required.

Servin noted, however, that social inequality was also an important reason for the Chambre de l'Edit to abolish this union. Henri Bullion and his mother were members of an eminent and honorable family, "above [the status of Gabriel] Durant, who has never been of any note."[55] The chamber judges would surely have known this already: Henri's father and maternal grandfather had both been royal magistrates, and his brother received a commission in the parlement's Chamber of Requests the very year this case was being heard. The Durants, however, were a disorderly and even disreputable family. Just prior to Marguerite's downfall, her father had been accused of forgery and suspended for two years from his office of

[53]A.N. X2b 286, 7 February 1615: l'estat et le public a interest de conserver [Coligny] et empescher que par quelques blandices, attachemens et abstraction d'espire ledict de Coligny se peust esloigner du conseil de sa Mere et parens en aulcune facon...pour entrer aulcun marriage inegal et conre le[ur] volonte.

[54] A.N. X2b 226, 19 July 1605.

[55]A.N. X2b 226, 19 July 1605: les parents de Bullion sont de condition eminente par dessus celle de Durant quand mesmes il n'auroit jamais eu aulcune note.

procureur. The Durants had also failed to supervise their daughter properly. "Whether by negligence or otherwise," Servin stated, "some of the fault lay with Marguerite Durant's father and especially her mother, who did not close the door or keep the keys as they should have done; this carelessness gave rise to the evil that occurred, for the daughter left her parents' house nightly."[56] Madame Durant had claimed that after finding the couple together in her home, she had cried out that marriage alone could restore Marguerite's honor—a proposition that Henri Bullion had accepted. Such protests did not impress the royal attorney: instead of dealing with the young man herself, she should have gone to the proper authorities immediately with a formal accusation of *rapt.* "I do not know what to make of this reticence," he noted severely, "which can lend a bad interpretation to the mother's actions in not doing what she could by invoking public authority."[57] At best, the Durants had been morally lax; at worst, they had deliberately contrived to bring about Marguerite's illegal union with Henri. Most of all, they had failed to remedy their daughter's unfortunate situation by "invoking public authority," that is, the law that made the marriage invalid and the judges who would enforce it.

Servin's arguments in this case highlight the connection between rapt and clandestine marriage, as well as the state's interest in prosecuting such crimes. He declared that the lawsuits involved "on the one side, an alleged *rapt* of a girl under the authority of her father and mother, [and] on the other, the clandestine union of the son of an honorable house, by deception of his mother and relatives, with a girl of lesser status."[58] His comments about the Durant family's "authority" over Marguerite implied that their misconduct outweighed Henri's deception. Yet in an unusual reference to judicial precedent, Servin recommended that Henri Bullion formally apologize to his mother before the court, just as Jerôme de La Planche had been ordered to do three years earlier. The court's verdict did not include that penalty, but the judges did nullify the marriage and forbade any further contact between Henri and Marguerite. In doing so, the Chambre de l'Edit effectively restored the social distance that should have existed between the son of a prominent robe family and the daughter of an insignificant lawyer.

---

[56]A.N. X2b 226, 19 July 1605: [il] y a de la faulte ou par negligence ou aultrement du coste du pere et principallement de la mere de Marguerite Durant car la maison estoit ouverte les pere et mere n'aiants faict fermer les portes ne pris les clefs devers eulx comme ils debvoient, ce manquement de soing a donne occasion au mal qui s'est faict par ce que la fille est sortie nuictamment.

[57]A.N. X2b 226, 19 July 1605: Je ne scay quelle odeur de ceste taciturnite qui peult faire mal interpreter ce qu'a faict la mere en ne faisant pas ce qu'elle pouvoit par invoquer le droict public.

[58]A.N. X2b 226, 19 July 1605: d'un coste un pretendu rapt d'une fille estant en puissance de pere et mere, de l'autre la conjonction clandestine d'un fils d'honneste maison au desceu de sa mere et de ses parents avec fille de moindre lieu.

For the royal advocate, *rapt* and clandestine marriage as revealed in this case reflected a lack of morality in society itself. "These unions are frequent in our era," Servin declared, "in which the corruption of morals has brought such great license that under the holy name of marriage such copulations take place between many persons of all ages."[59] Other lawyers and royal officials echoed his complaint in cases heard by the Chambre de l'Edit later in the century. Arguing before the court in 1635, a lawyer for Marie de Billy claimed that her opponent, Hierosme Puchot, sieur de Doinville, "should be condemned more severely than by an order of *contumace* since his crime [*rapt*] is frequent and often committed."[60] Royal advocate Jérôme Bignon agreed. Noting that technically *rapt* was punishable by death, he stated that "the accused should not benefit from the mercy which the court has shown, hoping to have the sum of forty thousand *livres* modified...which the court does on occasion so that by an excessive condemnation the person chooses marriage rather than pay the penalty."[61] In another case from the same year, a tax collector named Charles Payn complained that Patrix du Feu, also a local tax collector at Saint Florentin, had deceived and insulted his family. After contracting a marriage with Payn's daughter, du Feu had wed another woman in Paris. Yet Feu had written to Payn's daughter "as if he were not married, visited [Payn] as his father-in-law and [Payn's] daughter as his mistress, remaining a year at [Payn's] house." Du Feu's servants and friends were also fed and made welcome, until news of the Paris marriage made du Feu acknowledge his misconduct.[62] The royal advocate rejected as frivolous (*frivole*) du Feu's excuse that his union with Payn's daughter was invalid because she had never signed the marriage contract. "The law," Bignon declared, "establishes a penalty against those who do not honor betrothal...this was an obligatory contract." Following Bignon's recommendations, the chamber judges

---

[59]A.N. X2b 226, 19 July 1605: ces conjonctions sont frequentes en notre siecle ou la corruption des moeurs a apporte sy grande licence que soubs le sainct nom du Mariage telles copulations se font entre plussieurs personnes de toutes sortes d'aages.

[60]A.N. X2b 424, 6 June 1635: il doibt estre condemne plus hardiement que par l'arrest de contumace d'aultant plus que ce crime [rapt] est frequent et se commet souvent. Puchot apparently had not appeared to answer the charges, hence the threat of punishment for *contumace*.

[61]A.N. X2b 424, 6 June 1635: qu'il y ayt condemne de mort ainsy qu'il est accoustume, l'accuse ne doibt tirer a son adventage la douceur dont la court a use, esperant faire modifier la somme de querente mil livres...ce qu la court fait quelques fois affin que par l'exceds de la condemnation l'on face choix du marriage plustost que de payer la peyne. Despite Bignon's comments, the court released Puchot.

[62]A.N. X2b 424, 15 June 1635: "ensuitte de son Mariage escript des letters comme s'il n'eust este marie, visite l'appellant [Payn] comme son beaupere et sa fille comme sa maitresse, luy l'avoyt demeure un an en la maison de l'appellant noury et son lacquais et tous ceulx qui venoient de sa part les bienvenus ete depuis l'advis de son Mariage escript...et Recogneu sa faulte."

sentenced du Feu to pay six hundred *livres* in costs and damages, plus a donation of eighty *livres* for the Conciergerie prisoners' bread.[63]

Another aspect of the social disorder and immorality associated with *rapt* and clandestine marriage concerned the gender roles of those involved in such crimes. In *rapt* by abduction, women were usually the victims and sometimes the accomplices of men, but *rapt* by seduction could be committed by persons of either sex. Indeed, several cases heard by the Chambre de l'Edit featured women as accused perpetrators: Berthelemye Flé, Marguerite Durant, and Henriette Mortier were all portrayed by royal attorney Louis Servin as responsible for entangling their male victims in illicit marriages. A young Dutchman complained of similar female aggression before the court in 1649. Jean Vescure, who described himself as aged fifteen or sixteen, had been apprenticed to a merchant in Nantes named Domer. He argued that Anne Rutvelt, aged twenty-eight, and her widowed mother Cornelis Andrix had used both force and deceit to obtain his signature on a marriage contract. He stated that the two women,

> abusing his young age, simplicity and feebleness of mind, suborned him and attracted him to their lodging, where with force and violence they kept him for several days in a room, without the said Domer being able to discover where he was.[64]

Rutvelt and Andrix had denounced Vescure to a local magistrate, claiming that he had gotten Rutvelt pregnant. With the help of two *huissiers* (who threatened to kill him if he resisted), they forced Vescure to sign several documents that he allegedly did not understand because of his youth and his unfamiliarity with the French language. Vescure portrayed both women as "disreputable persons of no consequence who barely gain their living by selling beer and housing the captains of foreign ships," describing Rutvelt as a prostitute who had seduced several other young men.[65] In this case, however, the Chambre de l'Edit rejected the story of scheming women who had brought about a young man's downfall with a secret, unsuitable

[63]A.N. X2b 424, 15 June 1635: la loy establit une peyne contre ceulx qui ne tiennent les fiansailles.... C'estoit un contract obligatoire.

[64]A.N. XIb 4397, 12 May 1649: abusans de son bas aage simplicite et foiblesse d'esprit l'auroient suborne et attire a leur logis ou de force et violence ils l'auroient retenu quelques jours en une chambre sans que ledict Domer pust descouvrir ou il estoit.

[65]A.N. XIb 4397, 12 May 1649: "personnes mal notes et sans naissance qui gaignent a peine leur vie a vendre biere et a loger des maistres des navires estrangers...[elles] auroient suborne plusieurs autres heunes homes, ladicte fille estant de tres mauvaise vie et s'estant prostituee a plusieurs hommes et garcons."

marriage. The magistrates sentenced Vescure to pay Rutvelt 3000 *livres* to help her marry, 2700 *livres* to support her child, and another 400 *livres* in alms.[66]

Cases of *rapt* and clandestine marriage illustrate the Chambre de l'Edit's efforts to enforce royal ordinances that prohibited such unions, as well as to remedy the social disorders associated with illicit marriages. Accusations of *rapt* might reveal connivance and subornation of minors; on the other hand, spouses or their relatives might use such charges to attack a valid marriage. When adjudicating this kind of family dispute, the chamber magistrates acted to abolish illegal unions and punish the parties involved, but they also sought to protect those who had not broken the law. In doing so, the court not only enforced the relevant laws, but also acknowledged a "public interest" in preserving social and familial order.

The Chambre de l'Edit occasionally received requests to dissolve marriages without reference to the crimes of *rapt* or clandestine marriage. The magistrates could not pronounce on the sacramental or spiritual aspect of a union, but they could invalidate its civil effects. In 1648, damoiselle Marie d'Hertoghe d'Orsmael requested that the court dissolve her marriage to Hermant de Riperda, which had taken place a year earlier, by declaring it to be "null and invalidly contracted" [nul et non valablement contracté]. After questioning Marie and hearing the royal prosecutor's comments, the court granted her petition. Riperda was forbidden "to call himself her husband in future nor to attack her person and goods" and was condemned to costs and damages.[67]

The Chambre de l'Edit received a unique request to dissolve a marriage in November 1602, when Marthe Ranart appealed to have her union with Claude Pallier, sieur de Nitras, abolished on the grounds of impotence. Both canon law and Reformed disciplines recognized impotence as grounds for invalidating a marriage, but judges sometimes invoked an unusual mode of proof in such cases: the *essai de congrès*, in which a husband demonstrated his sexual capacity with his wife in the presence of witnesses.[68] The seneschal of Angoulême had ordered Pallier and

---

[66]A.N. XIb 4397, 9 April 1650. The document indicates that Jean Vescure's father Pierre, "marchand [h]olondais demeurant a Roterdam," had also tried to sue Rutvelt and Andrix for *rapt de séduction*. He was condemned to pay his share of the costs of the proceedings: see A.N. XIb 4397, 19 January 1650.

[67]A.N. XIb 4397, 7 September 1648: [La cour] faict deffences aud[it] de Riperda de se dire a l'advenir mary de lad[ite] d'Hertoghe ny atanter a sa personne et biens.

[68]On the *essai de congrès*, see Pierre Darmon *Damning the Innocent: A History of the Persecution of the Impotent in Pre-Revolutionary France*, trans. Paul Keegan (New York: Viking, 1986), 186–209; Wendy Gibson, *Women in Seventeenth-Century France* (New York: St. Martin's Press, 1989), 87. This procedure apparently had no clear basis in civil or canon law; according to jurist Pierre Guyot, it originated in the bishops' courts in the mid-sixteenth century and became part of French jurisprudence despite

Ranart to undergo this procedure in 1601, a decision which the Chambre de l'Edit confirmed a year later. Pallier refused to comply, however, and demanded a final judgment of the case. He and Ranart were summoned to Paris to satisfy the court's order, but he apparently failed the test: in January 1603, the Chambre de l'Edit annulled his marriage to Ranart and condemned him to return the 2000 *écus* he had received from her parents, as well as the clothes and jewelry she had brought to the marriage. Pallier was also assessed 4000 *livres* in damages plus legal costs. Finally, the court forbade him ever to marry again, while explicitly permitting Ranart to do so.[69]

Along with complaints about illegal marriage formation and petitions for marriage dissolution, the Chambre de l'Edit heard appeals for marital separations. By the seventeenth century, secular as well as ecclesiastical judges could award separations of person and property *(séparation de corps et biens)*. These could be obtained on the grounds of adultery, extreme hatred, and violent abuse that endangered a spouse's life or made cohabitation impossible. If awarded, such separations released couples from sharing households and conjugal duties, but neither spouse could legally marry someone else. A *separation de biens* alone dealt with a married couple's property and was usually occasioned by a husband's mismanagement of his wife's assets or his inability to support her. A wife who obtained this kind of separation might receive possession or use of the goods she had brought to the marriage and a share of the couple's community property.[70]

The Chambre de l'Edit reviewed appeals for marital separations, in some cases from wives who sought protection from both their husbands and the local courts. Olimpe de Lusignan, dame de Lespart, presented such an appeal in September 1649. Her husband, Antoine de Moulouzy, had refused to support her financially for the past two years. After he threatened her life, she took refuge with a relative and petitioned the court for a separation that would allow her access to revenues from the property she had brought to the marriage ten years earlier. Fearing her husband's influence with the local judges, Lusignan requested that the

---

the fact that it was "contraire à l'honnêteté et aux bonnes moeurs"; Pierre Guyot, *Répertoire universel et raisonné de jurisprudence* (Paris: Chez Visse, 1784), 4:471. Another jurist described it as a deplorable practice "qui offense les bonnes moeurs, le Religion, la Justice, et la nature même"; Ferrière, *Dictionnaire de droit et de pratique,* 1:362.

[69]A.N. X2b 211, 20 January 1603. See also X2b 210, 28 November 1602; X2b 211, 15 January 1603. Ranart was proceeding with the authority of her guardian, a *procureur* at Angoulême named Jacques Girard.

[70]Gaudemet, *Le Mariage en occident,* 244–63; Gibson, *Women in Seventeenth-Century France,* 85–87; Hanley, "Engendering the State."

chamber magistrates remand her case to the nearest royal judge; the court complied.[71] Philippes de Liscous likewise appealed to the Chambre de l'Edit to intervene in her lawsuit against her husband, Gabriel de Briqueville, marquis de Coulombieres. Liscous claimed that he had beaten her and planned to thwart her petition for a *séparation de biens* by intimidating witnesses. As a Protestant, Liscous could not use a *monitoire* (a public request for information about a crime, delivered by Catholic priests to their parishioners) to solicit testimony for her case. The chamber magistrates agreed to have the local royal prosecutor issue the *monitoire* on her behalf. Ironically, the court received a similar petition from Bricqueville himself a month later. According to him, it was Liscous and her relatives who threatened to prevent witnesses from telling the truth, or indeed from testifying at all, because of their influence in the region. The Chambre de l'Edit awarded Bricqueville (who was also Protestant) a *monitoire* under the royal prosecutor's name to pursue his case.[72]

In other cases, the chamber magistrates' task was to review previous judgments about marital separations. Suzanne Le Sueur had sought a *séparation de biens* from husband Jean de La Rue, *bailli* of Boulogne. The seneschal of Boulognais had dismissed the case in April 1604, ordering her to return immediately to her husband with the goods she had taken at her departure; La Rue was also ordered to treat his wife maritally. Four months later, the Chambre de l'Edit reviewed Le Sueur's appeal of this verdict, but she declared that she no longer wanted the separation. The court confirmed the original sentence and dismissed her suit without costs.[73] Daniel Imbert brought a different complaint about his wife's *séparation de corps et biens* before the court in June 1601. Noting that a royal judge at Poitiers had awarded Suzanne Arribat the separation without trying to make her reconsider, Imbert petitioned the Chambre de l'Edit to have her "sequestered in an honorable house and with a respectable woman to make her submit to her duty" [sequestrée en Maison honorable et avec femme d'honneur pour la Reduire à son debvoir]. Arribat's lawyer, however, countered that Imbert had already agreed to the separation, and that Arribat had had good reason to request it. The royal prosecutor neatly summarized the issues raised by Imbert's appeal: "[Imbert] complains that his wife is frequently with an adult girl who is accused of sorcery and

---

[71]A.N. XIb 4397, 7 September 1649.

[72]A.N. X2b 630, 30 July 1660 (petition from Liscous); X2b 631, 18 August 1660 (petition from Bricqueville). Liscous complained of "exceds, violences et voyes de fait commises en sa personne" by her husband. Bricqueville argued that "ladite de Liscous qui est puissante dans la province de Bretagne peut par ses menaces et ses parens Intimider les tesmoins qui peuvent deposer en l'information qu'il entend faire et par ce moyen les empescher de dire la verite mesme de deposer."

[73]A.N. X2b 220, 9 August 1604.

in whose home there is some loose living...it appears that [Imbert and Arribat] should not dwell together at this time, but the judges [at Poitiers] should not have decided this so much in advance as they did." The Chambre de l'Edit thus confirmed Arribat's separation but enjoined her "to withdraw to her house in Poitiers and live there according to her status in all modesty." The court also forbade Imbert to attack her in any way.[74]

Lawsuits concerning marital separations often gave rise to disputes about financial support, child custody, and insults to family honor. Catherine Febvrier's litigation against her husband Gilles de Chassy, sieur de Marant, began with her demand for a *séparation de corps et biens* before a local judge in 1602. Over the next six years, it mushroomed to include an appeal to the Chambre de l'Edit (in 1604), wrangling over Chassy's payment of pensions for his wife and children, and a custody battle. The parties also traded serious insults: Chassy accused his wife of adultery, while his sister Louise (who had joined his lawsuit) sued Febvrier for defamation, claiming that Febvrier had spread a rumor of incest between her and her brother. When the chamber judges delivered their verdict in February 1608, the case involved five separate legal actions. The court approved Febvrier's separation, ordering Chassy to pay her an annual pension of 2560 *livres* in quarterly installments. The couple's children would remain with their father, but the court commanded Chassy to allow Febvrier to see them whenever she wished.[75] The court also authorized Febvrier to pursue further legal proceedings without her husband's consent; she appears in the Chambre de l'Edit's records for January 1615, suing Louise de Chassy.[76] In a case from 1654, Magdelaine Merlat petitioned the chamber magistrates to maintain her status as *femme séparée de corps et biens* from Samuel Robert while increasing her financial settlement. Specifically, she demanded an annual pension of 1000 *livres* to support her, her daughters, and a female servant at a convent in Rainthes. Four years earlier, the presidial court there had sentenced Robert to pay her 400 *livres* a year after hearing the case, but apparently neither party was satisfied with that decision. Merlat continued to complain of the "abuse and ill treatment" [sevices et mauvaises traitemens] she had suffered, while Robert denied the charges and insisted that the court order his wife to

---

[74]A.N. X2b 201, 22 June 1601: l'appellant [Imbert] se plainct de ce que sa femme est ordinairement avec une fille de grand aage qu'on acuse de magye et en la maison de laquelle il y a quelque liberte de vye...il y a grande apparence qu'ils ne doibvent pour ceste heure demeurer ensemble Mais que les juges ne doibvent juger en si avant comme ils ont faict.

[75]A.N. X2b 240, 15 February 1608. For other documents related to the case, see X2b 217, 12 January 1604 and 10 February 1604; X2b 220, 3 August 1604; X2b 226, 11 August 1605; X2b 233, 11 December 1606.

[76]A.N. X2b 286, 9 January 1615.

return to her marital duties. After hearing the appeal, the Chambre de l'Edit ordered Merlat to be sequestered in the home of a Catholic relative, where Robert could visit her. He was to pay her 200 *livres* annually while a local judge investigated her accusations of abuse.[77]

The court also dealt with cases of marital discord that were not explicitly appeals for marital separations or dissolutions. Antoine Phelippes, sieur d'Espinay, tried to sue his wife Marguerite Le Jeune for adultery with Girard de Mannoury in 1617. But Le Jeune's lawyer protested that Phelippes had already been convicted of trying to kill her; the adultery charge was simply a legal ploy to evade his sentence of banishment, reparations, and fines. Royal prosecutor Cardin Le Bret argued that there was "great intimacy and familiarity" between Le Jeune and Mannoury, "more than shame, good morals and public honesty permitted." Yet this did not outweigh Phelippes's criminal conviction. The Chambre de l'Edit therefore ordered the royal prosecutor to take up the dispute about Le Jeune's alleged misconduct, effectively representing the husband's interests before the court.[78] In 1630, Guy de Salins, sieur de Nocle, appealed to the chamber magistrates to curb the "disobedience and rebellion" [desobeissances et rebellions] of his wife, Charlotte de Saint Gelais. According to Salins, she was conspiring with a suspected thief named Gadoulliere to kill him. Her legal maneuvers were equally alarming: at her request, the royal council had issued an *arrêt* against him. The Chambre de l'Edit agreed to submit "treshumbles remonstrances" to the king about the council's intervention in the case, and the court forbade any attacks against Salins's person or property.[79]

Wives were not the only ones accused of violent misconduct in such cases. When Abraham Barbier appealed his conviction by a seigneurial judge, the chamber judges reviewed a detailed account of his offenses against his wife, Suzanne Loyseau:

> Since his marriage with the said Loyseau [in June 1659], he daily [has] led Soldiers to his house to eat and drink at his expense, and by this means Dissipated the better part of his goods; sworn and blasphemed the holy name of God; spoken insulting words against the

[77]A.N. XIb 4397, 2 February 1654. Samuel Robert is identified as *lieutenant particulier* at Rainthes.

[78]A.N. X2b 297, 18 January 1617. Le Bret stated that "il y a lumiere de grandes privaulte et familiarite entre les appellants [Le Jeune and Mannoury] et plus que la pudeur Bonnes Moeurs et l'honnestete publicque ne permettoit." The court later ordered "que le procureur general demeurera seul partye" against the appellants, instead of acting jointly with Le Jeune's husband.

[79]A.N. X2b 389, 17 June 1630; there are two entries concerning Salins's case for this date.

honor and chastity of his wife, beaten her, and notably on 15 September 1659...threatened to sell her into prostitution, even to attack her life, and to this effect discharged three pistols and prepared to carry out his plan with his drawn sword.[80]

The fact that Barbier had also threatened to kill two local officials may explain his speedy conviction, just twelve days after the incident on 15 September. Barbier had been sentenced to nine years' banishment and a fine of ninety *livres,* while Suzanne Loyseau had received a *separation de corps et biens* which included the return of clothes, linens, furnishings, jewelry, and money as specified in her marriage contract. After questioning Barbier in Loyseau's presence, the Chambre de l'Edit rejected his appeal and ordered the original sentence carried out.[81] Barbier's abusive conduct was clearly a threat to public order, for it involved blasphemy and wastefulness as well as violence toward his wife. Indeed, it represented the mirror image of the type of marriage secular and religious authorities sought to promote and the law required as the basis of an orderly society.

As in cases of *rapt* and clandestine marriage, appeals for marital separations and complaints of violent discord between spouses reveal the centrality of marriage in family relations and social order. Regulating marriage meant not only establishing distinctions between legal and illicit unions, but also defining standards of conduct between husbands and wives. The Chambre de l'Edit, like other royal law courts, enforced the French crown's decrees on such matters, though such laws existed within a much larger context of regulations issued by Catholic and Reformed authorities, moralists' writings, and other depictions of family relationships. Faced with a wide variety of marital misconduct, the court dissolved some marriages while confirming others; the magistrates separated couples endangered by violence and prodigality while insisting that others attempt to resolve their conflicts. In turn, spouses and family members appealed to the court to resolve family conflicts over marriage or for protection from abusive spouses. In doing so, family members often had to reveal details of their family life for the

---

[80]A.N. X2b 630, 31 July 1660: depuis son marriage avecq ladite Loyseau [avait] mene et conduict journellement des cavaliers en sa maison boire et manger a ses depens et par ce moyen dissipe le meilleure partie de ses biens jure et blaspheme le sainct nom de dieu profferee des paroles injurieuses contre l'honneur et la chastete de ladite Loyseau sa femme, icelle battue et excedde a coups de baston, et notamment le 15 septembre audit an [1659]...l'avoit menasse de la vendre et livrer en prostitution mesme d'attenter a sa vie et a cet effet charge trios pistollets et avecq son espee nue s'estre mis en estat d'executer son dessein. At the time of Barbier's appeal to the Chambre de l'Edit, in 1660, Loyseau was joined by the local seigneur: Cesar d'Estrée, bishop of Laon and abbot of Saint Nicolas au Bois.

[81]A.N. X2b 630, 31 July 1660.

judges' scrutiny. For litigants as for magistrates, family discord over marriage threatened social order, and unlike Marguerite Durant's mother, many were willing to invoke the "public authority" of a royal law court in such matters. The Chambre de l'Edit's efforts to enforce legal marriages, abolish illicit unions, and punish violent spouses reflect both the importance and fragility of marriage in early modern France.

Disputes about the material and moral welfare of children also sparked lawsuits heard by the Chambre de l'Edit in which the conduct of parents and guardians was at issue. Parental authority was seen as a key feature of stable family life and an orderly society by Catholics and Protestants alike, and the views of moralists were reinforced by royal edicts which, as we have seen, made parental approval a condition of legal marriage. Despite an ideology of family relations that emphasized the authority of parents over children, conflicts between parents and children were hardly unknown. Indeed, Jonathan Dewald has suggested that during the seventeenth century, such conflicts raised serious questions about the value of both patriarchy and lineage as ideals of family relations.[82] In the absence of parents, guardians might have extensive control of a minor child's affairs. French law defined two kinds of guardianship: *tutelle*, which conferred responsibility for the ward's person, and *curatelle*, which involved managing the ward's property. An individual's family circumstances, as well as regional customs, might influence how guardians were chosen, and the distinction between *tutelle* and *curatelle* might become blurred if the same person served in both capacities.[83] A guardian's control over a ward's person, property, education, and marriage could provoke disputes among other family members, resulting in litigation. In some cases, the Chambre de l'Edit acted to protect the interests of minors whose guardians or parents acted illegally; in other instances, the court sought to enforce the child's or ward's obedience to family authority.

[82]Jonathan Dewald, "Deadly Parents: Family and Aristocratic Culture in Early Modern France," in *Culture and Identity in Early Modern Europe*, 223–36. See also Diefendorf, "Give Us Back Our Children," 265–307. On sixteenth-century Protestant views of parental authority, see Janine Garrisson, *Les Protestants au XVIe siècle* (Paris: Fayard, 1988), 88–89, 105–6.

[83]Jean Domat, "Traité des lois," in *Les Lois civiles dans leur ordre naturel* (Paris, 1777), 173–95; Antoine Loisel, *Institutes coutumières*, ed. André-Marie-Jean-Jacques Dupin and Edouard Laboulaye (Paris, 1846; repr. Geneva: Slatkine, 1971), 207–11; Brissaud, *History of French Private Law*, 235–50; Paul Viollet, *Histoire du droit civil français* (Paris: L. Larose et Forcel, 1893), 534–51; Paul Ourliac and Jean-Louis Gazzaniga, *Histoire du droit privé français: De l'an mil au Code Civil* (Paris: Albin Michel, 1985), 281–82; François Olivier-Martin, *La Coûtume de Paris: Traité d'union entre le droit romain et les legislations modernes* (Paris: Recueil Sirey, 1925), 34–37; Furetière, *Dictionnaire universel*, s.v. "Tutelle," "Tuteur, Tutrice," and "Curateur."

Rivalries and disagreements between guardians and other family members often revolved around a ward's marriage. The lawsuit between François de Vouhet, sieur de Villeneuve, and Jacques Desguilly, sieur de Chassy, illustrates this pattern. Desguilly and his wife were the guardians of eleven-year-old Marguerite de Bussieres and her sister Barbe. Desguilly had arranged for Marguerite to marry one of his wife's cousins, a boy who was also ten or twelve years old. Vouhet, who was the children's maternal uncle, opposed the marriage on the grounds that the intended spouses were too young. (An additional objection might have been that the match would allow Desguilly to keep Marguerite's property firmly tied to his own family's holdings, though this is not explicitly stated in the *arrêt*). Despite a judicial injunction against the union, Desguilly had allegedly summoned a priest to his home where, without any prior announcement or the approval of other family members, he had supervised Marguerite's wedding. Vouhet thus argued that Desguilly had committed *rapt* and abetted a clandestine marriage; he demanded that the union be dissolved and that Desguilly pay six thousand *écus* in reparations. For his part, Desguilly claimed that the marriage had been properly solemnized and endorsed by other family members. Moreover, arranging such a union for Marguerite was perfectly consistent with his responsibilities as her guardian. He attributed Vouhet's complaints to "ancient enmity" toward him, rather than concern for Marguerite's welfare, and demanded acquittal, costs, and damages from the Chambre de l'Edit.[84] After reviewing the evidence and questioning all of the parties (including Marguerite and her young husband), the chamber magistrates invalidated the marriage on the grounds of the spouses' youth, condemning Desguilly to pay legal costs as well as a charitable donation. In addition, the court deprived Desguilly of his guardianship and ordered a local judge to supervise the selection of a new guardian from eight of Marguerite's and Barbe's closest relatives—a group that specifically included François Vouhet. Finally, the court forbade the new guardian to arrange any marriage for the girls before they reached the canonical age of consent.[85]

Although the Chambre de l'Edit's verdict in the Vouhet-Desguilly case was based on a specific legal point (the spouses' age), the dispute also involved larger issues about responsible guardianship that the court sought to address. Similar concerns arose in 1606, when Louis de Saint Georges appealed to the court. As the guardian of fourteen-year-old Charlotte de Saint Gelais, he objected to the marriage being planned for his ward by her mother, dame Jeanne Dupuy. His misgivings apparently stemmed from the fact that the prospective bridegroom, Guy

---

[84]A.N. X2b 204, 12 December 1601.
[85]A.N. X2b 206, 23 April 1602.

de Salins, sieur de La Nocle, was a cousin of Dupuy's second husband: such a union would place Charlotte (and her property) more closely under the control of her stepfather's family. Fearing that Charlotte would become a victim of *rapt*, Saint Georges obtained an injunction forbidding Dupuy to arrange Charlotte's marriage without the consent of other relatives, but he had since received news that La Nocle had abducted the girl from her mother's house to marry her secretly. Dupuy's role in these events remained ambiguous. Saint Georges seemed to suspect her of being an accomplice in the abduction, but it is possible that she was unable or unwilling to intervene in a scheme concocted by her husband and his cousin. In any case, the Chambre de l'Edit granted Saint Georges's petition for further protection for his ward. The court ordered Charlotte returned to her mother's care but summoned Dupuy herself for questioning. The judges also prohibited La Nocle (and anyone else, for that matter) from contracting marriage with Charlotte. Jeanne Dupuy was forbidden to consent to any such plans, and "all notaries, priests, ministers and other public persons" [notaires, curés, ministres et aultres personnes publicqs] were commanded not to authorize any wedding involving the girl on pain of paying ten thousand *livres*.[86]

Two years later, Gilles de Machecoul, sieur de Saint Etienne et de La Grange Barbastre, likewise appealed to the Chambre de l'Edit to thwart a forced marriage involving his cousin, ten-year-old Catherine Giffart. His opponent in the case was the girl's maternal aunt, Catherine Heaulme, a widow who claimed to be her niece's legal guardian. In addition to accusing Heaulme of plotting *rapt*, Machecoul asserted that she had broken the law by marrying a cousin of her deceased first husband before the end of the legal waiting period. Machecoul apparently decided that the best way to protect Catherine Giffart from her aunt was to kidnap her first: "it is only a question of the seizure of the said minor by her relatives for her safety," his lawyer argued, "and to hinder the abduction which was to be carried out against her under the pretext of marrying her without their counsel."[87] Machecoul had voluntarily submitted to imprisonment in Paris while awaiting the transfer of his appeal from the presidial court at Nantes to the Chambre de l'Edit, but the chamber judges granted his request for release until his next summons to appear before the court.[88]

---

[86]A.N. X2b 231, 31 May 1606. Despite Saint Georges's efforts, the marriage with La Nocle was accomplished, and Charlotte de Saint Gelais later bedeviled her husband with legal actions that surface in the Chambre de l'Edit's records; see above, n. 79.

[87]A.N. X2b 240, 11 February 1608: n'est question que de la prise de ladite mineur par ses parens pour la seurete d'icelle et empescher le rap[t] qu'on veult faire de sa personne soubs pretexte de marriage sans leur advis.

[88]A.N. X2b 240, 11 February 1608.

Disagreements about a ward's marriage could also reflect conflicts over the disposition and management of a ward's property. While such concerns are only implied in the above cases, the lawsuit between André Blays, sieur de La Dorinière, and François Aubert, sieur de Malecoste, clearly shows the connection. Condemned to death for *rapt* by a royal judge at Saumur in 1599, Blays appealed his sentence to the Chambre de l'Edit the following year. Blays claimed that Aubert had encouraged him to court his niece and ward, Marie Renoul. As part of the marriage arrangements, however, Aubert had demanded a payment of three thousand *écus* and exemption from providing a *reddition de compte*—a formal account of his management of Marie's property during her minority. Blays withdrew from the match, but Marie's affections were engaged: she left her uncle's household and sought the aid of friends and relatives who helped reunite the couple. In petitioning the Chambre de l'Edit, Blays argued that since other family members knew and approved of the marriage, it could hardly be described as clandestine or illegal; Aubert's accusation of *rapt* stemmed from his own "boundless greed" [l'avarice insatiable]. Blays requested that the court dismiss the charges against him, award him costs and damages, and allow him full enjoyment of his wife's property.[89] The court's verdict, however, included a measure of punishment for both parties. Blays was formally rebuked for marrying Marie Renoul without her guardian's consent and sentenced to pay the costs of the proceedings. On the other hand, the chamber judges confirmed the marriage as valid, nullified Blays's death sentence, and ordered Aubert to deliver the long-awaited *reddition de compte* to one of the magistrates within two months. The Chambre de l'Edit thus weighed the circumstances of Blays's marriage to Marie Renoul against Aubert's dubious conduct as her guardian and punished both men for their actions.[90]

Not all of the guardians who appeared in the Chambre de l'Edit's records were men. Women—especially widows who were also mothers—also appealed to the court in their capacity as guardians (*tutrice* and/or *curatrice*). French customary law authorized a woman "to plead the affairs of her family," opening a way for women to enter the male world of the judiciary as active agents on their families' behalf.[91] French jurists conceded that women could be guardians of their own

[89]A.N. X2b 193, 18 February 1600. Marie is described as "engagee d'amytie envers le sieur de la Doriniere."

[90]A.N. X2b 199, 9 January 1601.

[91]Beaumanoir refers to the customary law that enabled a women to *plaider les affaires de sa famille*; see L. Moreel, "La Notion de famille dans le droit de l'Ancien Régime," in *Renouveau des idées sur la famille*, ed. Robert Prigent (Paris: Presses Universitaires de France, 1954), 20–26. Olivier-Martin also states that a woman was juridically capable "si elle agit dans son role normal de ménagère pour assurer la bonne marche de sa maison," Olivier-Martin, *La Coûtume de Paris*, 275. For additional

children but insisted that this was not the same as legal *tutelle* or *curatelle*, which were public functions available only to men. Writing in the seventeenth century, Jean Domat argued that a mother's natural authority and affection for her off-spring superseded the legal impediments to her serving as their guardian, though this did not permit her to act as guardian for anyone else.[92]

Such reasoning helps to explain how two widows named Françoise Haye and Marie Gourdon, acting as *tutrices* of their children, could sue eleven judicial officers from Vendômois for illegally condemning their husbands to death in November 1599. Two years later, the Chambre de l'Edit ruled in favor of their appeal. Along with formally restoring the dead men's good names, the court ordered the disgraced officials to pay a total of two thousand *écus* in reparations. This sum was to be divided equally between the two plaintiffs and managed by "a worthy citizen" [un notable bourgeois] so that the interest would support Gourdon, Haye, and their children until the latter reached adulthood.[93] Widow, mother, and *tutrice* Nicole Gaultier brought suit against Paul Roche, a "so-called gentleman" [soy-disant gentilhomme] from Piedmont, for seducing her daughter Estiennette. The chamber magistrates joined her appeal with that of another widow/*tutrice* named Guillemette Lirouard, who was suing Roche for the same crime against her under-age daughter. Having convicted Roche of debauching both girls, the provost of Paris had sentenced him to payments of three hundred *livres* for each victim, a formal judicial apology, and three years' banishment. The Chambre de l'Edit upheld this decision for Lirouard but ordered Gaultier's case to be reopened before the Paris judge.[94] Like François Vouhet, Louis de Saint Georges, and Gilles de Machecoul, these women used their position as guardians to prosecute those who had damaged their minor children's honor and material interests.

---

perspectives on women's agency in the legal system in early modern France, see Nadine Bérenguier, "Victorious Victims: Women and Publicity in *Mémoires Judiciaires*," in *Going Public: Women and Publishing in Early Modern France*, ed. Elizabeth C. Goldsmith and Dena Goodman (Ithaca: Cornell University Press, 1995), 62–78; Brunelle, "Dangerous Liaisons"; Hanley, "Engendering the State"; Jennifer Kermode and Garthine Walker, eds., *Women, Crime and the Courts in Early Modern Europe* (Chapel Hill: University of North Carolina Press, 1994).

[92]Domat, "Traité des lois," 173–95. On guardianship, see also Loisel, *Institutes coutumières*, 207–11; Brissaud, *History of French Private Law*, 235–50; and Viollet, *Histoire du droit*, 534–51.

[93]A.N. X2b 202, 17 August 1601. See also X2b 193, 19 February 1600; X2b 201, 20 June 1601; X2b 202, 11 July 1601. An *arrêt* from 1602 indicates that Haye and Gourdon were still trying to collect the full amount which the court had awarded them a year earlier: X2b 207, 22 May 1602.

[94]A.N. X2b 235, 8 March 1607.

Some of the lawsuits that parents and guardians brought before the Chambre de l'Edit dealt with other kinds of sexual and moral offenses. In cases concerning children born out of wedlock, the plaintiffs sometimes demanded that the child's father provide financial support for the mother and infant. Anthoine Moreau and Bertrande Poignart appealed to the court in January 1615, complaining that Jacques Thevet had secretly seduced their daughter Perrine. They had opposed a marriage between the two, but in the meantime Perrine had given birth to Thevet's child. The court ordered Thevet to pay sixty *livres* to feed Perrine and the infant, instead of the four hundred *livres* that Perrine's parents had originally requested.[95] René Paige, a wood merchant, and his wife similarly demanded that Paul Guichard assume financial responsibility for the child he fathered with their daughter, Rogere Marie. They requested not only a payment of twelve hundred *livres*, but also an order forbidding Guichard to attack Rogere Marie.[96] And as we have seen, the chamber judges condemned Jean Vescure to support Anne Rutvelt's child despite his claims that Rutvelt and her mother had forced him into marriage.[97]

In other cases, the Chambre de l'Edit's concern with the fate of illegitimate children went beyond financial support. For example, the provost of Paris condemned Zacarie Vigier to pay a total of twenty-four *livres* to Gillette Fernault for the costs of her pregnancy and childbirth; in addition, Vigier was ordered "to take the child which resulted from the pregnancy of the said Fernault in order to have him nourished and raised in the fear of God, and to have him learn a trade so that he may earn his living." Vigier petitioned the Chambre de l'Edit to revise this sentence two years later, but the court dismissed his appeal and thereby upheld the original verdict.[98] When widow Catherine Legeay became pregnant by lawyer Pierre Joly, the court required Joly to raise the child at his own expense.[99] The provost of Paris condemned Charles Restouble to pay seventy-two *livres* to Nicole Girault, the mother of his illegitimate child. Restouble and Girault were also forbidden to contact each other or "commit any shameful act" [commetre aulcun acte d'impudicité], but nothing was said about the child's future. When Nicole Girault appealed her case to the Chambre de l'Edit, the magistrates addressed that oversight:

---

[95]A.N. X2b 286, 7 January 1615.

[96]A.N. X2b 632, 7 September 1660. The *arrêt* does not contain the court's verdict.

[97]A.N. X1b 4397, 9 April 1650; for details, see above, nn. 64, 65.

[98]A.N. X2b 240, 7 February 1608: ledict Vigier auroit este condamne a prendre l'enfant qui proviendroit de la grossesse de ladicte Fernault pour iceluy faire nourir et eslever en la craincte de dieu et luy faire aprendre mestier pour gaigner sa vye.

[99]A.N. X2b 697, 20 May 1665.

> In that the said provost...omitted to make provision for the food and
> care of the child of the said Girault, procreated by the deeds of the
> said Restouble...[the court]...condemns the said Restouble to take
> charge of the said child, to nourish and maintain it, and to be con-
> strained by all due and reasonable means to do this.[100]

In addition to cases about the care and support of illegitimate children, the chamber magistrates dealt with other kinds of sexual and moral offenses involving parents and guardians. In December 1615, André Le Mer petitioned the court to hear his accusations of incest and clandestine marriage. A laborer named Guillaume Despreaux had allegedly tried to arrange a secret marriage between his pregnant stepdaughter, Andrée Boismartel, and Le Mer's son. Le Mer claimed that Despreaux himself was the father of Boismartel's child, having "suborned [her]...during the time that he was her guardian and having incestuously abused her both by force and by other illicit means." Since the charges brought against Despreaux in the local seigneurial court had been dismissed, the royal prosecutor joined Le Mer's lawsuit. The Chambre de l'Edit condemned Despreaux to five years' banishment from Brittany and Paris, along with a fine of eighty *livres* for the king.[101] Pierre Lievin appealed to the chamber magistrates after being condemned as "a blasphemer against God and the Catholic religion, seducer of youth and disobedient to justice" by the seigneurial judge at Essoues. The court upheld his conviction but revised his punishment, sentencing him to whipping, branding, and nine years' banishment.[102] Similarly, a Paris jeweler named Jean Pitan complained that one Simon Pierre Goutte was "corrupting the young people with card games and dice"; those led astray included Pitan's seventeen-year-old son. After reviewing these and other accusations against Goutte, the Chambre de

---

[100]A.N. X2b 257, 3 December 1610: en ce que ledict prevost...auroit omis a faire droict sur la nourriture et entretennement de l'enfant de ladicte Girault procree des oeuvres dudict Restouble en emendant ladicte sentence quant a ce a condamne et condamne ledict Restouble se charger dudict enfant, le faire nourir et entretenir et qu'a ce faire il sera contrainct par toutes voyes deues et raisonnables. The chamber judges' verdict suggests that they may not have believed the accusation of incest, since that was a capital crime.

[101]A.N. X2b 291, 24 December 1615: Ledict Despreaulx...d'avoir suborne Andree Boismartel, fille de Nicole Bretourault sa femme, pendant le temps qu'il en estoit tuteur et d'icelle en avoir incestueusement abuse tant de force que aultres voyes illicites. The chamber judges apparently did not believe the charge of incest against Despreaulx, since that was a capital crime.

[102]A.N. X2b 623, 29 January 1660: blasphemateur de dieu et de la Religion catholique apostolique et Romaine, seducteur de Jeunesse et desobeissant a Justice. Lievin had originally been condemned to be branded on the left shoulder with the abbot of Essoues's arms, but the Chambre de l'Edit changed this to branding on the right shoulder with the fleur-de-lys, symbol of the French monarchy.

l'Edit formally rebuked him and condemned him to pay three hundred *livres* in reparations to Pitan.[103]

Parents and guardians thus invoked the Chambre de l'Edit's authority to punish those who threatened minor children and wards. Such threats might involve a child's moral welfare or material interests, especially as they related to marriage. The danger might come from the child's own relatives or from outsiders like Simon Pierre Goutte, whom Jean Pitan described as "having come to take refuge in this city of Paris"—a clear contrast to Pitan's own status as a "merchant jeweler and citizen of Paris" [marchand joaillier bourgeois de Paris].[104] In appealing to the Chambre de l'Edit for their wards' and children's protection, parents and guardians often sought the court's reinforcement of their own authority—a situation that became especially complicated when family members quarreled among themselves over their conflicting plans for a young person's future. The judicial appeals of parents and guardians thus reveal another instance of families' seeking resolution of their disputes by recourse to the "public" authority of a royal tribunal, and of the judiciary's expanding role in preserving honor and order within families.

Along with ties of blood, marriage, and guardianship, families were bound together—and sometimes brought into conflict—by arrangements for the inheritance of property. Land, goods, and money were often transmitted from one person to another or from one generation to the next by means of wills, testaments, and marriage contracts. As in cases of disputes about marriage or parental authority, the Chambre de l'Edit was called upon to adjudicate such disagreements with an eye to restoring order among kinfolk in conflict.

Lawsuits involving contested inheritances might lead to accusations of other crimes, such as theft. For example, widow Marie Touppet and her two children became embroiled in a lawsuit against ten other Touppet relatives regarding their collective inheritance from Jehanne Touppet. After reviewing the appeals presented by both sides, the Chambre de l'Edit ordered Marie Touppet and her children to turn over "the coins, contracts, obligations and private debts, gold and silver money, silver dishes and other furnishings" that they had taken from Jehanne Touppet's estate after her death (but before the division of property among the family members) and to pay the costs of the proceedings.[105] Elizabeth de Villegagnon, another widow, complained to the court about "thefts, diversions,

---

[103]A.N. XIb 4397, 24 April 1648: debaucher les jeunes gens aux jeux de cartes et de die.

[104]A.N. XIb 4397, 24 April 1648. Goutte is described as "Albigeois de nation s'estant venu refugier en ceste ville de Paris."

[105]A.N. X2b 237, 2 July 1607: deniers, contrats, obligations et cedulles, or et argent monnoye, vayselle d'argent et autres meubles.

and fraudulently hidden items" [vols, divertissements et recelles] from the property of her late father-in-law, François de Piedefer. She was joined in her lawsuit by François's daughter and heir, Marguerite; the accused included Estienne Jauvon, a local priest, and eleven others.[106] When Phillibert de la Curée reported that his daughter Henriette's inheritance from her grandfather was being despoiled by another relative who insisted on cutting and stealing wood from the estate, the chamber magistrates forbade all such actions while the case was being heard by a local royal magistrate.[107] On the other hand, Antoinette de Malingnesan argued that her own children had forcibly dispossessed her of two estates. She claimed that the lands were rightfully hers according to her marriage contract with the late René de Rochchouart, sieur de Saint Annan; the fact that Malingnesan had remarried probably prompted her children's legal action. Again, the Chambre de l'Edit responded by restoring Malingnesan's property while a local judge settled the family's dispute.[108]

If a family's property or inheritance dispute involved a contested will, the litigation might involve charges of forgery—a serious accusation that could effectively transform a civil case into criminal proceedings. When Febvonie Raoul was ordered to give up a legacy from her husband and provide an inventory of his property, she argued that her accusers had used a forged document—her late son's will, dated June 1618—to make false claims against his estate. The Chambre de l'Edit agreed: the court officially suppressed the will and condemned Raoul's opponents to financial penalties and costs.[109] Pierre Lerot found himself embroiled in a dispute about a forged will which involved him and several others in a lawsuit against Robert Le Roy, priest and dean of the church at Beauvais. Acting as *curateur* for the estate of Thomas Barbanson, Lerot apparently inherited the lawsuit from Barbanson's late wife: she had accused Le Roy and a notary of falsifying a will for her brother, the previous dean at Beauvais. In this case, the chamber magistrates denied Lerot's claims and acquitted Le Roy.[110] The court likewise confirmed François de Bourzolles's possession of his late wife's property against the claims of her sister, dame Nicole de Vienne. Vienne had argued that a will drawn up by her sister in February

[106]A.N. X2b 625, 20 March 1660. See also X2b 628, 7 June 1660; X2b 631, 2 September 1660. *Recelles* derived from the verb *receler*, which meant to hide or withdraw items fraudulently, especially from an inheritance or estate; Hartzfeld and Darmesteter, *Dictionnaire de la langue française*, s.v. "receler."

[107]A.N. X1b 4397, 8 May 1654.

[108]A.N. X1b 4397, 3 July 1649.

[109]A.N. X2b 354, 20 January 1625. Raoul's main accusers were Jehan Fouyn, *sergent à verger* at the Paris Châtelet, and Richard Erondelle, master goldsmith of Paris.

[110]A.N. X2b 288, 27 June 1615.

1606 should supersede an earlier will in Bourzolles's favor, but after summoning notaries and writing experts to examine the documents, the court nullified the 1606 will. The judges ordered Nicole de Vienne to pay the costs of the proceedings and to seek payment of her sister's legacy from Bourzolles. He, in turn, was required to pay the back wages of his wife's servants and creditors, five of whom had joined him in the lawsuit.[111]

In 1615, the Chambre de l'Edit was faced with a unique case involving inheritance and charges of imposture. Gabriel de Hebles, sieur de La Vacqueresse, petitioned the court on behalf of his minor son, an heir of the late Jacques de Hebles, sieur du Ribert. La Vacqueresse was trying to protect Ribert's estate (and his own family's share of it) from two individuals who claimed to be Angelique and Scipion de Hebles, Ribert's natural children. Aided by a royal *archer* named Jean Le Noble, they had already won a pension of eighty *écus* in a previous judgment. The Chambre de l'Edit's inquiries, however, had revealed that "Angelique" was actually a woman named Catherine Rapin, while "Scipion" was really Marin Gombauld, a gardener's son. The investigating judge had also questioned one Jean Boisseret, described as "guardian of the alleged substitute children" [tuteur des enfans prétendus supposés]. The court ordered further interrogations of Rapin, Gombauld, Boisseret, and several possible accomplices, along with Gombauld's other relatives.[112]

As the above cases demonstrate, family members might find themselves drawn into a lawsuit because of their material stake in a relative's inheritance. Such disputes could implicate not only parents and children, but also siblings and other collateral relations. In 1605, Marie Larcher appeared before the Chambre de l'Edit as sole heir of her brother Gilles to sue his murderer, a Swiss gentleman named Noel Louis. Louis produced royal letters of remission regarding Larcher's death, but the chamber judges sentenced him to donate one hundred twenty *livres* in alms for his offense. Marie Larcher then presented a second petition that led the court to award the money to Marie herself, "to aid her in marrying and to have prayers said to God for her brother's soul."[113] Odet de La Noue continued a lawsuit begun by his father François, but which also involved Odet himself as an heir of his uncle, Charles de Teligny. The case concerned an allegedly forged contract made in January 1572 between Teligny and Guillaume de Grandies, sieur de Grandchamp et La Montague.[114] A case from June 1601 reveals a veritable genealogy of litigants on

---

[111]A.N. X2b 248, 12 May 1609.

[112]A.N. X2b 286, 23 February 1615; X2b 288, 19 May 1615. Neither document indicates the outcome of the case.

[113]A.N. X2b 226, 6 August 1605 and 19 August 1605: pour aider à la marier et f[air]e prier dieu pour l'ame dudict deffunt.

[114]A.N. X2b 208, 17 July 1602. The contract involved the substantial sum of 9400 *livres* but

both sides. Marie Bouvier, widow and guardian of her children by Charles Ferre, sieur de la Villesblanc, was pursuing her husband's appeal of a judicial verdict issued in 1583. (Charles Ferre had taken up the case for his brother.) Bouvier's opponents were dame Marie de Rieux, comtesse de Cheville, and Jehan Dubreuil, sieur de Pontbriant, both of whom replaced their fathers as litigants. The *arrêt* does not explain the exact nature of the disagreement, though a reference to "search and recovery of the said titles, papers and acts" suggests a property dispute of some sort.[115] In a final example, Jehan de l'Estrade's attempt to enforce certain contracts and agreements that his late father had made with a lawyer named Vaast Cormasson brought him into conflict with Cormasson's children and grandchildren, as well as their spouses and offspring—a total of ten persons from seven different families.[116] The fact that all of l'Estrade's opponents were Vaast Cormasson's heirs (and therefore potentially liable for his obligations) helps explain the number of Cormasson relatives who participated in the lawsuit. This case clearly shows how property and inheritance disputes could draw various kinfolk into litigation, sometimes allying them against a common threat to the family's wealth and honor.

Family members thus appealed to the Chambre de l'Edit to settle their disputes about property, inheritances, and financial obligations, as well as marriages and guardianship. By tying such disputes to accusations of theft, forgery, and even false identity, they used criminal litigation to contest wills and protect legacies. Occasionally, these cases also reveal a concern with the social and moral disorders that could accompany family conflicts over material goods. When Antoinette Malingnesan petitioned the court to enforce the property arrangements outlined in her marriage contract, she noted that

---

its details are not described. See also X2b 213, 16 May and 20 June 1603; X2b 214, 7 and 19 August 1603.

[115]A.N. X2b 201, 8 June 1601: la recherche et recouvrement de lesdicts tiltres, papiers et enseignemens.

[116]A.N. X2b 217, 27 February 1604; X2b 237, 11 August 1607. The contracts in question dated from 1572, 1577, 1581, and 1582. The defendants included Jehan Carré, a widower acting as guardian of his minor children by Mathurine Cormasson; Nicolas Henry and his wife Marthe Carré, one of Jehan Carré's adult daughters by Mathurine Cormasson; Mathieu Nyvert and his wife Jehanne Piau, daughter of Etienne Piau and Françoise Cormasson; Louis Jonye and his wife Catherine Cormasson; Honoré Potier and Jehanne Cormasson; and François Le Roy, acting as legal representative not only for his wife Madgelaine Cormasson, but also for Marthe and Marie Cormasson, the minor daughters of Jehan Cormasson. The *arrêt* dated 11 August 1607 omits the names of Jehan Carré, Honoré Potier, and Jehanne Cormasson (perhaps because they withdrew from the lawsuit) and indicates the court's decision to annul the disputed contracts.

The duty and respect owed her by her minor children should oblige them to contain themselves in their duty; nevertheless, by a disordered blindness, they expelled and threw her out of the said houses of Saint Annant and Montmoreau by force and violence, taking everything they desired.[117]

Malingnesan thus argued that her children's refusal to honor the terms of her marriage contract was not just a property dispute; it also reflected a violent and dangerous rejection of filial duty. The royal magistrates' intervention would quash this rebellion against parental authority, restoring her estates and dispelling her children's "disordered blindness." In supporting Malingnesan's request, the Chambre de l'Edit once again brought the power of royal justice to bear on family conflicts.

Criminal lawsuits could unite as well as divide families. Disputes about marriage, guardianship, and inheritance often pitted parents against children and siblings or collateral relatives against each other. On the other hand, members of several different families might join in a lawsuit if all were the beneficiaries of a single inheritance or alleged victims or perpetrators of the same crime. Litigants before the Chambre de l'Edit often called upon their relatives to provide evidence or lend support to their cases, creating extended "clans" of plaintiffs and defendants. Relatives might also take the place of a family member involved in legal proceedings. The Chambre de l'Edit's records thus offer a valuable perspective on family solidarities, as well as family conflicts.

Husbands and wives were often codefendants or coplaintiffs in judicial appeals presented to the chamber magistrates. While this was surely due in part to the fact that in general wives were considered legally subordinate to their husbands, some of the Chambre de l'Edit's cases indicate that spouses jointly participated in litigation to defend their mutual honor and interests. Jean Roiffé and his wife Michelle Motte had sued Louis Chevreau, sieur du Lizon, before the *lieutenant criminel* at Tours in 1601 because of Chevreau's insults to Motte. Dissatisfied with a verdict that included an apology but no monetary penalty, the couple appealed unsuccessfully to the Chambre de l'Edit.[118] Barbe Housset was joined by her second husband and two sons from her first marriage in a suit against Michel Revel, a laborer from Chateaufremont. After reviewing the case, the chamber judges condemned Revel to apologize formally before Housset's family and neighbors for

---

[117]A.N. XIb 4397, 3 July 1649: le debvoir et le respect a elle deub par ses enffans mineurs les deust obliger a se contenir en leur debvoir, neantmoins par un aveuglement desreigle ils l'auroient de force et violence expulsee, exspoliee et jettee hors desdites maisons de St. Annant et Montmoreau pris et emporte tout ce que [ils] auroient desire....

[118]A.N. X2b 212, 30 April 1603. See also X2b 210, 16 December 1602.

insulting her honor.[119] Husbands and wives might also be drawn into litigation concerning a spouse's collateral relatives. In 1602, Guillaume Roy and his wife Toussine Vernier sued Jehan Guiolot, a judge in the seigneury of Prelichy, for his condemnation of Toussine's uncle in 1587. The Chambre de l'Edit reprimanded Guiolot for his conduct, then dismissed the couple's appeal.[120]

The legal and familial ties between parents and children appear frequently in the Chambre de l'Edit's records. When Emery Lefebvre appealed a judicial verdict that required him to pay Guillemine Beaussier the sum of 100 *écus*, his opponents included not only Guillemine herself, but also her father and mother.[121] Gilles Buffiere joined his wife Marie Rollin in suing Anne Beauclerc and her servant for insults and violence against Rollin's daughter, Ysabel Picart.[122] In 1640, an artillery officer named Jean de Roussel and his wife Renée Mauclerc petitioned the Chambre de l'Edit; they were being sued by Renée Thonesvault, who claimed that her daughter had disappeared after entering Mauclerc's household as a chambermaid.[123] Not all parents participated in their children's litigation, however: Jean Grimault sought the court's permission to withdraw from a lawsuit involving his son Pierre, who was accused of assaulting Perrette Turaudiere. In a request dated 16 June 1635, Grimault noted that his son, aged twenty-eight, was "not living with him nor under his authority" [n'est demeurant aveq luy ny soubs sa puissance].[124]

Lawsuits involving brothers and sisters as judicial allies were also common. Siblings often acted to defend the interests of a parent or another relative, and such ties could extend to include brothers- and sisters-in-law as well. When Jacques, Noel, Jehan, and Pierre Marchant sued Antoine Hemard for the murder of their father, their three brothers-in-law joined in the suit on behalf of their wives, the Marchants' sisters.[125] A merchant named Claude Pautrais accused surgeon Jacques Dugue of having raped his widowed sister Estiennette, thus hastening her death.

---

[119] A.N. X2b 214, 26 August 1603.

[120] A.N. X2b 211, 11 January 1603. See also X2b 208, 16 July 1602; X2b 210, 18 December 1602. Guiolot had condemned Germain Vernier and another man to death for an unspecified crime.

[121] A.N. X2b 200, 15 March 1601, contains the court's verdict. See also X2b 193, 10 February 1600; X2b 199, 15 February 1601. The original sentence against Lefebvre, which the court upheld, was issued in 1595.

[122] A.N. X2b 424, 5 June 1635. Beauclerc's husband, a tailor, is not listed as a party in the dispute.

[123] A.N. X2b 456, 9 July 1640.

[124] A.N. X2b 424, 16 June 1635.

[125] A.N. X2b 202, 22 August 1601. See also X2b 204, 18 December 1601; X2b 207, 17 June 1602. The court absolved Hemard in June 1602, condemning the Marchants to pay 60 *écus* in damages and costs.

Dissatisfied with the verdict issued by the royal judge at Tours, Pautrais appealed to the Chambre de l'Edit, where he pursued his case for over a year. In doing so, Pautrais was fulfilling a double family role as Estiennette's brother and as guardian of her two daughters, aged eleven and fourteen.[126] David, Pierre, François, and Elisabeth Ovalles brought suit in 1630 against André Bauchaux and his son for the murder of their brother, Isaac Ovalles. Despite their letters of pardon, a La Rochelle court had sentenced the Bauchaux men to galley service; the Chambre de l'Edit commuted this to banishment and financial penalties.[127]

Siblings might also aid each other's legal proceedings in other ways, as the following case illustrates. Louis Briand, seneschal of Marans, became embroiled in a dispute with Etienne Franchard, the *procureur fiscal* at Marans. When he appealed to the Chambre de l'Edit in December 1601, Briand accused Franchard and his family of suborning witnesses; a month later, Briand complained specifically that Franchard and his brother Pierre were bringing charges against him in other jurisdictions "in order to prevent the suppliant [Briand] from defending himself and to harass and vex him in various places" [pour empescher que ledict suppliant se pu(i)sse justifier et le travailler et vexer en divers endroits].[128] When the litigants were ordered to pursue their case only before the Chambre de l'Edit, the Franchard brothers obliged: the Chambre de l'Edit's records for 1602 and 1603 abound with their petitions and charges against Briand and his alleged accomplices.[129] Although the outcome of the case is unknown, the court's records clearly show the Franchard brothers cooperating to multiply the legal proceedings against their opponent.

Whether as a legal tactic intended to overwhelm an opposing party or as an indicator of shared interest in a legal dispute, the practice of family members' aiding an individual's lawsuit suggests an extended concept of family ties. In December 1602, for example, Hubert Viollames and his wife appealed their condemnation for violence and insults against François Le Blanc and his wife Catherine Jolly. The court records show that six of Catherine's relatives had joined her and her husband in their lawsuit: *maître* Claude Jolly, a tax collector in the *élection* of Sezanne (possibly Catherine's brother or uncle); another Claude Jolly, widow of

---

[126]A.N. X2b 203, 15 September 1601. See also X2b 196, 3 and 28 August 1600; X2b 198, 13 December 1600; X2b 199, 1 February 1601; X2b 200, 13 April 1601; X2b 201, 11 May 1601. The court upheld Dugue's earlier conviction but increased the legal costs he had to pay.

[127]A.N. X2b 389, 21, 22, and 27 June 1630.

[128]A.N. X2b 204, 7 December 1601; X2b 205, 25 January 1602.

[129]A.N. X2b 207, 5 and 12 June 1602; X2b 209, 3 September 1602; X2b 210, 28 November and 10 December 1602; X2b 211, 22 January 1603; X2b 213, 6 May 1603; X2b 214, 2 July 1603.

Guillaume Cadet (possibly Catherine's sister); Benjamin and Claude Cadet; and Aymée Cadet and her husband Nicollas Boulle. *Maître* Claude Jolly's involvement in the case is understandable, since Viollames had called him a usurer, but the Cadets' participation shows that even more distantly related kin were willing to defend the Jolly family honor.[130] When Pierre Martin, sieur de Broisse, contested the legality of his son Guy's marriage to Magdelaine de Pilloner, Magdelaine's brother and two sisters joined her in opposing the charges. Moreover, Magdelaine responded with a countersuit involving no less than twelve of her other relatives, including several uncles and a brother-in-law. It is tempting to conclude that this rallying of support for Magdelaine's case (and in favor of her marriage) was what persuaded Pierre Martin to drop the charges against her and accept his son's marriage as valid.[131]

In addition to joining a lawsuit as coplaintiffs, codefendants, or intervening parties, relatives might take the place of family members involved in litigation. Such substitutions were usually caused by the death of one or more of the original parties in the case. Edmé de Breze, sieur de La Feullée and *lieutenant général* for the duchy of Epernon, contested a contract made with Pierre Fleury before a local judge in November 1601, but he lost his case. By the time Breze's appeal reached the Chambre de l'Edit, Fleury had died and his widowed daughter Jehanne had taken up her father's side in the dispute, petitioning the court herself. The court upheld the original verdict, sentencing Breze to pay damages and costs "for the imprisonment and undue vexation of the said appellant [Jehanne Fleury]."[132] Similarly, Marie Durant died before her legal dispute with Marguerite de Buffenant and several others was resolved, so her sister and heir Estiennette Durant took up the case. A year later, the Chambre de l'Edit dismissed the case but condemned Estiennette to pay the costs of her sister's litigation up to January 1599—a total of 50 *écus*.[133]

In contrast to the family ties and kinship networks revealed in the examples described above, many litigants pursued or faced their opposing parties before the Chambre de l'Edit without such support. It is not surprising to find men bringing lawsuits on their own (that is, without representation by or assistance from other

---

[130]A.N. X2b 210, 20 December 1602; X2b 211, 9 January 1603; X2b 212, 20 and 29 April 1603; X2b 214, 1 August 1603.

[131]A.N. X2b 244, 2 September 1608.

[132]A.N. X2b 212, 1 March 1603: [La cour] a condamné et condamne ledict de Breze en dommages et interests dudict emprisonnement et indeue vexation de ladite appellante. See also X2b 210, 11 December 1602; X2b 213, 16 May 1603.

[133]A.N. X2b 208, 10 July 1602. See also X2b 193, 5 and 21 February 1600; X2b 194, 27 March and 21 April 1600; X2b 197, 6 September 1600.

family members), but unmarried women who had attained their majority also appear in the court's records. Identified by the formula "fille usante et jouissante de ses droits" or "fille majeure," such women were legally independent of both paternal and marital authority, and they usually demanded legal redress for attacks against their honor or person. For example, Estiennette de Troyes successfully sued two soldiers in the royal guard who had insulted and physically abused her. After being condemned by the provost of Paris, the two men had obtained letters of pardon for their offense, but the Chambre de l'Edit vindicated Estiennette's appeal: the soldiers were ordered to affirm her honor before the court and then fulfill a year's military service at their own expense at a royal garrison in Guyenne.[134] *Fille majeure* Judith Bienfaict sued Louise Quillart, also *fille majeure*, and master sculptor and painter Simon Bigorne over their alleged interference with her inheritance from Verine Briet. After two years of litigation, the chamber magistrates ruled in favor of Bienfaict's claims.[135] On the other hand, *fille majeure* Louise Vergny lost her case against Etienne Bernard, sieur de Pressacq, whom she had accused of subornation and abuse: the Chambre de l'Edit reversed Bernard's conviction by the parlement of Brittany and sentenced Vergny to pay 80 *livres* in damages, plus the costs of the proceedings.[136]

One of the most poignant appeals presented to the court came from *fille majeure* Sebastienne Tronchet, a domestic servant from Abbeville who sued her mistress and two royal judicial officers for wrongful arrest and detention. When Tronchet attempted to leave the household of dame Marguerite Manessier because of abuse, Manessier retaliated by having Tronchet seized and taken before local magistrates for allegedly attempting to throw herself in a nearby river. Ignoring Tronchet's own complaints of mistreatment and claims to be "healthy in mind" [saine d'esprit], the local court admonished and imprisoned her. Both Tronchet's lawyer and the royal prosecutor in Paris argued that the Abbeville officials had exceeded their jurisdiction; moreover, their conduct implied collusion (or at least cooperation) with Manessier in her efforts to punish and intimidate her beleaguered servant. After reviewing her appeal, the Chambre de l'Edit absolved Tronchet of all blame and condemned her opponents to pay her 60 *livres* in costs and damages.[137] Tronchet's lawsuit clearly illustrates how a *fille majeure*

---

[134]A.N. X2b 204, 24 November 1601.

[135]A.N. X2b 629, 1 July 1660.

[136]A.N. X2b 697, 9 May 1665. The charges were originally brought by Louise Vergny's mother, who had since died; since her mother's *procureur* remained a party to the lawsuit, he was condemned along with Vergny in the Chambre de l'Edit's verdict.

[137]A.N. X2b 234, 24 January 1607.

could use criminal proceedings to defend herself against insult, attack, or injury, and how royal magistrates upheld her capacity to do so.

Married women could also pursue or defend their interests in litigation without their husbands' suing on their behalf or being formal parties to the lawsuit. Nicole Duchesne, wife of Antoine Lefebvre and "authorized by justice at the refusal of her husband" [femme autorisée par justice au refus de son mari], appealed her conviction for insulting behavior toward Gregoire Aubry before the Chambre de l'Edit in 1602.[138] In August 1603, another *femme autorisée par justice* named Magdelaine de Brouillard lost her suit against Anne de La Fontaine, sieur d'Esche et Orgerus, in a dispute over a forged receipt that dated from 1572. The chamber magistrates rejected her claim that the document was legitimate and sentenced her to pay the costs of litigation.[139] On the other hand, Jehanne Lefort found herself imprisoned because of a dispute over her repurchase of a bond *(rente)*. Claiming that her opponents had failed to pursue the case properly, this *femme autorisée* pleaded for her freedom in part to care for her husband, whom she described as "confined to bed, ill…and in the hands of doctors and surgeons" [detenu au lict malade…entre les mains des medecins et chirurgiens]. The court accepted her petition, ordered her release, and condemned her opposing parties to pay the costs of her appeal and imprisonment.[140] Whether as *filles majeures* or *femmes autorisées par justice*, women could and did appear before the Chambre de l'Edit as independent litigants, acting without the benefit of the kinship networks evidenced elsewhere in the court's records.

Lawsuits heard before the Chambre de l'Edit thus reveal family ties as well as family friction. Many cases involved conflicts among spouses, parents, and siblings, yet collateral relatives, such as aunts, uncles, cousins, and in-laws, might also be drawn into such lawsuits through their relationship to the principal parties. The guardians of minor children, who were often related to their wards by blood or marriage, further expanded the web of people who might join in litigation because of family ties and obligations. In some instances, lawsuits became a kind of legacy that was passed on from one generation to the next. Men and women also appeared as independent litigants before the court, demonstrating a certain level of agency for individuals of both sexes who lacked kin networks to support their legal proceedings (or whose families were unable or unwilling to provide such support). Although many of the cases adjudicated by the Chambre de l'Edit derived from conflicts within the nuclear family, evidence from the court's records

[138]A.N. X2b 207, 12 June 1602. Duchesne lost her case: the court upheld the sentence issued against her two years earlier and condemned her to pay the costs of the appeal.

[139]A.N. X2b 214, 7 August 1603. See also X2b 213, 3 June 1603.

[140]A.N. X2b 230, 19 April 1606.

also suggests that extended kin networks remained alive and well in early modern French society, sustained in part by the activity of criminal litigation.

Religious difference played an ambiguous role in family disputes heard before the Chambre de l'Edit. In some cases, a plaintiff's or defendant's religious status accounted for the judicial appeal: when the young Dutchman Jean Vescure petitioned the court in 1649, he did so explicitly as someone who professed "the so-called reformed religion."[141] But religious difference was not always central to conflicts among relatives, as in the case of André Blays and François Aubert. In the course of his dispute with his wife's uncle and guardian, the Catholic Blays claimed that the Protestant Aubert had received him at his home and encouraged the courtship of his niece even while Blays was serving the duc de Mercoeur, a member of the Guise family and leader in the Catholic League. Blays cited Aubert's lack of concern about his faith as further proof that Aubert's objections to his marriage were motivated by greed.[142]

Though it is not explicitly cited as such in the Chambre de l'Edit's records, religious difference might have been a factor in several of the cases involving *rapt* and clandestine marriage discussed above. For example, both Anthoine de La Planche and his son Jerôme are identified as Protestants; Jerôme affirmed that he had remained Protestant even after his secret wedding to Berthelemye Flé, which was conducted by a Catholic priest.[143] Similarly, Henri Bullion exchanged vows with Marguerite Durant in a Catholic church, and the couple had recorded their promise to wed without benefit of priest or notary.[144] (The fact that canon law retained the spouses' consent as the basis of a valid marriage may help account for La Planche's and Bullion's choice of Catholic marriage rites and venues. Indeed, no accusations of clandestine marriage conducted by Reformed ministers in their churches appeared in the Chambre de l'Edit's records used for this study.) The French Reformed churches' regulations concerning marriage condemned unions between Protestants and Catholics, so religious difference may have been a factor in the parental opposition to Jerôme de La Planche's and Henri Bullion's choice of marriage partners.[145] The principal arguments made in court, however, revolved around the royal edicts and social mores that these marriages had violated, rather than the issue of religious affiliation as an element in choosing a suitable marriage partner.

[141]A.N. X2b 209, 31 August 1602 (La Planche); X1b 4397, 12 May 1649 (Vescure).

[142]A.N. X2b 193, 18 February 1600.

[143]A.N. X2b 209, 31 August 1602.

[144]A.N. X2b 226, 19 July 1605; the *minute d'arrêt* contains the text of their marriage promise.

[145]On the condemnation of "mixed marriages" between Protestants and Catholics, see Garrisson, *Les Protestants*, 84–88.

On the other hand, some of the cases heard by the Chambre de l'Edit do reveal the disorders that could result from crossing confessional lines to marry. For example, Suzanne Clement had married Michel Denion with her parents' consent according to Protestant rites, but they had never consummated their union. She then married Jehan Le Devin and had several children with him. When Denion sued Clement and Le Devin, he described her second marriage as "adulterous and contracted by *rapt*" [adulterin et contracté par Rapt]. According to royal advocate Louis Servin, the court's principal task was to determine which of the two marriages should remain valid, and his comments about upholding the legitimacy of Clement's children implied that he supported confirming her union with Le Devin. The *arrêt*, however, merely records the judges' decision to deliberate further in private.[146] In 1654, Jeanne Andinet and her parents sued Pierre Rebecourt, an innkeeper from Loudun. He had wed Andinet in a Catholic ceremony in January 1653 but then abandoned her two months later, denying the marriage despite the fact that by then Andinet was pregnant with his child. When Rebecourt evaded prosecution by local judges, Andinet and her parents appealed to the Chambre de l'Edit. The court not only made Rebecourt responsible for the child's care and upbringing, but also sentenced him to pay Andinet 6000 *livres* in reparations to help her find another husband. Lacking the funds to pay her, Rebecourt and Andinet were married again—this time by a Protestant minister, in the presence of some friends and the court clerk.[147]

Disputes about guardianship sometimes explicitly involved conflicts about religious difference. In December 1607, the Chambre de l'Edit reviewed the complaint of widower Jean de Louvain about the guardianship of his children and their religious instruction. Although Louvain and his wife had raised their children as Catholics, Louvain had converted to the Reformed faith shortly before his wife's death. He argued that in accordance with the Edict of Nantes's provisions, he had never attempted to turn his children away from Catholicism, but had always behaved "as a true father" [comme vray pere]. Louvain's opponent was Henry Gamin, a Parisian merchant who claimed that before her death, Louvain's wife had taken steps to assure that her children would remain Catholic by entrusting their religious instruction to him and his wife. Other Catholic relatives (from Louvain's wife's family) had encouraged the Gamins to take custody of Louvain's son. When Louvain later encountered his son and Madame Gamin on an outing in her carriage, he had publicly insulted her—something which became an added charge in the lawsuit between the two parties. After reviewing the case,

[146]A.N. X2b 230, 18 March 1606.
[147]A.N. X1b 4397, 4 July 1654.

the chamber magistrates ordered Louvain to apologize formally for his insults but allowed him to retain guardianship of his children, provided that "he did not use any force against them in the matter of religion" [sans qu'il puisse user envers eux d'aulcune contraincte pour le faict de la Religion].[148]

In another case, religious difference was an important factor in a minor child's marriage. Jean Antoine de Couvers, baron de Sotinac, appealed to the court as guardian of his orphan niece, nine-year-old Anne Elizabeth. Couvers had convened a family council consisting of a dozen of Anne Elizabeth's relatives to meet before a local judge to arrange the little girl's education and other matters. His plans were blocked, however, by the person who actually had custody of Anne Elizabeth: her maternal grandmother, dame Jacqueline de Chioult. Chioult took increasingly drastic actions to oppose Couvers. After refusing to bring the little girl to the family council meeting, she appealed to the Chambre de l'Edit, then left France altogether with her granddaughter. Couvers claimed that she had taken Anne Elizabeth to Geneva "and threatened to make her contract a marriage" [mesnassoit (menaçoit) luy faire contracter mariage]. The chamber magistrates endorsed Couvers's petition that Chioult produce Anne Elizabeth before the court and forbade anyone, including any Reformed ministers, to participate in any marriage involving the little girl.[149]

For the Chambre de l'Edit, resolving family conflicts that were explicitly related to the problem of religious difference was yet another facet of the court's general mandate to maintain peace between Huguenots and Catholics. The family stood at the nexus of important power struggles between the two confessions; after all, marriage and religious education were two paths to conversion, which in turn could strengthen one group at the other's expense. The Huguenot minority was acutely aware of such dangers. During the sixteenth and seventeenth centuries, Reformed synods and consistories condemned "mixed marriages" between Catholics and Protestants, as well as other kinds of behavior and contact with Catholics that were deemed unacceptable for members of the Calvinists' godly communities.[150] As the most powerful arbiter of religious and legal disputes, the French crown and the royal judiciary perhaps benefited most from these family frictions. Huguenots and Catholics alike were subject to royal legislation concerning marriage, guardianship, and inheritance, and members of both confessions appealed to royal judges such as those of the Chambre de l'Edit for resolution of their family disputes.

[148]A.N. X2b 239, 22 December 1607.
[149]A.N. X1b 4397, 20 December 1647.
[150]Garrisson, Les Protestants, 51–78; Labrousse, Une foi, une loi, un roi?, 45–60, 95–112.

The Paris Chambre de l'Edit adjudicated many lawsuits that stemmed from disorder within families, notably conflicts over marriage, contested inheritances, and the authority of parents or guardians over minor children. These issues were often closely connected: a dispute about a marriage's validity, for example, could affect the spouses' ability to inherit property or bestow legacies, and relatives might challenge a guardian's plans for a minor child's marriage. Such cases reveal much about the dynamics of family life in early modern France, and the efforts of religious and political authorities to restore and maintain order within and among families. The court struggled to make family members' behavior conform to the ideals of conduct promoted by jurists, moralists, and church leaders of both confessions, ideals that emphasized parental authority over children, husbands' authority over wives, and often a general subordination of individual interests or will to the family's collective fortunes.

Although these ideals and the standards of behavior they implied were expressed in many forms, their reflection in laws and edicts issued by the French crown was perhaps most important for understanding the Chambre de l'Edit's handling of such cases. Unlike the Council of Trent's decrees and the French Reformed churches' ecclesiastical discipline, royal law applied to all French subjects. The Chambre de l'Edit's jurisdiction, though directly linked to the legal privileges of the Protestant minority, might also extend to Catholics who appeared before the court in conflict with Huguenots. Moreover, French kings could and did make use of family imagery to convey their claims to their subjects' full obedience. When Louis XIV described himself as "the common father of all our subjects" [père commun de tous nos sujets] in 1686, he echoed words used by his grandfather almost a century earlier to address magistrates from the Parlement of Paris. [151] Henry IV, however, had drawn upon this fatherly imagery to obtain the judges' approval of the Edict of Nantes; by 1686, Louis XIV had revoked that edict, using his royal (and paternal?) authority to determine the religion of his subjects/children.

Religious difference seemed to play an ambiguous role at best in most of the family-related cases heard by the Chambre de l'Edit. Instead, the court's work in such litigation highlights the common interests of Catholic, Protestant, and secular authorities in regulating marriage, parental authority, and inheritance. It

---

[151]"Declaration du Roy, concernant les formalitez necessaires pour les mariages des mineurs dont les peres, meres et tuteurs faisant profession de la R.P.R. sont absens," in *Recueil des édits, declarations et arrêts*, 347.

reflects the perception shared by all of these authorities that families were the foundation of moral, social, and political order. Conversely, the Chambre de l'Edit's work also reveals the complex dynamics of this policy, which depended for its operation on families themselves. Parents, spouses, and other relatives invoked royal laws and the court's authority to settle their differences, a key element in the chamber magistrates' efforts to implement those laws. As litigants before the Chambre de l'Edit, family members actively contributed to the extension of royal justice in regulating family affairs.

CHAPTER 5

"Que la force demeure au roi et à la justice"

Violence, Punishment, & Public Peace

IN JUNE 1602 THE PARIS CHAMBRE DE L'EDIT DECLARED HECTOR
Renault, baron de Bajaumont, his brother, and seven other men to be guilty of
murder. Only two of the condemned men were actually in custody, prisoners in
the Conciergerie (the Parlement of Paris's prison); the court sentenced them to
serve in the king's galleys. Renault, his brother Charles, and their other accomplices were convicted *par contumace* and condemned to death. If they could not be
apprehended, their executions were to be carried out using effigies. Finally, the
chamber magistrates ordered all of the men's property to be confiscated and
imposed a host of financial penalties, including a fine payable to the king and the
costs of all the legal proceedings. The court awarded a fine to Marguerite of Valois
in her capacity as Countess of Agenois, where the murder had occurred, as well as
reparations to the victim's widow and son.[1]

Two months after receiving this verdict, however, widow Jeanne de Preissac
and her son Anthoine de Malvin appeared before the Chambre de l'Edit again.
The chamber magistrates' decisions had proven impossible to enforce: Renault

[1]A.N. X2b 207, 22 June 1602. The victim was Charles de Malvin, sieur de Montazet et Guissac. Marguerite of Valois, Henry IV's former wife, had petitioned the court to award her the "fines
and reparations" [amandes et reparations] from Malvin's killers which were her due as Countess of
Agenois. The executions were to be carried out in Agen if done in effigy and otherwise in Paris; as
nobles, Renault and his brother were sentenced to beheading, while their accomplices were to be
hanged. The court costs probably would have been substantial: the case had been heard in 1600 by
the *sénéchaussée* of Agenois and remanded to the Paris Chambre de l'Edit by the royal council (*conseil
privé*) in 1601. See also A.N. X2b 202, 11 August 1601; X2b 207, 23 May 1602.

and his accomplices remained at large in Guyenne, aided by powerful supporters who were keeping them beyond the reach of royal justice. Preissac and Malvin therefore petitioned the court to order the local community to "sound the alarm" [sonner le toxin (tocsin)] and seek out the fugitives, and to treat Renault's supporters as traitors ("criminels de lese-Majesté"). The Chambre de l'Edit instead commanded local royal officials to make sure that the verdict was carried out: "in case of rebellion or resistance," the *arrêt* states, "the governor of Guyenne or his lieutenants will be admonished to lend a strong hand and have cannon brought before the places where the accused have taken refuge, and to act so that force remains with the king and justice."[2]

The Chambre de l'Edit's response to Preissac's and Malvin's appeal illustrates an important theme in the court's work: the importance of enforcing royal justice at the local level, especially in cases of violence and public disorder. Renault and his accomplices compounded their initial crime by defying the court's verdict, apparently with the aid of local supporters. The chamber magistrates responded by insisting that royal officials in Guyenne assure "that force remains with the king and justice," with the use of artillery if necessary. The Chambre de l'Edit dealt with instances of violence and public disorder in many forms, including insult, blasphemy, physical attacks, and abuses committed by judicial officials. Unlike lawsuits about memory and *oubliance*, these were usually crimes of the present, and they often had little to do with regulations concerning marriage, parental authority, or inheritance. Most of all, such violence threatened the goals of restoring public order and administering royal justice which were central to the Chambre de l'Edit's mandate according to the Edict of Nantes.

The Chambre de l'Edit's handling of crimes involving violence thus revolved around two policies. One emphasized keeping or restoring peace among those who had broken the law or caused public disorder (or both) by their actions; the other involved making sure that officials who administered justice at the local level did not abuse their authority—another source of disorder. Like other royal law courts, the Chambre de l'Edit had great latitude in assigning criminal punishments, but as a special court of appeal for France's Protestants, it also had a specific responsibility to redress their grievances. The chamber magistrates often dealt with cases of verbal violence with an eye to reconciliation, while corrupt or abusive judicial officials were punished harshly for their misdeeds. The common feature of

---

[2]A.N. X2b 208, 5 August 1602: en cas de Rebellion ou Resistance que le Gouverneur de Guyenne ou ses lieutenans seront admonestés de prester main forte et faire mener le canon devant les places et lieux ou seront reffugies lesdits accuses et faire en sorte que la force demeure au Roy et à la Justice.

such litigation was the court's effort to maintain peace and obedience among all of the king's subjects, as well as respect for justice at the local level.

Violence was endemic in early modern European societies, but it was not universally understood or condemned as a crime. Apart from the bloodshed and destruction that accompanied open warfare, violence was often a means of defending one's status and reputation—in a word, one's honor. Sixteenth-century French aristocrats thus claimed "the privilege of legitimated violence" not only because of their traditional role as military leaders, but also because they needed to assert and defend their honor.[3] Violence and honor remained closely linked to noble status, as symbolized by the issue of dueling: attempts to outlaw dueling in the seventeenth century proved difficult to enforce in part because they seemed to attack an essential feature of noble identity and status that the crown was reluctant to undermine.[4] Honor, however, did not belong to the nobility alone. Nonnoble persons and corporate groups, such as guilds, were also keenly aware of their honor, especially as it related to their perception of their rightful place in the hierarchical society of early modern France. Ordinary men and women demanded to be acknowledged as respectable persons ("homme ou femme de bien et d'honneur"); when challenged or affronted, they often responded with insults and violence of their own. If public order depended in part on recognizing personal and corporate honor at all levels of society, it might also be sacrificed in the name of defending honor with violence.[5]

Violence was also seen as a legitimate means to combat heresy in early modern France. During the sixteenth century, the spread of Protestant beliefs led to violent confrontations between Catholics and Huguenots, who attacked each other's beliefs, churches, and communities both before and during the Wars of Religion. Historians have argued that the religious riots of this era were not episodes of random or mindless violence, but rather the result of ordinary people battling to

[3]Kristen Neuschel, *Word of Honor: Interpreting Noble Culture in Sixteenth-Century France* (Ithaca: Cornell University Press, 1989), 204.

[4]François Billacois, *Le Duel dans la société française, XVIe–XVIIIe siècles: Essai de psychosociologie historique* (Paris: Editions de l'Ecole des Hautes Etudes en Sciences Sociales, 1986); A. Lloyd Moote, *Louis XIII, the Just* (Berkeley: University of California Press, 1989), 185–89.

[5]James R. Farr, *Hands of Honor: Artisans and Their World in Dijon, 1550–1650* (Ithaca: Cornell University Press, 1988); Arlette Jouanna, "Recherches sur la notion d'honneur au XVIe siècle," *Revue d'histoire moderne et contemporaine* 15 (1968): 592–623; Maurice Magendie, *La Politesse mondaine et les théories de l'honnêteté en France au XVIIe siècle, de 1600 à 1670* (Paris, 1925); Yves Castan, *Honnêteté et relations sociales en Languedoc, 1715–1780* (Paris: Plon, 1974).

preserve their communities from the danger that heresy represented. Since religious error threatened to pollute both polity and society, fighting heresy necessarily depended upon the use of violence.[6] Even after the military hostilities had ended, the perception of Protestants as enemies of true religion and order within society and polity persisted, and Catholic leaders often called upon the monarchy to abolish religious pluralism rather than uphold it. French Protestants, on the other hand, frequently argued that their obedience to the monarchy and the law made them more loyal subjects than their Catholic counterparts, who continued to disrupt the peace mandated by the king's edicts.[7]

Riots against taxes, rather than religion, provide another context for considering the nature and uses of popular violence. In this context, William Beik has argued that the numerous urban protests that occurred in seventeenth-century France reflected a "culture of retribution" in which crowds sought to punish municipal and royal officials who had failed to provide good governance. He links the protesters' actions to popular definitions of honor and methods of settling personal disputes, which were invoked at times of social and political rebellion to assert "a set of values about acceptable government behavior."[8] Ordinary people thus used violence to protest injustice, to punish official corruption, and to demand that ruling elites do a better job of fulfilling their responsibilities toward those they governed.

Despite the apparently legitimate uses of violence to defend honor, true religion, and justice, the notion of a "public order" that was threatened by such violence was also emerging.[9] In France as elsewhere, the central government played an active role in shaping the idea of public order and linking it to the control or

[6]Natalie Zemon Davis, "The Rites of Violence: Religious Riot in Sixteenth-Century France," in *Society and Culture in Early Modern France*, 152–87; Diefendorf, *Beneath the Cross*; Crouzet, *Les Guerriers de Dieu*; Philip Benedict, *Rouen during the Wars of Religion* (Cambridge: Cambridge University Press, 1980); Parrow, *From Defense to Resistance. Transactions of the American Philosophical Society* 83:6 (Philadelphia: American Philosophical Society, 1993); Mark Greengrass, "Hidden Transcripts: Secret Histories and Personal Testaments of Religious Violence in the French Wars of Religion," in *The Massacre in History*, ed. Mark Levene and Penny Roberts (New York: Bergahn Books, 1999), 69–88.

[7]G.W. Sypher, "'Faisant ce qu'il leur vient à plaisir': The Image of Protestantism in French Catholic Polemics on the Eve of the Religious Wars," *Sixteenth Century Journal* 11 (1980): 59–84. See also Dompnier, *Le Venin de l'hérésie*; Labrousse, *Une foi, une loi, un roi?* 77–112.

[8]Beik, *Urban Protest in Seventeenth-Century France*; 253.

[9]See especially Bruce Lenman and Geoffrey Parker, "The State, the Community and the Criminal Law in Early Modern Europe," in *Crime and the Law*, ed. Gatrell, Lenman, and Parker, 11–48. See also J.R. Hale, "Sixteenth-Century Explanations of War and Violence," *Past and Present* 51 (1971): 3–26; Thomas Kuehn, "Dispute Processing in the Renaissance: Some Florentine Examples," in his *Law, Family and Women: Toward a Legal Anthropology of Renaissance Italy* (Chicago: University of Chicago Press, 1991), 75–100.

repression of violence. Laws were issued that defined (or redefined) certain kinds of violence as crimes and determined how they should be punished; magistrates and other judicial officials were admonished to enforce the laws.[10] The French king, who was the ultimate source of justice, was also portrayed as the guarantor of public order in the realm. Of course, this process coexisted with more traditional ideas about what constituted criminal conduct, as well as alternative methods of settling disputes.[11] Although tensions between the central government and local authorities about crime, violence, and the administration of justice never completely disappeared, the struggle to impose "public order" at the local level tended to strengthen the monarchy's and the central government's power.

That struggle also forms an important context for examining the Paris Chambre de l'Edit's adjudication of disputes involving violence. The chamber magistrates dealt with a wide range of violent offenses, ranging from verbal attacks (insult, blasphemy, and seditious talk) to physical assaults. The court also heard cases involving judicial misconduct, in which local judicial officers engaged in corrupt or abusive behavior that threatened to compromise the administration of justice. Finally, the Chambre de l'Edit's records often contain information about subaltern judges' verdicts, which the chamber magistrates might confirm, overturn, or modify—including the assignment of specific punishments for crimes. All of this information allows us to analyze the Chambre de l'Edit's work, not only as a special court of appeal for Huguenots, but also as a royal tribunal engaged in the task of maintaining public order and obedience to royal justice among the king's subjects.

Crimes of violence, whether verbal or physical, featured prominently among the lawsuits heard by the Chambre de l'Edit. Table 5.1, based on a sample of 400 lawsuits from the court's records for the period of 1600 through 1610, illustrates the distribution of crimes according to five categories: verbal violence, physical violence, judicial misconduct, property crimes, and counterfeiting

The largest category—verbal violence—included blasphemy and seditious talk as well as insults aimed at individuals or their families. All were crimes that

[10]On crime and law in early modern Europe generally, see Bossy, ed., *Disputes and Settlement*; Weisser, *Crime and Punishment in Early Modern Europe*; Alfred Soman, "Deviance and Criminal Justice in Western Europe, 1300–1800: An Essay in Structure," *Criminal Justice History* I (1980): 3–28; Lenman and Parker, "The State, the Community and the Law." On developments in France, see Abbiateci et al., *Crimes et criminalité en France*; Gregory Hanlon, "Les Rituels de l'aggression en Aquitaine au XVIIe siècle," *Annales: Economies, Sociétés, Civilisations* 40 (1985): 244–68; Malcolm Greenshields, *An Economy of Violence in Early Modern France: Crime and Justice in the Haute Auvergne, 1587–1664* (University Park: Pennsylvania State University Press, 1994); Steven G. Reinhardt, *Justice in the Sarladais, 1770–1790* (Baton Rouge: Louisiana State University Press, 1991).

[11] Soman, "Deviance and Criminal Justice in Western Europe," 26–28.

Table 5.1: Crimes Identified in Sample Lawsuits
Adjudicated by the Chambre de l'Edit, 1600–1610

Crime Type	Cases (No.)
Verbal violence	127
Physical violence	106
Judicial misconduct	94
Property crimes	46
Counterfeiting	27
Total	400

essentially affected a person's honor, status, and/or reputation. Crimes of physical violence constituted the second largest category in the sample. These offenses ranged from fisticuffs to assaults involving weapons, such as swords and occasionally firearms. Judicial misconduct formed the third largest category of criminal offenses in the sample. In such cases, the accused were usually officials responsible for enforcing justice at the local level, and their offenses ranged from financial abuses to unlawful imprisonment. The most obvious property crimes were thefts of money, merchandise, and personal possessions, but this category also covered deliberate damage done to private lands and forests, and complaints about poaching or trespass on seigneurial lands. Finally, the crime of counterfeiting or fraud (*faux*) usually involved falsifying documents or objects. Most of these accusations centered on forged documents rather than counterfeit coin. It was not uncommon for litigants to accuse their opponents of having falsified evidence in a lawsuit, but this category includes only those cases where forgery was the principal issue.

Before taking a closer look at specific examples of such crimes, one should consider the penalties that the Chambre de l'Edit used to punish them. No formal code strictly prescribed how the court should assign punishments: like other royal judges, the chamber magistrates were bound by the variable authority of custom, precedent, and their own legal knowledge and discretion when deciding individual cases.[12] After reviewing the evidence, the royal prosecutor's recommendations and the *rapporteur's* summary of a case, the chamber president would determine the court's verdict from the magistrates' opinions on a case. A clerk would record the

---

[12] Allard, *Histoire de la justice criminelle,* 324–25. On the use of judicial precedent in the late medieval period, see André Sergène, "Le Précédent judiciaire au Moyen Age," *Revue historique de droit français et étranger,* 4th series, 39 (1961): 224–54, 359–70. The Chambre de l'Edit's records show little evidence of the judges' relying on previous decisions—even their own—when deciding a given lawsuit.

sentences, which were later announced publicly at court sessions and communicated to the accused persons who awaited the outcome of their trials in the Conciergerie.[13]

Criminal punishments fell into two general categories: afflictive penalties, which involved corporal punishment, and financial penalties. The Chambre de l'Edit judges used afflictive penalties such as whipping, banishment, service in the king's galleys, and death by hanging or beheading. Some contemporary forms of capital punishment, such as burning, burial alive (*enfouissement*), and being broken on the wheel (*la roue*) rarely appear in the chamber's records.[14] On the other hand, the court frequently imposed a ritual of public apology and dishonor called the *amende honorable*, which will be analyzed in detail below. The chamber magistrates also sentenced criminals to pay various kinds of financial penalties: reparations and damages (*reparations et dommages*) to compensate the successful party for injuries, wrongs and losses, fines (*amendes*) often payable to the crown or a local seigneur, and court costs (*dépens*).[15] The costs of litigation and subsequent judicial appeals, if any, were usually borne by the losing party, though judges could allocate the costs among litigants on both sides of a dispute. Of course, a judicial verdict did not always assure payment. The Chambre de l'Edit's records abound with examples of litigants' struggling (and suing) to collect the monies that the court had awarded to them. Finally, the court sometimes required payment of alms (*aumônes*), specifying both the amount and the recipient of the donation.

How often did the Chambre de l'Edit magistrates assign the various criminal penalties at their disposal? Table 5.2, column 2, based on a sample of 390 *arrêts* issued by the court between 1600 and 1610, shows the incidence of criminal punishments used. In 285 of the 390 *arrêts*, the court pronounced a verdict with one or more penalties; the remaining 105 cases were dismissed or remanded to another court. The chamber magistrates often imposed multiple punishments in a given case, sentencing a litigant to fines and reparations in addition to banishment or alms as well as an *amende honorable*. Thus, the total of 375 penalties exceeds the total number of *arrêts* in which they were recorded. The table also reflects certain penalties that were used for specifically relevant offenses, such as suspending convicted judicial officials from their offices or destroying counterfeit documents. On one occasion, the court sentenced a soldier to one year's military service in Calais

[13]Allard, *Histoire de la justice criminelle*, 324–30; Maugis, *Histoire du parlement de Paris* 1:286–302; Antoine, ed., *Guide des recherches*. See also Paul Guilhiermoz, *Enquêtes et procès: Étude sur la procédure et le fonctionnement du parlement au XIVe siècle* (Paris, 1892).

[14]Jean Imbert. *La Peine de mort: Histoire, actualité* (Paris: A. Colin, 1967).

[15]Ferriere, *Dictionnaire du droit et de pratique*, 1:81–82 (*amende pécuniaire en matière criminelle*), 1:464–68 (*dépens*), 1:497–98 (*dommages et intérêts*), 2:57–58 (*intérêts civils*), 2:518–19 (*reparations civils*).

at his own expense.[16] Since costs were generally required in any criminal conviction, they have not been included in the categories listed below.

TABLE 5.2: PENALTIES IMPOSED BY THE PARIS CHAMBRE DE L'EDIT.

PENALTY	CASES (NO.)	
	1600–1610	1615–1665
Afflictive		
Amende Honorable/ blaming/ admonishment	68	24
Banishment	40	16
Death	12	5
Galley service	9	3
Suspension from judicial office	7	2
Whipping	6	2
Counterfeit materials destroyed	5	4
Forced military service	1	—
Branding	—	1
Financial		
Reparations	67	16
Fines	58	27
Alms	39	15
Restitution of property or its value	36	4
Damages and *intérêts*	27	32
Total	375	151

Table 5.2, column 3, shows a second sample of 97 verdicts containing 151 penalties delivered during the period 1615 through 1665. The samples shown in column 3 reveal a similar distribution of penalties, as reflected in column 2.

Several factors complicate the interpretation of these figures. First, the Chambre de l'Edit's records often give details about such punishments but do not explain the magistrates' reasons for assigning them. In addition, crimes were not

[16]A.N. X2b 205, 8 January 1602. The court also ordered Pierre de Saint Clerc, sieur du Verger, to produce a certificate from the governor of Calais to prove that he had fulfilled the terms of his sentence.

always punished in precisely the same way. An infinite variety of special circumstances could influence the court's decision in a given case: the nature of offending remarks (including when and where they were made), the social status of the litigants, and the background of their immediate dispute. On the other hand, the fact that the Chambre de l'Edit heard most cases on appeal offers a useful perspective on the court's punishments. It is often possible to compare the subaltern court's verdict and penalties, if any, with the chamber magistrates' decisions.

While the Chambre de l'Edit rarely overturned the verdicts it reviewed on appeal, the court often modified the punishments assigned by lesser courts, something that was consistent with the Parlement of Paris's current judicial practice.[17] In some cases, the chamber magistrates confirmed a lower court's decision but altered the details of its execution. When the court upheld Raoul Bonny's conviction for the murder of Henry Guillaume in 1596 on appeal six years later, the judges also granted a petition by Guillaume's widow to have Bonny hanged in Paris, thus saving the expense of transporting him back to Brittany.[18] The court likewise ordered shoemaker Jean Boutrusche to be broken on the wheel in Paris rather than in Mayenne, where he had committed murder and highway robbery.[19]

In other cases, the Chambre de l'Edit modified a lesser court's verdict by substituting one punishment for another. Such modifications could increase or lessen a convicted criminal's penalty. For example, in amending a sentence issued by the *sénéchal* of Lyon, the court ordered Jerôme Maison, apprentice to a thread-dyer named Jehan Pusin, to be whipped for his involvement in the murder of Pusin's wife, instead of being merely forced to watch his master's execution.[20] On the other hand, the court sentenced teenaged Enterippe Bedeau to be whipped publicly once a week for two consecutive months and then banished from France forever, whereas the *bailli* of Provins had condemned Bedeau to be hanged.[21]

The chamber magistrates often used banishment in this fashion, perhaps because it was an inherently malleable penalty. In theory, perpetual banishment from the kingdom meant immediate execution for a condemned person who disobeyed the court's order, while banishment for more than nine years meant civil death: the banished person could not contract a marriage, inherit property, or confer legacies. Banishment for shorter periods of time or from a specific town or region, however, had less severe consequences. Convicted persons could return but

---

[17]Soman, "Aux Origines de l'appel de droit," 21–35.

[18]A.N. X2b 206, 18 April 1602; X2b 206, 20 April 1602.

[19]A.N. X2b 424, 16 June 1635.

[20]A.N. X2b 220, 8 July 1604.

[21]A.N. X2b 217, 5 January 1604. Bedeau is identified as being thirteen or fourteen years old. Whether the whippings were done in Paris or Provins is unclear.

were forbidden to hold public office in the jurisdiction from which they had been exiled.[22] Temporary banishment punished offenders by forcing them to leave their homes, families, and communities, but it also gave those communities a cooling-off period—a chance to let the passage of time and the criminal's absence alleviate any lingering hostility before he or she returned. The Chambre de l'Edit sometimes commuted capital punishment to banishment: Hector Bernier's death sentence for murder was changed to nine years' banishment from Poitou and the *prévôté et vicomté* of Paris, while Adrien de Thunes was condemned to five years' banishment from France instead of hanging.[23] André Bauchaux and his son Etienne obtained royal letters of pardon for the murder of Isaac Ovalles, but they were still sentenced to five years in the king's galleys. When the chamber magistrates heard the case on appeal in 1630, they commuted the galley service to banishment from Paris and La Rochelle—three years for André, five years for his son.[24] In contrast to these examples, the court condemned two men who gave false testimony in a lawsuit to whipping and perpetual banishment.[25]

It is difficult to assess the true severity of banishment as a criminal punishment. Unlike executions and whippings, banishment was difficult to enforce: it was quite possible for the "banished" person to remain in or around the area he or she was supposed to leave, especially if the local community did not object.[26] Moreover, condemned persons could petition to have their banishment delayed. A week after the Chambre de l'Edit delivered its verdict against André and Etienne Bauchaux, they requested six months to put their affairs in order before departing; the court granted a postponement of six weeks instead.[27] In June 1601 Jacques de Gaugy asked to delay his six-year banishment from Paris and Rouen, citing his responsibility for twelve motherless children, ruined lands, and numerous debts. The chamber magistrates gave him permission to remain in Paris and to visit Rouen legally for three months instead of the six he had requested. The court approved similar petitions submitted by Gaugy in August and December, though never for the full amount of time he had specified. Gaugy was still requesting—and receiving—such reprieves in 1603, when he pleaded arrangements for his oldest son's marriage to obtain another postponement of his banishment.[28]

[22]Ferrière, *Dictionnaire du droit et de pratique*, 1:175–76.
[23]A.N. X2b 242, 28 June 1608 (Bernier); X2b 338, 17 January 1623 (de Thunes). [AU: 338 is not in biblio.—is this correct?]
[24]A.N. X2b 389, 21 June 1630.
[25]A.N. X2b 230, 14 March 1606.
[26]Soman, "La Justice criminelle," 34–38.
[27]A.N. X2b 389, 27 June 1630.
[28]A.N. X2b 201, 6 June 1601; X2b 203, 17 August 1601; X2b 204, 20 December 1601;

Like banishment, galley service could be imposed for a specific number of years or in perpetuity. The Chambre de l'Edit often commuted death sentences to galley service, a practice that was consistent with the actions of other royal law courts in the sixteenth and seventeenth centuries.[29] Jacques Brouart was condemned to serve nine years in the king's galleys instead of hanging, while the court sentenced Jehan Clergeau to perpetual galley labor with the threat of summary execution if he tried to escape.[30] In one of its few dramatic reversals of judgment on appeal, the Chambre de l'Edit saved René de Chasseton, sieur de Malidor, from perpetual galley service as decreed by the *viséneschal* of Angoumois. Although the order for Chasseton's transport to Marseilles had been issued, he apparently managed to evade capture; after the chamber magistrates reviewed his case, they absolved him of his crime (murder), imposed heavy financial penalties on his accusers, and summoned several Angoumois judicial officials before the court to answer for their conduct.[31]

The Chambre de l'Edit also modified required payments of alms, often by distributing the funds differently than in the original sentence. The court tended to allocate donations to religious orders such as the Cordeliers or the Hôtel-Dieu in Paris, but sometimes the chamber judges ordered the money to be used for people incarcerated in Paris's prisons. Such funds were usually designated for "the Conciergerie prisoners' bread" [le pain des prisonniers de la Conciergerie], though other institutions might be chosen. Thus the Chambre de l'Edit upheld Etienne Dollaison's conviction by the *prévôt* of Paris but ordered that the donation of 16 *livres* he had been sentenced to pay for religious services should be used instead to

---

X2b 211, 5 February 1603. Gaugy's experiences highlight a paradox about banishment: since petitions for postponement were almost always granted, why not ignore the penalty altogether? Given magistrates' and lawyers' attention to procedural details, it seems possible that they did so to avoid further prosecution or worse punishment: as long as "banished" persons had permission to remain in the locality, they could not be accused of disobeying the court's orders.

[29]Marcel Aymard, "Chiourmes et galères dans la Méditerranée du XVIe siècle," in *Mélanges en l'honneur de Fernand Braudel*, vol. I: *Histoire économique du monde méditerannéan, 1450–1650* (Toulouse: Privat, 1973), 49–64; Marc Vigier and Muriel Wilder-Vigié, *Les Galériens du roi, 1661–1715* (Paris: Fayard, 1985); André Zysberg, *Les Galériens: Vies et destins de 60,000 forçats sur les galères de France, 1680–1748* (Paris: Seuil, 1987). Aymard argues that changes in the design and construction of galleys during the period 1550–1600 accentuated both the need for rowers and the complicity of royal law courts in answering that need through their verdicts, while Vigier stresses enforcement of the 1670 Ordonnance criminelle for the later seventeenth century.

[30]A.N. X2b 195, 23 June 1600 (Brouart); X2b 230, 13 March 1606 (Clergeau).

[31]A.N. X2b 209, 3 September 1602.

feed prisoners in the Châtelet.[32] On the other hand, in 1610 the court discharged a prisoner from paying 180 *écus* in alms: Jonathas Petit de Bretigny, himself a prisoner in the Conciergerie, claimed that he had never benefited from such monies and that releasing him from the forced donation was itself "a work of charity and pity" [oeuvre de charité et pitié]![33]

Diverting alms from religious charities to prisoners was consistent with the Chambre de l'Edit's general practice of modifying judicial sentences on appeal. It should be noted, however, that the court did not allocate such funds to Reformed churches or to support poor relief among Protestants. Indeed, Protestant prisoners in the Conciergerie complained to the court in 1608 that they had been excluded from receiving such alms because of religious prejudice. "Since last Easter," their petition stated, "some seditious persons, using insolent and blasphemous remarks, have incited the other Catholic prisoners to seize the box in which the alms are left and to distribute the money only among themselves."[34] The prisoners demanded restitution of their fair share of past donations, as well as access to such funds in the future. They also demanded that the chamber magistrates punish the Catholic malcontents by having them "separated...and locked up in dark cells" [sequestrés...et renfermés dans les cachots noirs]. The court responded by ordering a prison official—literally, "le concierge de la Conciergerie"—to distribute alms equally among Protestant and Catholic prisoners, with two senior prisoners of each confession supervising the process. The prisoners' other demands would require further investigation.[35]

Punishments such as galley service, whipping, and some financial penalties also carried personal and social dishonor. "Infamy" derived from criminal conviction and punishment could bar an individual from holding public office or from testifying in legal proceedings.[36] But infamy, too, could be modified by the chamber

---

[32]A.N. X2b 220, 30 July 1604. In the original sentence, the alms were to be used for "l'entretenement de la messe qui se dict et celebre en la chambre criminelle."

[33]A.N. X2b 253, 4 May 1610.

[34]A.N. X2b 242, 7 June 1608: depuis les festes de Pasques dernier aucuns seditieux usans d'insolences avec blasphemes auroient suscite les aultres prisonniers catolicques pour s'emparer de la boiste ou se met lesdicts aulmosnes et en fut la distribution entre eulx seuls sans y admettre esdicts supplians. The Protestant prisoners justified their demand to be included in the alms distribution by referring to the Edict of Nantes: "par article expres de l'edict ceulx de leur qualité peuvent participer aux aumosnes publicques qui se font à tous les pauvres prisonniers en general." See "Edict of Nantes," 45 (art. 22).

[35]A.N. X2b 242, 7 June 1608: "deux des plus anciens prisonniers catolicques et deux de ladicte Religion pretendue reformee."

[36]Ferrière, *Dictionnaire du droit et de pratique*, 2:23–24 *(infame, infamie)*. See also Pieter Spierenburg, *The Spectacle of Suffering: Executions and the Evolution of Repression from a Pre-Industrial Metropolis to the European Experience* (Cambridge: Cambridge University Press, 1984).

judges. When Marc Jousselin was condemned to pay fines, reparations, and costs for insults and malfeasance toward a merchant from La Rochelle, the chamber magistrates specified that Jousselin would not incur "any note of infamy" [aucune note d'infamie] because of his conviction. Moreover, they ordered that Jousselin's son could now be appointed to the office of *sergent royal;* his acceptance had been suspended because of the allegations against his father.[37] Whether the court's declaration made Jousselin a worthy man in the eyes of his neighbors and other local officials is a question that the *arrêt* alone cannot answer. The court's verdict did assure that he could continue in his office as clerk of a seigneurial court at Chastellaillon.

As these examples show, the Chambre de l'Edit disposed of a wide range of criminal punishments when reviewing criminal lawsuits on appeal. In assigning financial payments and afflictive penalties, the chamber magistrates often modified the decisions of subaltern judges. The crimes at issue in those cases merit closer examination, specifically those in three categories: verbal violence, physical attacks, and judicial misconduct.

When Protestant prisoners in the Paris Conciergerie petitioned the Chambre de l'Edit about "seditious persons" making "insolent and blasphemous remarks," they echoed complaints about verbal violence that occurred outside prison walls. This kind of violence came in many forms. Offensive words might be spoken, sung, or expressed in defamatory writings. Personal insults might be directed against one's relatives, neighbors, or strangers, while blasphemy usually involved offensive remarks about God, religious objects, beliefs, and practices. Similarly, seditious talk entailed insults about the king, his laws, or officials who represented his authority.[38] Despite the differences among these crimes, all were fundamentally linked to the concept of honor. A person or family could be dishonored by insults, just as blasphemy and seditious words offended the honor of God and the

[37]A.N. X2b 206, 1 April 1602. The *arrêt* does not explain the exact nature of Jousselin's crimes, though it seems he tried to foment a lawsuit against merchant Jehan Lecourt through a third party.
[38]Jean Delumeau, ed., *Injures et blasphèmes* (Paris: Editions Imago, 1989); Leonard Levy, *Treason against God: A History of the Offense of Blasphemy* (New York: Schocken Books, 1981); Arlette Farge, *Subversive Words: Public Opinion in Eighteenth-Century France,* trans. Rosemary Morris (University Park: Pennsylvania State University Press, 1995); Peter Burke, "Insult and Blasphemy in Early Modern Italy," in his *The Historical Anthropology of Early Modern Italy* (Cambridge: Cambridge University Press, 1987), 95–109; Donald Weinstein, "Fighting or Flyting? Verbal Duelling in Mid-Sixteenth-Century Italy," in *Crime, Society and the Law,* 204–20; Richard C. Trexler, "Reverence and Profanity in the Study of Early Modern Religion," in *Religion and Society in Early Modern Europe, 1500–1800,* ed. Kaspar von Greyerz (London: Allen & Unwin, 1984), 254–60; and J.A. Sharpe, *Defamation and Sexual Slander in Early Modern England: The Church Courts at York,* Borthwick Papers No. 58 (York: University of York, 1980).

king, respectively. Language was a powerful tool for asserting or attacking reputation, belief, and allegiance; it became downright dangerous when used in public places, such as market squares or church entrances, or expressed to an audience through song or print. When provocative words were uttered publicly, they could incite conflict and even physical violence.

The power of words to cause violent confrontations and reopen old wounds was reflected in the Edict of Nantes. The edict's terms explicitly prohibited Huguenots and Catholics from insulting or attacking each other "by word or deed," enjoining both groups to live in peace together or to be punished accordingly.[39] Article 17 specifically forbade preachers and other public speakers to use any speech that might lead to rebellious action; they, too, were ordered "to contain themselves and carry themselves modestly and to say nothing which was not to the edification and instruction of their listeners and for the maintenance of the repose and tranquility" which the king had established in France.[40] The edict thus condemned provocative speech by religious preachers as well as laypersons. Indeed, all of the king's subjects were ordered to exercise self-discipline in obedience to the law; offenders risked being treated as a threat to public peace itself. Despite these warnings, accusations of insult, blasphemy, and seditious talk were at the heart of many lawsuits heard by the Chambre de l'Edit.

Interpreting cases of verbal violence can be difficult because court records often describe insulting words simply as *injures, insolences, parolles scandaleuses, propos séditieux,* and *blasphèmes*—terms that tend to mask the exact nature of what was said and why it was offensive. Some of the Chambre de l'Edit's cases, however, do contain clues about the specific content of such speech. For example, in January 1602 the court reviewed the appeal of Tobie Boucher, who had been condemned by the *bailli* of Touraine for "boldly, meanly and seditiously... having uttered aloud the blasphemies against the mother of God contained in the *procès verbal.*"[41] Louis Dupront spoke "insults and blasphemies against the honor of God," for which the judge of Monthery (a seigneury belonging to the dean and canons of the church of Saint-Maur-des-Fosses) sentenced him to a public apology and perpetual banishment.[42] Claude Henry complained to the Chambre de l'Edit after he was convicted of blasphemy: he had met up with some fellow workers and "holding a paper, said, 'Here's a jubilee that gives a dispensation for eating meat during Lent; who will give me three *sols* for it?'" In response to Henry's appeal, the court

---

[39]"Edict of Nantes," 42 (art. 2).

[40]"Edict of Nantes," 45 (art. 17).

[41]A.N. X2b 205, 17 January 1602: themerairement, meschamment et seditieusem[ent] il avoit profere les blasphemes contre la mere de dieu contenus aud[it] process verbal.

[42]A.N. X2b 220, 3 August 1604: injures et blasphemes contre l'honneur de dieu.

reduced his fine but required him to pay court costs.[43] A royal judge at Châlons convicted Germain Hemet, a mason from the town of Saint Germain, for having spoken "scandalous words" [parolles scandaleuses]. After reviewing the case on appeal, the Chambre de l'Edit issued a verdict that, among other things, required Hemet to declare "that he had never said nor heard anything against the mystery of the holy trinity."[44]

Germain Hemet's case clearly illustrates the connection between blasphemy, public order, and rebellion against royal authority. The Chambre de l'Edit condemned Hemet for having spoken "ignorantly, scandalously, and indiscreetly in contravening the edicts of pacification." "In the future," the *arrêt* continued, "[the court] forbids all persons to provoke each other by arguments or otherwise regarding religion and to use words tending to sedition and scandal, but enjoins them to behave modestly following the king's edicts and ordinances."[45] The chamber judges likewise ordered Louis Dupront not to repeat his offense, but to "live well and conduct himself in the future according to the edicts."[46] After hearing the appeal of Antoine Le Varre and Nicollas Battereau in July 1605, the Chambre de l'Edit sentenced them to a formal reprimand for having spoken blasphemies, sung a scandalous song, and publicly argued about religion. The verdict stated:

> [The court] enjoins them and all others of the so-called reformed
> religion to live and conduct themselves according to the edicts on
> pain of being treated as infractors of the said edicts, perturbers of the
> public peace [and] rebels against the king and justice.[47]

The judges also decreed that their decision should be read at an open session of the law court in the *ville* and *châtellenie* of Venin, where Le Varre and Battereau

---

[43]A.N. X2b 245, 17 December 1610: rencontrant des ouvriers luy tenant un papier dict voila un jubillé qui donne disponce de manger la chair en Caresme, qu m'en vouldra donner trois sols, je luy en bailleray.

[44]A.N. X2b 206, 18 March 1602: n'avoir jamais dict ny entendu dire aulcune chose contre le mystere de la saincte trinité.

[45]A.N. X2b 206, 18 March 1602: ignoramment, scandaleusement et indiscretement en contrevenant aux edicts de pacification.... [La cour] faict deffences à toutes personnes à l'advenir se provoquer par disputes ou aultrement sur le faict de la Religion ny user de parolles tendantes à sedition et scandale, ains leur enjoint se comporter modestement suivants les edicts et ordonnances du Roy.

[46]A.N. X2b 220, 3 August 1604: luy enjoint de bien vivre et se comporter à l'advenir suivant les edicts.

[47]A.N. X2b 226, 25 July 1605: [La cour] leur a enjoinct et enjoinct et à tous aultres de la Relligion pretendue reformee de vivre et se comporter suivans les edicts sur peine d'estre procede contre les contrevenans comme infracteurs desd[its] edicts, perturbateurs du Repos public [et] Rebelles au Roy et à Justice.

lived, so that the entire community would be aware of the Chambre de l'Edit's injunction.[48]

In other cases, litigants accused of seditious talk had directly criticized the king and his edicts. A magistrate at Bourges condemned royal notary Anthoine Pastoureau for speaking "words [that were] scandalous and full of blasphemies against the honor of God and the edicts and ordinances of the king"; Pastoureau appealed his sentence to the Chambre de l'Edit in January 1600.[49] Ancelot Beauxavier, a traveling apprentice shoemaker (compagnon cordonnier) from the village of Rainvillier, likewise petitioned the court regarding his conviction for "scandalous and seditious words against the edicts of pacification."[50]

In all of the above lawsuits, local magistrates had sentenced the offender to perform an amende honorable, a criminal penalty that involved a ritual apology, public humiliation, and dishonor. Crimes of verbal violence were invariably punished with some form of judicial apology, but the most serious of these punishments was the amende honorable, in which the offender was condemned to appear bareheaded and barefoot, dressed in a chemise with a rope around the neck, and carrying a large lit candle. Kneeling, the offender then acknowledged aloud his or her misdeed and begged pardon of God, the king, and justice. The amende honorable was always performed in a public place specified by the judge—an open square on market day, the steps of a church, or during a law court's public session—to assure a large audience for the offender's repentance. In a sixteenth-century treatise on criminal procedure, French jurist Jean Milles de Souvigny described an amende honorable in which the offender apologized not only to God, the king, and justice, but also to the plaintiffs (plaignants) in his case.[51]

Other forms of judicial apology were essentially variations on the amende honorable. An amende seche required a person to apologize while bareheaded and kneeling before his judges; other witnesses might be present, but the punishment took place in the relative privacy of the court chambers and without the chemise, rope, and candle of the amende honorable. Magistrates sentenced some individuals to be blamed (à être blasmé), that is, to receive a severe official reprimand, while others were merely admonished (admonesté) and warned not to repeat their offense.[52]

---

[48] A.N. X2b 226, 23 July 1605.

[49] A.N. X2b 193, 20 January 1600: parolles scandaleuses et pleaines de blasphemes contre l'honneur de dieu et les edicts et ordonnances du Roy.

[50] A.N. X2b 255, 7 August 1610: propos scandaleux et seditieux contre l'edict de pacification.

[51] Jean Milles de Souvigny, Pratique Criminelle/par Jean de mille; translaté de latin en vulgaire françoys par Arlette Lebigre (Paris, 1541; repr. Moulins: Les Marmousets, 1983), 127–28.

[52] Ferrière, Dictionnaire du droit et de pratique, 1:55 (Admonesté), 200 (Blasmé), and 81 (Amende séche). The amende séche as described in Ferrière's work clearly matches the punishment as described in the

The *amende honorable* developed over several centuries in the context of religious as well as legal forms of apology. It closely resembled public penance, which similarly combined elements of humiliation and reconciliation. Mary C. Mansfield has noted that in thirteenth-century France, public penance was imposed "in ambiguous cases, where there was no unchallenged authority...[and] where the sin was partly spiritual, partly secular."[53] When assigned by the Parlement of Paris in the fifteenth century, the *amende honorable* often became a ritual inversion of the offense and a necessary element in restoring peace between the opposing parties. Medieval royal judges and prosecutors thus helped to conflate crime and sin, further transforming the public penance borrowed from ecclesiastical authorities into a criminal penalty that emphasized obedience to secular justice.[54]

During the first half of the sixteenth century, the *amende honorable* was a key feature of the French parlements' prosecution of heresy. In assigning this criminal penalty, parlement magistrates required condemned persons to renounce their errors, but their formulaic apology to God, the king, and justice did not offer much chance for spontaneous speech or preaching. The *amende honorable* also subjected heretics to public dishonor without the bloody spectacle of hanging or burning.[55] For those guilty of crimes other than heresy, an *amende honorable* sometimes preceded banishment or death; in this context, it became part of the spectacle of public execution, rather than an alternative to it.[56] Public apology and humiliation also remained in use by ecclesiastical authorities of both confessions. Although Protestant reformers rejected penance as a sacrament, Reformed communities throughout Europe used forms of public penance to both punish and reconcile wayward congregants who had violated the requirements of godly social discipline.[57]

Chambre de l'Edit's records, though the term *"amende séche"* does not appear in the *arrêts* examined for this study.

[53]Mary C. Mansfield, *The Humiliation of Sinners: Public Penance in Thirteenth-Century France* (Ithaca: Cornell University Press, 1995), 291.

[54]Gauvard, *"De Grace especial,"* 745–52.

[55]Monter, *Judging the French Reformation*, 185–87. See also Weiss, *La Chambre ardente.*

[56]Gauvard, *"De Grace especial,"* 705–52; M. Bée, "Le Spectacle de l'exécution dans la France de l'Ancien Régime," *Annales: Economies, Sociétés, Civilisations* 38 (1983): 843–63. On public executions as spectacles, see also Spierenburg, *The Spectacle of Suffering*; David Nicholls, "The Theatre of Martyrdom in the French Reformation," *Past and Present* 121 (1988): 49–73.

[57]The literature on social discipline, confession, and ritual in the Protestant Reformation is large and continually growing. I have benefited especially from the following: Lualdi and Thayer, eds., *Penitence in the Age of Reformations*; Susan C. Karant-Nunn, *Reformation of Ritual: An Interpretation of Early Modern Germany* (New York: Routledge, 1997); W. David Myers, *"Poor Sinning Folk": Confession and

As a criminal punishment, however, the *amende honorable* was more than a public act of apology and reconciliation akin to penance; it was literally a "fine of honor." Performing an *amende honorable* restored honor to the offended party by forcing the offender to sacrifice a portion of his or her honor through a ritual of humiliation. Condemned persons had to appear in a humble posture (kneeling) and without any outward marks of wealth or status (bareheaded, barefoot, and in a chemise) in order to acknowledge their offense publicly before a host of witnesses.

Publicity was an important key to measuring the penalty's level of dishonor and therefore the gravity of the punishment itself. The *amende seche*, blaming, and admonishment all required the condemned person's abasement in the magistrates' chambers—a venue far removed from the church entrances, public court sessions, and market squares where *amendes honorables* usually took place. The audience, too, was different: the less public forms of judicial apology did not occur in front of the indiscriminate mix of relatives, neighbors, acquaintances, and strangers who, along with local judicial and clerical officials, might witness an *amende honorable*. The *amende seche*, blaming, and admonishment were less serious penalties because they were less public rituals of apology, made without the dishonoring gestures and symbols required by a full-fledged *amende honorable*.[58]

The cases of blasphemy and seditious talk described above reveal a striking pattern in the Chambre de l'Edit's use of public judicial apologies, including the *amende honorable*. While local authorities were prepared to punish blasphemous and seditious speech with an *amende honorable*, the chamber judges tended to reduce that penalty to a less public (and therefore less humiliating) form of judicial apology. For example, the Chambre de l'Edit ordered notary Antoine Pastoureau "to declare in the council chamber of this court, being bare headed and on his knees,

---

Conscience in Counter-Reformation Germany (Ithaca: Cornell University Press, 1996); Thomas N. Tentler, *Sin and Confession on the Eve of the Reformation* (Princeton: Princeton University Press, 1977); John Bossy, "The Social History of Confession in the Age of the Reformation," *Transactions of the Royal Historical Society*, 5th series, 25 (1975): 21–38; Ronnie Po-chia Hsia, *Social Discipline in the Reformation: Central Europe, 1550–1750* (New York: Routledge, 1989); Edward Muir, *Ritual in Early Modern Europe* (Cambridge: Cambridge University Press, 1997).

[58]Jan Bremmer and Herman Roodenburg, eds., *A Cultural History of Gesture* (Ithaca: Cornell University Press, 1991); Julian Pitt-Rivers, "Honour and Social Status," in *Honour and Shame: The Values of Mediterranean Society*, ed. J.G. Peristiany (Chicago: University of Chicago Press, 1966), 21–77; Arlette Farge, "The Honor and Secrecy of Families," in *A History of Private Life*, vol. 3, *Passions of the Renaissance*, 571–607. For perspectives on honor, politics, and society outside France, see Mervyn James, *English Politics and the Concept of Honour, 1485–1642*, Past and Present Supplement, no. 3 (Oxford: Past & Present Society, 1978); Nancy Shields Kollmann, "Honor and Dishonor in Early Modern Russia," *Forschungen zur osteuropäischen geschichte* 46 (1992): 131–46.

that boldly, indiscreetly, and with poor judgment he uttered aloud the words mentioned in the said trial, which he repents in demanding pardon of God, the king, and Justice."[59] This was a far cry from Pastoureau's original sentence, which required him to perform an *amende honorable*—complete with chemise and burning candle—during a public session of the court at Bourges. Louis Dupront's punishment for blasphemy—an *amende honorable* during a plenary session of the local law court at Monthery—was similarly reduced to a formal apology before the Paris magistrates, as was Ancelot Beauxavier's *amende honorable* for seditious words about the king's edicts.[60] Germain Hemet had been sentenced to perform two *amendes honorables* for his inflammatory remarks about the trinity. The first was to take place at an open session of the local law court, after which Hemet was supposed to be taken "to the public place in the said Saint Germain where he held forth the said words, there to make a similar *amende honorable*."[61] The Chambre de l'Edit instead ordered him to appear bareheaded and kneeling and to be "blamed, admonished, and remonstrances made to him" [blasmé, admonesté et remonstrances à luy faictes] by the Paris judges themselves. After disavowing his scandalous remarks, Hemet would have to withdraw ("s'abstiendra") from Paris and Châlons for six months.[62] The chamber judges administered a "blaming" to Tobie Boucher, another blasphemer, before ordering him to withdraw from the town and suburbs of Tours for three years.[63] And Ambrois Boisguet, who had been sentenced by a royal judge at Tours to perform an *amende honorable* at the main entrance of one of the city's churches, was required instead to appear before the Chambre de l'Edit, kneeling and bareheaded, to beg pardon of God, the king, and justice for his "scandalous and seditious words" and then absent himself from Saint-Laurent-en Gastine for six months.[64]

The Chambre de l'Edit's decisions in these cases highlight the public nature of the *amende honorable*, as well as the crimes it was intended to punish. Blasphemous and seditious talk often involved remarks about religious differences and the laws governing them that were uttered "boldly," "indiscreetly," and "scandalously"—in other words, publicly rather than privately, and in a manner that could provoke

[59]A.N. X2b 193, 20 January 1600: declarer en la chambre du conseil d'icelle court estant nue teste et à genoux que temerairement, indiscretement et comme mal advise il a profere les parolles mentionnes aud[it] process dont il se repend en demander pardon à dieu au Roy et à Justice.

[60]A.N. X2b 220, 3 August 1604 (Dupront); X2b 255, 7 August 1610 (Beauxavier).

[61]A.N. X2b 206, 18 March 1602: en la place publicque dud[it] Saint Germain ou il avoit tenu lesd[its] parolles pour y f[air]e pareille amende honorable.

[62]A.N. X2b 206, 18 March 1602.

[63]A.N. X2b 205, 17 January 1602.

[64]A.N. X2b 193, 29 January 1600. Boisguet was condemned for blasphemy specifically "against the holy sacrament of the altar" [contre le sainct sacrement de l'autel].

whoever might be listening to argument and perhaps violent disagreement. For such offenses, an *amende honorable* seemed to represent an appropriately public punishment. Yet the Chambre de l'Edit often transformed the *amendes honorables* assigned by local authorities into judicial apologies or reprimands which were relatively private. Paradoxically, these "private" judicial apologies imposed by the Chambre de l'Edit emphasized the offenders' confrontation with the "public" authority that the chamber magistrates embodied as members of the Parlement of Paris.[65] The Chambre de l'Edit thus tended to transform a public ritual of humiliation and dishonor into judicial apologies that required a more private submission to the court and the royal justice it represented.

The Chambre de l'Edit, however, did not always revise or reduce the verdicts of local authorities in cases of blasphemy and seditious talk, as in the case of a notary named Jehan François. He had been summoned before the *lieutenant criminel* of the Châtelet in Paris for speaking "oaths and seditious and scandalous words against the honor of God, the authority of the king, his parlement, and public peace, and insults against the honor of [the priest Jehan] Tireul and the safety of his person." While being questioned by the Châtelet judges, François made further inflammatory remarks: he declared that "he would prefer that his child die without baptism than receive the baptism that [the child] would have received" in the church of Saint-Etienne-du-Mont, where Tireul worked.[66] François was condemned to apologize formally for the incident and personally to Tireul, and his offending remarks were to be stricken from the court records "as defamatory and indiscreetly written against the honor of the said Tireul and his order [and] to the prejudice of the modesty commanded by the king's edict to his subjects to live peaceably as brothers, friends, and fellow citizens under obedience to him." In this case, the Chambre de l'Edit upheld the original sentence, ordering François not to provoke or threaten Tireul in the future.[67] The notary's potent combination of

[65]On the variable connotations of "public" and "private" in early modern France, see Ariès's introduction to *The History of Private Life*, vol. 3, *Passions of the Renaissance*, 9. On the "public sphere" and the legal world for a later period, see David A. Bell, "The 'Public Sphere,' the State and the World of Law in Eighteenth-Century France," *French Historical Studies* 17 (1994): 912–34; Maza, "Le Tribunal de la nation," 73–90.

[66]A.N. X2b 198, 1 December 1600: "Il auroit dict et profere...les jurements et propos seditieux et scandaleux contre l'honneur de dieu, l'auctorite du Roy, de son parlement et du repos public et injures contre l'honneur dudict Thireul et seurete de sa personne.... Il auroit repondu et dict en ses interrogatoires qu'il eust mieulx ayme que son enfant fust mort sans baptesme que d'avoir receu le baptesme qu'il auroit receu en ladict eglise."

[67]A.N. X2b 198, 1 December 1600: "comme diffamatoires et indiscretement escriptes contre l'honneur dudict Thireul et de son ordre, [et] au prejudice de la modestie commande par l'edict du Roy à ses subjects pour vivre paisiblement comme frères, amys et concitoyens soubs son obeissance."

blasphemy, sedition, and personal insult—which included remarks about the parlement itself—apparently did not merit a reduced judicial apology.

In adjudicating cases of blasphemy and seditious talk in the early seventeenth century, the Chambre de l'Edit struggled to enforce the Edict of Nantes's decree of orderly public behavior. Offenders such as Louis Dupront, Germain Hemet, Nicollas Bettereau, and Antoine Le Varre were condemned for provocative speech and warned to conduct themselves "according to the edicts." By the same token, the court tended to modify the penalty most often assigned by local judges—the *amende honorable*—by reducing it to less public forms of apology that would be less likely to further inflame local passions over the offender's words. The chamber magistrates' selective use of public apology and dishonor to punish blasphemous and seditious talk reflects their effort to keep the peace between Catholics and Huguenots.

The crimes of blasphemy and seditious talk remained linked as such cases continued to appear in the court's records later in the seventeenth century. In June 1620, for example, Marthe Angoumois appealed to the Chambre de l'Edit after being condemned to perform an *amende honorable* in the royal law court at Saumur to atone for blasphemy. The chamber magistrates "admonished" her themselves and reduced her financial penalties from 50 *livres* to four *livres.* Finally, the judges ordered her "to comport herself according to the edicts" [se comporter suivant les edicts].[68] When Jean Clerget petitioned the Chambre de l'Edit in January 1625 to prevent his arrest for blasphemy, the royal prosecutor told the court that several witnesses could attest to Clerget's having used "very bad words...against the faith and the belief of Catholics" [tres mauvaises parolles...contre la foy et la creance des Catholicques] which constituted "a public scandal" [un scandal publicq] and would lead to sedition. The chamber magistrates ordered Clerget to be returned as a prisoner to Langres to answer the charges against him.[69] André Martin appealed to the Chambre de l'Edit after a royal judge at Baugency had convicted him of "having spoken badly and insolently against the holy sacrament of the altar" [d'avoir mal et insolement parlé contre le sainct sacrement de l'autel]. Martin was sentenced to a reprimand before the court at Baugency and a fine of 100 *livres,* part of which would be used to pay for a candle to be burned before the altar of the Holy Sacrament in the church of Saint Fremin at Baugency. He was also told not to repeat his offense "or cause any scandal or sedition" [ny causer aucun scandalle

---

[68] A.N. X2b 319, 22 June 1620. The chamber judges "admonished" Angoumois. Her original fine was divided in thirds and allocated to the king, the Hôtel-Dieu at Saumur, and for reparations to the local prison; the Chambre de l'Edit ordered her reduced fine to be used for the Conciergerie prisoners' bread.

[69] A.N. X2b 351, 18 January 1625.

ny sedition] in the future. After reviewing his case, the Chambre de l'Edit carried out the "blaming" that the original sentence had required and reduced his fine to eight *livres*.[70]

Throughout the seventeenth century, then, the Chambre de l'Edit dealt with cases of blasphemy and sedition as a form of verbal violence. The two crimes were closely connected, for inflammatory speech about religious beliefs, practices, and objects contravened the king's laws forbidding such remarks. A key feature of these crimes was that the offending words were uttered "scandalously" and "indiscreetly" in public places or circulated in writing or song. The speakers thus failed (or refused) to practice the "modesty" and self-discipline required to keep the peace; instead, their words produced public disorder and conflict. Given the public nature of both the crimes and the threat they represented, the chamber magistrates punished such offenses with a selective use of judicial apology, often situating the punishment within the judges' own chambers and delivering the reprimands themselves rather than exposing the offender (and his or her inflammatory words) to further publicity.

Not all of the Chambre de l'Edit's cases concerning verbal violence, however, involved blasphemy and sedition. Personal insults also led to numerous lawsuits before the court. Although these offending words were usually directed against individuals, their spouses, or their families rather than God or the king and his edicts, personal insult still involved dishonor and threatened public order. As in cases of blasphemy and seditious talk, some kind of apology was required in order to restore honor to the offended party. Instead of an *amende honorable, amende seche,* or other formal judicial reprimands, however, the Chambre de l'Edit usually required the offender to apologize directly to the insulted person.

The court's records of such cases often lack details about the insulting words at issue, describing them simply as *injures, propos scandaleux,* and *insolences.* Regardless of the specific nature of the insults, the offended person's honor was always at stake. When Magdelaine Dufour was insulted by René Nepveu and his two sons, she and her husband sued before the royal judge at Chinon, but he simply ordered the Nepveus to behave in the future. After reviewing the case on appeal, the Chambre de l'Edit sentenced the Nepveus to appear before the judge at Chinon and, in the presence of Dufour, her husband, and four of the couple's relatives, to declare "that they did not intend to maintain the words…uttered against the honor of [Magdelaine] Dufour and begged her to forget them, and that they knew nothing

---

[70]A.N. X2b 629, 12 July 1660. Martin was "mandé en la chambre estant à genoux a esté blasmé." The court also upheld the provision for the candle, but the remainder of Martin's reduced fine was allocated for the Conciergerie prisoners' bread.

about her but goodness and honor." The Nepveus were also condemned to pay the costs of both the original lawsuit and the appeal.[71] Similarly, Orienne Dauthon and two others were convicted of insulting Etienne Sableau and his family. According to the lower court's verdict, Dauthon and her accomplices had to acknowledge the Sableaus "as honorable and respectable people of good descent, [who] were in no way stained by the insults mentioned in the proceedings"; the apology had to be made in the presence of four of the Sableaus' relatives or friends. The chamber magistrates rejected Dauthon's appeal and ordered the original sentence to be carried out.[72]

In some cases, the court records hint at slurs that were professional as well as personal. The Chambre de l'Edit upheld widow Claudine Minarval's condemnation for the "slanderous accusation" [calumnieuse accusation] she had made against Louis Serres, a medical doctor from Lyon. The presidial court at Lyon had sentenced Minarval to pay legal costs and to be reprimanded in court ("blasmé en la chambre du conseil"), and the chamber magistrates rejected her appeal.[73] The Chambre de l'Edit confirmed a sentence issued against Jehan Barbier, a *vigneron* from Gie-sur-Seine who had insulted a Reformed minister named Jehan Parisot during legal proceedings involving the two men. Barbier was condemned to declare before Parisot and six witnesses that he acknowledged the minister to be a respectable person who fulfilled his clerical responsibilities well, and to provide a written declaration to that effect.[74]

The Chambre de l'Edit's punishment of Jehan Barbier illustrates a common feature of apologies for personal insult: they often had to be made in writing. The court frequently sentenced offenders not only to apologize before witnesses, but also to make a formal declaration before a court clerk acknowledging their opposing party's honor and good reputation. For example, in 1606 the chamber judges reviewed a petition from Joseph de Mahier. He had successfully sued Pierre Amyot and his wife Rachael Dermal for insult, but another judge had dismissed the charges, accepting Dermal's claim that she had already retracted her angry

---

[71]A.N. X2b 193, 10 February 1600: ils n'entendent soustenir les propos...proferes contre l'honneur de ladicte Dufour et la prier de les oublyer et qu'ils n'ont sceu et ne scavent en elle qu de bien et honneur. Unlike the Chambre de l'Edit, the judge at Chinon had condemned the parties to pay their own legal costs ("chacun à leur regard").

[72]A.N. X2b 219, 25 June 1604: gens de bien et d'honneur et de bonne lignes, et n'estre nullement tasches des injures mentionees audict proces. In the *arrêt* Sableau is identified as *procureur fiscal* of the seigneury of Vivonne.

[73]A.N. X2b 389, 6 June 1630.

[74]A.N. X2b 218, 13 April 1604: "homme d'honneur, bon religieux et bien vivant en sa profession, non coupable des injures mentionnees au process, dont seroit dresse acte et delivre audit Parisot."

remarks against Mahier. To settle the case, the Chambre de l'Edit ordered Dermal to obtain a written record of the retraction she had made and deliver it to Mahier.[75] Daniel Mouflier appealed to the court in 1635 regarding his conviction for insulting and violent behavior toward Marie de La Creuse. He had been sentenced to apologize for his behavior before La Creuse, her husband, and two or three witnesses of their choice, declaring that "he was sorry to have beaten and attacked the said de La Creuse whom he acknowledged as an honorable woman who had never behaved badly." In revising his punishment, the chamber magistrates ordered Mouflier to file a written declaration to that effect at the local law court in Montreuil.[76] When widow Nicole Le Doux was condemned for insulting François Doyenne, sieur de Rougemont, and his wife, a local judge ordered her to apologize verbally to the couple and four witnesses of their choice for "the injurious words mentioned at the trial [and] to pray that they would forget them" [les paroles injurieuses mentionnees au proces (et) les prieroit de les oublier]. In response to Le Doux's appeal, the Chambre de l'Edit required her to file a written *acte* with the local court clerk acknowledging Doyenne and his wife as honorable persons.[77]

By making offenders apologize for personal insults before witnesses or in writing, the Chambre de l'Edit again used the relative publicity of such punishments to help restore honor to the offended parties. While witnesses could attest to the fact that the apology had been made, written apologies could be used to publicize the offender's retraction even more widely. After a royal judge at Niort condemned Marie Moynier for insulting André Hersant and his wife, he ordered Moynier to provide a written record of her declaration that they were "persons of honor and good reputation" [personnes d'honneur et de bonne renommée] and to pay the costs of the legal proceedings. Moynier petitioned the Chambre de l'Edit to review her case, but to no avail. The chamber judges not only confirmed the sentence, but also authorized Hersant and his wife to publicize Moynier's written admission of their good character. The difference between the parties' social class may have been a factor in the court's decision: Hersant is identified as "peer and citizen of the city of Niort" [pair et bourgeois de ladicte ville de Niort], while Moynier was a shoemaker's wife. Publicizing Moynier's apology would have been

[75]A.N. X2b 229, 18 January 1606. The *arrêt* indicates that Dermal claimed to have made her statements against Mahier "in anger" [par Collere].

[76]A.N. X2b 424, 16 June 1635: il estoit marry d'avoir battu et excede ladite de La Creuse laquelle il tiendroit pour femme de bien et n'estre jamais mal comportee.

[77]A.N. X2b 628, 21 June 1660: Le Doux was ordered "bailer acte au greffe à ses depens qu'elle reconnoist led[it] Doyenne et [Suzanne] Dauphin sa femme pour gens de bien et d'honneur non entaches des injures par elle proferes."

an important factor in restoring Hersant's and his wife's reputations.[78] Similarly, the Chambre de l'Edit confirmed a sentence issued against Guillaume Charpentier, Simon Gigot, and Hellie Voillant for insulting Toussaint Millien and Jean Guerin while they were embroiled in litigation before the *lieutenant criminel* of Nevers. By the time the chamber magistrates reviewed the case, Guerin had been replaced in the lawsuit by his widow, Leonarde Ursin. Charpentier and his accomplices were ordered to file an *acte* stating "that they knew nothing but good and honor of the person and family of the said Guerin and Millien" [qu'ils ne scavent que bien et honneur en la personne et famille desdits Guerin et Millien]. The court also authorized the offended parties to publicize this declaration in their church and community and decreed that the insulting words should be stricken from all of the local court records.[79]

In some cases, personal insults were expressed in legal documents themselves. Martin Nesmond, sieur de Bunes, accused Pierre de Marc of inserting insults about Nesmond's wife in a deposition that he had given in a separate legal proceeding. The Chambre de l'Edit decreed that the deposition should be suppressed and ordered Marc to acknowledge the lady's honor before a local court clerk.[80] The court received a similar petition from Jean Poullain and his wife, whose insulting comments about Jean Du Boys and his wife, Jeanne Sarazin, were recorded in a formal declaration. As a result, a subaltern judge had ordered Poullain and his wife to admit "that they had not intended to speak of Du Boys in their complaint, whom they acknowledged along with his wife as honorable persons" [qu'ils n'avoient entendu par leur plainte parler dudit Du Boys lequel avec sa femme ils recognoistroient pour gens de bien et d'honneur] and to provide Du Boys with a written declaration to that effect. A month later Poullain and his wife were threatened with fines and imprisonment if they insulted or attacked Du Boys or his family. The chamber magistrates upheld these condemnations after reviewing the case, sentencing Poullain to pay the costs of his unsuccessful appeal.[81]

Of course, insults as well as apologies could be expressed in writing, as the following cases illustrate. When Nicolas Thevenot and several other men, including a Reformed minister, wrote and printed an inflammatory "declaration," the

[78]A.N. X2b 205, 23 January 1602.

[79]A.N. X2b 480, 1 August 1644: "lequel acte lesdits Guerin et Millien pouvoit faire publier aux prosnes desdites eglises parochialles de leur domiciles et autres lieux...[la cour] ordonne que les parolles injurieuses mentionnees esdites interrogatoires...seront rayees et biffees tant des grosses que minutes par le plus proche judge royal des lieux...."

[80]A.N. X2b 243, 27 August 1608.

[81]A.N. X2b 424, 4 June 1635: "de ne mesdire ny meffaire audit Du Boys et les siens à peine d'amende arbitraire et prison." Poullain's wife is not named in the document.

Chambre de l'Edit ordered the document destroyed. The court also forbade the publication and distribution of any other "libelous books and defamatory writings," specifically invoking the Edict of Nantes's prohibitions against disturbing the public peace with scandalous language.[82] Several years later, Charles Mocquet, sieur de l'Essart, complained to the Chambre de l'Edit about threats and insults made by a group of university students at Saumur. A local court had already condemned the students for their actions, but this had only provoked further outrages. The students had "caused several scandals in derision of the said court order, violating the authority of justice and public liberty"; moreover, they had displayed "several placards and defamatory writings against the honor of the suppliant and his family, [with] threats against their lives." The chamber magistrates ordered Mocquet to pursue his case before the *lieutenant criminel* at Angers, but they also placed him and his dependents "under the protection of the king and the court" [en la protection du Roy et de ladict cour]—technically making any future actions against them comparable to an attack on the king and the court as well.[83]

Cases of personal insult like those described above thus represented another aspect of the Chambre de l'Edit's struggle to maintain "le repos public" by punishing verbal violence against individuals and families. Because such violence was not directly aimed at religious or political authority, it did not merit the same kinds of penalties imposed in cases of blasphemous or seditious talk. Yet such insults still required some kind of public reparation to satisfy those whose personal honor had been besmirched. The court therefore required offenders to apologize directly to the insulted person before witnesses, or to register their apologies as written legal documents that could be publicized.

In addition to cases of verbal abuse, the Chambre de l'Edit also dealt with accusations of physical violence. Here too the court records' language often masks the exact nature of such confrontations with bland legal formulas: *exceds, violances, voies de faict*. For example, in 1635 the Chambre de l'Edit agreed to review the complaint of Gilles Buffiere, his wife, and her daughter Ysabel, who had been attacked

[82]A.N. X2b 200, 13 April 1601: "la cour a ordonné et ordonne que ladicte declaration et les coppies d'icelle imprimees seront supprimees, [et] faict inhibitions et defenses audict Thevenot et à toutes personnes d'user d'aulcunes mots et parolles scandaleuses ny faire imprimer, publier, et vendre aulcuns livres libelles et scripts diffamatoires, Et à tous libraires de les imprimer, sur les peines contenues es edicts de pacification et d'estre procedé contre les contrevenans comme infracteurs de paix et perturbateurs du repos public." Unfortunately, the *arrêt* gives no details about the specific content of Thevenot's declaration.

[83]A.N. X2b 252, 1 March 1610: "[ils ont] faict et commis plusieurs scandals en derision dudict arrest violant l'auctorité de la Justice et liberte publicque et encores este mis plusieurs placards et libelles diffamatoires contre l'honneur dudict suppliant et des siens [avec] menasses d'attentat à leurs vyes."

by Anne Beauclerc and her servant with "atrocious words and violence" [parolles atroces et exceds].[84] In other cases, however, the court records contain detailed accounts of confrontations between Huguenots and Catholics that went beyond assault between individuals. Rather, such incidents highlight the court's struggle to maintain both religious coexistence and public order as mandated by law.

Historians have noted that like religious conflict, religious coexistence often depended upon local conditions, and that ordinary people shaped the law's requirements to suit their needs and priorities. The shared concerns and interests of local community members could aid in keeping the peace, so that Huguenots and Catholics might conduct business and even marry across confessional lines. Yet such actions were often opposed by those who believed that peace depended upon retaining confessional boundaries, including the legal privileges that distinguished Huguenots from Catholics.[85] The Chambre de l'Edit's records show evidence of such disputes, indicating the kinds of issues that challenged religious coexistence at the local level and led to violent confrontations between Huguenots and Catholics.

Cemeteries and burials were one such issue. The Edict of Nantes's general articles mandated separate cemeteries for Catholics and Protestants. The secret articles noted that in the past Protestants had sometimes buried their dead in Catholic cemeteries; royal officials were ordered to prevent any inquiries into such cases.[86] When local traditions or practices conflicted with the law's requirements, however, they sometimes resulted in lawsuits and petitions to the Paris Chambre de l'Edit. For example, in 1610 Louis de La Gresille, sieur de Mihoudy, and four other Huguenot seigneurs requested that the court intervene in a dispute about La Gresille's mother, who had wanted to be buried in the cemetery of the local parish church. Since La Gresille's family had possessed burial privileges ("un droit particullier de sepulture") there for several generations, he had not expected any trouble in fulfilling her dying request. The parish priest and another local seigneur, however, had complained about the funeral to the *prévôt des maréchaux* of Loudun, who ordered the funeral participants arrested. In his appeal to the Chambre de l'Edit, La Gresille contested the *prévôt's* legal competence to handle such a dispute, though he had already reburied his mother's body "to remove all

[84]A.N. X2b 424, 5 June 1635.

[85]On religious coexistence in the seventeenth century, see Labrousse, *Une foi, une loi, un roi?* 77–94; Gregory Hanlon, *Confession and Community in Seventeenth-Century France: Catholic and Protestant Coexistence in Aquitaine* (Philadelphia: University of Pennsylvania Press, 1993); Benedict, "Un roi, une loi, deux fois," 65–93; Luria, "Rituals of Conversion," 63–81.

[86]"Edict of Nantes," 46 (arts. 28, 29); 63 (Secret Articles, art. 45). The parlements never ratified the secret articles, which complicated their enforcement.

subject of complaint from the priest and all others" [pour ôter tout subject de plaint audict cure et tous aultres]. The chamber magistrates agreed to investigate the matter further and forbade any further attacks against La Gresille and his cohorts in the interim.[87]

In another case concerning cemeteries, the petitioners were three Huguenots from the village of Jumeauville: Etienne Piedesac (or Perdesac), his son Michel, and Etienne Frere. They stated that for more than fifty years, Jumeauville's Protestants and Catholics had been interred without distinction in the village cemetery, an arrangement that had provoked no opposition from the local clergy or the village's seigneur. Yet in August 1601, the customary practice was suddenly challenged. Robert Moulin, "calling himself the priest in the parish church of Jumeauville" [prenant seulement qualité de prebstre en l'eglise parroschialle dudict Jumeauville], objected loudly to the burial of a Protestant woman named Mathurine Vassac. Moulin not only demanded that Vassac's body be disinterred, but also had local judges arrest Etienne Piedesac and his fellow suppliants. After reviewing the three men's petition in November 1601, the chamber magistrates ordered them released from prison while their appeal was under consideration.[88]

When the case reappeared in the Chambre de l'Edit's records four years later, the dispute about Vassac's burial had mushroomed to include Jumeauville's Catholic inhabitants; Marin de Fredel, the village's seigneur; and the clergy of Chartres. All three appeared as intervening parties in the lawsuit, with lawyers to represent their interests in the case. The *arrêt* does not contain details about their arguments, but it does include royal advocate Louis Servin's summary of the case. Servin declared that although Mathurine Vassac's burial had contravened royal edicts about such matters, compassion and the passage of time should mitigate any penalty:

> The long time which has since passed must be considerable [i.e., of considerable importance] in the dispute...those of both religions buried in the said cemetery could be said to be joined together and cannot be distinguished...[it] is necessary to bring [to the situation] some Christian humanity by a reconsecration and reconciliation of the cemetery which could be done without difficulty, for unity and peace.[89]

[87] A.N. X2b 253, 22 May 1610: "lesdicts suppliants, pour ôter tout subject de plaint audict cure et tous aultres, auroient ote le corps de ladite Bonnevin [Perrine Bonnevin, La Gresille's mother] et enleve de ladict eglise et incontinent inhume en aultre lieu."

[88] A.N. X2b 204, 23 November 1601.

[89] A.N. X2b 226, 20 July 1605: Le long temps qui est passé depuis doibt estre considerable en la cause...les [morts] de l'une et de l'autre Religion inhumes audict cymetiere se pouvoit dire estre joincts ensemble et ne pouvoient estre decernes...estant requis d'y apporter de l'humanite chrestienne

The chamber magistrates, however, did not entirely support Servin's recommendations. The court explicitly forbade Jumeauville's Protestants to bury their dead in the village cemetery, or indeed in any parish cemetery within the diocese of Chartres. As for the "reconsecration and reconciliation" of Jumeauville's cemetery, the court referred that matter to the bishop of Chartres. In the meantime, the court ordered local authorities to provide without cost "a separate place in the said parish of Jumeauville where Protestant remains may be buried in the future."[90] The chamber magistrates thus chose to try and maintain order in Jumeauville by rejecting the village's customary burial practices in favor of the separate cemeteries mandated by royal edicts, while at the same time acknowledging the jurisdiction of other authorities (specifically, the bishop of Chartres) in the matter.

Violence also occurred when Huguenots tried to exercise their privilege of public worship as assured by the Edict of Nantes. Jean Troyon and Abraham Poret—a clockmaker and jeweler, respectively—appealed to the Chambre de l'Edit in 1600 after local judicial officials in Poitiers tried to arrest them. According to their account, Protestants had royal permission to hold public worship services at a place at a suburb of Poitiers called La Cuelle. The journey there was already treacherous: there was "only one road bordered on one side by cliffs and on the other by huge rocks, which road [the Protestants] must necessarily take to go to their church" [ne contient qu'un seule chemin borne d'un coste de precipices et de l'autre de grands rochers, par lequel chemin il leur faut necessairement passer pour aller à leur temple]. The Catholics of La Cuelle had suddenly erected a cross on this route, "in order to prepare occasions for sedition every day, announcing, as they have already done several times, that those of the said religion [Protestants] scandalize Catholics before this newly built cross, which is a pure calumny" [pour se preparer tous les jours des occasions de sedition en publyant comme ils ont desja faict plusieurs foys qu ceux de ladicte Religion scandalisoyent les Catholiques à l'endroit de ceste croix de nouveau constructe et eslevee, qui est une pure calumnye]. Fearing more violent attacks, Troyon and Poret requested that the ringleaders receive exemplary punishment, so that "every person may do his duty within the terms of the peace treaties" [afin que...à leur exemple chascun se puisse retenir en son debvoir et dedans les termes des edicts de pacification].[91] The Chambre de l'Edit's verdict, issued three months later, was much more

---

par une rebenediction et reconciliation du cymetiere, laquelle se peult faire sans trouble pour l'unite et la paix.

[90] A.N. X2b 226, 20 July 1605: un lieu separe en ladicte paroisse de Jumeauville pour y estre enterres à l'advenir les corps de ceulx de ladicte Religion pretendue reformee et sans depens.

[91] A.N. X2b 194, 13 May 1600.

restrained: the court simply ordered the parties to obey the king's edicts and not to provoke each other with insults or other behavior that might threaten the public peace.[92]

The Chambre de l'Edit received a similar complaint from the Protestant inhabitants of Beaufort. René Sinault, Antoine Chavury, Ollivier Phelippeau, and Jullien Tronchon, acting on behalf of their coreligionists, claimed that a local priest and a visiting monk named Brother Jony had used their Lenten sermons to incite violence among Beaufort's Catholics. As a result, "the suppliants were attacked and insulted; the Catholics even threatened to drown and kill them, having committed several assaults and outrages against them." The four appellants pointed out that the edicts of pacification specifically forbade seditious preaching and other provocations, yet Beaufort's royal prosecutor and *lieutenant criminel* had not enforced the law: indeed, they had ordered Protestants to stop meeting in the town or suburbs of Beaufort for religious worship, effectively siding with the Catholics in the dispute. The Chambre de l'Edit responded by prohibiting local judicial officials from interfering with Reformed religious activities while the case was being considered.[93]

Even Huguenots imprisoned in the Conciergerie demanded that the Chambre de l'Edit uphold their privileges regarding public worship. In March 1608, they petitioned the court to designate an appropriate place in the prison where they could hold Reformed worship services. The chamber magistrates cautiously approved the request:

> The jailer is ordered to provide a chamber or commodious place in the Conciergerie for the said prisoners professing the so-called reformed religion so that they may pray according to the rites of their church, all the same without any preaching or administration of sacraments by the said church, nor may [the prisoners] sing psalms or be heard outside the said chamber or place in which they are praying; with prohibitions against all other persons of the said religion who are not prisoners to attend their prayers. [The court] orders the said jailer to separate the said prisoners from the Catholics during their prayers and to observe and enforce the observance of this decree.[94]

[92]A.N. X2b 196, 9 August 1600.

[93]A.N. X2b 225, 17 June 1605: preschant audict lieu…en sorte que lesdicts suppliants estoient atacques et injuries, mesmes que lesdicts Catholicques les auroient menacés de les noyer et tuer, leurs ayans commis plussieurs exceds et oultrages.

[94]A.N. X2b 241, 29 March 1608: [La cour] ordonne qu'il sera baillee par ledict geollier une chambre ou lieu commode en ladicte Conciergerie ausdicts prisonniers faisans profession de ladicte

The chamber magistrates' instructions suggest that even within the Conciergerie, the edict's provisions for Reformed religious worship would be upheld but strictly enforced. Like those who had to travel through hostile communities to worship in outlying areas, Protestants within the Conciergerie were to be isolated from Catholics, as well as from Protestants outside the prison walls.

By contrast, in 1602 it was the Catholic inhabitants of Houdan who requested that the Chambre de l'Edit intervene in their conflict with local Huguenots over the latter's public worship. Their petition accompanied an appeal by Pierre Aubey, a Protestant *menusier* who wanted the court to review his conviction for assault. A legal spokesman *(procureur sindic)* for Houdan's Catholics argued that Aubey and other Protestants from the area were accustomed to walking through the town on their way to worship in the suburbs; he requested that the Chambre de l'Edit order the Huguenots to stay behind the town's walls when making their journey.[95] The chamber magistrates denied this request and forbade the *procureur sindic* from presenting any other such petitions in the future; the judges also ordered that their verdict should be read at the next public session of Houdan's law court.[96] The court's decision also essentially cleared Pierre Aubey, for the judges forbade "all persons to provoke by words or otherwise the said Aubey and others professing the said religion, but enjoins them together with those of the said religion to live tranquilly and peaceably with each other according to the edicts of pacification."[97]

Unlike cases of fights or assaults among individuals, these cases reflected violent confrontations over the conditions of religious coexistence, specifically public

---

religion pretendue reformee pour faire leurs prieres selon la forme de leurdicte eglise sans toutesfois aucune predication ny administration de sacremens de ladicte eglise ny qu'ils puissent psalmodier ou estre entendus hors ladicte chambre ou lieu dans lequel ils feront lesdictes prieres; faict deffences à toutes personnes de ladicte religion non prisonniers d'y assister. Enjoint audict geollier de separer lesdict prisonniers d'avec les Catholiques pendant lesdictes prieres et de garder et faire garder le present arret.

[95]A.N. X2b 207, 6 May 1602: "Requete presentee à ladicte cour par le procureur syndic des manans et habitans dudict Houdan...à ce que ledict Aubey et aultres de la rellligion pretendue reformee allans et retournans du lieu estably pour l'exercice de leurdict relligion n'eussent à passer par l'enclos de leurdict ville ains par deriere les murs d'icelle."

[96]A.N. X2b 207, 6 May 1602: "Et quant à ladicte requete [la cour] a deboutte et deboutte ledict procureur sindic de l'entherinement d'icelle, faict deffences de plus presenter telles requetes, et sera le present arrêt leu au siege dudict Houdan les plaids tenans."

[97]A.N. X2b 207, 6 May 1602: [La cour] faict deffences à toutes personnes de provoquer par parolles ou aultrement ledict Aubey et aultres faisant profession de ladict Rellligion, ains leur enjoint ensemble ausdicts de ladict Relligion vivre doucement et paisiblement les unes avec les aultres suivant l'edict de pacification.

worship and burial. They also illustrate the Huguenots' efforts to depict themselves as loyal, law-abiding subjects—and to portray their opponents as the true threat to peace and public order. According to the lawyer who argued before the Chambre de l'Edit on behalf of Jean Troyon and Abraham Poret, the two men had "always lived with all the modesty one could desire of good and peaceable citizens, and in the exercise of their religion, which is permitted to them by the king's edicts; they have not given any subject for scandal to anyone."[98] By contrast, their Catholic opponents were "forever accustomed to sedition and still unable to forget the craft they practiced earlier during their rebellion, daily seeking pretexts to quarrel with and defame those of the reformed religion who live in the city of Poitiers."[99]

Later seventeenth-century petitions to the Chambre de l'Edit also illustrate the Huguenots' struggle to define themselves as law-abiding subjects. In May 1645, four Protestants complained of abusive treatment by the seigneur of Houday Sainte Croix because of their religion. One plaintiff named Nicollas Barbichon had been assaulted and told that "he had the plague and wanted to haunt good people; [the seigneur] forbade him to appear in public in the future and ordered him to stay closed up in his house."[100] Viban Desbordes described how the local priest had summoned him to his house one day, where the two men began to discuss religion; their talk ended with the priest throwing Desbordes to the ground and whipping him. The priest was also accused of pressuring local Catholics to take oaths and sign agreements assuring "that they would not associate with the suppliants [that is, the four Protestants] in the future for any reason whatsoever."[101] Barbichon, Desbordes, and the other plaintiffs protested that all of these actions were outlawed by "the edicts of pacification." In response to their appeal, the Chambre de l'Edit remanded the case to the *lieutenant criminel* at Vitry-Le-François.

[98] A.N. X2b 194, 13 May 1600: ils ayent tousjours vecu avecq toute la modestie qu'on peult desirer de bons et pacificques citoyens et qu'en l'exercice de leur religion qui leur est permis par les edicts du Roy ils n'ayent donne subject de scandale à personne quelconques.

[99] A.N. X2b 194, 13 May 1600: de tout temps accoustumes à la sedition et qui ne peuvent encor oublyer le mestier qu'ils faisoient par cy devant pendant leur rebellion, recherchent tous les jours des pretexts pour quereles et calumnier ceux de la religion reformee qui demeurent en la ville de Poitiers.

[100] A.N. X2b 485, 11 May 1645: luy disant qu'il avoit la peste et qu'il vouloit hanter des gens de bien, qu'il luy deffendoit de se trouver à l'advenir en compagnie et luy enjoignoit de se tenir reclus en sa maison.

[101] A.N. X2b 485, 11 May 1645: qu'ils s'obligent ne frequanter doresnavant les suppliants pour quelque occasion que ce soit, toutes lesquelles procedures sont aultant des contraventions aux edicts de pacification et une oppression contre les subjects du Roy.

The complaints presented by Barbichon, Desbordes, and their fellow Protestants echoed issues that were brought before the Chambre de l'Edit earlier in the century. In disputes over cemeteries and privilege of public worship, Huguenots faced hostility and outright violence from Catholics. Such behavior not only threatened their lives, but also the peace and public order that was supposed to prevail under the king's edicts, and that royal law courts were supposed to uphold. On the other hand, Catholics (like those of Houdan) expected the court to enforce the legal limitations on France's Protestant minority, and each group portrayed the other as the true source of trouble in the local community. Such conflicts highlighted the tensions surrounding religious coexistence: the law might require that confessional communities remain separate, but activities like burying the dead or walking to church brought Protestants and Catholics into contact with each other. When the seigneur and priest at Houday Sainte Croix tried to isolate local Protestants by force, Nicollas Barbichon and Viban Desbordes claimed that the law gave them a legitimate place in their community, despite religious difference.

Judicial abuses were defined by the nature of both the crime and the offender. Local judicial officials of every sort—magistrates in subaltern royal tribunals or seigneurial law courts, prosecutors, clerks (greffiers), bailiffs (huissiers), the sergents who carried out summonses and other court orders, the archers who acted as a kind of local constabulary—appear as the accused in such cases. They were charged with a host of misdeeds related to the exercise of their offices: prolonging litigation to collect excessive fees; colluding with one party in a lawsuit against his or her opponent; and unlawfully imprisoning individuals. Judicial misconduct was in some respects the worst threat to public order, for it could undermine the effectiveness and validity of justice itself at the local level.

The Chambre de l'Edit sometimes received complaints about judicial misconduct in the context of other legal disputes. For example, when René Sinault petitioned the court about threats and assaults from Catholics at Beaufort, he also reported that local judicial officials had publicized their decision to ban Reformed worship, despite the fact that their decree should have been suspended once the matter was under appeal. Small wonder that Sinault specifically requested that the chamber magistrates forbid the local judge, prosecutor, sergents, and huissiers to enforce the ban until the case had been decided.[102] After the chamber magistrates

[102]A.N. X2b 225, 17 June 1605: Sinault asked the court to "faire deffences particullieres audict substitut dudict procureur general et lieutenant audict Beaufort et tous aultres qu'il appartiendra de passer oultre ny faire executer leurdict jugement et à tous huissiers sergens et aultres de les mettre à l'execution."

cleared Pierre Aubey, they summoned the local judge and prosecutor from Houdan to explain their conduct in his case. The two men were suspended from office until they fulfilled the court's order and were later permitted to resume their responsibilities.[103]

In other cases, however, judicial misconduct was the substance of the legal dispute itself. Litigants who appealed to the Chambre de l'Edit sometimes complained that judicial officials had deliberately interfered in legal proceedings to favor one party over another. For example, Charles Michel Dubois, sieur Dufresne, requested a three-month delay in the Chambre de l'Edit's review of his case because he claimed to have royal letters of pardon to present to the court. He needed time, however, to recover the relevant documents from Jean Boistel, a clerk whom Dubois suspected of having colluded with his opponents to keep the lawsuit in limbo. "It appears that there is an understanding between the said Boistel and Dubois's adversaries," his lawyer argued, "who nevertheless wish to have his dispute decided, which is unreasonable given that this defense and the registration of his letters of *abolition* depend upon the [missing] records."[104] François Daubanel, sieur de Saint Roman, likewise petitioned the court regarding judicial collusion. Daubanel had successfully appealed his case against Jacques Vallat and two other men from Montpellier to Nîmes, but the Montpellier judge had blocked his efforts. Daubanel argued that this was because the Montpellier judge "is conspiring and devising with the said Vallot the ruin of the suppliant and those who are helping him." The chamber magistrates accepted Daubanel's appeal and forbade the Montpellier judge to handle any further proceedings in the case.[105]

François Advisard's complaint against Nicolas Dupont, *lieutenant criminel* of Marchesnoir, combined charges of collusion with kidnapping. While embroiled in a lawsuit not described in his *requête*, Advisard had successfully appealed to gain his release from prison, but Dupont had prevented this:

> [Advisard] was violently and with great animosity abducted from the prisons of Marchesnoir and transferred to the prisons of the diocesan jurisdiction of Chartres, where several cruel and inhuman acts were committed against him...the suppliant, in order to be healed, was

[103]A.N. X2b 207, 6 May 1602; an *arrêt* dated 13 May 1602 records their appearance and the court's decision.

[104]A.N. X2b 253, 14 May 1610: Il y a grande apparence que c'est une intelligence qui est entre ledict Boistel et les parties adverses dudict Dubois qui ce pendent veullent faire juger son process, ce qui ne seroit raisonnable d'aultant que de cette information depend sa justification et l'entherinement de ses lettres d'abolition.

[105]A.N. X2b 562, 13 May 1655: concerte et conspire avec ledit Vallot la ruine du suppliant et de ceux qui l'assistent.

forced to make a declaration before the *official* of Chartres his party [i.e., his opponent in the original dispute]....[106]

According to Advisard, Dupont had effectively transferred his case (and his person) to the jurisdiction of his opposing party, the diocese of Chartres. The chamber judges responded forcefully to Advisard's claims: they ordered the diocesan officials to release Advisard and to forward the records of their proceedings against him to the Paris court's clerk immediately. As for Dupont, he was summoned to Paris to answer for his conduct, and the judges specifically commanded the local royal prosecutor to assure that he complied.[107]

Later that same year, a merchant from Poitou named Isaac Chassay complained to the Chambre de l'Edit about similar mistreatment by the *visénéchal* of Fontenay-le-Comte. Chassay reported that since the beginning of September, the *visénéchal* "had detained him in a private house, without having put him in prison, but transferring him from one place to another, wherever he pleased."[108] At first Chassay attributed this misconduct to his captor's violent nature, claiming that he had acted "to avenge his passions and without cause" [pour venger ses passions et sans subject]. Yet Chassay offered another explanation for the *visénéchal*'s actions. Chassay was involved in a lawsuit before the presidial court at La Rochelle but expected the case to be sent to another court at Poitiers. Thus "by an evil course of action...the said *visénéchal* kidnapped the suppliant [Chassay] from the city of La Rochelle" on the eve of the transfer.[109] In response, the chamber magistrates ordered the official to release Chassay and to send all documents related to Chassay's case to the *presidial* at La Rochelle.

In these cases, judicial officials were accused of using their authority in an arbitrary way, thus violating the complainant's legal proceedings as well as his physical safety. The Chambre de l'Edit condemned other instances of arbitrary justice that amounted to abuses of judicial authority. For example, in July 1600, the court scolded eight officials from Vendôme for a variety of misdeeds. *Bailli*

---

[106]A.N. X2b 252, 4 March 1610: Il [Advisard] auroit este violemment [et] avec grande animosite enleve des prisons dudict Marchesnoir et traduict es prisons de l'officialite de Chartres ou il luy auroit este commis plusieurs cruaultes et inhumanites...ledict suppliant pour en estre soulage auroit este contrainct de faire quelque declaration devant l'official de Chartres sa partie....

[107]A.N. X2b 252, 4 March 1610.

[108]A.N. X2b 257, 23 November 1610: il ayt detenu ledict suppliant en maison privee sans l'avoir mis en aulcune prison, mais traduict de lieu en aultre ou bon luy a semble.

[109]A.N. X2b 257, 23 November 1610: par une mauvaise fasson [façon] de faire...ledict viseneschal auroit enleve de nuict de ladict ville de la Rochelle ledict suppliant. Chassay's petition says nothing about the original lawsuit that instigated the jurisdictional tug-of-war between the presidial courts at La Rochelle and Poitiers.

Benjamin Rigoureau was ordered "not to sound the *tocsin* in the future for any occasion whatsoever unless it be for rescue from fire and to summon assemblies concerning taxes in the usual manner," while his assistant Jacques Degennes was warned "not to conduct legal proceedings in his home, but in a place worthy for the execution of justice, and to conform to what is decided by the majority of opinions."[110] An assistant to the local royal military commander named Philippes Augron was told "not to undertake... jurisdiction or cognizance of legal matters" [n'entreprendre... jurisdiction ne cognoissance des affaires de la Justice].[111] The specific abuses noted in the chamber magistrates' rebuke suggest that Rigoureau and his cohorts were not yet accustomed to administering justice in peacetime, and that the distinction between military and civilian jurisdiction, which might have been blurred during the recent civil wars, needed to be reestablished at Vendôme.

In another case, the chamber magistrates confirmed a lower court's sentence against Daniel Ducos, chief jailer for the prisons at La Rochelle, and his assistant Jean François. Ducos and François had been sued for allowing a prisoner to escape, but the authorities at La Rochelle had also condemned a combination of laxity and brutality in the two men's conduct in running the city's prison. Ducos and François were ordered to stop abusing prisoners "by deed and words" [de faict et par parolles]. They were also warned not to allow prisoners to confer with anyone, nor to put prisoners in solitary confinement, nor to give prisoners pen, ink, and paper without a judge's permission. Finally the two men were commanded to post a copy of the court's decree where the prisoners themselves could see it. The chamber magistrates rejected Ducos's and François's appeal of this sentence.[112]

In contrast to accusations that local judicial officials had abused their power by acting arbitrarily or intervening unfairly in legal proceedings, some individuals

[110]A.N. X2b 196, 7 July 1600: ledict Rigoureau bailly de ne faire à l'advenir sonner la cloche du tocquesaint pour quelque occasion que se soit sinon pour le secourts au feu et pour faire les assembleees pour les tailles en la maniere accoustumee, et ledict Degennes de ne juger les proces en sa maison ains au lieu d'estime pour l'execution de la Justice, et se conformer à ce que sera arrester par la pluralite des opinions.

[111]A.N. X2b 196, 7 July 1600. Other men named in the *arrêt* were Pierre Joubert, jailer in charge of Vendôme's prisons, three of Rigoureau's servants, and Guillaume Joubert, servant to Degennes and probably a relative of the jailer.

[112]A.N. X2b 286, 22 January 1615: "ne laisser à l'advenir parler ny conferer aulcuns personnes avec les accuses de crime reserves en cachots ou chambres closes jusque à ce que par les juges en eust este autrement ordonne, Et ne donner ausdicts prisonniers ancre, plume ne pappier, ne mettre aulcun prisonnier dans les cachots...sans ordonnance de justice...et que le dispositif de ladite sentence seroit affiche par le greffier contre la porte de la sale commune desdits prisons à ce que les prisonniers en peussent avoir cognoissance."

argued that officials had not done enough to fulfill their responsibilities. As we have seen, Jeanne de Preissac called upon the Chambre de l'Edit to make local authorities enforce the judgment she had obtained against Hector Renault and his accomplices, who were at large in Guyenne. In June 1625, two widows named Marie de Lorride and Anne de La Febriere appealed to the court regarding their husbands' murderers. The three men accused of this crime, along with several accomplices, had been permitted to stay at large in Paris, where they were using threats and persuasion to drive away witnesses in the case. Noting that the investigating magistrate could not go after the witnesses, the two women requested that the Chambre de l'Edit intervene to halt their opponents' "intimidation, threats, and violence"; the court accepted their appeal.[113] Sara Buffier protested that the two men charged with murdering her husband had also evaded local authorities; witnesses had been frightened into silence about the crime, and the accused were free to roam the country and affront Buffier at every opportunity. This was unjust, Buffier complained, "and against the King's intention and the court's orders." The chamber magistrates summoned the men to Paris to answer her charges or face arrest and imprisonment.[114] Incidents such as these suggest that when subaltern judicial officials were unable (or unwilling) to prevent accused criminals from intimidating witnesses and their accusers, litigants appealed to royal magistrates—including those of the Chambre de l'Edit—to intervene.

Religious prejudice was sometimes invoked to explain abuses committed by local authorities. In 1601, Georges Chevalleau, sieur de La Thifardiere, claimed that he had been seized without cause by the *prévôt des maréchaux* for an alleged attack against two other noblemen. Chevalleau had rejected the judge's authority in the matter, however, "as much because of his [Chevalleau's] status as a gentleman...as because he publicly professed the so-called reformed religion" [tant à cause de sa qualité de gentilhomme...que au moien de ce qu'il est de la religion pretendue reformee et en a de tout temps faict profession publicque]. Since judges in the presidial court at Poitiers shared this animosity toward Protestants, they supported the *prévôt*'s actions: Chevalleau appealed to the Chambre de l'Edit to hear his case

---

[113]A.N. X2b 354, 16 June 1625: "ils ont praticque et suborne les tesmoins qui peuvent deposer des assassinats...par prieres et menasses et fait evader aulcuns des tesmoins, et...le conseiller commis par les arrets ne peust se donner loisir d'aller sur les lieux pour l'instruction du proces." The two women requested permission to have the court investigate "des pratiques, intimidations, menasses et viollances dont lesdits accuses ont uses et usent journellement tant allencontre des tesmoins que desdites suppliants."

[114]A.N. X2b 632, 6 September 1660: "[ils] sont dans le pais aussy triomphent de leurs crimes et luy font insultes...ce qui n'est poinct juste et ce qui est contre l'intention du Royet contre les arrests de la cour."

and deny the local courts jurisdiction. The chamber magistrates agreed, forbidding the magistrates at Poitiers from taking any further action until Chevalleau had been heard before the Paris court.[115] Similarly, Pierre Marin petitioned the Chambre de l'Edit regarding mistreatment at the hands of judicial officials in Ribemont, where he was a prisoner. According to Marin, the local royal prosecutor and *lieutenant criminel* had imprisoned him not only to ruin him with legal costs ("pour consommer ledict supliant en frais"), but also because of religious prejudice ("par animosite à cause de sa qualité de la religion pretedue reformee"). Even Marin's crime (of which he claimed to be innocent) was nothing more than "words allegedly spoken about his said [religious] status." The court ordered Marin released from prison and a further hearing of his accusations.[116]

Religious prejudice may have been a factor in other cases of judicial abuse, even if complainants did not cite it specifically in their grievances to the Chambre de l'Edit. When Nicolas Dupont threw François Advisard into the diocesan prison at Chartres, he might have been acting out of religious animosity, since Advisard was most likely Protestant. In another case, three university students from Poitiers argued that both family connections and religious prejudice accounted for their unjust treatment by the *lieutenant criminel*. In their petition to the chamber magistrates, Louis Draud, Pierre Beau, and Jacques Riffault explained that while walking around the streets of Poitiers with friends in February 1609, their companions had thrown stones at a local nobleman named René de La Lande, sieur de Breult de Vernon, and his servants. "They were neither wounded nor offended in any other way by this," the account continued, "and besides the suppliants were innocent of the action and the one who supposedly threw the stones had left."[117] Unfortunately for the three students who remained behind, the *lieutenant criminel* of Poitiers was La Lande's brother-in-law. He may have regarded the incident as an affront to his family's honor, or as a crime committed by disorderly students against a local notable, or even as a chance to strike out at Protestants—all three students described themselves as "professing the reformed religion." In any case, Draud, Beau, and Riffault were seized and imprisoned, though as students they claimed that they

---

[115]A.N. X2b 199, 11 January 1601: "Et toutesfois par une animosite et en haine de sadicte Relligion auroyt este ledict prevost par les presidiaux dudict Poitiers declare competant."

[116]A.N. X2b 288, 9 May 1615: "parolles pretendues dictes au sujet de sadite qualité."

[117]A.N. X2b 247, 21 March 1609: "[Les suppliants] se seroient trouves en la compagnie d'aultres escolliers lesquels se promenant par la ville...ils auroient jecte quelquees coups de pierres au sieur de La Lande dudict Poitiers et ses serviteurs dont ils n'auroient este aultrement blesses ny offenses. Et encores que lesdicts suppliants fussent innocens dudict faict et celuy que l'on pretend avoir jecte lesdict coups de pierres s'estant absente."

were not subject to the *lieutenant criminel*'s jurisdiction; hence their appeal to the Chambre de l'Edit.

An *arrêt* from May 1609 reveals the outcome of both the proceedings at Poitiers and the students' appeal to the Paris Chambre de l'Edit. For "having wanted to assassinate de La Lande and his servant Frere," the three students had been sentenced to perform an *amende honorable* in open court and to pay damages, fines, alms, and costs totaling 3,000 *livres*.[118] The chamber magistrates did not reverse this verdict, though they did reduce the severity of its penalties: the students were ordered to apologize to La Lande and six witnesses of his choice in the *lieutenant criminel*'s court chambers and to pay 540 *livres* in alms and damages to La Lande and his servant. A notation on the reverse side of the court's *arrêt* declares that after fulfilling the terms of their sentence, the three students would have to absent themselves from Poitiers for one year. Finally, the court ordered its verdict to be announced publicly in the city streets, no doubt to discourage other such incidents.[119]

Cases of arbitrary use and abuse of judicial authority, however, were far less common than accusations of financial misdeeds. In such cases, the Chambre de l'Edit intervened to punish judges and other officials who had unfairly profited from the administration of justice at the local level. For example, the chamber magistrates ordered royal *sergent* Ozée Laurens and two accomplices to pay Mathieu Baudouin, sieur Dupeux, the just value of a doe which the three men had poached on Baudouin's lands. The court, however, also reprimanded the magistrate at La Rochelle who had first adjudicated the dispute for making Baudouin pay unnecessary fees: he was ordered to send the money to the Paris court clerk, who would assure that it was returned to Baudouin.[120]

In other cases, the Chambre de l'Edit admonished subaltern magistrates to "judge summarily," that is, to use their authority to settle certain kinds of disputes without recourse to lengthy, expensive proceedings. For example, in 1608 the court reviewed a lawsuit between Simon de Nezard and Guillaume Rouveau concerning insults exchanged between them and their wives. In summarizing the case, the royal advocate took note of illegal actions by the local magistrate at Fort

[118]A.N. X2b 248, 22 May 1609: the formula for the students' *amende honorable* states that they were to declare que termerairement et malicieusement ils auroient voullu assassiner ledict de La Lande et Frere son serviteur. They were also declared to be individually and collectively responsible ("chacun d'eux seul et pour le tout") for the financial penalties that the local court had imposed.

[119]A.N. X2b 248, 22 May 1609.

[120]A.N. X2b 220, 30 July 1604. The court reduced the La Rochelle judge's fees by one half, as well as ordering him to return an unspecified sum taken for the witnesses' interrogations. On the other hand, the court left the determination of the doe's value to experts ("selon l'estimation qu'en seroit faicte par gens au cognoissance.")

Levesque: he had used procedures normally applied to more serious crimes, thereby "consuming the parties in legal costs" [consommant les parties en frais] and probably increasing his own profits from the case. Although the chamber magistrates confirmed the local judge's verdict, they also ordered him to repay the money he had received by unnecessarily prolonging the lawsuit and "to do justice summarily" [sommairement faire droict] in the future.[121] When Salomon Potin and his wife appealed to the Chambre de l'Edit in 1620, they were dissatisfied with the judgment they had received from the judge at Chastel Chinon who had condemned them for insults to Paul Etignard. Royal advocate Jacques Talon and the chamber magistrates, however, focused on the judge's conduct more than the litigants' offense. Talon pointed out that since it was a case of "verbal insults spoken in heat" [injures verballes dictes par challeur], the judge should have heard the parties' oral arguments and delivered a verdict. Instead, he had required written proceedings to increase the litigants' costs ("pour les vexer et travailler en frais"), in violation of proper procedure for such cases. Since Potin had already filed a written declaration acknowledging Etignard as a respectable man ("homme de bien et d'honneur"), the chamber magistrates simply ordered him and his wife to avoid future confrontations with Etignard, but the court also admonished the judge at Chastel Chinon to handle cases of verbal insult properly in the future.[122]

Magistrates were not the only local judicial officials accused of abusing their offices with unfair financial exactions. In 1609, the Chambre de l'Edit forbade notary François Herbault to conduct official business until the court had finished investigating the charges of forgery and financial misdeeds made against him.[123] A royal *sergent* named François de Baudet appealed to the court when he was accused of "malversations, exactions et concutions"—terms indicating some kind of financial misconduct. The *lieutenant criminel* of Tours had sentenced Baudet to penalties that included a formal rebuke, six months' suspension from his judicial office and a fine of six *écus*, but all parties were dissatisfied with this decision. The royal prosecutor protested that the sentence was too lenient, while Baudet and Videlot launched their own appeals. For Baudet, this proved to be a mistake: the Chambre de l'Edit deprived him of his post and declared him incapable of holding any royal or public office in the future. The chamber magistrates also ordered

---

[121]A.N. X2b 245, 28 November 1608: Specifically, the local judge had issued a summons to appear in court on pain of arrest *(decret de pris de corps)* and had witnesses provide written depositions followed by face-to-face confrontations with the parties *(recolement et confrontation)*, neither of which was necessary for a case of insult *(injures verballes).*

[122]A.N. X2b 316, 15 January 1620: "de traicter les matieres d'injures sommairement suivant les ordonnances."

[123]A.N. X2b 247, 27 March 1609.

him to perform an *amende honorable* during an open session of the Paris parlement's Grand Chambre. There he would have to declare that "boldly and maliciously he committed the financial abuses mentioned in his trial, which he repents and asks pardon." The court then banished him from Paris and Touraine for five years.[124]

A case involving forgery and five royal *sergents* from Poitou came before the court in 1604. Pierre Barré, Jehan Vinet, André Bonniveau, and René and Pierre Tressart (father and son, respectively) had fabricated a legal document in which two merchants were accused of counterfeiting coin. The crime of "faulce monnoye" constituted treason and would have meant death for the two merchants had they been found guilty; the accusation alone might have damaged their professional reputations. But the merchants were cleared of the counterfeiting charges by a subaltern judge in Poitiers who suspended Barré and Vinet from office and ordered them to pay financial penalties totaling 20 *livres*. The Poitevin judge, however, had simply condemned *sergents* for having produced an *information* against the merchants without the proper commission from the local royal prosecutor.[125] When the case was reviewed on appeal, the fact that the *sergents* had forged the document came to light, and the Chambre de l'Edit's verdict was more severe. Bonniveau and René Tressart were condemned to an *amende honorable*—complete with ropes around their necks and candles in their hands—in the Palais Royal at Poitiers; during the ceremony, the forged legal document would be torn into pieces. The two men's fines and reparations were also increased to 700 *livres*. Pierre Barré was ordered to attend his accomplices' public humiliation, and all three men were dismissed from their offices and banished from Poitou and Paris. Since Jean Vinet and Pierre Tressart had apparently fled before their appeal was concluded, the chamber magistrates convicted them *par contumace* and sentenced them to be hanged. Finally, the court authorized the two merchants who had been maligned by the *sergents'* forgery to publicize this decision in neighboring towns.[126] It is worth noting that in this case, as in the one involving François de Baudet, the court altered its usual pattern of reducing an *amende honorable* to a less public form of judicial apology. Instead, the court deliberately used the *amende honorable* to punish incidents of judicial misconduct by publicizing the dishonor of the men who had committed such crimes, and whose actions brought royal justice itself into disrepute.

[124]A.N. X2b 208, 5 August 1602: themererement et malicieusement il a faict et commis les malversations, exactions et concutions mentionnees audict process dont il se repent et en demande mercy et pardon.
[125]A.N. X2b 218, 3 April 1604. The *lieutenant criminel* of Poitiers had forbidden Barré and Vinet "faire à l'advenir aulcuns informations à la requeste dudict substitut [du procureur general du roi à Poitiers] seullement, sans avoir commission ou mandement de ce faire sur peyne de faux."
[126]A.N. X2b 221, 4 September 1604.

In responding to charges of judicial abuse, the Chambre de l'Edit faced a double battle. The court's actions reveal an effort to make local judicial officials enforce the law and keep the peace as mandated by the king's edicts. This meant not only following established procedures for investigating and punishing crimes, but also fulfilling their responsibilities with discipline and integrity. When the chamber magistrates rejected an appeal from Edmé Nicot, a *procureur fiscal* in Nivernois, they ordered him to "behave modestly without further using words [which are] insolent, scandalous, and contrary to royal edicts and ordinances...and to render justice to those who demand it."[127] Local authorities whose conduct was arbitrary, unfair, or scandalous threatened "le repos public"; their actions compromised the effectiveness and the honor of royal justice. The Chambre de l'Edit acknowledged as much when it admonished Abraham Cuzin, Nicot's opponent in their lawsuit, to "show honor and respect to justice" [porter honneur et respect à justice] when he returned to Nivernois.[128] As in cases of provocative speech or violent confrontation, the chamber magistrates sought to enforce a standard of orderly behavior that had been mandated by law. It was essential that local judicial officials should embody that standard.

On the other hand, maintaining public order also depended upon ordinary people, for they, too, were expected to obey royal laws and conduct themselves with restraint. When faced with cases of inflammatory speech or violent confrontation, the Chambre de l'Edit invoked the edicts that forbade such behavior. Moreover, the court tended to punish such crimes with an eye to emphasizing the offender's submission to royal justice over public humiliation. French men and women, however, expected justice to be administered in the same fashion: with fairness and discipline. To be worthy of honor, respect, and obedience, the power of royal justice could not be exercised in an arbitrary or corrupt manner. Ordinary people who encountered abuses of judicial authority by local officials appealed to superior royal magistrates to prevent or punish such misconduct. Thus litigants like Sara Buffier, whose husband's accused murderers had been "wrested from the hands of justice with open force," called upon the Chambre de l'Edit to assure "that force remains with the king and justice."[129]

---

[127]A.N. X2b 319, 22 June 1620: se comporter modestement sans plus user de parolles insolents, scandaleuses et contraires aux edits et ordonnances royaux...et de rendre la justice à ceux dont il seroit requis.

[128]A.N. X2b 319, 22 June 1620.

[129]A.N. X2b 632, 6 September 1660: arrachés d'entre les mains de la justice à force ouverte.

CHAPTER 6

"An annihilation of justice"

The Huguenots & the Law Revisited

IN 1665, LOUIS XIV RECEIVED A COMPLAINT ABOUT PROTESTANT magistrates who offered favorable treatment to beleaguered Catholic litigants—if they were willing to convert. "From this a great number of perversions occur every day," the *mémoire* stated, "such that we have the shame and displeasure of seeing the loss of souls and the annihilation of justice."[1] To anyone familiar with the history of France's Protestant minority during the seventeenth century, the statement seems absurd. Surely it was Huguenots who were pressured to abjure their faith, and it was they who feared (with some justification) partisan judgments in French law courts. Yet the complaint reflected issues that had existed in French society for decades before they were expressed in the *mémoire*: how could peace and order be restored to a society that remained divided between two religious confessions? How could justice exist when the laws themselves seemed fraught with contradictions?

In the aftermath of the Wars of Religion, law seemed to offer the best chance for overcoming past conflicts and achieving the peace that was necessary to rebuild the kingdom. Though he became king in 1589, Henry IV did not easily inherit the loyalty or obedience of his subjects; he won them over through a combination of military conquest, recompense, and amnesty. His public conversion to Catholicism strengthened his legitimacy as king of France, but as one recent biographer

---

[1] A.N. TT430, dossier 31, no. 97, "Mémoire du Duc d'Elzès," 2: de là il arrive tous les jours grand nombre de perversions, en sorte que nous avons la honte et le deplaisir de voir la perte des ames et l'aneantissement de la justice.

has noted, he realized that "as a reigning monarch he had obligations to protect the welfare of all Frenchmen, not just Huguenot or Catholic Frenchmen."[2] In the Edict of Nantes Henry IV effectively declared (or rather reiterated) that Catholicism was the kingdom's official religion. Yet the edict offered privileges to the Huguenots that made them a protected though vulnerable confessional community within the larger society and polity. The Edict of Nantes was not only a peace treaty, but also a contract among the crown, Huguenots, and Catholics, and it contained a blueprint for religious coexistence backed by royal authority.

The edict, however, was fragmented from within. Its component parts did not have the same legal standing or validity; the general edict, which was eventually ratified by France's parlements, contained provisions that were often modified by the conditions set forth in the two *brevets* and secret articles. Language in the general edict's preamble stated that this "clear, precise, and absolute" law was intended to settle past and present conflicts—"insofar as the spirit of the times will permit."[3] Henry IV and many of his Catholic subjects might have regarded the edict as a temporary measure, but for Huguenots it became a permanent point of reference that defined their status in law. As other sources of protection were weakened or abolished, Huguenots continually invoked the law and the crown's authority to help maintain their collective identity and what they saw as their legitimate if separate place in the French state.

Special access to royal justice was one of the most important and lasting privileges outlined for Huguenots in the Edict of Nantes. Bipartisan law courts allowed Huguenots to obtain offices in the royal magistracy, as well as offering the possibility of some protection when they appeared before such courts as plaintiffs or defendants. The Paris Chambre de l'Edit was one such tribunal. It offered few opportunities for judicial office, since it included only one Huguenot magistrate. Yet its affiliation with the Parlement of Paris—arguably the most powerful law court in the French judicial hierarchy—gave it an enormous geographical and legal jurisdiction. Men and women from across the spectrum of French society appealed to the Chambre de l'Edit, and their criminal lawsuits open a perspective on the tensions surrounding religious coexistence, public order, and the expansion of royal power.

Criminal litigation, of course, usually denoted conflict and disorder, two themes that pervaded the Chambre de l'Edit's work. Though the Edict of Nantes had decreed that the wartime violence of the later sixteenth century was to be

[2]Ronald S. Love, *Blood and Religion: The Conscience of Henri IV, 1553–1593* (Kingston and Montréal: McGill-Queen's University Press, 2001), 306.

[3]"Edict of Nantes," 42.

forgotten, there were exceptions to the law of *oubliance*. Litigants took advantage of this to open new disputes about past events, demanding that the court restore property and honor that had been lost, stolen, or compromised in the heat of civil and religious war. The Chambre de l'Edit, however, usually responded to such demands for remembrance by emphasizing that past conflicts and losses had to be put aside in the interest of peace. Obedience to royal law, including the law of *oubliance*, would provide a firm foundation for France's recovery and renewal.

The family was another such foundation. Many contemporaries viewed the family as both a microcosm and a building block of society; the relationship between father and child, which ideally combined affection and authority, provided a powerful metaphor for the connection between king and subject. This image of paternal power, which Bourbon monarchs invoked at various times during the seventeenth century, was already enshrined in sixteenth-century royal edicts regulating marriage formation, inheritance, and guardianship. Although the Catholic Church's canon law and the French Reformed churches' ecclesiastical disciplines also established requirements for valid marriages, it was royal law that the Chambre de l'Edit applied and upheld in criminal lawsuits. Such litigation often stemmed from conflict within families, but it also revealed the extent and strength of kinship networks, as relatives joined in legal proceedings to protect common interests or inherited an unfinished lawsuit from a parent, spouse, or sibling. Bringing order to disorderly families was another facet of the Chambre de l'Edit's effort to implement royal law and maintain a peaceful, civil society.

Violence of all sorts represented a third challenge to the court's accomplishment of that task, and another source of criminal lawsuits adjudicated by the chamber magistrates. Though separated by the legal privileges related to their religious confession, Huguenots and Catholics were supposed to avoid insulting and assaulting each other because of past or present differences. Instead, they were commanded to discipline themselves to live in friendship, brotherhood, and harmony—or at the very least within the bounds of civil order. Those who could not or would not conform their speech and behavior to this standard would be punished for threatening the public peace.[4] Living according to the edict's requirements, of course, was another matter, as illustrated in the Chambre de l'Edit's adjudication of disputes involving blasphemy, seditious speech, personal insult, and other confrontations. Administering justice fairly and effectively at the local level was essential to maintain public order and obedience to the law. The court investigated and sometimes harshly punished judicial misconduct by subaltern

---

[4]"Edict of Nantes," 42 (art. 2).

officials because their abuses dishonored royal justice itself. Like religious coexistence, religious conflict and judicial misconduct were often shaped by local conditions in villages, towns, and communities, but the Chambre de l'Edit struggled to implement laws that applied to all French subjects.

Did the court fulfill its tasks successfully? Records of the Chambre de l'Edit's criminal litigation offer little evidence that the court provided much protection or many sympathetic judgments for French Protestants, though this is hardly surprising. Unlike the chambres mi-parties affiliated with the parlements of Toulouse, Bordeaux, and Grenoble, this bipartisan chamber had no bloc of Huguenot magistrates, and from its inception the Paris chamber was fully integrated into the Parlement of Paris. The Chambre de l'Edit's character as the Huguenots' special law court thus derived more from its jurisdiction than its composition.

That jurisdiction included all kinds of cases and litigants, for Huguenots could appear before the court as plaintiffs or defendants—and frequently did. When Huguenots invoked or accepted the court's authority, they made its legal mandate a reality; when they petitioned its magistrates for redress, they exercised a legal privilege that reinforced their individual and corporate identity as a protected religious minority. Ironically, Catholics too could participate in this process by appealing their lawsuits against Huguenots to the Chambre de l'Edit. Small wonder that many Catholics viewed the Huguenots' legal privileges—including their special law courts—as "an annihilation of justice" long before the 1665 *mémoire* quoted above.

Yet litigants of both confessions often sued before the court, and herein lies its contribution to religious coexistence, absolutism, and the cultural creation of national identity. Throughout its adjudication of criminal lawsuits, the Chambre de l'Edit emphasized obedience to laws that applied to all French subjects. Some of those laws (like the Edict of Nantes) existed because of religious difference, while others (like those condemning *rapt* and clandestine marriage) did not. Even the Edict of Nantes, which defined the privileges that separated Huguenots and Catholics, also defined the principal thing the two groups shared: obedience to the king and his laws. In the aftermath of bitter civil and religious warfare, peace and public order depended upon such obedience. Thus the Chambre de l'Edit, like other institutions in the central government, strove to promote the ideal of the loyal, law-abiding French subject whose primary allegiance was to the monarchy. Conversely, French men and women of both confessions appealed to the court, demanding justice in return for their loyalty and obedience. Their initiatives, combined with the chamber magistrates' efforts to assure "that force remains with the king and justice," became part of a dynamic process that generally served to enhance and expand the king's power. One cannot say that the magistrates or the crown triumphed completely in these endeavors: complaints about judicial misconduct continued, and the seventeenth and eighteenth centuries are full of examples of rebellion, religious conflict, and resistance to absolutism. But in working to instill a common obedience to royal law among Huguenots and Catholics alike, the Chambre de l'Edit contributed to the history of religious coexistence and the formation of the French nation state in the seventeenth century.

Bibliography

MANUSCRIPT SOURCES

Archives Nationales (Paris):

Série X2b: Parlement de Paris, Criminel: Minutes d'Arrêt

X2b 193–98	1600	X2b 316–19	1620
X2b 199–204	1601	X2b 338	1623
X2b 205–10	1602	X2b 354–55	1625
X2b 211–16	1603	X2b 389	1630
X2b 217–22	1604	X2b 424	1635
X2b 223–28	1605	X2b 456	1640
X2b 229–33	1606	X2b 480	1644
X2b 234–39	1607	X2b 483–85	1645
X2b 240–45	1608	X2b 562	1655
X2b 246–51	1609	X2b 623–32	1660
X2b 252–57	1610	X2b 697	1665
X2b 286–91	1615		

Série X2a: Parlement de Paris, Criminel: Registres

X2a 150–52	1600
X2a 152–53	1601
X2a 154–56	1602
X2a 156–58	1603
X2a 158–61	1604
X2a 161–65	1605
X2a 165–67	1606
X2a 168–70	1607
X2a 170–72	1608
X2a 172–75	1609
X2a 175–77	1610
X2a 237	1630

Parlement de Paris, Chambre de l'Edit

XIa 9682	*Registre de la Chambre de l'Edit, Paris.*
XIb 4397	*Arrêts de la Chambre de l'Edit:* two collections of *arrêts civils* (1667–1668) and one of *arrêts criminels* (1647–1654).

X2a 1369   *Registre des Productions de la Chambre de l'Edit, Paris.*

Série TT, Affaires Protestantes:

Folio 430

Bibliothèque Nationale (Paris)

Collection Dupuy, v. 323:

Folios 38–44   Excerpt from *Chambre de l'Edit registers,* 1598.
Folios 53–55   Organization of *Chambre de l'Edit* for Rouen, 1599.
Folio 72   Instructions to royal commissioners sent to Castres regarding chambre mi-partie.
Folios 63–66   Arrêts du conseil concerning *Chambre de l'Edit.*
Folios 119–26   Arrêts du conseil concerning *Chambre de l'Edit.*
Folios 275–85   Cahier of royal decisions in favor of Protestants, 1623.
Folios 297–318 Cahier of requests from Protestant assembly of Loudun, 1620.

Collection Dupuy, v. 857:

Folios 125–29   *Chambre de l'Edit arrêts.*
Folios 145–48   *Arrêts du Conseil d'Etat,* 1609.
Folios 158–71   *Arrêts du Conseil Privé,* 1605.
Folios 180–87   *Arrêts du Conseil Privé,* 1606.

Bibliothèque de la Société de l'Histoire du Protestantisme Français (Paris)

MS Papiers Duplessis-Mornay, no. 753

Feuille 100 (Letter from deputies general of reformed churches to Philippe Duplessis Mornay, 1618) and Feuille 101 (*Letter from François Le Coq,* Chambre de l'Edit magistrate, to Duplessis-Mornay, 1618).

MS 2857   Dubief, Catherine. "La Chambre de l'Edit du Parlement de Paris." Unpublished Mémoire pour le diplôme d'études supérieures d'histoire du droit et des faits sociaux, Université de Paris II, 1972.

SELECTED SOURCES:

Abbiateci, André, et al. *Crimes et criminalité en France sous l'Ancien Régime, XVIIe–XVIIIe siècles.* Paris: A. Colin, 1971.

Airo-Farulla, Joseph. "Les Protestants et l'acquisition des offices à la fin du XVIe siècle." *Bulletin de la Société de l'Histoire du Protestantisme Français* 116 (1970): 509–12.

Allmand, Christopher. *The Hundred Years' War: England and France at War, c. 1300–c. 1450.* Cambridge: Cambridge University Press, 1988.

Amussen, Susan D. *An Ordered Society: Gender and Class in Early Modern England.* Oxford: Blackwell, 1988.

Anderson, Benedict. *Imagined Communities: Reflections on the Origin and Spread of Nationalism.* 2d ed. London: Verso, 1991.

Anquez, Léonce. *Histoire des assemblées politiques des réformés en France, 1573–1622.* Paris: A. Durand, 1859.

Antoine, Michel, ed. *Guide des recherches dans les fonds judiciaires de l'Ancien Régime.* Paris: Archives Nationales, 1958.

Ariès, Philippe. *Centuries of Childhood: A Social History of Family Life.* Translated by Robert Baldick. New York: Knopf, 1962.

———, ed. *A History of Private Life,* vol. 3: *Passions of the Renaissance.* Edited by Roger Chartier and translated by Arthur Goldhammer. Cambridge: Harvard University Press, 1989.

Aubert, François. *Le Parlement de Paris de l'origine à François Ier, 1250–1515.* Paris, 1894.

Aymard, Marcel. "Chiourmes et galères dans la Méditerranée du XVIe siècle." In *Mélanges en l'honneur de Fernand Braudel, vol. 1: Histoire économique du monde méditerannéan, 1450-1650,* 49-64. Toulouse: Privat, 1973.

Babelon, Jean-Pierre. *Henri IV.* Paris: Fayard, 1981.

Baker, Keith Michael. "Memory and Practice: Politics and the Representation of the Past in Eighteenth-Century France." *Representations* 11 (1985): 134–64.

Barbiche, Bernard. *Les Institutions de la monarchie française à l'époque moderne.* Paris: Presses Universitaires de France, 1999.

Bardet, Pierre. *Recueil d'arrests du parlement de Paris pris des mémoires de feu Maître Pierre Bardet, ancien avocat en la cour.* Paris: Besoigne, 1690.

Barnavi, Elie. *Le Parti de dieu.* Louvain: Nauwelaerts, 1980.

Barnavi, Elie, and Robert Descimon. *La Sainte Ligue, le juge et la potence.* Paris: Hachette, 1985.

Bataillard, Charles. *Moeurs judiciaires de la France du XVIe siècle au XIX siècle.* Paris, 1878.

Beaune, Colette. *The Birth of an Ideology: Myths and Symbols of Nation in Late Medieval France.* Translated by Susan Huston. Berkeley: University of California Press, 1991.

Bée, M. "Le Spectacle de l'exécution dans la France de l'Ancien Régime." *Annales: Economies, Sociétés, Civilisations* 38 (1983): 843–63.

Beik, William. *Absolutism and Society in Seventeenth-Century France.* Cambridge: Cambridge University Press, 1985.

———. *Urban Protest in Seventeenth-Century France: The Culture of Retribution.* Cambridge: Cambridge University Press, 1997.

Bell, David A. *Lawyers and Citizens: The Making of a Political Elite in Old Regime France.* New York: Oxford University Press, 1994.

———. "Lingua Populi, Lingua Dei: Language, Religion and the Origins of French Revolutionary Nationalism." *American Historical Review* 100:5 (1995): 1403–37.

———. "The 'Public Sphere,' the State and the World of Law in Eighteenth-Century France." *French Historical Studies* 17 (1994): 912–34.

Bels, Pierre. *Le Mariage des protestants français jusqu'en 1685.* Paris: Librairie général de droit et de jurisprudence, 1968.

Benedict, Philip. *The Huguenot Population of France, 1600–1685: The Demographic Fate and Customs of a Religious Minority.* Transactions of the American Philosophical Society, 2d series, 81:5. Philadelphia: American Philosophical Society, 1991.

———. *Rouen during the Wars of Religion.* Cambridge: Cambridge University Press, 1980.

Bérenguier, Nadine. "Victorious Victims: Women and Publicity in *Mémoires Judiciaires.*" In *Going Public: Women and Publishing in Early Modern France.* Edited by Elizabeth C. Goldsmith and Dena Goodman, 62–78. Ithaca: Cornell University Press, 1995.

Bergin, Joseph. *Cardinal Richelieu: Power and the Pursuit of Wealth.* New Haven: Yale University Press, 1985.

———. *The Rise of Richelieu.* New Haven: Yale University Press, 1991.

Bertheau, Solange. "Le Consistoire dans les églises réformées du Moyen Poitou au XVIIe siè-cle." *Bulletin de la société de l'histoire du protestantisme français* 116 (1970): 332–59, 513–49.

Billacois, François. *Le Duel dans la société française, XVIe–XVIIIe siècles: Essai de psychosociologie historique.* Paris: Editions de l'Ecole des Hautes Etudes en Sciences Sociales, 1986.

Blet, Pierre. *Le Clergé de France et la monarchie: Étude sur les assemblées générales du clergé de 1615 à 1666.* 2 vols. Rome: Librairie éditrice de l'Université grégorienne, 1959.

Bodin, Jean. *Six Books of the Commonwealth.* Translated by M. J. Tooley. New York: Barnes & Noble, 1967.

Bonifas, Ernest-Charles-François. *Le Mariage des protestants depuis la Réforme jusqu'à 1789.* Paris: L. Boyer, 1901.

Bonney, Richard. "Absolutism: What's in a Name?" *French History* 1 (1986): 93–117.

Bossy, John. "The Social History of Confession in the Age of the Reformation." *Transactions of the Royal Historical Society,* 5th series, 25 (1975): 21–38.

———, ed. *Disputes and Settlements: Law and Human Relations in the West.* Cambridge: Cambridge University Press, 1982.

Bouwsma, William. *A Usable Past: Essays in European Cultural History.* Berkeley: University of California Press, 1990.

Bremmer, Jan, and Herman Roodenburg, eds. *A Cultural History of Gesture.* Ithaca: Cornell University Press, 1991.

Briggs, Robin. *Communities of Belief: Cultural and Social Tension in Early Modern France.* Oxford: Clarendon Press, 1989.

Brissaud, Jean. *A History of French Private Law.* Translated by J. Garner. Continental Legal History, vol. 9. New York: Rothman, 1969.

Brucker, Gene A. *Giovanni and Lusanna: Love and Marriage in Renaissance Florence.* Berkeley: University of California Press, 1986.

Brundage, James A. *Law, Sex and Christian Society in Medieval Europe.* Chicago: University of Chicago Press, 1987.

Brunelle, Gayle K. "Dangerous Liaisons: Mésalliance and Early Modern French Noblewomen." *French Historical Studies* 19 (1995): 75–103.

Bryant, Lawrence M. *The King and the City in the Parisian Royal Entry Ceremony.* Geneva: Droz, 1986.

Buisseret, David. *Henry IV.* London: George Unwin & Allen, 1984.

Burke, Peter. "History as Social Memory." In *Memory: History, Culture and the Mind.* Edited by Thomas Butler, 97–113. Oxford: Blackwell, 1989.

———. "Insult and Blasphemy in Early Modern Italy." In Burke, *The Historical Anthropology of Early Modern Italy,* 95–109. Cambridge: Cambridge University Press, 1987.

Butler, Jon. *The Huguenots in America: A Refugee People in New World Society.* Cambridge: Harvard University Press, 1983.

Cameron, Keith, ed. *From Valois to Bourbon: Dynasty, State and Society in Early Modern France.* Exeter: University of Exeter Press, 1989.

Canons and Decrees of the Council of Trent. Translated by Henry Joseph Schroeder. St. Louis: B. Herder, 1941.

Capot, Stéphane. *Justice et Religion en Languedoc au temps de l'Edit de Nantes: La Chambre de l'Edit de Castres, 1579–1679.* Paris: Ecole des Chartes, 1998.

Carey, Robert. *Judicial Reform before the Revolution of 1789.* Cambridge: Harvard University Press, 1981.

Carsalade du Pont, Henri de. *La Municipalité Parisienne à l'époque d'Henri IV.* Paris: Éditions Cujas, 1971.

Castan, Nicole. *Justice et repression en Languedoc à l'époque des Lumières.* Paris: Flammarion, 1980.

Castan, Yves. *Honnêteté et relations sociales en Languedoc, 1715–1780.* Paris: Plon, 1974.

Chartier, Roger. *Cultural History: Between Practices and Representations.* Translated by Lydia Cochrane. Ithaca: Cornell University Press, 1985.

Cheyette, Frédéric. "La Justice et le pouvoir à la fin du moyen âge français." *Revue historique de droit français et étranger,* 4th series 40:3 (1963): 373–94.

Church, William F. *Constitutional Thought in Sixteenth-Century France.* Cambridge: Harvard University Press, 1941.

————. "France." In *National Consciousness, History and Political Culture in Early Modern Europe.* Edited by Orest Ranum, 43–66. Baltimore: Johns Hopkins University Press, 1975.

Collins, James B. *The State in Early Modern France.* Cambridge: Cambridge University Press, 1995.

Connerton, Paul. *How Societies Remember.* Cambridge: Cambridge University Press, 1985.

Cottret, Bernard. *L'Edit de Nantes.* Paris: Perrin, 1997.

Cressy, David. *Bonfires and Bells: National Memory and the Protestant Calendar in Elizabethan and Stuart England.* Berkeley: University of California Press, 1990.

Crouzet, Denis. *Les Guerriers de Dieu: La violence au temps des troubles de religion, vers 1525–1610.* 2 vols. Paris: Seyssel, 1990.

Cruz, Anne J., and Mary Elizabeth Perry, eds. *Culture and Control in Counter-Reformation Spain.* Minneapolis: University of Minnesota Press, 1992.

Cummings, Mark. "Elopement, Family and the Courts: The Crime of *Rapt* in Early Modern France." *Proceedings of the Annual Meeting of the Western Society for French History* 4 (1976): 118–25.

Damien, André. *Les Avocats du temps passé: Essai sur la vie quotidienne des avocats au cours des âges.* Versailles: H. Lefebvre, 1973.

Darmon, Pierre. *Damning the Innocent: A History of the Persecution of the Impotent in Pre-Revolutionary France.* Translated by Paul Keegan. New York: Viking, 1986.

David, René. *French Law: Its Structures, Sources, and Methodology.* Trans. Michael Kindred. Baton Rouge: Louisiana State University Press, 1972.

Davis, Natalie Zemon. "Boundaries and the Sense of Self in Sixteenth-Century France." In *Reconstructing Individualism: Autonomy, Individuality and the Self in Western Thought.* Edited by Thomas Heller et al., 53–63. Stanford: Stanford University Press, 1986.

————. *Fiction in the Archives: Pardon Tales and Their Tellers in Sixteenth-Century France.* Stanford: Stanford University Press, 1987.

————. "Ghosts, Kin and Progeny: Some Features of Family Life in Early Modern France." *Daedalus* 106:2 (1977): 87–114.

————. *The Return of Martin Guerre.* Cambridge: Harvard University Press, 1983.

————. *Society and Culture in Early Modern France: Eight Essays.* Stanford: Stanford University Press, 1975.

Davis, Natalie Zemon, and Randolph Starn. "Introduction to Special Issue on Memory and Counter-Memory." *Representations* 26 (1989): 1–6.

Dawson, John P. *A History of Lay Judges.* Cambridge: Harvard University Press, 1960.

Dean, Trevor, and Kate Lowe, eds. *Crime, Society and the Law in Renaissance Italy.* Cambridge: Cambridge University Press, 1994.

Decisions royales sur les principales difficultez de l'Edict de Nantes. Par Responses et Expressions faites et ordonées au Conseil d'Estat, sur les Cayers des plaints et remonstrances qu'en esté presentées au Roy. Paris, 1643.

DeKlerk, Peter, ed. *Renaissance Reformation and Resurgence: Colloquium on Calvin and Calvin Studies.* Grand Rapids: Calvin Theological Seminary, 1976.

Delachanel, Roland. *Histoire des avocats au parlement de Paris, 1300–1600.* Paris, 1885.

Delumeau, Jean, ed. *Injures et blasphèmes.* Paris: Editions Imago, 1989.

Desplat, Christian. "Louis XIII and the Union of Béarn to France." In *Conquest and Coalescence: The Shaping of the State in Early Modern Europe.* Edited by Mark Greengrass, 68–83. London: Edward Arnold, 1991.

De Waele, Michel. "Les Opinions politiques d'un avocat parisien sous Henri IV: Antoine Arnauld." *Renaissance and Reform/Renaissance et Réforme* 17 (1993): 51–60.

———. *Les Relations entre le parlement de Paris et Henri IV.* Paris: Publisud, 2000.

Dewald, Jonathan. *Aristocratic Experience and the Origins of Modern Culture: France, 1570–1715.* Berkeley: University of California Press, 1980.

———. *Formation of a Provincial Elite: The Magistrates of the Parlement of Rouen, 1499–1610.* Princeton: Princeton University Press, 1980.

———. "The 'Perfect Magistrate': Parlementaires and Crime in Sixteenth-Century Rouen." *Archiv für Reformationsgeschichte* 67 (1976): 284–99.

Deyon, Solange. *Du Loyalisme au refus: Les protestants français et leur député général entre la Fronde et la Révocation.* Lille: Université de Lille III, 1976.

Diefendorf, Barbara B. *Beneath the Cross: Catholics and Huguenots in Sixteenth Century Paris.* New York: Oxford University Press, 1991.

———. "Give Us Back Our Children: Patriarchal Authority and Parental Consent to Religious Vocations in Early Counter-Reformation France." *Journal of Modern History* 68 (1996): 265–307.

———. "Houses Divided: Religious Schism in Sixteenth-Century Parisian Families." In *Urban Life in the Renaissance.* Edited by Susan Zimmerman and Robert Weissman, 80–99. Newark: University of Delaware Press, 1989.

———. *The Paris City Councillors in the Sixteenth Century.* Princeton: Princeton University Press, 1983.

Diefendorf, Barbara B., and Carla Hesse, eds. *Culture and Identity in Early Modern Europe: Essays in Honor of Natalie Zemon Davis.* Ann Arbor: University of Michigan Press, 1993.

Domat, Jean. "Traité des lois." In *Les Lois civiles dans leur ordre naturel.* Paris, 1777.

Dompnier, Bernard. *Le Venin de l'hérésie: L'Image du protestantisme et combat catholique pendant le XVIIe siècle.* Paris: Le Centurion, 1985.

Doucet, Roger. *Les Institutions de France au XVIe siècle.* 2 vols. Paris: Picard, 1948.

Doyle, William. *Venality: The Sale of Offices in Eighteenth-Century France.* New York: Oxford University Press, 1996.

Duguit, Léon. "Etude historique sur le rapt de séduction." *Nouvelle revue historique du droit français et étranger* 10 (1886): 586–685.

Dupin, A., ed. *Profession d'avocat: Recueil des pièces concernant l'exercice de cette profession.* Paris, 1832.

Dupuy, Christophe. *Jacques-Auguste de Thou and the Index: Letters from Christophe Dupuy, 1603–1607.* Edited by Alfred Soman. Geneva: Droz, 1972.

"The Edict of Nantes with Its Secret Articles and Brevets." Translated by Jotham Parsons. In *The Edict of Nantes: Five Essays and a New Translation.* Edited by Richard L. Goodbar, 41–68. Bloomington, Minn.: National Huguenot Society, 1998.

Edits, declarations et arrests concernans la religion prétendue réformée, 1662–1751, précédés de l'Edit de Nantes. Paris: Fischbacher, 1885.

Esmein, Adhémar. *Cours élémentaire d'histoire du droit français.* Paris: Recueil Sirey, 1921.

———. *Histoire de la procédure criminelle en France.* Paris: L. Larose et Forcel, 1882.

———. *Le Mariage en droit canonique.* 2 vols. Paris: Recueil Sirey, 1935.

Estèbe, Janine, and Bernard Vogler. "La Genèse d'une société protestante: Etude comparée de quelques registres consistoriaux languedociens et palatins vers 1600," *Annales: Economies, Sociétés, Civilisations* 31 (1976): 362-88.

L'Estoile, Pierre de. *Mémoires-Journaux.* Edited by G. Brunet et al. 12 vols. Paris: Librairie des Bibliophiles, 1879.

Farge, Arlette. *Subversive Words: Public Opinion in Eighteenth-Century France.* Translated by Rosemary Morris. University Park: Pennsylvania State University Press, 1995.

Farr, James R. *Authority and Sexuality in Early Modern Burgundy, 1550–1730.* New York: Oxford University Press, 1995.

———. *Hands of Honor: Artisans and Their World in Dijon, 1550–1650.* Ithaca: Cornell University Press, 1988.

Ferrière, Charles-Joseph. *Dictionnaire de droit et de pratique.* 2 vols. Paris, 1762.

Filleau, J. *Décisions catholiques: Ou, recueil général des arrêts rendus en toutes les cours souveraines de France en l'exécution ou interpretation des edits qui concernent l'exercice de la religion prétendue réformée.* Poitiers: Fleuriau, 1668.

Finley-Croswhite, Annette. *Henry IV and the Towns.* Cambridge: Cambridge University Press, 1999.

Flandrin, Jean-Louis. *Families in Former Times.* Translated by Richard Southern. Cambridge: Cambridge University Press, 1979. Originally published as *Familles: Parenté, maison. Sexualité dans l'ancienne Société.* Paris: Hachette, 1976.

Ford, Caroline. *Creating the Nation in Provincial France: Religion and Identity in Brittany.* Princeton: Princeton University Press, 1993.

Forster, Robert, and Orest Ranum, eds. *Family and Society: Selections from the Annales: Economies, Sociétés, Civilisations.* Translated by Patricia Ranum and Elborg Forster. Baltimore: Johns Hopkins University Press, 1976.

Franklin, Julian H. *Jean Bodin and the Sixteenth-Century Revolution in the Methodology of Law and History.* New York: Columbia University Press, 1963.

———, ed. *Constitutionalism and Resistance in Sixteenth-Century France.* New York: Pegasus, 1969.

Furetière, Antoine. *Dictionnaire universel.* La Haye and Rotterdam, 1690. Reprint Geneva: Slatkine, 1970.

Garrisson, François. *Essai sur les commissions d'application de l'Edit de Nantes, règne Henri IV.* Montpellier: Déhan, 1950.

Garrisson, Janine. *L'Edit de Nantes et sa révocation: Histoire d'une intolérance.* Paris: Seuil, 1985.

———. *Henri IV.* Paris: Seuil, 1984.

———. *Les Protestants au XVIe siècle.* Paris: Fayard, 1988.

———. *Les Protestants du Midi, 1559–1598.* Toulouse: Privat, 1980.

Gatrell, V.A.C., et al., eds. *Crime and the Law: The Social History of Crime in Western Europe since 1500.* London: Europa Publications, 1980.

Gaudemet, Jean. *Le Mariage en occident: Les moeurs et le droit.* Paris: Cerf, 1987.

Gauvard, Claude. *"De Grace Espécial": Crime, état et société en France à la fin du Moyen Age.* 2 vols. Paris: Publications de la Sorbonne, 1991.

———. "L'Image du roi justicier en France à la fin du Moyen Age, d'après les lettres de rémission." In *La Faute, la répression et le pardon: Actes du 107e Congrès National des Sociétés Savantes,* vol. I, 165–92. Brest: Comité des travaux historiques et scientifiques, 1982.

"The Generall and Particular Acts and Articles of the Late National Synod of the Reformed Churches of France, Assembled by the Permission of the King at Charenton near Paris, beginning the 26th of December 1644." London, 1645.

Gibson, Wendy. *Women in Seventeenth-Century France.* New York: St. Martin's Press, 1989.

Giesey, Ralph. "The King Imagined." In *The Political Culture of the Old Regime.* Edited by Keith Michael Baker, 41–59. New York: Pergamon Press, 1988.

———. *The Royal Funeral Ceremony in Renaissance France.* Geneva: Droz, 1960.

———. "Rules of Inheritance and Strategies of Mobility in Pre-Revolutionary France." *American Historical Review* 82:2 (1977): 271–89.

———. "State-Building in Early Modern France: The Role of Royal Officialdom." *Journal of Modern History* 55 (1983): 191–207.

Giesey, Ralph, Lanny Haldy, and James Millhorn. "Cardin Le Bret and Lèse Majesty." *Law and History Review* 4 (1986): 23–54.

Gillis, John, ed. *Commemorations: The Politics of National Identity.* Princeton: Princeton University Press, 1994.

Ginzburg, Carlo. *The Cheese and the Worms: The Cosmos of a Sixteenth-Century Miller.* Translated by John and Anne Tedeschi. Baltimore: Johns Hopkins University Press, 1980.

Golden, Richard, ed. *The Huguenot Connection: The Edict of Nantes, Its Revocation, and Early French Migration to South Carolina.* Dordrecht: Kluwer Academic Publishers, 1988.

Goody, Jack, et al. *Family and Inheritance: Rural Society in Western Europe, 1200–1800.* Cambridge: Cambridge University Press, 1976.

Gordon, Daniel. *Citizens without Sovereignty: Equality and Sociability in French Thought, 1670–1789.* Princeton: Princeton University Press, 1994.

Gottlieb, Beatrice. *The Family in the Western World from the Black Death to the Industrial Age.* New York: Oxford University Press, 1993.

Grandjean, Michel, and Bernard Roussel, eds. *Coexister dans l'intolérance: L'Edit de Nantes (1598).* Geneva: Labor et Fides, 1998.

Gravdal, Kathryn. *Ravishing Maidens: Writing Rape in Medieval French Literature and Law.* Philadelphia: University of Pennsylvania Press, 1991.

Greenblatt, Stephen J. *Renaissance Self-Fashioning: From More to Shakespeare.* Chicago: University of Chicago Press, 1980.

Greengrass, Mark. *The French Reformation.* Oxford: Blackwell, 1987.

———. "Hidden Transcripts: Secret Histories and Personal Testaments of Religious Violence in the French Wars of Religion." In *The Massacre in History.* Edited by Mark Levene and Penny Roberts, 69–88. New York: Bergahn Books, 1999.

Greenshields, Malcolm. *An Economy of Violence in Early Modern France: Crime and Justice in the Haute Auvergne, 1587–1664.* University Park: Pennsylvania State University Press, 1994.

Grell, Ole Peter, and Bob Scribner, eds. *Tolerance and Intolerance in the European Reformation.* Cambridge: Cambridge University Press, 1996.

Groshens, J.-C. *Les Institutions et le régime juridique des cultes protestants.* Paris: Librairie générale de droit et de jurisprudence, 1957.

Guilhiermoz, Paul. *Enquêtes et procès: Étude sur la procédure et le fonctionnement du parlement au XIVe siècle.* Paris: 1892.

Guyot, Pierre. *Répertoire universel et raisonné de jurisprudence.* 12 vols. Paris: Chez Visse, 1784.

Haag, Eugène, and Émile Haag. *La France protestante.* 10 vols. Paris: J. Cherbuliez, 1846–59.

Halbwachs, Maurice. *The Collective Memory.* Translated by Francis and Vida Ditter. New York: Columbia University Press, 1980.

———. *On Collective Memory.* Edited and translated by Lewis A. Coser. Chicago: Chicago University Press, 1992.

Hale, J.R. "Sixteenth-Century Explanations of War and Violence." *Past and Present* 51 (1971): 3–26.

Hamscher, Albert N. *The Conseil Privé and the Parlements in the Age of Louis XIV: A Study in French Absolutism.* Transactions of the American Philosophical Society 77:2. Philadelphia: American Philosophical Society, 1987.

———. *The Parlement of Paris after the Fronde, 1653–1673.* Pittsburgh: University of Pittsburgh Press, 1976.

Hanley, Sarah. "Engendering the State: Family Formation and State Building in Early Modern France." *French Historical Studies* 16 (1989): 4–27.

———. "Family and State in Early Modern France: The Marriage Pact." In *Connecting Spheres: Women in the Western World from 1500 to the Present.* Edited by Marilyn Boxer and Jean Quataert, 53–63. New York: Oxford University Press, 1987.

———. *The Lit de Justice of the Kings of France.* Princeton: Princeton University Press, 1983.

———. "Social Sites of Political Practice in France: Lawsuits, Civil Rights and the Separation of Powers in Domestic and State Government, 1500–1800." *American Historical Review* 102 (1997): 27–52.

Hanlon, Gregory. *Confession and Community in Seventeenth-Century France: Catholic and Protestant Coexistence in Aquitaine.* Philadelphia: University of Pennsylvania Press, 1993.

———. "Les Rituels de l'aggression en Aquitaine au XVIIe siècle." *Annales: Economies, Sociétés, Civilisations* 40 (1985): 244–68.

Harding, Robert. "Corruption and the Moral Boundaries of Patronage in the Renaissance." In *Patronage in the Renaissance.* Edited by Guy Fitch Lytle and Stephen Orgel, 41–64. Princeton: Princeton University Press, 1981.

Hardwick, Julie. *The Practice of Patriarchy: Gender and Household Authority in Early Modern France.* University Park: Pennsylvania State University Press, 1998.

Harisse, Henry. *Le Président de Thou et ses descendants.* Paris, 1905.

Hayden, J. Michael, and Malcolm R. Greenshields. "The Clergy of Seventeenth-Century France: Self-Perception and Society's Perception." *French Historical Studies* 18 (1993): 145–72.

Herman, Arthur L. "Protestant Churches in a Catholic Kingdom: Political Assemblies in the Thought of Philippe Duplessis-Mornay." *Sixteenth Century Journal* 21 (1990): 543–57.

Hobsbawn, Eric J., and Terence O. Ranger, eds. *The Invention of Tradition.* Cambridge: Cambridge University Press, 1983.

Hoffman, Philip. *Church and Community in the Diocese of Lyon, 1500–1789.* New Haven: Yale University Press, 1984.

Holt, Mack P. *The French Wars of Religion, 1562–1629.* Cambridge: Cambridge University Press, 1995.

———. "Putting Religion Back into the Wars of Religion." *French Historical Studies* 18:2 (1993): 524–51.

Hsia, Ronnie Po-chia. *Social Discipline in the Reformation: Central Europe, 1550–1750.* New York: Routledge, 1989.

Hudson, Elizabeth K. "The Protestant Struggle for Survival in Early Bourbon France: The Case of the Huguenot Schools," *Archiv für Reformationsgeschichte* 76 (1985): 271–95.

Hunt, Lynn, ed. *The New Cultural History.* Berkeley: University of California Press, 1989.

Huppert, George. *Les Bourgeois Gentilhommes: An Essay on the Definition of Elites in Renaissance France.* Chicago: University of Chicago Press, 1977.

——. *The Idea of Perfect History.* Urbana: University of Illinois Press, 1970.

Hutton, Patrick H. *History as an Art of Memory.* Hanover, N.H.: University Presses of New England, 1993.

Imbert, Jean. *La Peine de mort: Histoire, actualité.* Paris: A. Colin, 1967.

——. *Quelques procès criminels des XVIIe et XVIIIe siècles.* Paris: Presses Universitaires de France, 1964.

Isambert, François-André, et al. *Recueil général des anciennes lois françaises.* 26 vols. Paris: Belin-Leprieur, 1833.

James, Mervyn. *English Politics and the Concept of Honor, 1485–1642.* Past and Present Supplement, no. 3. Oxford: Past and Present Society, 1978.

Jensen, DeLamar. *Diplomacy and Dogmatism: Bernardino de Mendoza and the French Catholic League.* Cambridge: Harvard University Press, 1964.

Johnson, Douglas. "The Making of the French Nation." In *The National Question in Europe in Historical Context.* Edited by Roy Porter and Mikulás Teich, 35–62. Cambridge: Cambridge University Press, 1993.

Jouanna, Arlette. *Le Devoir de révolte: La noblesse française et la gestation de l'état moderne, 1559–1661.* Paris: Fayard, 1989.

——. "Recherches sur la notion d'honneur au XVIe siècle." *Revue d'histoire moderne et contemporaine* 15 (1968): 592–623.

Jouhaud, Christian. *Mazarinades: La Fronde des mots.* Paris: Aubier, 1985.

Kagan, Richard L. *Lucrecia's Dreams: Politics and Prophecy in Sixteenth-Century Spain.* Berkeley: University of California Press, 1990.

Kaiser, Colin. "Les Cours souveraines au XVIe siècle: Morale et Contre-Réforme," *Annales: Economies, Sociétés, Civilisations* 37 (1982): 15–31.

Karant-Nunn, Susan C. *The Reformation of Ritual: An Interpretation of Early Modern Germany.* New York: Routledge, 1997.

Kelley, Donald R. *The Foundations of Modern Historical Scholarship: Language, Law and History in the French Renaissance.* New York: Columbia University Press, 1970.

Keohane, Nannerl O. *Philosophy and the State in France: The Renaissance to the Enlightenment.* Princeton: Princeton University Press, 1980.

Kermode, Jennifer, and Garthine Walker, eds. *Women, Crime and the Courts in Early Modern Europe.* Chapel Hill: University of North Carolina Press, 1994.

Kettering, Sharon. *Judicial Politics and Urban Revolt in Seventeeth-Century France: The Parlement of Aix, 1629–1659.* Princeton: Princeton University Press, 1978.

Kettering, Sharon. *Patrons, Brokers and Clients in Seventeenth-Century France.* New York: Oxford University Press, 1986.

Kingdon, Robert M. *Geneva and the Coming of the Wars of Religion in France.* Geneva: Droz, 1956.

——. *Geneva and the Consolidation of the French Protestant Movement.* Geneva: Droz, 1967.

Klaits, Joseph. *Printed Propaganda under Louis XIV.* Princeton: Princeton University Press, 1976.

Klapisch-Zuber, Christiane. "La 'Mère cruelle': Maternité, veuvage et dot dans la Florence des XIV–XVe siècles." *Annales: Economies, Sociétés, Civilisations* 38 (1983): 1097–109.

Kleinman, Ruth. "The Unquiet Truce: An Exploration of Catholic Feeling against the Huguenots in France, 1646–1664," *French Historical Studies* 4 (1965): 170–88.

Knecht, R. J. *French Renaissance Monarchy: Francis I and Henry II.* London: Longman, 1984.

Kollmann, Nancy Shields. "Honor and Dishonor in Early Modern Russia." *Forschungen zur osteuropäischen geschichte* 46 (1992): 131–46.

Konnert, Mark. "Urban Values versus Religious Passion: Châlons-sur-Marne during the Wars of Religion." *Sixteenth Century Journal* 20 (1989): 387–406.

Kuehn, Thomas. "Dispute Processing in the Renaissance: Some Florentine Examples." In Kuehn, *Law, Family and Women: Toward a Legal Anthropology of Renaissance Italy,* 75–100. Chicago: University of Chicago Press, 1991.

La Chesnaye-Desbois, François. *Dictionnaire de la noblesse.* 3d ed. 19 vols. Paris: 1863–77.

Labrousse, Elisabeth. "The Wars of Religion in Seventeenth-Century Huguenot Thought." In *The Massacre of Saint Bartholomew: Reappraisals and Documents.* Edited by Alfred Soman, 243–51. The Hague: M. Nijhoff, 1974.

————. *Une Foi, une loi, un roi? La révocation de l'Edit de Nantes.* Geneva: Labor et Fides, 1985.

Langbein, John. *Prosecuting Crime in the Renaissance.* Cambridge: Harvard University Press, 1974.

————. *Torture and the Law of Proof.* Chicago: Chicago University Press, 1976.

Lebigre, Arlette. *Les Institutions de l'Ancien Régime.* Paris: Les Cours de Droit, 1976.

————. *La Justice du roi: La vie judiciaire dans l'ancienne France.* Paris: Albin Michel, 1988.

————. *La Révolution des curés: Paris, 1588–1594.* Paris: Albin Michel, 1980.

Le Goff, Jacques. *History and Memory.* Translated by Steven Rendall and Elizabeth Claman. New York: Columbia University Press, 1992.

Lesdiguières, François de Bonne, duc de. *Lettre et Advis envoyé au Roy, par Monsieur le Mareschal de Lesdiguières.* Tours, 1610.

Levy, Leonard W. *Treason against God: A History of the Offense of Blasphemy.* New York: Schocken Books, 1981.

Ligou, Daniel. *Le Protestantisme en France de 1598 à 1715.* Paris: S.E.D.E.S., 1968.

Loisel, Antoine. *Institutes coutumières.* Edited by Andre-Marie-Jean-Jacques Dupin and Edouard Laboulaye. Paris, 1846. Reprint Geneva: Slatkine, 1971.

Loride, Pierre. *Sommaire des procès, differens et contestations qui arrivent ordinairement dans l'exécution des edicts de pacification.* Paris: Gentil, 1661.

Love, Ronald S. *Blood and Religion: The Conscience of Henri IV, 1553–1593.* Kingston and Montreal: McGill-Queen's University Press, 2001.

Lowenthal, David. *The Past Is a Foreign Country.* Cambridge: Cambridge University Press, 1985.

Lualdi, Katherine Jackson, and Anne T. Thayer, eds. *Penitence in the Age of Reformations.* Aldershot: Ashgate, 2000.

Luria, Keith P. *Territories of Grace.* Berkeley: University of California Press, 1991.

Luria, Keith P. "Separated by Death? Burials, Cemeteries, and Confessional Boundaries in Seventeenth-Century France." *French Historical Studies* 24 (2001): 185–222.

Magendie, Maurice. *La Politesse mondaine et les théories de l'honnêteté en France au XVIIe siècle, de 1600 à 1670.* Paris, 1925.

Mandrou, Robert, et al. *Histoire des Protestants.* Toulouse: Privat, 1977.

Mansfield, Mary C. *The Humiliation of Sinners: Public Penance in Thirteenth-Century France.* Ithaca: Cornell University Press, 1995.

Margolf, Diane C. "The Edict of Nantes' Amnesty: Appeals to the Chambre de l'Edit, 1600–1610." *Proceedings of the Annual Meeting of the Western Society of French History* 16 (1988): 49–55.

Martin, Victor. *Les Origines du gallicanisme.* 2 vols. Paris: Bloud & Gay, 1939.

Martines, Lauro. *Lawyers and Statecraft in Renaissance Florence.* Princeton: Princeton University Press, 1968.

Maugis, Edouard. *Histoire du parlement de Paris de l'avènement des rois Valois à la mort d'Henri IV.* 3 vols. Paris, 1914–16. Reprint New York: Burt Franklin, 1967.

Maximes à observer aux jugements des partages faicts par MM. Les commissaires executoires de l'Edit de Nantes, avec réponse de Loride des Galinières. N.p., 1661.

Maza, Sarah. "Le Tribunal de la nation: Les mémoires judiciaires et l'opinion publique à la fin de l'Ancien Régime." *Annales: Economies, Sociétés, Civilisations* 42 (1987): 73–90.

Medick, Hans, and David Sabean, eds. *Interest and Emotion: Essays on the Study of Family and Kinship.* Cambridge: Cambridge University Press, 1984.

Mentzer, Raymond A. "Bipartisan Justice and the Pacification of Late Sixteenth-Century Languedoc." In *Regnum, Religio et Ratio: Essays Presented to Robert M. Kingdon.* Edited by Jerome Friedman, 125–32. Kirksville, Mo.: Sixteenth Century Journal Publishers, 1987.

———. *Blood and Belief: Family Survival and Confessional Identity among the Provincial Huguenot Nobility.* West Lafayette: Purdue University Press, 1994.

———. "'Disciplina Nervus Ecclesiae': The Calvinist Reform of Morals at Nîmes," *Sixteenth Century Journal* 18 (1987): 89–115.

———. "Ecclesiastical Discipline and Communal Reorganization among the Protestant of Southern France," *European History Quarterly* 21 (1991): 163–83.

———. "The Formation of the Chambre de l'Edit of Languedoc," *Proceedings of the Annual Meeting of the Western Society for French History* 8 (1980): 47–56.

———. "The Reformed Churches of France and Medieval Canon Law." In *Canon Law in Protestant Lands.* Edited by Richard Helmholz. Berlin: Duncker & Humblot, 1992.

———. "The Self-Image of the Magistrate in Sixteenth-Century France." *Criminal Justice History* 5 (1984): 23–43.

———, ed. *Sin and the Calvinists: Morals Control and the Consistory in the Reformed Tradition.* Kirksville, Mo.: Sixteenth Century Journal Publishers, 1994.

Merrick, Jeffrey. *The Desacralization of the French Monarchy.* Baton Rouge: Louisiana State University Press, 1990.

Milles de Souvigny, Jean. *Pratique Criminelle/par Jean de Mille; translaté de latin en vulgaire françoys par Arlette Lebigre.* Paris: 1541. Reprint Moulins: Les Marmousets, 1983.

Miskimin, Harry A. "Widows Not So Merry: Women and the Courts in Late Medieval France." In *Upon My Husband's Death: Widows in the Literature and Histories of Medieval Europe.* Edited by Louise Mirrer, 235–76. Ann Arbor: University of Michigan Press, 1992.

Molin, Jean-Baptiste, and Protais Mutembe. *Le Rituel du mariage en France du XIIe au XVIe siècle.* Paris: Beauchesne, 1976.

Monter, E. William. *Judging the French Reformation: Heresy Trials by Sixteenth-Century Parlements.* Cambridge: Harvard University Press, 1999.

Moote, A. Lloyd. *Louis XIII, the Just.* Berkeley: University of California Press, 1989.

———. *The Revolt of the Judges: The Parlement of Paris and the Fronde, 1643–1652.* Princeton: Princeton University Press, 1971.

Moreel, L. "La Notion de famille dans le droit de l'Ancien Régime." In *Renouveau des idés sur la famille.* Edited by Robert Prigent, 20–26. Paris: Presses Universitaires de France, 1954.

Mours, Samuel. *Les Eglises réformées en France.* Paris: Librairie Protestante, 1958.

————. *Essai sommaire de géographie du protestantisme français au XVIIe siècle.* Paris: Librairie Protestante, 1966.

————. *Le Protestantisme en France au XVIe siècle.* Paris: Librairie Protestante, 1959.

Mousnier, Roland. *L'Assassinat d'Henri IV.* Paris: Gallimard, 1964.

————. *La Famille, l'enfant et l'éducation en France et Grande Bretagne, XVIe au XVIIIe siècles.* Paris: Centre de documentation universitaire, 1975.

————. *The Institutions of France under the Absolute Monarchy, 1598–1789.* Translated by Brian Pearce. Chicago: Chicago University Press, 1979.

————. *La Vénalité des offices sous Henri IV et Louis XIII.* 2d ed. Paris: Presses Universitaires de France, 1971.

Muir, Edward. *Ritual in Early Modern Europe.* Cambridge: Cambridge University Press, 1996.

Myers, W. David. *"Poor Sinning Folk": Confession and Conscience in Counter-Reformation Germany.* Ithaca: Cornell University Press, 1996.

Neuschel, Kristen. *Word of Honor: Interpreting Noble Culture in Sixteenth-Century France.* Ithaca: Cornell University Press, 1989.

Nicholls, David. "The Theatre of Martyrdom in the French Refomation." *Past and Present* 121 (1988): 49–73.

Nora, Pierre. "Between Memory and History: Les Lieux de Mémoire." *Representations* 26 (1989): 7–25.

————, ed. *Les Lieux de mémoire.* 3 vols. Paris: Gallimard, 1984.

Olier, Nicolas-Edouard. *Journal de Nicolas-Edouard Olier, conseiller au Parlement, 1593–1602.* Edited by L. Sandret. Paris, 1876.

Olivier-Martin, François. *La Coûtume de Paris: Traité d'union entre le droit romain et les législations modernes.* Paris: Recueil Sirey, 1925.

————. *Histoire du droit français des origines à la Révolution.* Paris: Domat Montchrestien, 1951.

Ourliac, Paul, and Jean-Louis Gazzaniga. *Histoire du droit privé français: De l'an mil au Code Civil.* Paris: Albin Michel, 1985.

Pacilly, Georges. "Contribution à l'histoire de la théorie du rapt de séduction: Etude de jurisprudence." *Tijdschrift voor Rechtsgeschiedenis* 13 (1934): 306–18.

Pagden, Anthony, and Nicolas Canny, eds. *Colonial Identity in the Atlantic World, 1500–1800.* Princeton: Princeton University Press, 1987.

Pannier, Jacques. *L'Eglise réformée de Paris sous Louis XIII, 1610–1621.* Paris, 1922.

————. *L'Eglise réformée de Paris sous Louis XIII, 1621–1629.* 2 vols. Paris: H. Champion, 1931.

Parker, David. "The Huguenots in Seventeenth-Century France." In *Minorities in History.* Edited by A.C. Hepburn, 11–30. New York: St. Martin's Press, 1979.

————. *The Making of French Absolutism.* London: Edward Arnold, 1983.

————. *La Rochelle and the French Monarchy: Conflict and Order in Seventeenth-Century France.* London: Royal Historical Society, 1980.

————. "The Social Foundations of French Absolutism, 1610–1630," *Past and Present* 53 (1971): 67–89.

————. "Sovereignty, Absolutism and the Function of Law in Seventeenth-Century France." *Past and Present* 122 (1989): 36–74.

Parrow, Kathleen A. *From Defense to Resistance: Justification of Violence during the French Wars of Religion.* Transactions of the American Philosophical Society 83:6. Philadelphia: American Philosophical Society, 1993.

Peters, Edward. *Inquisition*. New York: Free Press, 1988.

Piqué, Nicolas, and Ghislain Waterlot, eds. *Tolérance et réforme: Eléments pour une généalogie du concept de tolérance*. Paris: L'Harmattan, 1999.

Pitt-Rivers, Julian. "Honour and Social Status." In *Honour and Shame: The Values of Mediterranean Society*. Edited by J.G. Peristiany, 21–77. Chicago: University of Chicago Press, 1966.

Pocock, J.G.A. *The Ancient Constitution and the Feudal Law*. 2d ed. Cambridge: Cambridge University Press, 1987.

Popoff, Michel, ed. *Prosopographie des gens du parlement de Paris, 1266–1753*. Saint-Nazaire-le-Désert: Références, 1996.

Powis, Jonathan K. "Order, Religion and the Magistrates of a Provincial Parlement in Sixteenth-Century France." *Archiv für Reformationsgeschichte* 71 (1980): 180–97.

Prestwich, Menna, ed. *International Calvinism, 1541–1715*. Oxford: Clarendon Press, 1985.

Quéniart, Jean. *La Révocation de l'Edit de Nantes: Protestants et catholiques en France de 1598 à 1685*. Paris: Desclée de Brouwer, 1985.

Quick, John. *Synodican in Gallia Reformata: Or, the Acts, Decisions, Decrees and Canons of Those Famous National Councils of the Reformed Churches in France*. 2 vols. London: Parkhurst & Robinson, 1692.

Rabb, Theodore K. *The Struggle for Stability in Early Modern Europe*. New York: Oxford University Press, 1975.

Rabut, Elisabeth. *Le Roi, l'église et le temple: L'exécution de l'Edit de Nantes en Dauphiné*. Grenoble: Editions La Pensée Sauvage, 1987.

Ranum, Orest. *Artisans of Glory: Writers and Historical Thought in Seventeenth-Century France*. Chapel Hill: University of North Carolina Press, 1980.

Recueil des edicts de pacification, ordonnances, declarations, etc. faîtes par les rois de France, en faveur de ceux de la Religion Prétendue Réformée. Geneva: Estienne, 1658.

Recueil général des edits, declarations de Louis le Grand, arrêts du Conseil et de toutes les cours souveraines du royaume. Le Reolle: Labottiere, 1684.

Reinhardt, Steven G. *Justice in the Sarladais, 1770–1790*. Baton Rouge: Louisiana State University Press, 1991.

Richet, Denis. *De la Réforme à la Révolution: Etudes sur la France moderne*. Paris: Aubier, 1991.

———. "Sociocultural Aspects of Religious Conflicts in Paris during the Second Half of the Sixteenth Century." In *Ritual, Religion and the Sacred: Selections from the Annales*. Edited by Robert Forster and Orest Ranum. Translated by Elborg Forster and Patricia Ranum, 182–212. Baltimore: Johns Hopkins University Press, 1982.

Roelker, Nancy L. *One King, One Faith: The Parlement of Paris and the Religious Reformations of the Sixteenth Century*. Berkeley: University of California Press, 1996.

Roper, Lyndal. *The Holy Household: Women and Morals in Reformation Augsburg*. New York: Oxford University Press, 1989.

Rosa, Susan. "'Il était possible aussi que cette conversion fût sincere': Turenne's Conversion in Context." *French Historical Studies* 18 (1994): 632–66.

Rothrock, George. "The Gallican Resurgence after the Death of Henry IV," *The Historian* 24 (1961): 1–25.

Rousselet, Marcel. *Histoire de la magistrature*. 2 vols. Paris: Plon, 1956.

Sacaze, M. "Les Chambres mi-parties des anciens parlements: La Chambre de l'Edit du Languedoc, 1576–1679," *Bulletin de la société de l'histoire du protestantisme français* 3 (1855): 362–77.

Safley, Thomas Max. *Let No Man Put Asunder: The Control of Marriage in the German Southwest, A Comparative Study, 1550–1600*. Sixteenth Century Essays & Studies, vol. 2. Kirksville, Mo.: Sixteenth Century Journal Publishers, 1984.

Sahlins, Peter. *Boundaries: The Making of France and Spain in the Pyrenees*. Berkeley: University of California Press, 1989.

——. "Fictions of a Catholic France: The Naturalization of Foreigners, 1685–1787." *Representations* 47 (1994): 85–110.

Sales, François de. *Introduction to the Devout Life*. Translated by John K. Ryan. London: Longmans, Green, 1953.

Salmon, J.H.M. *Renaissance and Revolt: Essays in the Intellectual and Social History of Early Modern France*. Cambridge: Cambridge University Press, 1987.

——. *Society in Crisis: France in the Sixteenth Century*. New York: Methuen, 1975.

——. "Storm over the Noblesse." *Journal of Modern History* 53 (1981): 252–57.

Sawyer, Jeffrey. "Judicial Corruption and Legal Reform in Early Seventeenth-Century France." *Law and History Review* 6:1 (1988): 95–188.

——. *Printed Poison: Pamphlet Propaganda, Faction Politics, and the Public Sphere in Early Seventeenth-Century France*. Berkeley: University of California Press, 1990.

Schalk, Ellery. *From Valor to Pedigree: Ideas of Nobility in France in the Sixteenth and Seventeenth Centuries*. Princeton: Princeton University Press, 1986.

Scott, James. *Domination and the Arts of Resistance: Hidden Transcripts*. New Haven: Yale University Press, 1990.

Scoloudi, Irene, ed. *Huguenots in Britain and Their French Background, 1550–1800*. London: Macmillan Press, 1987.

Sergène, A. "Le Précédent judiciaire au Moyen Age." *Revue historique de droit français et étranger*, 4th series, 39 (1961): 224–54, 359–70.

Sharpe, J. A. *Defamation and Sexual Slander in Early Modern England: The Church Courts at York*. Borthwick Papers, no. 58. York: University of York, 1980.

Shennan, J.H. *The Parlement of Paris*. Ithaca: Cornell University Press, 1968.

Soman, Alfred. "Deviance and Criminal Justice in Western Europe, 1300–1800: An Essay in Structure." *Criminal Justice History* I (1980): 3–28.

——. "La Justice criminelle aux XVIe–XVIIe siècles: Le parlement de Paris et les sièges subalternes." In *La Faute, la répression et le pardon. Actes du 107e Congrès National des Sociétés Savantes*. Brest: Comité des travaux historiques et scientifiques, 1982, I:15–52.

——. "Aux Origines de l'appel de droit dans l'Ordonnance Criminelle de 1670." *XVIIe Siècle* 32 (1980): 21–35.

Soman, Alfred, and Elisabeth Labrousse. "Le Registre consistorial de Coutras, 1582–1584." *Bulletin de la société de l'histoire du protestantisme français* 126 (1980): 195–228.

Spierenburg, Pieter. *The Spectacle of Suffering: Executions and the Evolution of Repression from a Pre-Industrial Metropolis to the European Experience*. Cambridge: Cambridge University Press, 1984.

Starr, June, and Jane F. Collier, eds. *History and Power in the Study of Law: New Directions in Legal Anthropology*. Ithaca: Cornell University Press, 1989.

Stone, Lawrence. *The Family, Sex and Marriage in England, 1500–1800*. Abridged edition. New York: Harper & Row, 1977.

Strayer, Joseph. "France: The Holy Land, the Chosen People and the Most Christian King." In *Action and Conviction in Early Modern Europe*. Edited by Theodore K. Rabb and Jerrold E. Siegel, 3–16. Princeton: Princeton University Press, 1969.

Sunshine, Glenn S. "French Protestantism on the Eve of St. Bartholomew: The Ecclesiastical Discipline of the French Reformed Churches, 1571–1572." *French History* 4 (1990): 340–77.

———. "Geneva Meets Rome: The Development of the French Reformed Diaconate." *Sixteenth Century Journal* 26 (1995): 329–46.

Sutherland, N.M. *The Huguenot Struggle for Recognition.* New Haven: Yale University Press, 1980.

———. "Was There an Inquisition in Reformation France?" In *Princes, Politics and Religion, 1547–1589,* 13–29. London: Hambledon Press, 1984.

Sypher, G.R. "'Faisant ce qu'il leur vient à plaisir': The Image of Protestantism in French Catholic Polemics on the Eve of the Religious Wars." *Sixteenth Century Journal* 11 (1980): 59–84.

Taber, Linda. "Religious Dissent within the Parlement of Paris in the Mid-Sixteenth Century: A Reassessment," *French Historical Studies* 16 (1990): 684–99.

Taillandier, Pierre. *Le Mariage des protestants français sous l'Ancien Régime.* Clermont-Ferrand, 1919.

Tentler, Thomas N. *Sin and Confession on the Eve of the Reformation.* Princeton: Princeton University Press, 1977.

Thou, Jacques-Auguste de. *Mémoires.* In *Nouvelle collection des mémoires pour servir à l'histoire de France,* 1st series, vol. 11. Edited by Joseph François Michaud and Jean-Joseph-François Poujoulat. Paris: 1838.

Timbal, Pierre-Clément. "L'Esprit du droit privé au XVIIe siècle." *XVIIe Siècle* 58–59 (1963): 30–39.

Traer, James F. *Marriage and the Family in Eighteenth-Century France.* Ithaca: Cornell University Press, 1980.

Très-humbles et très-veritables remonstrances à Sa Majesté: Par les officiers de la Religion Prétendue Réformée de la Chambre de l'Edit de Guienne, sur le sujet de la dernière declaration de 1656. Montauban: Bertié, 1657.

Turchetti, Mario. "'Concorde ou tolérance' de 1562 à 1598." *Revue historique* 56 (1985): 341–55.

———. "La Qualification de 'perpétuel et irrévocable' appliquée à l'Edit de Nantes (1598)." *Bulletin de la société de l'histoire du protestantisme français* 139:1 (1993): 41–78.

Valone, James S. *Huguenot Politics, 1601–1622.* Lewiston, N.Y.: Edward Mellen Press, 1994.

Van Kley, Dale. *The Religious Origins of the French Revolution.* New Haven: Yale University Press, 1996.

Vigier, Marc, and Muriel Wilder-Vigié. *Les Galériens du roi, 1661–1715.* Paris: Fayard, 1985.

Viollet, Paul. *Histoire du droit civil français.* Paris: L. Larose et Forcel, 1893.

Voeltzel, René. "Le Droit matrimonial dans les anciennes églises réformées de France, 1550–1660." *Revue de droit canonique* 29 (1977): 154–77.

Von Greyerz, Kaspar, ed. *Religion and Society in Early Modern Europe, 1500–1800.* London: Allen & Unwin, 1984.

Wachtel, Nathan. "Memory and History: Introduction." *History and Anthropology* 2 (1986): 207–24.

Weiss, Nathaniel. *La Chambre ardente: Etude sur la liberté de conscience en France sous François Ier et Henri II.* Paris, 1889. Reprint Geneva: Slatkine, 1970.

Weisser, Michael. *Crime and Punishment in Early Modern Europe.* New Jersey: Humanities Press, 1979.

Wells, Charlotte. *Law and Citizenship in Early Modern France.* Baltimore: Johns Hopkins University Press, 1994.

Wheaton, Robert, and Tamara Hareven, eds. *Family and Sexuality in French History.* Philadelphia: University of Pennsylvania Press, 1980.

Wolfe, Michael. "Amnesty and Oubliance at the End of the French Wars of Religion." *Cahiers d'histoire* 16 (1996): 45–68.

————. *The Conversion of Henri IV.* Cambridge: Harvard University Press, 1993.

————, ed. *Changing Identities in Early Modern France.* Durham: Duke University Press, 1997.

Yardeni, Myriam. *La Conscience nationale en France pendant les guerres de religion, 1550–1590.* Louvain: Nauwelaerts, 1971.

Zysberg, André. *Les Galériens: Vies et destins de 60,000 forçats sur les galères de France, 1680–1748.* Paris: Seuil, 1987.

Index

All locations and institutions are in France unless otherwise indicated. Page references to tables are indicated by a *t*.

Edict of Nantes, *continued*
    on kinship, marriage, 111 (*see also* family litigation)
    on memory/forgetting (*see* memory/ forgetting)
    oubliance policy of, 76, 77, 79, 95 (*see also* memory/forgetting)
    as peace treaty vs. religious statement, 3, 191
    perpetual silence imposed on royal prosecutors, 78
    on public/private worship, 5–6
    ratification of, 48–49, 99–100, 146
    religious conflict/coexistence/toleration associated with, x, xii, 32, 79, 191
    revocation of, xii, xiv, 2, 71n.118, 98, 146
    and royal power over the judiciary, 17, 193
    on schools and offices, 36n
    on seditious talk, 161
    on Wars of Religion (*see* memory/ forgetting)
Edict of Poitiers (1577), 11
Edict of Saint Germain (1570), 10
Edict of Union (1588), 12
Erondelle, Richard, 134n.109
essai de congrès, 120–21, 120–21n.68
Estates-General (Paris, 1593), 47–48
Etignard, Paul, 187
Eveschan, Epipheman, 64
évocation, 71
execrable cases (*cas execrables*), 77–78, 80–81
execution. *See* capital punishment

family
    definition of, 102
    emotional/moral support from, 103
    extended, 139–40
    nuclear, 103
    patriarchal, 103–4, 192
    and public vs. private life, 105
    and the state, 100, 104, 192
    See also family litigation; marriage
family litigation, 99–147
    on adultery, 124
    on child custody, 123
    and family unity/division, 102–3, 133–43, 192
    on financial support, 123–24

on forgery, 134–35
on guardianship/parental behavior, 102, 126–33, 144–45
on illegitimate children, 130–31
on imposture, 135
on inheritance, 102, 115, 135–36
on marriage, validity of, 102, 115nn, 192 (*see also* marriage)
    by married women, 142
    and patriarchy, 103–4, 126
    religious difference in, 102, 105–6, 143–47, 193
    by unmarried women, 140–42
on wills, 134–35
women's initiative in, 104
Fatin, Nicolas, 113
Faucanbourg, Louis de, 66
Favereau, Jean, 114
favoritism, 42, 59, 60, 66, 73
Febvrier, Catherine, 123
Fernault, Gillette, 130
Ferre, Charles, sieur de la Villesblanc, 135–36
Figeac synod (1579), 28
Finistère, xvii
First President (*prémier président*), 37
Fizes, Pierre, 114
Flavigny court, 46
Flé, Berthelemye, 113, 119, 143
Fleix, Treaty of (1580), 5, 11
Fleury, Pierre, 140
foreign wars, financing of, 16
forgery, 134–35, 153
Forget, Jean, 50, 53
Fouyn, Jehan, 134n.109
Franchard, Etienne, 139
Franchard, Pierre, 139
Francis I, king of France, 15–16, 41
François, Jean, 183
François, Jehan, 167
Fredel, Marin de, 175–76
French Calvinists. *See* Huguenots
French Reformation, 97
French Revolution (1789), xvi–xvii
Frere, Etienne, 175–76

Gagnieres, Claude, 113
galley service, 154, 157, 158, 158n.29
Gallicanism, 8–9, 36–37, 44, 97, 101

litigants, *continued*
   nobles among, 63–64
   plaintiffs vs. defendants, 65, 65n.92
   wealthy vs. poor, 63
   See also under Chambre de l'Edit; memory/
     forgetting; violence
lits de justice, 44
Lorride, Marie de, 184
Louet, Jeanne, 91
Louis, Noel, 135
Louis XII, king of France, 41
Louis XIII, king of France, 18–19
   on the chambres mi-parties, 58–59
   on chambres mi-parties' jurisdiction, 22,
     22n.61
   chambres mi-parties protected by, 33
   Code Michaud issued by, 58–59
   Huguenot rebellion against, 98
   on marriage, 105
   on proof of Huguenots' legal status, 23–
     24
Louis XIV, king of France
   absolutism of, xvi
   Edict of Nantes revoked by, xiv, 2, 98, 146
   fatherly image of, 146
   Huguenots repressed by, 18
Louvain, Jean de, 144–45
Loyseau, Suzanne, 124–25
Lusignan, Olimpe de, dame de Lespart, 121–
   22
Luther, Martin, 107
Lyon synod (1563), 27, 29–30

Machecoul, Gilles de, sieur de Saint Etienne et
   de La Grange Barbastre, 128
magistrates
   allegiance of, 17
   authority of, 16
   in the consistory, 27–28
   corruption of, 45–46
   divisions among, 16–17
   in exile in Tours, 46, 46n.27
   favoritism among, 59, 66, 73
   as guardians of law/political integrity, 43–
     44, 46, 48, 49
   Huguenot, in the chambres mi-parties,
     26–27, 36
   Huguenot grievances as, 35–36

importance in governance, 39–40, 44, 69
jurisdiction over marriage, 108, 110, 120
monarchy's tensions with, 16
moral influence of, 40
the perfect magistrate/exemplary figure,
   40, 42, 49, 60
power of, 41
professional, need for, 15
and prosecution of heretics, 44–45
royal, authority of, 33
See also under Chambre de l'Edit; judges
Mahier, Joseph de, 170–71, 171n.75
Maison, Jerôme, 156
maîtres des requêtes, 37
Malingnesan, Antoinette de, 134, 136–37
Malvin, Anthoine de, 148–49, 148n
Malvin, Charles de, sieur de Montazet et
   Guissac, 148–49, 148n
Mandat family, 57
Manessier, Marguerite, 141–42
Mannoury, Girard de, 124
Mansfield, Mary C., 164
Marc, Pierre de, 172
Marchant, Jacques, 138, 138n.125
Marchant, Jehan, 138, 138n.125
Marchant, Noel, 138, 138n.125
Marchant, Pierre, 138, 138n.125
Marguerite of Valois, countess of Agenois,
   148–49, 148n
Mariette, Ysaac, sieur de La Tousche, 75
Marin, Magdelon, sieur de Laulnay, 91
Marin, Pierre, 185
marriage
   betrothals, 107–8
   clandestine, 105, 109–10, 112–13, 115–
     20, 143, 193
   as a contract, 106
   and divorce/separation, 107, 109, 121–
     23, 125
   impediments to, 106
   impotence in, 120–21, 120–21n.68
   magistrates' jurisdiction over, 108, 110,
     120
   mixed, 145
   parental consent for, 108–10, 112–14
   via *rapt,* 112–20, 120n.66, 143, 193
   records of, 23, 109
   religious difference in, 143–44